COMMUNITY ORGANISING AGAINST RACISM
'Race', ethnicity and community development

Edited by Gary Craig

First published in Great Britain in 2018 by

Policy Press
University of Bristol
1-9 Old Park Hill
Bristol
BS2 8BB
UK
t: +44 (0)117 954 5940
pp-info@bristol.ac.uk
www.policypress.co.uk

North America office:
Policy Press
c/o The University of Chicago Press
1427 East 60th Street
Chicago, IL 60637, USA
t: +1 773 702 7700
f: +1 773-702-9756
sales@press.uchicago.edu
www.press.uchicago.edu

© Policy Press 2018

British Library Cataloguing in Publication Data
A catalogue record for this book is available from the British Library

Library of Congress Cataloging-in-Publication Data
A catalog record for this book has been requested

ISBN 978-1-4473-3376-0 paperback
ISBN 978-1-4473-3374-6 hardcover
ISBN 978-1-4473-3377-7 ePub
ISBN 978-1-4473-3378-4 Mobi
ISBN 978-1-4473-3375-3 ePdf

The right of Gary Craig to be identified as editor of this work has been asserted by him in accordance with the Copyright, Designs and Patents Act 1988.

The statements and opinions contained within this publication are solely those of the editor and contributors and not of the University of Bristol or Policy Press. The University of Bristol and Policy Press disclaim responsibility for any injury to persons or property resulting from any material published in this publication.

Policy Press works to counter discrimination on grounds of gender, race, disability, age and sexuality.

Cover design by Lyn Davies
Front cover image: istock
Printed and bound in Great Britain by Clays Ltd, St Ives plc
Policy Press uses environmentally responsible print partners

This book is dedicated to the
memory of Ratna Lachman
(died 2017), who fought for
racial justice throughout her
adult life, inspiring many by
her energy and commitment;
and to all those who have done
likewise.

How does it feel to be constantly regarded as a potential threat, strip-searched at every airport? Or to be told that, as an actress, the part you're most fitted to play is the 'wife of a terrorist'? How does it feel to have words from your native language misused, misappropriated, and used aggressively towards you? How does it feel to have a child of colour say in a classroom that stories can only be about white people? How does it feel to go 'home' to India when your home is really in London? What is it like to feel you always have to be an ambassador for your race? How does it feel to always tick 'other'? Why does society appear to deem people of colour as bad immigrants – until by winning Olympic races, or baking good cakes, or being conscientious doctors, they cross over and become good immigrants?

Nitesh Shukla (ed) (2016) *The good immigrant*,
London: Unbound

The Chipko tell a story in the villages about a fox that comes wearing a tiger's coat to terrify the people. When the real tiger comes, however, it wears a fox's coat. The Chipko argue that 'we should beware of those who come saying they love the people', and should treat their claims with this same degree of scepticism.

Traditional tale

Contents

List of figures

Author biographies

Dr Asif Afridi is Deputy CEO of a UK-based national equality and human rights charity called brap. He is also Chair of the Equality and Diversity Forum, a UK-based network of equality and human rights charities. With a background in international human rights work, Asif has published research on a range of subjects including: poverty reduction; inequalities; promoting human rights and effective regulation; social cohesion and the political engagement of minority groups.

Morris Beckford has been actively involved in education and social services sector for over 15 years and is currently the Director of Community Health and Wellness at Access Alliance Multicultural Health and Community Services and is a PhD candidate in Social Work at York University. Morris believes that having physical spaces in communities where people can gather and help to build their own health and well-being is a key determinant of good health that both the public and private sectors need to nurture. To that end he has worked with numerous property management companies to help revitalise decaying spaces. He believes that these gathering places can help to foster and facilitate difficult conversations about the state of our society, including the lack of diversity in many sectors across the country. His new passion is shining light on the lack of diversity at the leadership level in the non-profit sector in Canada.

Brian Belton is a senior lecturer at the YMCA George Williams College in East London. Brian has been involved in youth work for over 40 years as a practitioner, trainer and educator. He has a global profile in the study of Gypsy and Roma identity as well as youth work. His work is widely published, including in almost 70 books on a range of subjects. Brian has worked on several international research projects, practising and lecturing in four continents and dozens of countries.

Dr Rick Bowler is a senior lecturer at the University of Sunderland. His pedagogical interests focus on transformative educational approaches to critical youth work practice. Rick has extensive community youth work experience connecting therapeutic with socio-cultural explanations to the life-worlds of young people. Rick draws upon an intersectional critical race theory lens to challenge the white standards that perpetuate British racism. Rick was chairperson of Young Asian Voices youth project from its birth in 1996 until 2003.

Shane Brady is Assistant Professor in the School of Social Work, University of Oklahoma, and a community organiser. His major research area is developing empowerment-based participatory community development interventions through utilising community organising and asset-based community development methods to address local challenges, build capacity and advocate for social change. He has over 15 years of experience as a community organiser, community outreach worker, social worker and social services administrator, along with extensive university teaching experience.

Linda Briskman was recently appointed to the Margaret Whitlam Chair of Social Work at Western Sydney University. She previously held the position of Professor of Human Rights at the Swinburne Institute for Social Research in Melbourne. Linda's areas of research and advocacy include Indigenous rights, asylum-seeker rights and challenging Islamophobia. She publishes extensively in each area. Her most recent book is *Social work with Indigenous communities: A human rights approach* (Federation Press, 2014).

Professor Colin Clark teaches at the University of the West of Scotland (UWS). His research is mainly located within the fields of Romani studies and ethnic and racial studies, with a special interest in issues of identity, migration and citizenship, publishing widely in these areas. Outside of UWS, Colin sits on the Board of Directors of the Glasgow-based anti-racist Coalition for Racial Equality and Rights. He is also a Trustee of the Roma Rights group Friends of Romano Lav.

Louisa Cocris is a community education worker in Fife. Louisa has extensive experience of living and working in Romania, beginning over 25 years ago in the immediate aftermath of the regime change there in 1989. Louisa has recently started to contribute in an academic way to the subject of youth work in Romania. Her grounding in and understanding of the topic are drawn from first-hand experience.

Gary Craig is Professor Emeritus at the Wilberforce Institute for the study of Slavery and Emancipation, University of Hull and Visiting Professor at the universities of Newcastle upon Tyne and York and at Hong Kong Baptist University. His career covers 20 years of working in community development projects and almost 30 years in academic life. He has written widely and been an activist on community development, 'race' and ethnicity and, more recently, on aspects of modern slavery.

Lis de Vries was the National Manager for Migration Support Programs at the Australian Red Cross during a time when asylum-seekers arriving by boat grew to a relatively high number in Australia. The Red Cross was the primary provider of support for asylum-seekers around Australia. Lis has worked for 25 years in the not-for profit sector in Tasmania and Victoria, specialising in migration and international issues. She has a Bachelor's degree in Social Work and a Master's in International Politics and received a Churchill Fellowship to research on international responses to unemployment in small island states. She is currently working in the Department of Social Work at the University of Melbourne and is the chair of the Refugee Council of Australia.

Mick Doyle is Head of Operations at Scottish community development centre and worked in community development and equalities for 30 years as a practitioner, manager, policy maker and researcher in the public and third sectors. He managed Scottish Refugee Council's community development team, including support to refugee communities and receiving community organisations. Mick led the implementation of the organisation's community development strategy, widening the involvement of other communities and community development workers providing sanctuary in Scotland.

Kwok-kin Fung is an assistant professor in the Department of Social Work at the Hong Kong Baptist University. He is also a board member of the International Association for Community Development and an international advisor for the *Community Development Journal*. His areas of interest include community development, social policy, globalisation, gender and welfare.

Larry M. Gant's research focuses on neighbourhood-based responses to health disparities and social-economic challenges in post-industrial cities in the United States and urban metropolitan areas in Europe, sub-Saharan African and China. Another strand of research includes the use of visual and performance arts-based settlement house programmes to create indigenous creative groups of residents ready for community development. Gant's research has been supported by the National Institutes of Health, Centers for Disease Control and Prevention and numerous private foundations.

Margaret Greenfields is Professor of Social Policy and Community Engagement at Buckinghamshire New University in the UK. Her practice and policy activities with refugee and asylum-seeking women are part of an overall 30-year focus on supporting marginalised communities to 'speak to power' to bring about positive change. In addition to working on co-production with community groups, she has provided input for policy development in the UK and EU as well as lecturing and delivering training in numerous countries.

Robert Gregory has worked as a community development worker and more recently as a senior local government officer in the UK. He undertook his Master's in Applied Anthropology and Community Development at Goldsmiths College, London and has led practice development at home and overseas. He is currently a board member for the International Association for Community Development.

Lorraine Gutierrez is a professor in the School of Social Work, Psychology, and Latino Studies at the University of Michigan. Her teaching and scholarship focus on multicultural praxis in communities, organisations and higher education. She has engaged in community-based practice and research in multi-ethnic communities in Chicago, New York, San Francisco, Seattle and Detroit. Her most recent focus is on arts-based methods for multicultural community change. She is currently an editor of the *Journal of Community Practice*.

Stuart Hashagen is Chair of the European Community Development Network and an advisor with the Scottish Community Development Centre. He is a board member of Crossroads Youth and Community Association, which works with Roma and other migrant groups. By his involvement in both very local and pan-European networks he hopes to encourage community development to gain a persuasive voice in challenging inequality, xenophobia and exclusion and in arguing the case for greater investment in this.

Suet-lin Hung (Shirley) is an associate head and associate professor in the Department of Social Work, Hong Kong Baptist University. She is also the Director of the Social Work Practice and Mental Health Centre of the University, Regional Director of the International Association for Community Development and the chairperson of the Social Workers Registration Board 2010–2013. In addition to research, she has been delivering training in collective narrative practice, advanced group work and feminist social work with women. She was honoured with the award of Outstanding Social Worker by the Hong Kong Social Workers Association in 1996 and the 60th Anniversary Distinguished Alumni Award by the University of Hong Kong in 2010. Her areas of interest include gender, family, social work and social policy, narrative practice and group and community work.

Brian Keenan has worked in the field of community development for over 20 years in Ireland, the UK and Europe. He is a passionate community activist and has been involved in campaigns focusing on social housing, gentrification, racial discrimination, community health and environmental protection. Brian previously worked for Crossroads Youth and Community Association in Glasgow, which features in 'Cultural identity, migration and community development in Glasgow'. He currently works for Inspiring Scotland's Link Up programme and is based in Saltcoats, Scotland.

Dr Athena Lathouras is a lecturer in the Social Work programme of the School of Social Sciences at the University of the Sunshine Coast, Australia. She teaches courses in community development and social action and in critical social policy analysis. Athena engages in participatory action research projects exploring community development and citizen-led social movements that work for social justice and human rights.

Carlos Moreno-Leguizamon conducts research on health inequalities in the provision of services to black and minority ethnic (BME) groups in the South East of England and has been promoting the use of the Learning Alliance methodology as a way to increase the socio-economic impact of research projects. The project presented here relates to the implementation of a Learning Alliance in a research project on palliative care and end-of-life services for BME groups. He is a senior lecturer at the University of Greenwich.

Holly Notcutt has worked for the last 10 years in the UK voluntary and public sectors, in both front-line community development roles and managerial roles. She studied social psychology and, later, international development, with a particular research focus on marginalised people, gendered and racial inequalities and poverty reduction in 'developed countries'. She currently works in the UK in local government, leading on cross-sector initiatives to developing grassroots approaches to supporting marginalised communities.

Mohita Roman is currently working at Australian Red Cross and has 15 years' experience in the international development sector. Her current work focuses on building practice standards within the humanitarian sector and capacity building of migrant communities. Mohita holds a PhD from Monash University and a Master's in International Relations from Yonsei University in South Korea. Her research has covered a broad range of topics, including development and culture, memory and war, gendered violence, sexual slavery and human trafficking, with a particular focus on East Asia. She has lectured on gender relations in Asia, war and women, global changes and changing identities in East Asia.

Dr Dyann Ross teaches in the Social Work programme at the University of the Sunshine Coast, Australia, in the areas of ethics and professional practice; the sociology of health and mental health; and complexity in social work practice. She researches the nature of love and social justice ethics in the social welfare sector, particularly mental health services and also in the mining industry. Recent publications relate to corporate social irresponsibility and madness of privileged groups as violence in mental health systems and universities.

David Smith is a principal lecturer in sociology at the University of Greenwich. His research interests include the impact of socioeconomic and policy changes on working-class and other marginalised groups. He has published widely on issues related to the accommodation, health and well-being of Gypsies, Roma and Travellers and has recently completed a research project with Carlos Moreno-Leguizamon exploring access and experiences of palliative and end-of-life care among BME groups.

Ranjit Sondhi has been involved with community action projects in the inner city of Birmingham since the early 1970s. He worked with the Handsworth Action Centre, the Lozells Social Development Group, the Handsworth Law Centre and the Birmingham branch of the Joint Council for the Welfare of Immigrants and was the founder-director of the Asian Resource Centre. He was a senior lecturer in the Youth and Community Work department at Birmingham College. He continues to be involved with the Birmingham Hope projects for destitute asylum-seekers.

Angela Summersgill is a tutor of applied social work at Tai Tokerau Wānanga (NorthTec) Whangarei, New Zealand. She completed a Master's in Critical Pedagogy and Social Justice at the University of Cumbria, UK. Her commitment to personal, social and environmental transformation was born in communities in the North West of England, where she spent many years in grassroots community-work practice focusing on 'bridge building across difference'. Her current role as a social work educator encourages the synthesis of her community and statutory social work experience in a pedagogical approach that promotes authentic, deeply connected and critically aware practice.

Lynn Tang is an assistant professor at Tung Wah College, Hong Kong. She worked in Mental Health in Higher Education, an interdisciplinary network in the UK, and gained her PhD in Sociology from the University of Warwick. Her main research interests are mental health, sociology of health and social inequalities. Her work appears in peer-reviewed journals such as *Community Development Journal*, and her book *Recovery, mental health and inequality: Chinese ethnic minorities as mental health service users* will be published by Routledge.

Phil Ware is an associate fellow of the Third Sector Research Centre (TSRC) at Birmingham University, working on research with BME community groups, linked to TSRC's Below the Radar programme. His background is in community development, working in the voluntary and statutory sectors in Birmingham and Dudley. Phil's research has focused on the voice and influence of BME community groups in urban and rural settlements, using primary research undertaken in the West Midlands, the North West and the South West, and with national strategic organisations.

List of abbreviations

BME	black and minority ethnic
ESF	European Social Fund
NDC	New Deal for Communities
PAR	participatory action research
RASW	Refugee and Asylum-Seeking Women
SCD	structural community development
SRB	Single Regeneration Budget
VCS	voluntary and community sector

Introduction

Gary Craig

This book aims to help fill a huge gap in the literature around community development policy, training and practice. It is remarkable that, despite the salience of 'race' and ethnicity in public policy debates, at least at the level of communities if not within government, and the growing threat of racism – in all its manifestations: nationalism, chauvinism, fascism, ethnic cleansing, genocide, modern slavery – across the world, there is only one major book about community development, and that 35 years old, which took as its main focus working with black and minority ethnic (BME)[1] groups (Ohri et al, 1982). That book, reporting largely on the experience of racialised minorities within the United Kingdom (UK), observed that the dimension of 'race' was then hardly on the agenda of government and outlined, in a series of case studies, the struggle of minorities to achieve some leverage against the racism that was then endemic in British society. The editors exhorted community workers (then mainly white) to ensure that minorities were fully engaged in their work and warned of the dangers facing British society if the issue of 'race' continued to be ignored.

Beyond this book, the issue of 'race' and ethnicity from a community development perspective is poorly represented in the wider literature: the *Community Development Journal*'s Cumulative Index, for example, lists only 10 articles in the first 35 years of publication, with a few published more recently, including a special issue on working with refugees.[2] Thirty-five years on from that single book, with race-related disturbances in many parts of the UK (provoked by a combination of the continuing immiseration of most minorities, racist policing practices, the racist-related murders of more than 100 black and Asian people since 1997 and the failure of public policy effectively to deal with the consequences of a wider racism – Craig, 2013), this cocktail of widespread hostility – or, in many cases, passive tolerance – towards minorities in the policies and practices of most private and public agencies, not to mention the attitudes of the public at large (as demonstrated in the spike of racist attacks following the UK's 2016 EU referendum – Burnett, 2016), suggests that this warning seems well justified. And while the particular combination of circumstances and responses may differ between countries, it is clear that this is an issue that now faces very many countries. Hence the need for a book that also seeks to draw together experience from across the world. Its aims are therefore

- to help to fill a substantial gap in the literature on community development work;
- to outline the history and theory of community development work with minority groups;
- to explore, through case studies from different parts of the world, how different approaches to community development work can empower minority ethnic communities to overcome social disadvantage; and
- to encourage a wider debate and writing about this area of work.

The aim of this introduction is specifically to provide an overarching historical, theoretical and political context for the detailed analyses and accounts of local work that follow. This is important because community workers are now increasingly struggling at the local level against political, social and economic trends generated at the global level, making their work more difficult but more urgent than ever before.

Most countries can now appropriately be described as multicultural, whether or not this fact of life is reflected in the policies of governments, which have in fact generally abandoned the notion of multiculturalism (if they had ever adopted it) and returned to a more controlling and oppressive notion of assimilation.[3] The political origins of and attacks on the concept of multiculturalism are addressed in particular here by Afridi (Chapter One) and Sondhi (Chapter Five). The particular form that the ethnic mix has taken in any particular country is the result of a combination of factors, some historical, most of all the existence or not of First Nations (aboriginal) people (as, for example, in such disparate countries as Canada, Australia, New Zealand/Aotearoa, the US, Botswana and Northern Scandinavian countries; two chapters (Chapters Thirteen and Nineteen) focus on their experience); economic migration (which has a history stretching back several hundred years and not, as many commentators suggest, starting in 1948 or even in the last twenty or so years); migration driven by wars, poverty, conflict and climate change (leading to the largest movements of people seeking asylum ever in recorded history); and demographic change within each country as migrants have settled, formed families and moved around. This has led to a situation where the populations in some parts of many major towns and cities – including some represented in this book – contain people from as many as 100 differing national or ethnic origins, whose members may in fact now constitute a numerical majority in certain districts.[4]

The phenomenon of migration[5]

The 33rd Session of the UN Commission on Population and Development heard in 2000 from the Director of the UN Population Division that 'international migration' would become the major demographic issue of the 21st century (United Nations Non-Governmental Liaison Service, 2000), leading to changes in language, religion, ethnicity and nationality and to what he circumspectly described as 'negative public sentiment and xenophobia'. More positively for community development workers, he suggested that it might also lead to innovation, revitalisation and tolerance.

His negative predictions have become reality remarkably early in this century; the world's media are now full of images and stories of migrants – whether those seeking asylum or simply a sustainable life – embarking on perilous journeys such as across the Mediterranean from North Africa, from Mexico into the US or from Indonesia to Australia (resulting in death for many), only to be met with official hostility, public fear and rejection. Citizenship, the reasonable goal of most migrants (Castles and Davidson, 2000), has now, certainly for most poor migrants, become conditional, temporary and, above all, profoundly difficult to obtain. The wave of populism spreading across Europe at present will worsen this situation for many migrants of whatever kind. Across the world, governments have been elected, and from Hungary to the US politicians have stood on platforms, espousing neofascist views with regard to 'immigrants'. These views have in turn impacted on the lives of those migrants/minorities who have been long-settled in many countries where they are now regarded, despite their long-standing contributions to their adopted countries, as unwelcome visitors. Following the EU referendum in the UK, many minorities, whether recently arrived Polish workers or long-standing third-generation Pakistani residents with UK birth and citizenship, were told to 'go back to their own countries', and at the time of writing there remains considerable uncertainty about the status of EU nationals residing in the UK. Quite apart from the many millions of those who are moving across national boundaries within the global marketplace, searching for better living conditions – in some cases forced by dispossession of their livelihoods as a result of climate change or the destruction of their own local economies – there are currently upwards of 30 million people worldwide displaced by war or violence within their own countries. Half of these are refugees. Most of these migrants are particularly affected by racism in some form or another. There are probably around 200 million international migrants, half of them women, representing 3% of the world's population. Many millions more are affected by individual and structural racism within their own societies, even where that has not taken the extreme form of war or inter-ethnic violence.

A brief historical account of racism

Inter-ethnic conflict, itself a legacy of imperial exploitation and division, has led in the past twenty years to hundreds of thousands dead in Uganda, Rwanda, Sudan, Nigeria, Sierra Leone, Congo, Angola, Mozambique, South Africa, Algeria, Indonesia, in most Balkan countries and much of South East and Central Asia. In some countries, as in South Africa before 1994, Uganda under Idi Amin and Fiji to the present, racism was given a constitutional basis. In Zimbabwe, the cloak of anti–imperialist rhetoric was used to justify inter-ethnic conflict between Shona and Ndebele. It is of course hardly surprising that racism is such a powerful force in post-colonial societies, since it was racism that was used by imperial powers to justify both European domination of colonies and its specific economic manifestations such as slavery, and that manipulated inter-ethnic divisions to ensure control of local economies.

Racism – often framed within cultural and religious imperialism – drove much of the conflict and exploitation that characterised the global South for hundreds of years. Nor are the issues of 'race' and migration and of both individual and state-sponsored racist responses to minorities new phenomena within the domestic landscape of the UK or other 'developed' countries. Eight hundred years ago, for example, the entire Jewish population of York, in England, was burned to death by a mob incited by local landowners who wanted to avoid repaying their debts. Two hundred years later, to paraphrase Fryer (1984, p 36), 'ethnocentric myths [encouraged by the church] about dark-skinned people from over the sea eased European consciences about enslaving Africans', thus encouraging the slave trade on which the economic fortunes of many European and American millionaires (and political leaders) still rest. This approach to those of presumed inferiority was adopted by all the major imperial powers.[6]

The hostility of wealthy countries towards those of different skin colour extended to their behaviour towards the First Nations 'minorities' colonised during the era of imperialism. For example,

4

the Treaty of Waitangi in 1840 ceded government of Aotearoa (New Zealand) to the British Crown but offered some protection to the Maori in terms of continuing possession of and authority over their lands and property, giving them the 'rights and privileges of British subjects'. The legal basis of the Treaty is now disputed but it was introduced in the expectation, as in Australia, that those Maori (or in Australia the Kuri, and in the US native American Indians) who had survived the wars carried out by those wishing to seize their land would die out as a result of imported European diseases such as influenza, or become incorporated into the new Western culture.

In Australia the Aboriginal Kuri, having initially been regarded as not existing at all under the imperial doctrine of Terra Nullius, and despite making some gains, such as the establishment of the Aboriginal and Torres Strait Islanders Council and some successful traditional land claims, still do not have anything like the benefits of full citizenship of Australia. This situation faces all First Nations people, such as the San in Botswana, who are dominated politically and economically by the Botswana government (representing the dominant Tswana ethnic group), which appears to want to drive the San out of existence, Aboriginal Indians in Canada (where, unlike in Australia, the First Nations people have at least been offered a statement of reconciliation by the federal government); or the First Nations people of Hawaii and the Pacific Islands nations, whose case has yet properly to be heard in other parts of the world. Despite some advances in their status over the past 200 years, First Nations minorities are still disproportionately represented among those who are unemployed, living on low incomes, in prison, who have poor education and health outcomes and among who are dying prematurely. Although aboriginal people have generally had their civil rights and, eventually, their political rights at least partially protected, they have yet to achieve full social citizenship. This is one arena where community or social development can have an important role to play, as accounts here demonstrate.

Everyday contemporary racism

Now the historical process of migration is reversed. Those without economic prospects from Southern countries are migrating in increasing numbers to richer countries in search of better work and life opportunities, despite the dangers presented to them during that process of migration.[7] Their slogan is 'we are here because you were there'. What they will find is that within the so-called 'developed' countries of the North, racism towards non-white residents and migrants alike is an everyday experience. Within the UK, for example, every aspect of Britain's welfare state, for long held to be one its most progressive political and social achievements, remains characterised by racism at both institutional and individual levels (Craig, 2007a). One opinion poll in 2014 found that roughly one-third of the UK population were prepared to admit that they had racist attitudes. There have been at least 100 racially motivated murders in Britain since 1997, across the whole of the UK. Research in many countries demonstrates that minorities are disproportionately represented among the poorest and are living overwhelmingly in the more deprived communities, where community development workers are more likely to be plying their trade. It is the continued deprivation of many of the minority populations in many countries – for example, their failure to access welfare or the labour market on anything like equal terms, together with the failure of their own elders to provide effective leadership – that, it is argued, has provoked the increasingly frequent disturbances in many cities over the past few years. One community response has been these disturbances; another is for young black and Asian community workers to build new forms of leadership, instances of which are reflected in this collection (see for example Chapters One, Two and Three). A common response of those in power has been to blame the immiseration of these poor on the victims themselves, as if it were some sort of cultural trait they brought with them rather than the result of their treatment at the hands of the dominant majority.

This structured racism is certainly not limited to the UK. For example, the experience of minorities entering the labour market across European countries, from Sweden to Hungary, shows similar patterns, shaped by the same structural response of racism that drives many aspects of European national policy making. Structural racism is experienced by recently immigrant and settled minorities alongside the longer-standing resident native or First Nations ethnic minorities such as the Saami of northern Scandinavia, the Roma of East and Central Europe, and the Basque of northern Spain and southern France. Racism specifically affects the opportunities of minority or migrant groups in the labour market through blocking opportunities for training or decent work (Craig et al, 2003), while local populations blame migrants for bringing down wages and creating unemployment among the host population (Craig, 2015). I make no apology for including separate coverage here of work with Roma, Gypsy and Traveller populations within Europe; indeed I would have liked to have had more chapters to share. These populations have suffered the most oppressive forms of racism over hundreds of years, yet still remain largely 'below the radar' as far as official policy and research are concerned (Hills, 2010).[8]

Racism has taken new forms in recent years. The whole of Europe, including countries hitherto regarded as tolerant, and other countries such as the US and Australia are gripped in an intense political debate about refugee and asylum policy that itself builds on longer-standing structural racism. Economic recession and the growth of right-wing populist governments has led to growing calls for further immigration controls and the repatriation of existing 'foreigners', lending support to xenophobic campaigns in populist media and to increasing levels of racist violence against religious, ethnic and cultural minorities in countries with vastly differing histories and cultures. Europe, North America and Australia seem bent on becoming 'gated' continents. Although immigration has been part of nation building in countries such as Australia and New Zealand (as it was briefly in post-war European countries), it is clear from the Australian government's response to boat people travelling from Indonesia that a fortress mentality now dominates. The growth of racist violence makes the social and economic position of migrants and many long-settled minorities more precarious, adding to their political and economic marginalisation. As several writers note, too, the Brexit vote in the UK referendum and similar currents elsewhere across the world appear to have legitimised everyday racism that had not gone away but was lurking beneath the surface of many allegedly tolerant societies.

Many European and 'developed' countries, responding to campaigns and evidence, have attempted to create structures, policies and legislation over the past 30 years which, although frequently ineffective in practice, offer some limited protection for minorities against discrimination.[9] At the same time, however, these calls for immigration control have grown steadily and the increased flow of refugees and migrants sharpens these contradictions. The treatment of refugees and asylum seekers is increasingly harsh and racist, starting generally from the assumption that they are actually not fleeing from a well-founded fear of persecution, but simply seeking a better economic standard of living. 'Northern' governments are attempting to build barriers to trade in labour to their own advantage, in a way that mirrors their trade in goods, services and commodities. At the same time as global corporations are increasingly manipulating the local economies of poor countries and driving many to migrate in search of work, access to that work is increasingly being managed by rich countries in ways that ensure that migrants deliver their work with as little call on the resources of rich economies as possible. Those relatively few migrants who achieve refugee status are provided with the poorest housing and a subsistence income below that of even the poorest settled minorities, a treatment that largely correlates with skin colour; meanwhile white migrants from Commonwealth countries and returning citizens, who actually form significant groups of immigrants, are welcomed. One obvious recent example is that of the *aussiedler*, people deemed to be of German origin and who, despite having lived in Poland or Russia for years, are treated as Germans when they decide to return to live in Germany, protected by their whiteness and German bloodline; meanwhile long-standing 'German' residents of Turkish or Yugoslav origin struggle for citizenship. The ideological significance of whiteness is explored in Bowler's chapter (Two).

Within 'developed' societies (or the global North), racism now performs two functions: first, it allows people of different skin colour to continue to be exploited economically, and secondly, it creates the conditions for them to be used as political scapegoats, for example in relation to crime and drug taking or more general economic decline. Many countries claiming to be peacefully multicultural, such as Britain, France and Germany, are, as Favell (2002) and Fekete (2009) have argued, already deeply polarised, and worse may follow. Their huge disparities in income and wealth, often strongly associated with ethnicity and a direct result of their adoption of unregulated market forces, are now impacting strongly on traditional white working-class communities that have proved to be fertile recruiting grounds for the parties of the political far Right. What many governments and many of their populations appear to have failed to grasp is the increasing dependency of their economies on both settled minorities and continuing immigration to sustain a range of industrial sectors, not least health and social care, public transport, cleaning services and leisure provision, in the face of an ageing host demography. This is becoming clear in the UK in the aftermath of the Brexit vote as many businesses, from engineering to food production, are now recognising their dependence on migrant labour. Nor is it widely understood that the economic contribution of migrants to national economies is largely positive (see, for example, Portes and Glover, 2001; Dustmann et al, 2010), challenging the narrative that migrants and minorities are 'a burden' on national economies. In many 'developed' economies there remain shortages of highly skilled workers, including doctors and IT personnel. Governments' responses to this have increasingly tried to develop systems that privilege high skill as well as key professional occupations, a policy that is simultaneously undermining the ability of many 'sending' countries to sustain their own economies and health and social systems.

'Race' and ethnicity

Although many countries have had a mix of ethnic groups within their borders for thousands of years (for the case of the UK see Olusoga, 2016), one of the major social and economic trends of the post-Second World War period has been the increasing globalisation of migration, as discussed above. This has increased the mix of minority populations now living alongside a settled majority (many of them descendants of migrants also), all generally defined in terms of their 'race' or ethnicity. 'Race' is a commonplace term and has generated a number of other related terms or concepts such as racism or 'race' relations. It is, however, a social construct, although it is still widely used as a shorthand. To quote from a recent book (Craig et al, 2013, p 27):

> In the past, within social sciences, 'race' and ethnicity were treated as different analytical concepts; 'race', implying nature or relatedness through genealogy or blood, while ethnicity suggested relatedness through common history and culture. This corresponded with notions of citizenship by *jus sanguinis* (by genealogical link [as in Germany]) and *jus soli* (place of birth or soil [as in France]). The two categories, of course, imply each other and cannot be treated as mutually exclusive. Just as ethnicity evokes a sense of common heritage, kinship and descent, 'race' and racism are not only descriptive terms for physical difference but involve potent cultural metaphors and value judgements attempting to justify negative/discriminatory attitudes.

This is reflected in many modern states' recognising both types of claims to citizenship, although the two notions of citizenship are still problematic to reconcile in countries such as France and Germany.

The theory of distinct biological 'races' that can be hierarchically arranged, and that predict intellectual, moral and social qualities, was extensively challenged during the 1940s/1950s, in the aftermath of the Holocaust. It is now well recognised that there is a huge variation in physical characteristics within as well as between 'racial' groups, and that the boundaries of racial groups are fluid, due to constant movements and intermingling of peoples from different geographical parts of the world, earlier associated with particular racial 'types'. The idea of there being such distinct racial groups, therefore, has become unsustainable, even though racism still remains a pervasive theme within our social and political domains. Thus, although 'race' thus has no clear intellectual meaning, it continues to be prominent in social and political discourse. It features strongly in accounts in this book, often as a shorthand, although the dominant concept should more properly be ethnicity. This describes a collective identity and is based on the assumption that 'a collectivity has its roots in common ancestry, heritage, religion, culture, nationality, language and a territory' (Afkhami, 2012, p 14). While this may bring some conceptual clarity to the book, it also opens up the boundaries of what might be discussed within it. Essentially, I have sought to include contributions based on community development work where the prime focus was on ethnicity, although, as noted, the language of 'race' continues to be widely used. However, acknowledging the current global realities, reflected here in the wide range of responses to calls for contributions to the book, the impact of migration in shaping local 'communities' and requiring policy, service and community development responses is also a central theme.

The response of community development

How can community development play a role in confronting these processes on behalf of the poorest and most marginalised people, and particularly the BME people who are disproportionately represented among them? The growth of racism is perhaps one of the greatest challenges confronting the most basic values of community development. The conditions created by globalisation – of economic exploitation and division, with concomitant political division – are precisely those under which racism thrives, placing the weakest economic actors at greatest risk. This is now the global, and thus national and local, context in which community development has to find a role in order to ensure the development of a socially just society that fully includes those who offer their labour and skills, who seek to be full members of 'developed' communities and upon whom these countries' basic welfare structures and services now increasingly depend.

Community development is both a practice, with a set of skills and techniques, and a broad philosophical approach to working with people; one that strives to give ordinary people a voice for expressing and acting on their needs and desires and, through the process of participating in this approach to social change, offers people, particularly the most powerless and deprived, support for their empowerment. It is a practice whose potential for positive and peaceful social change has been recognised worldwide (Craig and Mayo, 1995; Budapest Declaration, 2004; see also www.iacdglobal.org). First of all, then, community development's response has to be to promote its value base; it should, for example, challenge the appearance of racism in whatever form it takes and, in collaboration with local minorities and majority populations, support the development of local, national and international responses and solutions to social and economic problems. In many countries, faced with an increase in racism at a local level, community development workers have often had agendas defined for them by local racist victimisation; it is here that some obvious and immediate responses of community development are being made (*Community Development Journal*, 2003; and see many of the chapters in this volume). Building on local knowledge, networks and experience, community development workers have also organised to challenge the racist pronouncements of government.

Community development now has also to work in the local context of the arrival of both migrant workers and refugees and asylum seekers, usually in fairly hostile environments, where there is competition for basic resources, where there frequently has been little history of previous migrant settlement and where little development work has been done with local residents before substantial numbers of such migrants arrive. These contexts are also the focus of many of the chapters below, which demonstrate the varying ways in which community development can challenge dominant racist discourses, publicity, local media fabrications and, increasingly, even 'fake' news.

This book

Historically, most mainstream community development literature has been focused on the notion of community as a geographical community, and on working with communities that have variously been described as in poverty, deprivation or social exclusion. The goal of this work has been to develop the ability of deprived communities to gain greater leverage over services, increase their share of resources, build their power base and so on within what would generally be understood as a pluralist context. The working definition of this form of community development is largely captured by the opening phrases of the International Association for Community Development's Budapest Declaration (2004), which argues:

Community development is a way of strengthening civil society by working with people in communities which privileges their actions and perspectives in the development of social, economic and environmental policy. It seeks the empowerment of local communities, taken to mean both geographical communities, communities of interest or identity and communities organising around specific themes or policy initiatives. Community development strengthens the capacity of people as active citizens through their community groups, organisations and networks; and the capacity of institutions and agencies (public, private and non-governmental) to work in dialogue with citizens to shape and determine change in their communities. It plays a crucial role in supporting active democratic life by promoting the autonomous voice of disadvantaged and vulnerable communities.

This broad consensual definition is not intended to be prescriptive but provides the territory within which this book is situated, based again on the core values of social justice, equality and respect for difference and diversity, values that allow us also to challenge much that goes under the rubric of community development but in reality is not true to those values – most of all top-down initiatives often in recent years characterised also as 'community capacity-building' (Craig, 2007b). The definition also recognises that community development may have different meanings and take different forms in differing contexts. For most minorities, community as geography may be far less salient than community of interest (often spanning national borders)[10]. Community development has, to emphasise this point, different specific meanings in different contexts.

As noted, the global process of migration (happening for thousands of years, but accelerating rapidly since the 1940s) brings a very specific demographic picture within each country from which case studies of community development may be drawn. These case studies should be seen within the country-specific policy and practice context in which community development has emerged. The ethnic mix in any individual country, and its changing demography, is formed by its unique mix of historical and contemporary forms of migration, including some or all of the following.

1. *Migration to 'mother'/metropolitan countries from former colonial territories* (generally in the period 1940s to the present)

These metropolitan centres are generally former European imperial nations, including the UK, France, Netherlands, Spain, Portugal, Belgium and, to a lesser extent, Germany, Italy and Denmark. This form of migration generated what are now regarded as 'settled' minorities within many countries: for example, Pakistanis and Nigerians within the UK, North Africans and Senegalese within France, Angolans within Portugal, Surinamese and Indonesians within the Netherlands and Congolese within Belgium. These 'settled' minorities now constitute between 5% and 15% of Western European country populations and have been the objects of a range of 'integrative' policy instruments variously called 'race'/community relations or community cohesion policies. In some countries, very restrictive attitudes towards citizenship status have left these minorities with the experience of being treated as second-class citizens, quite apart from the continuing forms of racism directed towards them through policy and service provision.[11] As this migration started generally in the 1940s, these communities now contain third and fourth generations, many of them born and raised within the metropolitan centres.[12] Of course many countries outside Europe have witnessed significant forms of migration shaped not necessarily by colonial relationships but, for example, by geographical proximity, as with migrants moving to the US from Mexico and to Australia from a range of European as well as South East Asian countries.

2. *Economic migrants*
Although the migration described above has largely been economic in its motivation (that is, the desire of migrants to achieve a 'better life'), more recently migration has also had an explicitly economic motive but within a different context – that is, one in which the possibility of return to a migrant's home country is also common.[13] This has been notably the case recently within Europe since the 2004 and 2007 accessions of 10 East and Central European countries where hundreds of thousands of migrants have moved towards the west within Europe, seeking work for a limited period of time (see Gregory, Chapter Seven). Frequently, many have then settled within host countries, building sustained lives there, although the possibility of occasional, frequent or even permanent return to their country of origin remains.[14] This is also a global phenomenon, with migrant workers spending anything from months to years in more wealthy countries in order to generate cash that can be remitted back to families in their poorer countries of origin (as with domestic and

construction workers in the Gulf states from Nepal, Malaysia and the Philippines). Many countries of the world, driven by right-wing populist policies, are now, as described earlier, seeking to halt the flow of economic migrants to their countries unless they bring with them significant assets such as skills and money with which, effectively, they can purchase citizenship rights. The boundary between what is properly a refugee and what is an economic migrant is one that is, in any case, increasingly blurred (although exploited often for political reasons). For example, someone fleeing the desertification of their homeland might be regarded equally as a climate-change refugee and as an economic migrant.

3. *Internal migration*
   In most countries of the world, significant internal disparities of income and wealth remain and indeed, by most accounts, have increased as a result of the marketisation of economic policy and practice. This has generated substantial internal migration, which is most obvious within larger countries such as China, Russia and India, where rural migrants have had, sometimes, to travel thousands of miles to find adequate paid work.[15] Within these countries, the general picture is of a poorly organised, heavily exploited population of migrant workers, living on the periphery of urban centres, moving in and out of poorly paid and often dangerous work, and enjoying few of the rights of full citizenship. This is a process that generates significant demographic change in the towns, cities and rural areas of many countries and is an important contributory factor to the increasing ethnic mix (and, in some cases, inter-ethnic tensions) in many areas, but presents particular difficulties for community organisers. The experience of First Nations people (see below) is also often one of forced internal migration. Internal migration is also consequent on ethnic or religious tensions, as for example with the Muslim Rohinga in northern Myanmar, who are currently the subject of what might be categorised as ethnic cleansing.

4. *Refugees and those seeking asylum*
   Since the end of the Second World War and the introduction of various refugee Conventions, it has been – at least technically – open to those fleeing persecution to seek asylum in other countries. The numbers of those seeking asylum or being automatically granted refugee status under various UN schemes accelerated substantially from the 1980s until the last few years for a variety of reasons, but most obviously from the growth of conflict within and between

nation–states, leading to moral panics within many receiving countries and increasingly repressive refugee policy regimes. These conflicts have often had an ethnic basis in which religion has also played a dominant part: obvious examples in the past twenty years include the conflicts in Bosnia and Kosovo, in northern Nigeria, in the Eastern Congo region (including Rwanda and Uganda), Sudan, Somalia, Malaya, the Caucasus, Iraq, Iran, Afghanistan and Syria. Considerable community development work has been done on the ground in receiving countries to build refugee community organisations, providing a voice for people who are frequently found at the bottom of the hierarchy of migrants, and this work has been well reported elsewhere (see, for example, Zetter et al, 2005). The 'migrant crisis' currently being experienced in Europe, with millions of refugees fleeing war and starvation in Syria has become a major focus for debate about migrants and migrations, partly because the language of many politicians has been crude and hostile and has deliberately mis–characterised most of those fleeing towards Europe as economic migrants.

5. *First Nations*

In many countries of the world (see above) there are ethnic groups referred to most widely now as First Nations groups – groups that have migrated to, within and/or lived within particular territories for thousands of years but that have been displaced by colonial conquest and settlement or, since the last century, by the processes of industrialisation and urbanisation. These groups have often been corralled into narrowly defined sites (often bearing little relationship to their original 'lands'), becoming alienated both from their historic ways of life and from more 'modern' forms of existence. The struggle of these groups to maintain their identity and achieve their aspirations for self–determination has begun to be acknowledged, albeit unevenly, since the last thirty or so years, with some forms of protective policy and practical interventions, although basic demands for the restoration of land rights, particularly in the face of mineral exploitation, remain the most problematic area.[16] Accounts in this book from Australia and New Zealand/Aotearoa reflect this on-going struggle.

This combination of forms of migration has produced a huge variety of ethnic mixtures within individual national demographies that, in the most extreme cases, are now being referred to as superdiverse countries. Community development work with local populations can (or at least should) now therefore hardly fail to address the issue of ethnicity in a context driven by the consequences of migration, although for a variety of reasons, notably individual and institutional racism, it often frequently does. What these various 'migrant' groups share is a common experience, typically of poverty, exclusion and marginalisation. Their organisation through community development work produces many challenges: one reason why there may be a relative paucity of accounts of this work is that the work may itself be quite dangerous, with workers identifying with one ethnic group sometimes facing hostility and violence from another.[17]

Because the political, historical and demographic context is critical, seeking to offer an overarching theoretical or conceptual context to this work is problematic and this book does not attempt that beyond this introduction. Providing a global theoretical context that reflects also on work in the global South would be even more problematic. Instead, the book provides a range of examples from so-called 'developed' countries, with their varying historical experiences of migration as context and a broadly common understanding of the practice of community development focusing on work with minorities. This may include working between so-called 'host country nationals' and minorities, between differing minorities (for example, recent or more long-standing minority groups) or within particular minority groups. The book has one particular small sub-focus in relation to Gypsy, Roma and Traveller groups. As probably the most marginalised of all minorities, they are more mobile and present particular challenges in community organisation. In the case of Roma groups, as well as being among the most persecuted of all European minorities, they demonstrate issues of transnational organisation pursued by Roma-led organisations.[18]

The book is organised into five sections, all of them focused on the main theme of the book – addressing racism through community development work – together with this overarching contextual chapter and a small concluding section which includes two chapters written in a more personal and ideological reflective style. This seemed appropriate to the topic of the book, since working across cultural boundaries has been and remains a challenging enterprise, with many workers facing hostility or at best indifference at their attempts to help to organise or build bridges in support of campaigns against racism. The other sections group chapters by theme, with a brief summarising introduction to each section.

The chapters were collected as a result of several calls for contributions through a series of national and international networks, a process that took more than 12 months before a final collection was agreed upon. The final selection attempted to provide a good geographical spread across the world and range in terms of the focus of the work, the context and approaches used (that is, working with minorities, working with specific minority groups, or working between 'host communities' and minorities). One of the editor's personal priorities was to include chapters on working with First Nations people (there are three in the book) and on working with Roma communities (again there are three chapters in the book), which together are probably the most marginalised by racism and yet the least reported on either in the literature or in policy and political discourse. One very difficult decision concerned the question of work in global South countries. In many countries of the global South ethnic conflicts, driven by a mix of racism and religious difference, have resulted in wars that have often had to be resolved through international interventions: Bosnia, Rwanda, Syria, Sri Lanka, Myanmar, India and Bangladesh are just a few of the very many examples that could be cited here. While there has no doubt been an enormous amount of local development work attempting to mitigate the impact of these conflicts, this is largely unrecorded and, to the extent that there is a literature, it seemed to us for several reasons (including size) that this should in any case be the subject of a separate volume. This book therefore takes the global North as its focus, with a typical historical context involving various mixes of First Nations (aboriginal) peoples, colonial settlers (who have become the dominant majority) and minorities including refugees, economic migrants and other settlers, alongside, in many cases, 'host' populations that have developed – including as a result of invasion and colonialisation – over thousands of years. The selection here cannot be described as truly representative in a scientific sense, if such a goal were possible to define and achieve, but does, I believe, provide a representative selection of contexts and approaches that allow workers from the whole of this global North context to understand the range of work currently in progress and to draw on it in shaping their own campaigns and organising. One other area that, for obvious reasons is perhaps less well-represented is work done at a very local level by local BME community organisations, work that has also been described elsewhere as 'under the radar'.[19] I have argued elsewhere (Craig, 2011) that the BME voluntary and community sector (VCS) in the UK has been historically underfunded, its work under-reported, and has recently suffered disproportionately as a result of government financial austerity measures; doubtless the same situation applies in other countries.

Section One provides two longer theoretical, historical and policy-oriented chapters on working with minority groups, providing important contexts to the more descriptive work that follows. Although I have argued elsewhere that the term 'community capacity building' has been used in recent years simply as a way for organisations – including governments – to claim that they are engaged in a form of practice that differs from community development, in reality capacity building, as understood by the authors of the chapters in Section Two, is about community development in the sense of empowering local BME communities of differing kinds and through a variety of vehicles – such as health, housing and arts and culture – to take more control over their own lives. Section Three brings together a series of three chapters about work with Roma, Gypsies and Travellers, addressing the serious lacuna in accounts of work with these most marginalised of communities. It is hoped that many more such accounts will emerge – indeed, some of the more prominent Roma-led organisations are now publishing their own accounts. Section Four offers a range of accounts of community development work with minorities from a range of countries across the world, all driven by the need to confront racism in its various forms. Across all of these sections, chapters focus on work with the differing forms of minorities described earlier – economic migrants, long-settled minority communities, First Nations people and refugees and asylum seekers. The final section includes two chapters that have a strong personal, reflective feel to them and that raise issues familiar to anyone who has worked within a multi-ethnic context. This is followed by a short conclusion drawing out some of the key lessons for community development workers that are raised by the accounts in this book.

Racism has long been a global phenomenon; but economic globalisation – with its positive and negative drivers for migration from global South to global North – now promotes the growth of new, dangerous forms of racism and ethnic division, some of which have been adopted by the new breed of political leaders. The examples in this book suggest ways in which community development can contribute both locally and globally to anti-racist work. Recent terrorist attacks in the US, the UK, Bali, France, Belgium and Germany, the wider globalising context of growing migration both within economic and refugee contexts and the growing right-wing and at times fascistic response to minorities and migrants of all kinds suggest that the task of combating racism needs to grow. For those concerned with the values of social justice and equality, key to the endeavours of community development workers in their personal and professional practice is helping to create the conditions for both mood and action, at whatever level and in whatever forums they work, against the crime of racism. It remains an urgent task.

Notes

[1] Various common formulations are used for this aggregation of 'non-host country nationals' such as BME, BAME, minority ethnic, ethnic minority. I happen to use BME without prejudice to other forms.

[2] *Community Development Journal* (2005) Special Issue, *Community development with refugees*.

[3] This is not the place to embark on a long description of the various models of integration experimented with by governments of different hues across the world. There is an extensive international literature in this area regarding multiculturalism and the attacks on it, which the reader is encouraged to consult, for example Kymlicka (1995), Modood and Werbner, P. (1997), Parekh (2002) and Lewis and Craig (2014).

[4] In two boroughs in London, Brent and Newham, minorities are in fact a majority. Others will follow.

[5] Some of this section draws on an earlier article by the author from 2002. Sadly, many of the negative predictions made then about racism have become true.

[6] For a longer account of the history of slavery and the links between historical slavery and present-day slavery see Quirk (2009) and Olusoga (2016).

[7] As for example in the tens of thousands of migrants drowned while attempting to cross the Mediterranean Sea from North Africa to Europe and the thousands more who have fallen into the hands of people traffickers.

[8] See www.peer-review-social-inclusion.eu/network-of-independent-experts/2011/promoting-the-social-inclusion-of-roma.

[9] See, for example, 'Policy and politics', chapter 3 in Craig et al, 2013.

[10] For many refugees, 'community' now has a transnational meaning as connections are made with co-nationals residing in other countries.

[11] See, for example, Craig (2007a); Craig (2013).

[12] Almost half of the minority population within the UK was born in the UK.

[13] It is worth remembering that the original migration of Pakistanis to the UK was also understood to be a temporary phenomenon: it was only 20 years after that particular migration started on a large scale that books such as the *Myth of Return* (Anwar, 1979) finally dispelled this aspiration as a myth.

[14] The earliest example of this form of migration within Europe, which has no connection with historical colonial links, is of the many tens of thousands of Greek, Turkish and Italian workers who moved to Northern, more industrialised, European countries, especially Germany, in the 1950s and 1960s.

[15] In China for example, of the 700 million residents of larger towns and cities, 200 million are rural migrants who are denied a hukuo certificate, thus preventing them from accessing welfare services for at least five years.

[16] The more organised First Nations groups often, however, reject outside intervention, arguing that they simply need the political and economic space to maintain a traditional way of life. Here is a Kuri (Aboriginal) spokesman responding to questions about capacity building in Australia. 'To restore capacity in our people

is to be responsible for our own future. Notice that I talk of restoring rather than building capacity in our people ... we had 40 to 60,000 years of survival and capacity. The problem is that our capacity has been eroded and diminished [by white colonialists] – our people do have skills, knowledge and experience ... we are quite capable of looking after our own children and fighting for their future.' Cited in Craig (2007b).

[17]   One example of this was work across 'the peace line' in Northern Ireland during the worst period of what came to be known as 'The Troubles' when community development workers attempted to bridge between nationalist and Unionist communities from differing religious persuasions. Some paid with their lives for this work, which is still under-recorded.

[18]   See, for example, www.errc.org.

[19]   See the workstream of the Third Sector Research Centre, www.birmingham. ac.uk/tsrc.

References

Afkhami, R. (2012) *Ethnicity: Introductory user guide*, Swindon: Economic and Social Data Service.

Anwar, M. (1979) *Myth of return*, London: Heinemann.

Budapest Declaration (2004) *The Budapest Declaration*, Edinburgh: IACD.

Burnett, J. (2016) *Racism and the Brexit state*, London: Institute of Race Relations.

Castles, S. and Davidson, A. (2000) *Citizenship and migration*, Basingstoke: Macmillan

Community Development Journal (2003) Special Issue, *Citizenship and participation in the new Europe*, vol 39, pp 1.

Craig, G. (2007a) 'Cunning, unprincipled, loathsome': the racist tail wags the welfare dog', *Journal of Social Policy*, vol 36, no 4, pp 605–23.

Craig, G. (2007b) 'Community capacity-building: something old, something new ...?', *Critical Social Policy*, vol 27, no 3, pp 335–59.

Craig, G. (2011) 'Forward to the past: can the UK black and minority ethnic third sector survive?', *Voluntary Sector Review*, vol 2, no 3, pp 367–89.

Craig, G. (2013) 'The invisibilisation of "race" in public policy', *Critical Social Policy*, November, pp 712–20.

Craig, G. (2015) *Factors promoting the integration of migrants*, Milan: KING.

Craig, G. and Mayo, M. (eds) (1995) *Community empowerment*, London: Zed Books.

Craig, G., Dietrich, H. and Gautie, J. (2003) 'Excluded youth or young citizens? Ethnicity, young people and the labour market in three EU countries', in J. Hoof and H. Bradley (eds) *Young people, labour markets and social citizenship*, Bristol: Policy Press.

Craig, G., Atkin, K., Chattoo, S. and Flynn, R. (eds) (2013) *Understanding 'race' and ethnicity*, Bristol: Policy Press.

Dustmann, C., Frattini, T. and Halls, C. (2010) 'The fiscal costs and benefits of A8 migration to the UK', *Fiscal Studies*, vol 31, pp 1–41.

Favell, A. (2002) 'Exposing the nation-state's true colours', *Times Higher Education Supplement*, 19 September.

Fekete, L. (2009) *A suitable enemy: Racism, migration and Islamophobia in Europe*, London: Pluto Press.

Fryer, P. (1984) *Staying power*, London: Pluto Press.

Kymlicka, W. (1995) *Multicultural citizenship*, Oxford: Oxford University Press.

Hills, J. (Chair) (2010) *An anatomy of economic inequality in the UK*, London: National Equality Panel.

Lewis, H. and Craig, G. (2014) '"Multiculturalism is never talked about": community cohesion and local policy contradictions in England, *Policy and Politics*, vol 42, no 1, pp 21–38.

Modood, T. and Werbner, P. (1997) *The politics of multiculturalism in the New Europe*, Basingstoke: Palgrave Macmillan.

Ohri, A., Manning, B. and Curno, P. (eds) (1982) *Community work and racism: Community work seven*, London: Routledge and Kegan Paul.

Olusoga, D. (2016) *Black and British*, London: Macmillan.

Parekh, B. (2002) *Rethinking multiculturalism*, Cambridge, MA: Harvard University Press.

Portes, J. and Glover, S. (2001) *Migration: An economic and social analysis*, RDS Occasional Paper no 67, London: Home Office.

Quirk, J. (2009) *Unfinished business*, Paris: UNESCO.

United Nations Non-Governmental Liaison Service (2000) 'Human rights of migrants', *Roundup*, March, New York: UNNGLS.

Zetter, R., Griffiths, D. and Sigona, N. (2005) 'Social capital or social exclusion: the impact of asylum-seeker dispersal on refugee community organisations', *Community Development Journal*, vol 40, no 2, pp 169–81.

Section One
Community development with ethnic minorities: history, theory, policy

Introduction

Gary Craig

The two chapters in this introductory section offer differing but complementary perspectives on community development with minority ethnic groups, each incorporating elements of the ideological, political, theoretical and historical.

Afridi traces the historical development of public policy towards racialised minorities in the UK, particularly through the lens of the concept of representativeness, showing how the British state has historically pursued a divide and rule strategy, working with what it regards as 'good minorities', that is, those that can be relied upon to accept the state's analysis of the origins and nature of social and political problems and can thus be accredited with the description of being representative of minorities, and dismissing those that do not (and, for example, take their protests to the streets) and that are therefore marginalised further by being labelled as unrepresentative and thus remain effectively unheard in any real political sense. As the British state has become more confident of its ability to control the way in which the issue of 'race' is defined (or indeed, as recent events have shown, 'invisibilised': see, for example, Craig, 2013), many organisations at local and national level that might lay real claim to some degree of representativeness have been closed or undermined, leaving the voice of minorities in the hands of informal selected (more accurately, patronised) groups and individuals. 'Race' is now, in the view of the British (and doubtless other) state/s, an issue of the past.

Bowler goes to the invisible heart of the matter when he brings into view the underlying 'white standards' that, he argues, underpin dominant cultural practices and that have been have been a 'core component perpetuating racialised hostile environments since the British state's [legislative and political whitewashing] of national citizenship'. This dominant (but denied) white supremacy is demonstrated at present in the UK, where, as Afridi also argues, government claims that we live in a post-racial society are set against a backdrop of rising forms of racism against all forms of minority 'other' (whether asylum seeker, settled minority citizen or migrant worker), and in all areas, whether housing significant minority populations or not. Whiteness is a hidden form of privilege that does not require of those owning it the same standards that are demanded of the 'other'; marginalised minorities are thus left alone with the responsibility of addressing the ills visited on them by a racist state.

Reference

Craig, G. (2013) 'The invisibilisation of "race" in public policy', *Critical Social Policy*, vol 33, November, pp 712–20.

ONE

BME community engagement in the UK and public policy: a brief retrospective

Asif Afridi

Introduction

Ethnic minorities in the UK have played, for some years, a relatively clear role in public policy making as 'communities of interest' in a pluralist conception of a wider system of electoral politics (Cooke and Vyas, 2008, p 14). Ethnic minority 'community leaders' and ethnic minority community-based organisations have been integrated (some would say incorporated) into public policy making and the state, and are drawn upon – albeit unevenly – to share views on how public policy should respond to issues of race inequality (Smith and Stephenson, 2005). Indeed, Hall et al (1978, p 213) argue that the representation of ethnic minorities through civil society and the state has been defined for some time as an everyday, 'technical' matter of managing political and social consent. The role of ethnic minorities in this system has been defined and enforced via race equality legislation and driven via various national and local policy initiatives. Yet, in this drive for procedural and technical refinement of community engagement processes, rarely are broader questions asked about what we mean by 'representation' and whether these forms of representation are appropriate for contemporary society.

This chapter provides one broad political and policy context for the book, complementing the historical and demographic context outlined by Craig (see Introduction) by outlining the ways in which ethnic minorities have been represented through 'community engagement' work and the close relationship between British race relations policy and the development of a BME community and voluntary 'sector' since the Second World War. After outlining this policy context, I suggest that the relationship between the state and BME communities has been restrained (even contained) and has impeded progress on race equality.

I argue that new forms of community engagement may ultimately be required to help progress race equality in the UK, but this requires a re-evaluation of societal views on what it means to 'represent' and achieve 'equality'. This chapter focuses specifically on community engagement, an important part of community development in its broadest sense. There is no widely agreed definition of 'community engagement' and associated terms like 'participation' and 'involvement' (Myhill, 2012). For my purposes, I define community engagement simply as a form of strengthening civil society by encouraging and drawing upon the perspectives of communities in the development of public policy.

A brief history of BME community engagement in Britain

There are historical records of BME community action and mutual support as far back as the 18th century (White, 2013). However, it was perhaps not until the 1950s and the development of a discernible black and Asian-British working class, following post-war immigration, that 'BME community engagement' developed in the more organised form we have come to know. It was arguably these new immigrants' experience of overt racism, lack of access to jobs and poor housing conditions on arriving in the UK that fuelled the development of more wide-scale and coordinated forms of BME community engagement. The death of Kelso Cochrane, a carpenter from Antigua, at the hands of a white gang and days of riots in Notting Hill, London in the previous year prompted the government's first inquiry into race relations in 1959. Yet the government's response to race equality through the 1960s was still largely placatory and tokenistic. Initiatives to build a National Advisory Committee for Commonwealth Immigrants (NACCI) were underfunded (Foot, 1965; Williams, 1989) and attempts to introduce early versions of a Race Relations Act (1965 and 1968) included only partial attempts to limit already widespread discrimination in public services and housing. The principal approach to race relations was one of 'assimilation', where migrants were supported to fit in and adapt to British society. Assimilation assumed that immigrants could be 'assimilated' swiftly into the 'host' community (Alibhai-Brown, 2000).

During this period, community engagement of minority groups was aimed largely at educating new arrivals and supporting them to understand what it was to be British (Grosvenor, 1997). Minority groups did not have an opportunity to offer alternative standpoints based on their cultural (or other) preferences in the political realm and were not expected to contribute information about particular needs or demands that they had. At this time a raft of restrictive immigration policy was being introduced through the Commonwealth Immigrants Bill of 1962 (limiting the number of immigrants and their citizenship rights), and mainstream politicians were drawing upon anti-immigration sentiment to build support, with Conservative MP Enoch Powell's 'Rivers of Blood' speech in 1968 being perhaps the most (in)famous example of this.

Throughout the 1950s and 1960s, black and Asian workers began collectively to organise and undertook a series of strikes and industrial action to argue for the same pay and conditions as their colleagues (Fryer, 1984). Similarly, with the support of the NACCI, Community Relations Councils began to provide advice to immigrant groups and, in time, began to advocate on their behalf and provide services to encourage 'harmonious community relations' (Law et al, 2008, p 17). The historical development of a BME VCS, much as we know it today, had commenced, and is outlined in Craig (2011b). At the same time, multiculturalism developed as a distinct strand of official public policy in the UK. This began as an educational approach in schools in the late 1960s and later expanded to the provision of public services in other fields and to the funding and empowerment of civil society groups working on behalf of particular ethnic, cultural or religious groups. By valuing, respecting and teaching others about the value and nature of other cultures, multiculturalism offered in principle a different approach to previous 'assimilationist' approaches.

Yet the introduction of the Race Relations Act in 1976 and continued action of the NACCI and other forms of grassroots voluntary action did not reduce the level and ferocity of racist attacks in many of Britain's towns and cities. Growing community tensions erupted in 1981 with mass mobilisation and demonstrations by largely black and Asian communities in response to far-Right activity and oppressive policing. 'Riots' in 1981 spread quickly from Brixton to other cities. The subsequent Scarman Inquiry, initiated by the government, found there to be strong evidence of discriminatory use of 'stop and search' powers by police against black people. In addition to changes in policing codes of practice, the final Scarman Report (1981) also highlighted the need for preventative work to address discrimination and the lack of opportunities for BME young people in the nation's urban neighbourhoods. This led to a raft of funding programmes such as the government's Urban Programme and bolstering of Section 11 funding for local authorities (under the Local Government Act, 1966) that were used, often by BME-led organisations, to tackle race inequality and disadvantage.

Towards the end of the 1980s the Commission for Race Equality supported the development and standardisation of Community Relations Councils and their name was typically changed to Race Equality Councils. Many of these ethnic-minority community-led organisations had begun to develop funded relationships with local authorities and other public agencies and were now regularly called upon to offer scrutiny and advice on issues of public policy (Smith and Stephenson, 2005). Engagement and consultation with BME communities and their involvement in public policy were becoming more organised.

By the time the Labour government was elected in 1997, there was already a discernible 'sector' of BME VCS groups and Race Equality Councils in the UK, responsible for a range of voluntary and publicly funded activities in fields such as education, health and housing (McLeod et al, 2001). Much of this activity involved direct provision of services to BME communities as well as advice and support in accessing mainstream public services. In addition, the political mobilisation of ethnic minorities had by now been encouraged and supported for decades by a strong pluralist conception of multiculturalism that had encouraged BME community groups and individuals to engage directly in the public policy process. Indeed Modood (2005, p 471) characterised ethnic minority political mobilisation in the UK as 'without parallel in Europe', due to the strength of its ideological assertiveness and impact on civic institutions.

The New Labour government saw its opportunity to draw on this 'BME third sector' in its vision for a modern multicultural Britain. Over the following decade the government and other parts of the voluntary and charitable trust sector also sought to regularise and improve the services provided by BME third sector organisations through local commissioning relationships and the funding of regional BME networks and 'infrastructure' organisations across the country to support and represent those local groups (Afridi, 2007; D'Angelo, 2013). Various guides for local authorities, explaining how they could improve the technical process of engagement with BME communities, appeared in this period (Page et al, 2007; Scottish Centre for Regeneration, 2007; Perry and Azim Al-Hassan, 2008). Following the introduction of the Race Relations Amendment Act (2001), which placed a positive duty on public authorities to address institutional racism, there were also a range of community development-focused activities for BME people run from within public sector organisations themselves. The Department of Health's 'Delivering Race Equality' programme (2005–09) is a good example; this saw the recruitment of many BME community development workers by mental health trusts to improve BME engagement and patient experience (Department of Health, 2005; Craig and Walker, 2012).

Yet, alongside this commitment to a modern, 'multicultural' Britain, following violence in northern mill towns in the UK in the summer of 2001 and the events of 9/11 and later 7/7,[1] the New Labour government began to show signs that its commitment to 'multiculturalism' and support for community groups that helped specific ethnic or faith groups was waning. The advent of 'community cohesion' policy can be seen as a response to some of the competition and (at times violent) conflict in northern English towns – which was reportedly exacerbated by the lack of contact and communication between different ethnic and religious communities associated with previous multicultural policies (Cantle, 2001) – as well as to provocation by far Right political groups. Local authorities were encouraged to promote a common vision and a sense of belonging for all communities through developing positive relationships between people from different backgrounds at the neighbourhood level. While community cohesion policy placed significance emphasis on participation and community engagement (Commission on Integration and Cohesion, 2007), related government guidance (CLG, 2009) offered little, often contradictory, direction on desirable models for the representation and engagement of minority groups in public decision making (Lewis and Craig, 2014).

By 2010 and the election of a Coalition government, 'race' was rapidly slipping down the political agenda (Craig, 2013). In 2011, Prime Minister Cameron signalled the government's retrenchment from multiculturalism both as a normative ideal and as a set of useable public policies in the face of the global financial crisis and extremism. He asserted the 'failure of state multiculturalism' and the need to replace 'passive tolerance' of faith groups with a more 'muscular liberalism' based on British values. This was accompanied by policy announcements that heralded a clear move away from the communitarian 'identity politics' of the past, in favour of a liberal individualist approach based on individual needs (HM Government, 2010, p 6). The Home Office funding for regional BME voluntary sector networks ended in 2012; similarly, at a national level, the funding for all of the central government's Office for Civil Society's strategic 'race'-related partners was withdrawn in 2011.

In 2010 a coalition of larger national race-equality organisations made a statement calling on the government to place more focus on race equality and develop targeted programmes, with the help of BME VCS organisations, to promote the civic and political engagement of

BME communities (CORE, 2010). Yet, across the country the number of smaller local community-based organisations specifically supporting BME communities was already shrinking in size and number in the face of increasing competition for funding and local contracts and lack of discretionary public spending for race-equality initiatives (V4CE, 2009; ROTA, 2011). Initial evidence suggested that significant funding cuts to local authorities have had a profound impact upon the ability of many local areas to respond to people's needs and entitlements (Asenova and Stein, 2014). These funding cuts are concentrated particularly in local authority districts that have historically been more deprived (SPERI, 2014), and it is traditionally excluded groups (such as women and ethnic minorities) in particular that have been most affected by benefits changes and austerity policies (Women's Budget Group, 2014; Runnymede Trust, 2015).

Yet, at a time when issues of inequality are a significant concern for many local areas and when strong public governance processes are required in order to involve BME groups (and indeed other traditionally excluded groups) in decisions about effective public resource allocation, local authorities have also faced significant pressures in relation to their wider engagement through public and democratic functions. For example, in 2013 Birmingham City Council, the largest local authority in Europe, proposed a reduction of some £14 million between 2014 and 2017 in its 'support costs', which include: corporate policy making, representing local interests, duties arising from public accountability and support work to ensure that there is good governance. This reduction in the capacity of local authorities to engage with BME communities in traditional ways (such as through investment in race equality-focused consultation exercises and forums for local BME communities) has also been accompanied by a significant shake-up in the way public authorities have been asked to respond to their legal equality obligations. The introduction of the Equality Act in 2010 and subsequent reviews of this legislation have created an environment in which public authorities have fewer specific duties and have been asked to respond to a broader range of inequalities. Public authorities have more autonomy to decide how they respond and prioritise action in addressing inequality across nine protected characteristics (including 'race'). National bodies such as the Equality and Human Rights Commission and the government's own Equalities Office have also been subject to severe funding cuts (Craig, 2013).

Thus, by 2016 the voluntary sector, race equality and indeed 'equality' itself as a policy agenda were under significant pressure. The political space afforded to those campaigning to promote race equality has diminished significantly. The nature of BME community engagement has also arguably begun to shift too, from the relatively formalised and well-resourced engagement of BME communities of the 1990s and 2000s to something more voluntary and sporadic. Race equality and the provision of discretionary funding for activities or public services to address inequalities faced by BME communities has been eclipsed by concerns about the wider impact of public spending cuts and the slashing of benefits on those for whom, overwhelmingly, the welfare state is most necessary. Despite some progress in the UK's responses to race inequality (in fields like school attainment), a number of persistent and systemic race inequalities remain. Babies born to Black Caribbean and Pakistani origin British families are still twice as likely to die in their first year as White British babies. Gypsies and Travellers and some types of migrants are still much more likely to face negative attitudes, and some social groups face much higher barriers of discrimination and inequality in the worlds of work, education and public life (EHRC, 2015).[2] The disproportionate impact of the government's austerity policies on race inequality has also been accompanied by an increasingly narrow and hostile focus and framing of 'race' in the media and politics in relation to issues of immigration (Blinder and Jeannet, 2014).

The narrowing of political space to discuss issues of race inequality and exclusion has also made it harder for those experiencing or affected by immigration to share their views. The UK's EU referendum and decision to leave the European Union has thrown into stark relief some of the (often unspoken) challenges the country is facing in its response to immigration and the inequalities and tensions that this can cause between communities. The voices of new migrants are rarely heard in policy making as local authorities struggle to deliver basic services to the whole population (Guma, 2015), let alone engage with and monitor new residents who arrive in their localities (Aspinall, 2012; Sachrajda and Griffith, 2014). Indeed, gone are the days when many local areas could involve a handful of 'migrant' representatives (largely from Commonwealth countries) in public decision making and fairly confidently suggest that they had achieved a level of representation that mirrored the local population. Many of these towns and cities are now 'superdiverse' (Vertovec, 2007) with people from 150+ nationalities, various identities and migration statuses living within their boundaries. We face new and unique challenges in responding to this complexity at a local level. Not only do BME communities face the practical challenge of understanding what people from different backgrounds value, and translating that into public policy within the broader context of the decline of many traditional organised forms of BME community engagement. They also face the challenge of balancing a wide range of diverse social groups' needs and responding to a range of inequalities that have become, in some cases, more entrenched in the face of welfare austerity.

So what next for the UK?

The interpretation of the development of 'BME community engagement' in the UK that is offered above is of course selective and benefits from hindsight. I have emphasised the close relationship between the state and the BME VCS that has been responsible for organising or mediating much BME community engagement over the last twenty years or so. This relationship has not always been either healthy or smooth. I have shown how state-funded initiatives helped to establish a discernible BME VCS and formalised routes for influence and scrutiny of public policy. Yet, at the same time, in the same way that government intervention helped to improve the visibility of 'race' in public policy, recent withdrawals of public funding for BME VCS organisations and a narrowing of the political space afforded to issues of race equality have led to an invisibilising of 'race' in public policy discourse and practice (Craig, 2013). This is problematic, given contemporary tensions in society surrounding issues of immigration, integration, growing levels of deprivation and persistent patterns of systemic race inequality.

Indeed the purposive or unintentional (mis)appropriation of community engagement activities by the public sector has been a common theme in wider studies of community development. Craig (2011a, p 12) cites the 'old tensions' of community development associated with 'manipulation of communities, misappropriation of terminology, co-option of activists, conditional funding and state-controlled power games such as divide and rule'. Building on Craig's critical analysis I suggest that there are three key challenges associated with the influence of the state and wider powerful forces in society that have limited the progress of BME community engagement and action on race equality. I argue that if we are to improve our response to race inequality in the future, then we will need to engage with these challenges and develop new approaches to progress 'representation' and 'equality' (see also James, 2008).

First, much BME community engagement has started from a 'deficit model' in relation to the state. There is often an assumption on the part of public sector organisations that they know too little about the BME community in question, and this is almost invariably seen to be the community's 'fault'. The community is seen to be so different from the 'mainstream' and so 'hard to reach' that public service providers cannot be expected to meet their specific needs without further research, consultation and scoping.[3] Addressing this deficit of knowledge, or lack of engagement with 'hard to reach' groups should become central to the state's response to many new initiatives to address race equality in a diverse range of policy areas. Initiatives and funding to encourage BME community engagement have been designed using this model. Yet rarely is the 'deficit' framed conversely, in terms of the inability of public authorities to convince BME communities that their concerns will be acted upon. One official indicator used to gauge the appropriateness of democratic activity in English local authorities has been the percentage of people who 'feel they can influence decisions in their locality'. This indicator has been disaggregated by ethnicity in the past and can help in understanding perceptions of influence (Gill and Cave, 2011). Yet, on its own, an indicator like this is limited in terms of its ability to capture how people really feel about their representation in the policy-making process (Chanan and Miller, 2013). Arguably, questions that address 'deficits' in the state's response to inequality, such as whether people feel that representatives are 'acting on their behalf', or whether representatives are helping to 'improve responses to race inequality', are equally if not more pertinent in this context.

Second, perhaps our lack of understanding and monitoring of how BME communities feel about their 'representation' reveals deep-seated attitudes about the type of representation BME communities have been led to expect when engaging with public authorities. Currently, the predominant model that is aspired to when engaging BME communities in public policy making is 'descriptive representation' (Judge, 2014). In this model, representatives are sought with particular attributes (such as ethnicity or nationality) who can share the views of a larger group of others with that attribute. As Pitkin (1967, p 61) puts it, focus is placed upon 'what he is or is like, on being something rather than doing something'. For many public authorities, measuring the ethnic profile of those involved in community engagement activities and developing a sufficiently nuanced list of local communities of interest that reflects the population has been a strong indicator of their ability to achieve 'equality' in community engagement (Blake et al, 2008, p 32). This has driven efforts to improve the reach and accessibility of public services. And certainly achieving descriptive representation has been a hard-fought struggle for many traditionally excluded minority groups. Indeed, it is hardly surprising that continued race inequalities in society have reinforced public calls for more BME politicians and more BME people to be involved in policy making in order to help to respond to the persistent nature of racism and discrimination in society. Yet rarely are questions asked about whether this model is all we should be aiming for in terms of representation and what its contribution has been to addressing race inequality in society. It also ignores serious questions about the highly gendered and often elder-dominated notions of 'community leaders' that are often accepted without question by public bodies as representative of minorities.

When descriptive representation is judged as a goal in itself to be achieved by public authorities, this can help to show one aspect of BME groups' engagement with the public policy process. Yet, when descriptive representation is judged as a proxy for other forms of representation such as 'substantive representation', then we are on less solid ground. 'Substantive representation' refers to the ability of representatives to further the policy preferences and interests of the represented (Pitkin, 1967). I have argued elsewhere that often the purpose of efforts to improve representation in policy making for excluded groups is unclear (Afridi, 2016). In the context of BME community engagement, I would argue that for many public authorities the achievement of descriptive representation has been seen as sufficient. Focus is placed squarely on the 'point of entry' to public engagement processes and less focus has been placed on the levels of power and equality that those representatives have to influence policy once inside the process (substantive representation). Many BME community groups and representatives have sought to improve the levels of power and substantive representation that they are able to progress within the policy-making process. Yet I would argue that repeated exposure to state-sponsored, formalised and technocratic forms of BME community engagement that favour descriptive representation as an end-goal have shaped our experience and ultimately conditioned many people's expectations of what can be achieved through BME 'representation' in the policy-making process. The expectations of those in power are conservative in scope and should be subjected to greater public debate. More conscious efforts to progress and measure substantive representation for those furthering the interests of race equality (whether from BME backgrounds or not) in policy making are required.

Third, and perhaps most damaging of all, has been a tendency for the state to treat the public's input on race equality-related policy issues as something that can be achieved only through the engagement of specific forms of BME community engagement. Specific forms of BME community leadership (often, as noted, male, older and heterosexual[4]) and the engagement of specific BME community-based organisations have been nurtured and called upon to represent the views of their community (sometimes with more passive and compliant organisations being 'chosen' to participate with government, rather than organisations that might have a more assertive voice). This has, nevertheless, been a significant if circumscribed advance in the rights of BME people to self-determination and political mobilisation and has come a long way since the early work of Community Relations Councils in the 1960s. Yet, at the same time, these advances have come at a cost. Established models of BME community engagement can be problematic not only because of the well-established criticisms of 'essentialism' and lack of representation of the interests of women, young people and other excluded groups by self-appointed community leaders (Murphy, 2012). Existing models of BME representation in the public policy process can also fail to keep pace with the complex and subtle ways in which racism is changing. For example, the relationship between race and class can be downplayed when BME representatives are expected to 'look' a particular way (with authenticity and legitimacy linked closely to representatives' ethnic minority background). This has, arguably, limited the voice of other majority and minority groups who do not 'fit the mould' that is expected for 'BME representatives'. Indeed, opportunities for collective action and solidarity between 'majority' and 'minority' groups in response to the everyday effects of government austerity and growing wage inequality in the UK are weakened as BME community engagement practice encourages representatives to emphasise their differences as opposed to their commonalities in order to secure entitlements and progress on race equality.

But more than this, 'racism' is reinforced in other ways in society too. It can be found in discrimination based on people's accents, on their postcodes, on the way they dress and the way they choose to name their children. Different types of racism are also being felt by new arrivals with different immigration statuses. In the wake of the UK's decision to leave the EU in June 2016 there are, as noted above, widespread reports of markedly growing racism and xenophobia against both established and newer EU migrants as well as asylum seekers and refugees. New patterns of migration are likely to force policy makers to reassess their approaches to the engagement and representation of BME communities and their approaches to allocating (increasingly scarce) public resources to respond to race inequality. I would argue that increasing focus on and purposeful monitoring of issues of 'substantive' representation by policy makers, and whether BME community engagement is furthering the preferences of local people on race inequality, should be an important part of that equation.

Yet focusing on substantive representation does not mean that we should forget about descriptive representation and ensuring that our policy-making processes mirror the characteristics of those that are routinely racialised. This is an important sign of equitable access to the democratic process. The two types of representation are not mutually exclusive. Indeed, Lentin (2016) acknowledges how definitions of racism have become wider in recent years. Yet she also warns against the growing 'motility' of racism, which, as a consequence, becomes generalised, applicable in a range of circumstances and polyvalent:

> As racism becomes more motile, in the sense of being made to apply – according to a post-racial logic – to an ever-increasing variety of circumstances and population, the permission for the racialized to define racism is consequently foreclosed. (Lentin, 2016, p 36)

In a UK context, this will mean finding resources (be those voluntary or state funded) to support the voiceless to share their experiences of racialisation. Yet, at the same time, as I have suggested in this chapter, this will need to be on BME communities' own terms. The pursuit of simple, convenient forms of descriptive representation that have supported the technology of local governance and the management of social and political consent are unlikely to respond to the systemic and adaptable nature of racism in our society. Certainly these technologies of community engagement have struggled to achieve this so far. We will need to demand more from public governance and community engagement processes. More systematic assessment of people's levels of substantive representation in the process is a good start. Those who are sharing their opinions about how race inequality should be addressed in our society need more power and respect in the policy-making process. And this process is unlikely to be easy. Responding to diversity is difficult, messy and not always comfortable. It requires us to acknowledge different ways of looking at the world and to understand, at times, our own complicity in replicating and sustaining forms of inequality. Engagement processes that support and manage these types of awareness raising, conflict and debate are our best chance of progressing race equality. In short, we need to put the 'politics' back into BME community engagement, and policy makers need to be ready for this and to embrace it with open arms because it will help all of us.

Notes

[1] 9/11 was the attack on the twin towers of the World Trade Center in New York in September 2001, and 7/7 the London bombings of July 2005.

[2] The issue of hate crime against minorities achieved prominence after the Brexit vote of June 2016 – the Leave vote being understood by some to have been driven substantially by racism and xenophobia – with a sharp rise in the numbers of incidents reported to the police, themselves a fraction of the number of actual incidents.

[3] The same issue dogs the funding of research, where many researchers and funders have argued that it is too difficult to research minority ethnic groups because their numbers are too small or it is too expensive to include the costs of effective translation and interpretation in their research projects (Katbamna and Craig, 2012).

[4] A classic example was the meeting with community leaders called by former Prime Minister Tony Blair at Downing Street in the wake of the 7/7 bombing: all of those 'leaders' – chosen by Blair's advisers – were male and aged over 50.

References

Afridi, A. (2016) 'Identity, representation and the acceptable face of equalities policy-making in Britain', *Journal of Poverty and Social Justice*, vol 24, no 1, pp 77–83.

Afridi, A. (2007) *Performance and Race Equality Project Report*, London: ChangeUp.

Alibhai-Brown, Y. (2000) *After multiculturalism*, London: Foreign Policy Centre.

Asenova, D. and Stein, B. (2014) *Assessing the social and community risks of council spending cuts in Scotland*, York: Joseph Rowntree Foundation.

Aspinall, P.J. (2012) 'Answer formats in British census and survey ethnicity questions: does open response better capture "superdiversity"?', *Sociology*, vol 46, no 2, pp 354–64.

Blake, G., Diamond, J., Foot, J., Gidley, B., Mayo, M., Shukra, K. and Yarnit, M. (2008) *Community engagement and community cohesion*, York: Joseph Rowntree Foundation.

Blinder, S. and Jeannet, A.M. (2014) 'Numbers and eaves, the illegal and the skilled: the effects of media portrayals of immigrants on public opinion in Britain', Working Paper no 116, Oxford: COMPAS.

Cantle, T. (2001) *Community cohesion – a report of the Independent Review Team*, London: Home Office.

Chanan, G. and Miller, C. (2013) *Rethinking community practice: Developing transformative neighbourhoods*, Bristol: Policy Press.

CORE (Coalition of Race Equality Organisations) (2010) Position statement on race equality, www.raceequalityfoundation.org.uk/advisory-groups/core/position-statement, accessed 29 June 2016.

Commission on Integration and Cohesion (2007) *Our shared future*, London: COIC.

CLG (Communities and Local Government) (2009) *Guidance for local authorities on how to mainstream cohesion into other services*, London: HM Government.

Cooke, S. and Vyas, D. (2008) *Votes and voices: The complementary nature of representative and participative democracy*, London: LGA.

Craig, G. (2011a) 'Reflections on community development, community engagement and community capacity-building', *Concept*, vol 2, no 2, pp 7–13.

Craig, G. (2011b) 'Forward to the past: can the UK black and minority ethnic third sector survive?', *Voluntary Sector Review*, vol 2, no 3, pp 367–90.

Craig, G. (2013) 'The invisibilisation of '"race"in public policy', *Critical Social Policy*, vol 33, issue 4, November, pp 712–20.

Craig, G. and Walker, R. (2012) 'Race on the welfare margins', *Community Development Journal*, vol 46, no 3, pp 491–505.

D'Angelo, A. (2013) 'Migrant and BME organisations in the UK: navigating the perfect storm', paper presented at the Social Policy Association Annual Conference, University of Sheffield.

Department of Health (2005) *Delivering race equality in mental health care: An action plan for reform inside and outside services and the Government's response to the independent inquiry into the death of David Bennett*, London: Department of Health.

EHRC (Equality and Human Rights Commission) (2015) *Is Britain fairer?*, London: EHRC.

Foot, P. (1965) *Immigration and race in British politics*, London: Penguin.

Fryer, P. (1984) *Staying power: The history of black people in Britain*, London: Pluto Press.

Gill, B. and Cave, K. (2011) 'What do we know about the extent of community engagement in different communities?', in R. Tunstall, R. Lupton, A. Power and L. Richardson (eds), *Building the Big Society*, London: CASE.

Grosvenor, I. (1997) *Assimilating identities: Racism and education policy in post-1945 Britain*, London: Lawrence and Wishart.

Guma, T. (2015) *Ethnicisation of need: Questioning the role of ethnicity in the provision of support and services for post-accession migrants in Glasgow*, policy paper, Glasgow: University of Glasgow.

Hall, S., Critcher, C., Jefferson, T., Clarke, J. and Roberts, B. (1978) *Policing the crisis: Mugging, the state, and law and order*, Birmingham: Critical Social Studies

HM Government (2010) *The equality strategy: Building a fairer Britain*, London: HM Government.

James, M. (2008) *Interculturalism: Theory and practice*, London: Baring Foundation.

Judge, D. (2014) *Democratic incongruities: Representative democracy in Britain*, Basingstoke: Palgrave Macmillan.

Katbamna, S. and Craig, G. (2012) '"Race"and social policy research', *Understanding research for social policy and social work* (2nd edn), Bristol: Policy Press, pp 141–6.

Law, I., Hunter, S., Osler, A., Swann, S., Tzanelli, R. and Williams, F. (2008) Working paper 3: *Ethnic relations in the UK*, Leeds: University of Leeds.

Lentin, A. (2016) 'Racism in public or public racism: doing anti-racism in "post-racial" times', *Ethnic and Racial Studies*, vol 39, no 1, pp 33–48.

Lewis, H. and Craig, G. (2014) '"Multiculturalism is never talked about": community cohesion and local policy contradictions in England', *Policy and Politics*, vol 42, no 1, pp 21–38.

Mcleod, M., Owen, D. and Khamis, C. (2001) *Black and minority ethnic voluntary and community organisations: Their role and future development in England and Wales*, York: Joseph Rowntree Foundation.

Modood, T. (2005). 'Ethnicity and Political Mobilisation in Britain', in G.C. Loury, C. Glenn, T. Modood and S.M. Teles (eds), *Ethnicity, social mobility and public policy*, Cambridge: Cambridge University Press, pp 457–74.

Murphy, M. (2012) *Multiculturalism: A critical introduction*, Abingdon: Routledge.

Myhill, A. (2012) *Community engagement in policing: Lessons from the literature*, London: National Police Improvement Agency.

Page, J., Whitting, G. and Mclean, C. (2007) *Engaging effectively with black and minority ethnic parents in children's and parental services*, London: Department for Children Schools and Families.

Perry, J. and Azim Al-Hassan, A. (2008) *A guide to engaging Muslim communities*, London: Chartered Institute of Housing.

Pitkin, H. (1967) *The concept of representation*, Berkeley, CA: University of California.

ROTA (Race on the Agenda) (2011) *The impact of the economic downturn on BAME education services*, London: ROTA.

Runnymede Trust (2015) *The 2015 budget: Effects on black and minority ethnic people*, London: Runnymede Trust.

Sachrajda, A. and Griffith, P. (2014) *Shared ground: Strategies for living well together in an era of high immigration*, London: Institute for Public Policy Research.

Scarman, L. (1981) *The Scarman Report into the Brixton Disorders*, Harmondsworth: Penguin.

Scottish Centre for Regeneration (2007) *Community engagement how-to guide: Engagement and equalities – how to engage with minority ethnic communities*, Edinburgh: Scottish Centre for Regeneration.

SPERI (Sheffield Political Economy Research Institute) (2014) *Local authority spending cuts and the 2014 English local elections*, SPERI British Political Economy Brief no 6, Sheffield: University of Sheffield.

Smith, G. and Stephenson, S. (2005) 'The theory and practice of group representation: reflections on the governance of race equality in Birmingham', *Public Administration*, vol 83, no 2, pp 323–43.

Vertovec, S. (2007) 'Super-diversity and its implications', *Ethnic and Racial Studies*, vol 30, no 6, pp 1024–54.

V4CE (Voice4Change England) (2009) Letter to Director General of Office of the Third Sector, 23 December, www.voice4change-england.co.uk/webfm_send/45, accessed 29 June 2016.

White, J. (2013) *A great and monstrous thing: London in the eighteenth century*, London: Vintage.

Williams, F. (1989) *Social policy: A critical introduction*, Cambridge: Polity Press.

TWO

Critical youth and community work and its struggle with white standards

Rick Bowler

Where are we heading? How do we begin to dream ourselves out of this dark place of death and destruction and war, from this suffocating place where anyone who is not down with the war plan could be labelled a traitor? (Kelley, 2002, p 196)

Introduction

The ideas set out here emerged from a talk the author gave to the UK North East region[1] regional Hate Crime Conference organised as a partnership between the North East Race Equality Forum (NEREF)[2] and the Office of the Northumbria Police and Crime Commissioner (PCC) in late 2015. In that talk the environments of hostility encouraged by elements of the political establishment (Withnall, 2013; Syal, 2014) were identified as an important contextual reality in the everyday lives of BME young people in the city of Sunderland (Bowler, 2006; Saeed, 2007).

The chapter looks back on a 20-year developmental process to offer reflections on the place of 'white standards' (Lorenz, 1996, p 174) impacting upon a small intercultural youth work[3] project. I argue that the white standards underpinning dominant cultural practices have been a core component perpetuating racialised hostile environments since the British state's whitewashing of national citizenship in the 1950s (Paul, 1997). It has been argued that whiteness is performed, yet appears to operate imperceptibly to those who embody it (Ahmed, 2004). This performance of whiteness is illuminated in the current moment where dominant establishment claims of a post-racial society (Nayak, 2006) are juxtaposed against rising forms of xeno-racism (Fekete, 2001), articulated through a focus upon anti-asylum, anti-immigrant and anti-Muslim activity. The resurgence of white authoritarian nationalism has accompanied a rise in racist violence, particularly in dominant monocultural white geographies across the UK (Burnett, 2013). This violence has been further accentuated by the 2016 decision of the UK to leave the EU and the neofascist comments made by prominent 'Brexiteers'.

The chapter counters the dominant idea that Britain is post-racial. The counter-story illuminates attempts by BME and white youth workers to work with BME and white young people to encourage intercultural relationships in predominantly white spaces. The author explores the changes and continuities in the British state's relationship to its own formations of racism. It does this through a reflective exploration from a youth and community work initiative arising out of a community struggle for justice located in Sunderland in the North East of England. This inner-city youth project is called Young Asian Voices (YAV); it emerged in a place where the privileged status of whiteness operates as the primary marker of the everyday norm.[4] The author steps back from describing the young people or the community youth work in order to place in the spotlight the different faces of the hostile environment that have been a continuous presence throughout YAV's 20-year history.

The front story thus focuses on whiteness as a system of privilege that keeps alive racial logics, maintains social division and leaves critical conversations about intercultural futures outside of mainstream planning. The backstory utilises key moments in YAV's work with young people across that 20-year time frame. It offers an association that shows that while youth work offered hope by seeking anti-racist intercultural futures for young people focused on place, the white standards underpinning dominant decisions about resourcing these futures perpetuate logics that (re)produce race (Mills, 1999).

We begin by setting out conceptual and contextual concerns. This is followed by an exploration of how white standards operated to undermine critical youth work processes throughout YAV's journey. The author concludes with a call for community youth work to resist white standards by helping young people in dreaming about a better world.

Conceptualising white standards

> Whiteness in a racist, corporate-controlled society is like having the image of an American Express card or Diners

> Club card stamped on one's face: immediately, you are 'universally accepted'. (Marable, 1997, p 3)

British racism, critiqued through the lens of Critical Race Theory (CRT)[5] enables a theorising of practice that acknowledges that despite 'race' being a social construct, it persists, through processes of racialisation, as a 'lived reality' (re)produced discursively (Hylton et al, 2011). Twine (2004) defines one important aspect of lived reality as a 'racial reality', identifying that all people have one but not everyone has the racial literacy to enable them critically to engage with it. One major gap in the British political landscape has been the absence from policy decisions of an understanding that white identities are also racialised (Garner, 2007).

In conceptualising white standards it is necessary to recognise whiteness as a privileging social system (Gillborn, 2006, 2008; Preston, 2009). Whiteness as a privileging social system perpetuates unequal relations of power and identity and this requires exposure because, as Bonnett (1996, pp 97–8) observes, 'Whiteness is a peculiar identity [...] invisible, largely undiscussed'. The lack of discussion about whiteness has been a major source of difficulty for YAV because it leaves white standards outside of critique. The absence of dialogue about how white people develop their racial literacies is a necessary component of an explanatory framework in building intercultural pedagogies with young people. Furthermore, Garner (2012, p 446) has identified how whiteness as a system of 'moral economy' is an influencing factor in the (re)production of 'white as a position of relative privilege'.

How this positioning of relative privilege performs in the local contexts of the North East region and the city where YAV developed is an important consideration because 'race' always intersects with other social divisions. White standards overlap with and are woven into dominant norms about class, gender, heteronormativity, age and ability. The anti-racist knowledge assembled from the community of practice of critical anti-racist youth work requires that youth workers have a professional responsibility critically to consider the community contexts in which young people learn about the world (Bowler, 2103). In adhering to this responsibility the core components of the community contexts influencing young people's personal, social, spiritual and political literacies about the world require situating[6]

How the youth worker situates the life-worlds of young people requires an explanatory framework that is itself literate about the socio-cultural orientations in which life-worlds are constituted (Grunwald and Thiersch, 2009). The youth work within YAV was focused on bridging differences between racially categorised young people. The purpose was to develop intercultural literacy. In doing this, the community/youth worker engages young people in educational processes that explore a socio-cultural reading of how their worlds are racialised.

I cannot find an example of where a local or national policy maker has openly discussed how they had challenged their own racial illiteracy on their journeys to recognising how the British state could come to terms with its own racist past and present. This is despite the empirical work identifying the different ways that the logics of race underpin everyday ideas about whiteness, British/English identity and entitlement (Clarke and Garner, 2010; Garner, 2012). In her critique of cultural racism in the decade leading up to YAV's formation, Murray (1986, p 2) identified how anti-racism was attacked in pursuit of 'national pride and the liberation of the white majority'. In this reformulation of a very particular whitewashed British national identity, the die was cast through an enactment of 'unashamedly racist "white culturalism"' (Murray, 1986, p 3).

We argue that it is these cultures of white standard policy making that require to be changed if the desire to move beyond race by ending racism is to be achievable. These white standards hinder critical work with communities and young people, limiting any approaches on the ground that try to challenge endemic ignorance about Britain's racial realities.

Some thoughts about whiteness and context

[P]eople need to create modes of belonging, accountability, and justice that are not predicated on someone else's denigration and dehumanization. (Ioanide, 2015, p 112)

As Lorenz (1996, p 174) uncovered in his analysis of youth work and anti-racism, there has been collusion with 'white standards', thus diminishing the realities of racism. In his work on pedagogical principles for anti-racist intercultural possibilities, Lorenz locates white as inside the 'ethnicity' box and thus confronts directly the misconception in dominant European thought that posits white as the default norm for an identity that belongs.

In the period of the British state when the Empire was in decline and anti-colonial struggles were shifting the tectonic plates of 'white rule', the British establishment set out to bring conceptions of white supremacist thought back into the metropole (Schwarz, 1996, 2011).

In this (re)production, 'scientific' racism was socially engineered into the concept of Britishness, with British identity becoming literally 'whitewashed' (Paul, 1997). The 2016 vote by British people to exit the EU has demonstrated how ideas about Britishness retain a deep connection to issues of 'race', sovereignty and belonging (Chowdhury, 2016; Rose, 2016).

In the two decades before YAV was established in 1996, Britain's BME youth were experiencing extreme levels of racist political violence combined with deeply embedded state racism (Sivanandan, 1982; Ramamurthy, 2013). These were formative times for all those citizens learning about their place in society. The 1980s saw a resurgence of 'nostalgia for past greatness and xenophobia' that generated 'a kinetic energy to racist ideology' (Murray, 1986, p 7). This was the England in which the second generation of Bengalis in Sunderland were brought up and from which YAV emerged.[7] This national context underwent some structural change, following the 1997 election of a New Labour government, that culminated in a framework for equality and human rights (TSO, 2010). Despite a relatively strong equality and human rights policy frame, British society remained divided, in part because of its cultural attachment to the racial coding of whiteness (Parekh, 2000; Garner, 2012).

The region where YAV developed is a predominantly monocultural white setting (Bowler, 2006). This backdrop is a crucial component in any explanatory frame about how whiteness as a privileging social system interacts with the identity formations of young white or BME people growing up in places such as Sunderland, a fairly typical formerly industrialised city where skilled manual work has been replaced by low-paid service sector work and high levels of unemployment. We know that racialised identities, whether BME or white, are complex, nuanced and constituted in relation to place (Nayak, 2003). The city itself is of course also racialised within the wider national narrative.

The North East region has been identified by some national media narratives as containing the whitest place in England and Britain (Manzoor, 2006; Casciani, 2008).[8] This identification of white cannot be adequately understood outside of its historical connection to whiteness (Bonnett, 2008). White is a racialised social construct. The middle-class media portrayals of 'white' culturally produce an identification of whiteness as if this has meaning outside of race and place (Lloyd, 2008; Martin, 2008; Mukherjee, 2008). In the construction of white by sections of the white middle-class media, public education about the region foregrounded identity politics over the politics of redistribution. This left the historical legacy of British racism, its white racial logic and the on-going racialisation of material inequalities as absent considerations. The white logics woven into the white standards performed by sections of the media were not opened up by them for critique. This is because white norms construct 'white identities [...] as cultureless' (Perry, 2001, p 57).

The regional geography of the North East is much more complex and nuanced, although it is an area where racist violence persists in everyday life (Saeed, 2007; Craig et al, 2012; NERCJRRN, 2012). As a white highland region it also contains 'some of the most deprived areas in England', experiencing poor socio–economic and health indicators across age, gender, class and ethnic backgrounds (Fleming, 2012, p 2).

The public narration of white as whitest onto a community context that was recovering from the devastation of the industrial closures (of mining, engineering and shipbuilding) imposed brutally by a neoliberal government in the 1980s, lacked the reality that whiteness is simultaneously at the core of racial logic but invisible in public policy concerns. These impositions of white standards are part of a process of 'fact faking' embedded within dominant cultural messages that obscure an open dialogue about sociocultural contexts framing young people's lives (Alexander, 2000, p 243). What was meant by white as it relates to the racialisation of identity and the stratification of inequality in these portrayals about the North East region and its containment of the whitest place in Britain requires the framing of 'race' and the exposure of racism to be accurately located and adequately put, literally and figuratively, in their place.

Critical youth and community work, YAV and the trouble with white standards

> [C]ontrolling images and the cultural myths associated with them are not simply imposed from outside their bodies, but deeply internalized psychologically-speaking. (Hancock, 2016, p 174)

It is now generally accepted that young people in Britain are navigating their transition to adulthood within an ever more challenging and complex world, in localities that are themselves unequal and fraught with social divisions (Grattan, 2009). This changing landscape in which young people negotiate and mediate their inter/independence places demands upon them to be more empowered and socially and emotionally literate so that 'Personal change in their lives [...] can lead to positional change in their circumstances' (McNeil et al, 2012, p 6).

The community youth work in YAV was driven by a desire to challenge both the external racism embedded in the state as well as the cultural myths that young people can come to believe. These dominant cultural myths, familial, communal and societal, can mask the vulnerabilities that young people experience while leaving them feeling not worthy (Tyler, 2013). Critical youth workers thus require knowledge that can help young people to work with complex intersectional identifications and be vigilant of the specific influences of 'particularly vulnerable locations' (Hancock, 2016, p 158). For youth workers working across these different formations of vulnerability, a focus on challenging the injustices experienced by young people in their local regions is needed.

The ethical practice of community/youth workers in this domain is of absolute importance in establishing a way of working with young people that can help them to navigate route maps out of vulnerable locations (Sercombe, 2010). In everyday practice a critical youth work approach recognises the importance of 'situational contingency' (Hancock, 2016, p 110) to help young people explore how contexts and identity connect. The understanding that knowledge as power is relational (Collins, 2000) enabled YAV workers to think beyond single-strand influences on life-worlds and to explore their situated intersecting orientations. For youth workers to help young people to challenge the vulnerabilities generated from growing up in unequal places, there is a requirement for them to also challenge how the culture of white standards has ordered their behaviour. This also includes the youth worker engaging in a critical reflexive process to understand their 'own inclinations towards colonial behaviour' (Skott-Myhre et al, 2007, p 56).

As Lorenz (1996) identified , white people need reflexively to analyse their own place in the (re)production of racism. The youth work underpinning YAV set out to challenge the essentialism of racial logic woven into British racism. It did this with all the young people in its domain so as to ensure that the codes of whiteness at the centre of dominant constructions of national/local identity were no longer absent from the critique of racism's elite and everyday operations. In this nuanced view the racialised identities of white people are not assumed to carry within them a fixed racist pattern but are considered 'as a core problematic' (Garner, 2012, p 225) that requires a more critical pedagogical intervention.

YAV had two strategic aims. The first was to create an anti-racist safe space for BME young people. The second was to generate work that enabled all young people across the cityscape to be empowered intercultural activists. How YAV set out to achieve this was to enshrine in all its youth-work practices an anti-racist ethical stance that was itself intersectional. How racism was to be challenged needed to take cognisance of other social divisions, not in some reductive additive fashion but through the recognition of, for example, how class or gender are racialised. One fundamental mistake was to assume that policy makers and implementers were interested in this.

In 1990 the Commission for Racial Equality undertook empirical research to identify the situation facing Bengali people in Sunderland. The subsequent report, titled *We're Here Too*, identified several problems located within the dominant mindset in the local governance of the city. These included a monocultural and silo agency approach, no community participation and a paternalistic as well as patronising approach to the needs of minoritised communities (Field, 1990). This was the immediate local context in which YAV was developed. The failure to provide culturally competent services for BME young people was because there was 'professional indifference' (Jones, 1999, p 6) within the dominant culture that ignored the reality of racism.

By 1997, YAV had built up a strong practice base with primarily Bengali-heritage British young people. It also established its first transnational intercultural exchange with its twinned German city of Essen, developing a partnership project with Shonnebeck Youth Centre. The area of Essen where Shonnebeck was based had a multi-ethnic mix similar to that of the area of Hendon, Sunderland where YAV was housed. The rationale for this work was to explore intercultural experiences, with a focus on the developing social and political climate across Europe where racism and Islamophobia were apparent realities. The backdrop for the young people of both Shonnebeck and YAV was a situation in which racist harassment was a common experience. The young people were tasked to produce an aim, and they focused on how they could become valued and responsible citizens of Europe.

The manifestation of this backdrop of vulnerability to racial harassment culminated in the near-murder in 1998 of a 16-year-old young man (Sunderland Echo, 1998). The violent racist attack was carried out by a white man known to have close contact with far-Right racist organisations. The attack was witnessed by up to 20 white young people who did not intervene to stop it. Many of those white young people had been regular attenders at a local white youth project that worked closely with YAV. The racist attack and the youth projects all were located in the same area of Sunderland. This sister youth project was dismayed by the behaviour of its young people and, as a consequence of this, YAV responded by developing a locally based anti-racist intercultural project focused on white and BME young men and women to explore intercultural futures as citizens of the city. The project was named PROUD: 'people respecting others understand difference'.

The PROUD project was devised in 1998 and obtained funding from the National Youth Agency (Hingorani, 2004), and engaged 56 young people over a two-year period. The young men and women were supported in exploring their life-worlds and orientations, including how literate they were about racism and other forms of hate. The project began in 1999 with an original three-year plan, but funding was made available for only two years. At the end of the two years all the white and BME young men and women expressed an interest in continuing the work. In 2001, as the PROUD project was ending and the evaluation finalised (Bowler et al, 2002), two specific events occurred to alter the environment. The first was the summer 'riots' in northern towns of England, which generated the official policy of community cohesion (Cantle, 2001; Kundnani, 2001). The second was the violent 9/11 attacks on the US, from which emerged the 'war on terror' (Kundnani, 2007). As these events unfolded, YAV believed that it was in an informed space to share the empirical evidence from its intercultural work.

The project evaluation team sought a meeting with the chief executive of a regional quango[9] to share with it the lessons learned. At that meeting the chief executive refused to hear the evidence. Without listening, he judged the work of a BME-led youth project, from the perspective of his own white cultural norms, to be a call for 'segregation', articulating a view that post 9/11 nothing was going to be the same. 'You people need to understand the world has changed', was his asserted wisdom. What he meant by this was never forthcoming. His decision making informed YAV that BME-led youth projects were a thing of the past. He was adamant that youth work needed to be 'integrated', which was also never explained.[10] His resolute position, underpinned by white standards, did not question why white youth work projects remained almost exclusively white and were failing to deal with the racist mindsets identified by their youth workers. YAV had discovered the difficulty in helping white young people to challenge the illiteracies in their knowledge construction of how their worlds were racialised (Bowler, 2006). The absence of any racial literacy in the chief operating officer of a major regional policy-making organisation was more disturbing.

In 1996 the white standards foundational to the racism experienced by BME young people had created an intimidating and unwelcoming environment (CRE 1987; Field, 1990; Dadzie, 1997). In 2002 the whitewashed thinking at the head of the regional quango ensured that the environmental hostility in everyday street life would be replicated in regional strategic plans. The New Labour years from 1997–2010 have themselves been critiqued as a political project that reinvigorated assimilationist explanations, leaving the whiteness at the heart of the British state outside of critique (Back et al, 2002). This national absence of a critique about white standards increased the vulnerability for young people using the YAV project.

Since 2010 and the governmental response to the 'war on terror', there has been a reduction in systematic funding for intercultural youth work approaches aimed at building social cohesion through empowering processes that enable young people to transform their lives (Bowler, 2006, 2013; Thomas, 2011, 2012; Cantle and Thomas, 2014). By 2012 the Coalition government was developing the policy process of a 'secretive' working group given the name 'the hostile environment working group' (Aitkenhead, 2013). These changing forms of environmental hostility, impacting upon the young people at the heart of YAV's concerns certainly, add complexity to any contextual critique. They also provide continuity to the apparent inability of many potentially influential decision makers to reduce their resistance to the exposure of their white standards for critique.

YAV in 2016 continues to pursue its anti-racist intercultural dream. The project has 300 multi-ethnic young men and women as members alongside a diverse and vibrant staff team of mainly volunteers. The management committee is also an example of Parekh's (2000) vision of an intercultural community of communities. This work continues in a context where the white standards embedded within media stories positing possibly all young Muslims as a potential threat to the value base of British society are now limiting the life-worlds of young Muslims (Khan, 2013).

This dominant discourse, driven by white logic, foregrounds 'culturalist and/or reformist explanatory frames' (Kundnani, 2015, p 115) that mark children and young people who are or look like Muslims as dangerous to the 'British' way of life. In his articulation of the shifting complexion of his Islamic political identity, Saeed (2008) identifies critical moments, including 9/11 and the 'war on terror', that suggest that his sense of self 'is sutured in history' (Venn, 2002, p 58). These realities are a reminder that we are all social beings, and this mindfulness about our dreams for a collective humanity are at the heart of YAV's development and central to the present story.

The youth work underpinning YAV was driven by a desire to challenge the racialised cultural practices that had come to be so dominant in a monocultural northern landscape. In the post-industrial space of Sunderland 'race is mobilised' (Shire, 2008, p 15) so that the recodified racisms of previous generations become an explanatory device through which local fears and beleaguered expressions of the changing British landscape can become articulated (Clarke and Garner, 2010). One of the powerful realities of the now dominant radicalisation policy agenda is the way that the exceptional – grotesque acts of political violence (and not just, of course, in the UK) – has become normalised as if a potential characteristic of all Muslim people. The current Islamophobic narration by much of the British media (Versi, 2016) creates the context for the rise in hate experienced by British Muslims (Dodd, 2015) while taking no account of the political contexts that have contributed to the rise of groups such as Daesh (Cockburn, 2015).[11]

Conclusion

The arguments raised here have identified the changing contexts influencing the always dynamic ways in which young people co-create their identities and live out their realities in the world. Macpherson (1999, p 8), reflecting on the racist murder of Stephen Lawrence, argued that for racism to be 'eliminated from our society there must be a coordinated effort to prevent its growth', and this has been a significant failure despite the potentially strong legislation set out in the Equality Act 2010.[12] The context of continuing xeno-racism, with increasing hate crimes targeted at young Muslim women (Rawlinson, 2016), is further evidence that the anti-asylum/migrant, anti-Muslim rhetoric of dominant political and media sources keeps those white standards to the fore.

Neoliberal governance has articulated a narrative that places the responsibility for managing the economy, economic and moral, onto those most negatively affected by it. So, despite the history of work and the processes of de-industrialisation including the racial realities underpinning colonisation, the precarious reality of everyday life for working-class white and BME young men and women in places such as Sunderland has now become their own responsibility to resolve. The dominant story narrated by the British establishment about immigrants, asylum seekers and Muslims has altered the landscape of concern (Kundnani, 2007; Fekete, 2012; Khan, 2013). Young Muslims are now at risk from the state if they engage in public discussions about their personal, social, spiritual and political literacies, including any questioning of the political landscape shaping the world. In early 2017, children as young as three years have been reported to the police for mentioning words or singing songs allegedly having some connection with terrorism.

These pedagogical concerns that enable young people to engage in democratic practices that challenge unjust authority are viewed as potential acts of 'radicalisation' by the white standards underpinning current policy (Kundnani, 2015). In this, the essential logic of Islamophobia homogenises disparate and diverse communities as if they are singular and a threat. This 'othering' replicates the essentialist logic at the core of the European colonial project grounded in white supremacist ideology, where white men were concerned to 'civilise' all those whom they marked as subordinate (Schwarz, 2011). This leaves the political contexts in which young people come to know the world outside of critique, while simultaneously imposing the meaning of 'concern' without engaging young people, as active and equal citizens of the state, in defining their own realities.

If journalists can claim to be writers of the history's first draft (Cockburn, 2016, p 19), then community/youth workers are undoubtedly the first attentive listeners to developments in the ways young people read the world. These early signs alert to how the changing landscape of society impacts upon the life-worlds of young people. The everyday normative enactment of white standards repeats acts of erasure, (re)producing ideas that suggest to the majority population that the minoritised have contributed nothing to the state's wealth, nor to the collective culture of the society. As Žižeck (2008, p 140) articulates, 'habits are the very stuff our identities are made of'. Our interior worlds are interwoven with and by external forces.

Neoliberal governance and its new forms of austerity have trashed the resource base for critical forms of youth work (Gil, 2014; Unison, 2016). The current governing strategy of closing community cohesion work in order to pursue a surveillance of Muslim youth takes no account of the empirical evidence drawn from youth work (Thomas, 2009, 2011, 2012). This leaves the difficult mediated conversations about identity, belonging, systems of power and radicalisation under the resourcing decisions of white standards. If the institutions of the state and its policy advisors do not recognise their own racial realities (and the British state only formally began to do this in 1999 [Macpherson, 1999, p 8]), then critical youth workers have a duty of care to be vigilant and to collectivise the 'coordinated effort' to critique the systemic failings of those in positions of power, helping them to become literate about their own racial realities. How young people read their world and how much they know about the governing decisions that order the world requires community/youth workers to continue to engage in difficult democratic conversations so that we can continue to dream about and fight for shared intercultural futures.

Notes

[1] The North East region, population about 2.6 million, covers 12 local authorities in England bounded by the Pennine Hills to the west and the sea to the east, between Yorkshire and the Scottish border.

[2] NEREF is itself a partnership between the five regional universities in the North East alongside a range of voluntary and community sector and statutory organisations. NEREF is concerned to build racial equality through research, outreach and education, and one of its tasks is to generate a critical pedagogical space that can directly challenge the logics of race that persist in elite discourses and everyday practice. Bizarrely, and perhaps adding further strength to the basic premise of this chapter, the University of Durham's School of Applied Social Sciences decided in 2016 that 'race' would no longer be a priority for its research work and its involvement in NEREF is therefore now under question.

[3] Youth work in a community context (as opposed to buildings-based youth work or work within uniformed organisations), can be described as community youth work, youth and community work or simply community work with young people. These terms are used interchangeably in this discussion.

[4] Sunderland was one of the local authority areas that voted most strongly in the EU referendum to leave the EU. Overall the leave vote was predicated largely, it is widely accepted, on an 'anti-immigrant' vote.

[5] CRT is a compound theoretical framework that begins by acknowledging that racism is 'ordinary, not aberrational' (Delgado and Stefancic, 2001, p 6). It consists of different intellectual vantage points for the purpose of troubling racism's complex reach and is thus 'a radical lens through which to make sense of, deconstruct and challenge racial inequality in society' (Rollock and Gillborn, 2011, p 1).

[6] The importance of the community context is crucial in this analysis where young people's cultural knowledge cannot be understood outside of the dominant parental, communal and societal knowledge systems (Hall and Jefferson 1976). Of course in an allegedly multicultural context where white remains the dominant ethnic imagery, it becomes even more difficult for young people to decode issues around their own identity.

[7] The primary reasons for first-generation migration of, initially, Bangladeshi men to Sunderland were economic. This migration and settlement pattern was intimately connected to the historical imprint of the British state where, prior to 1962, all Commonwealth citizens were British subjects. By the 1980s the now settled Bangladeshi community increased, due to the secondary migration of mainly wives and children. By 1990 their employment patterns were primarily as entrepreneurial owners and workers in the restaurant trade.

[8] Indeed, one analysis suggests that a nearby small town, Easington, is the place in the UK as a whole where a white resident has the smallest chance of bumping into someone from a different ethnic background.

9   A quasi-autonomous non-governmental organisation, that is, a semi-public administrative body outside the civil service but receiving financial support from the government, which makes senior appointments to it.
10 The shift from multiculturalism to community cohesion and the government pressure to end BME-led projects is discussed in Lewis and Craig (2014).
11 One of the contexts that is not discussed is the fact that 2016 marks the centenary of the development of the Sykes-Picot line, a covert agreement between French and British governments to carve up the Middle East into a range of new countries (mainly populated by Muslims but, ironically, bearing ancient Jewish names such as Lebanon, Syria, Jordan and Palestine) without regard to traditional ethnic loyalties or identities. The resulting nation-states, as we see on a bloody daily basis, were inherently unstable.
12 There have in fact been more than 100 racist murders since the death of Stephen Lawrence.

References

Ahmed, S. (2004) 'Declarations of whiteness: the non-performativity of anti-racism', *Borderlands e-journal*, vol 3, no 2, www.borderlands.net. au/vol3no2_2004/ahmed_declarations.htm, accessed 25 June 2016.

Aitkenhead, D. (2013) 'Sarah Teather: "I'm angry there are no alternative voices on immigration', *Guardian*, 12 July, www. theguardian.com/theguardian/2013/jul/12/sarah-teather-angry-voices-immigration, accessed 22 March 2016.

Alexander, C. (2000) *The Asian gang: Ethnicity, identity, masculinity*, Oxford: Berg.

Back, L., Keith, M., Khan A., Shukra, K. and Solomos, J. (2002) 'The return of assimilationism: race, multiculturalism and New Labour', *Sociological Research Online*, vol 7, no 2, www.socresonline. org.uk/7/2/back.html.

Bonnett, A. (1996) 'Anti-racism and the critique of "white" identities', *New Community*, vol 22, no 1, pp 97–110.

Bonnett, A. (2008) 'Whiteness and the west', in C. Dwyer, and C. Bressey (eds), *New geographies of race and racism*, London: Ashgate, pp 17–28.

Bowler, R., Hill, I. and Reid, P. (2002) 'Final report: people respecting others understand difference', Sunderland: University of Sunderland (for a copy of this report please e-mail rick.bowler@sunderland.ac.uk, sending your name and postal address).

Bowler, R. (2006) 'Countering racisms: reflections from working with young people', in RShardFutR, Belfast: Northern Ireland Youth Council, pp 17–19, accessed at https://www.community-relations. org.uk/sites/crc/files/media-files/09-CRED-RShaRdFutR.pdf

Bowler, R. (2013) 'The risky business of challenging risk: youth work and young people through the lens of "race"', in J. Kearney and C. Donovan (eds), *Constructing risky identities: Consequences for policy and practice*, Basingstoke: Palgrave, pp 146–62.

Burnett, J. (2013) *Racial violence: Facing reality*, London: Institute of Race Relations.

Cantle, T. (2001) *Community cohesion – a report of the Independent Review Team*, London: Home Office.

Cantle, T and Thomas, P. (2014) 'Taking the Think Project forward – the need for preventative anti-extremism educational work', Project Report: The Think Project, Swansea, http://eprints.hud. ac.uk/19790/1/Think_project_report.pdf, accessed 10 June 2016.

Casciani, D. (2008) 'The whitest place in England', *BBC News Magazine*, 6 March, http://news.bbc.co.uk/1/hi/magazine/7281107. stm, accessed 27 May 2016.

Chowdhury, A. (2016) 'Brexit would be a victory for racists', *Huffington Post*, 15 June, www.huffingtonpost.co.uk/areeq-chowdhury/eu-referendum_b_10431872.html, accessed 24 June 2016.

Clarke, S. and Garner, S. (2010) *White identities: A critical sociological approach*, London: Pluto Press.

Cockburn, P. (2015) *The rise of Islamic State: ISIS and the new Sunni revolution*, London: Verso Books.

Cockburn, P. (2016) 'The first draft of history', *i*, 18 April, London, Johnston Publications Ltd, http://www.independent.co.uk/voices/the-first-draft-of-history-afghanistan-iraq-syria-libya-isis-taliban-patrick-cockburn-on-the-front-a6988001.html

Collins, P.H. (2000) *Black feminist thought: Knowledge, consciousness, and the politics of empowerment* (2nd edn), London: Routledge.

Craig, G., Atkin, K., Chattoo, S and Flynn, R. (eds) (2012) *Understanding 'race' and ethnicity: Theory, history, policy, practice*, Bristol: Policy Press.

CRE (1987) *Living in terror: A report on racial violence and harassment in housing*, London: Commission for Racial Equality.

Dadzie, S. (1997) *Blood, sweat and tears*, Leicester: Youth Work Press.

Delgado, R and Stefancic, J. (2001) *Critical race theory: An introduction*, London: New York University Press.

Dodd, V. (2015) 'Majority of British Muslims have witnessed Islamophobia – study', *Guardian*, 11 November 2015, www.theguardian.com/world/2015/nov/11/majority-of-british-muslims-have-witnessed-islamophobia-study, accessed 12 April 2016.

Fekete, L. (2001) 'The emergence of xeno racism', *Race and Class*, vol 43, no 2, pp 23–40.

Fekete, L. (2012) *Pedlars of hate: THE violent impact of the European far right*, London: Institute of Race Relations, www.irr.org.uk/wp-content/uploads/2012/06/PedlarsofHate.pdf, accessed 22 March 2016.

Field, A. (1990) *We're here too! The results of a research project into the needs of the Bangladeshi Community in Sunderland*, Sunderland: TUC Unemployed Centre and Commission for Racial Equality.

Fleming, M. (2012) *Population health profile: Easington locality*, County Durham and Darlington NHS, http://content.durham.gov.uk/PDFRepository/DDES_CCG-EasingtonPHP-February2012.pdf, accessed 16 April 2016.

Garner, S. (2007) *Whiteness: An introduction*, Abingdon: Routledge.

Garner, S. (2012) 'A moral economy of whiteness: behaviours, belonging and Britishness', *Ethnicities*, vol 12, no 4, pp 445–64.

Gil, N. (2014) 'Robbed of their futures: how austerity cuts hit young people hardest', *The Guardian*, 17 November, At www.theguardian.com/education/2014/nov/17/robbed-of-their-futures-how-austerity-cuts-hit-young-people-hardest, accessed 19 June 2016.

Gillborn, D. (2006) 'Rethinking white supremacy: who counts in "Whiteworld"', *Ethnicities*, vol 6, no 3, pp 318–40.

Gillborn, D. (2008) *Racism and education: Coincidence or conspiracy?*, London: Routledge.

Grattan, A. (2009) 'Segregated Britain: a society in conflict with its "radicalised" youth?', *Youth and Policy*, no 102, pp 35–52.

Grunwald, K and Thiersch, H. (2009) 'The concept of the "'lifeworld orientation" for social work and social care', *Journal of Social Work Practice*, vol 23, no 2, pp 131–46.

Hall, S. and Jefferson, T. (eds) (1976) *Resistance through rituals: Youth subcultures in post-war Britain*, Centre for Contemporary Cultural Studies, Birmingham: Harper Collins Academic.

Hancock, Ange-Marie (2016) *Intersectionality: An intellectual history*, Oxford: Oxford University Press.

Hingorani, M. (2004) *Justice, equality, our world: Supporting young people's active involvement in strengthening communities*, Leicester: The National Youth Agency.

Hylton, K., Pilkington, A., Warmington, P. and Housee, S. (eds) (2011) *Atlantic crossings: International dialogues on critical race theory*, Birmingham: Sociology, Anthropology, Politics (CSAP), The Higher Education Academy Network, University of Birmingham.

Ioanide, P. (2015) *The emotional politics of racism: How feelings trump facts in an era of colourblindness*, California: Stanford University Press.

Jones, R. (1999) *Teaching racism – or tackling it? Multicultural stories from white beginning teachers*, Stoke-on-Trent: Trentham Books.

Kelley, R.D.G. (2002) *Freedom dreams: The black radical imagination*, Boston: Beacon Press.

Khan, M.G. (2013) *Young Muslims, pedagogy and Islam: Contexts and concepts*, Bristol: Policy Press.

Kundnani, A. (2001) 'From Oldham to Bradford: the violence of the violated', in 'The Three Faces of British Racism', *Race and Class*, vol 43, no 2, pp 105–110.

Kundnani, A. (2007) *The end of tolerance: Racism in 21st century Britain*, London: Pluto Press.

Kundnani, A. (2015) *The Muslims are coming! Islamophobia, extremism and the domestic war on terror*, London: Verso.

Lewis, H. and Craig, G. (2014) '"Multiculturalism is never talked about": community cohesion and local policy contradictions in England', *Policy and Politics*, vol 42, no 1, pp 21–38.

Lloyd, J. (2008) 'White men unburdened', *Financial Times*, 1 March www.ft.com/cms/s/2/8943a7d0-e650-11dc-8398-0000779fd2ac. html (paywall).

Lorenz, W. (1996) 'Pedagogical principles for anti-racist strategies', in A. Aluffi-Pentini and W. Lorenz (eds), *Anti-racist work with young people*, Lyme Regis: Russell House Publishing, pp 159–77.

Macpherson Report (1999) *The Stephen Lawrence Inquiry, Report of an Inquiry by Sir William Macpherson of Cluny*, London: The Stationery Office, Cm 4262-1.

Manzoor, S. (2006) 'My week in the whitest place in Britain', *Guardian*, 6 December, www.guardian.co.uk/society/2006/dec/06/communities, accessed 27 May 2016.

Marable, M. (1997) 'Rethinking black liberation: towards a new protest paradigm', *Race and Class*, vol 38, no 4, pp 1–13.

Martin, N. (2008) 'BBC series "labels" white working class racist', *Telegraph*, 12 March, www.telegraph.co.uk/news/uknews/1581438/BBC-series-labels-white-working-class-racist.html.

McNeil, B., Reeder, N. and Rich, J. (2012) *A framework of outcomes for young people*, London: The Young Foundation, http://youngfoundation.org/wp-content/uploads/2012/10/Framework-of-outcomes-for-young-people-July-2012.pdf, accessed 14 April 2016.

Mills, C. (1999) *The racial contract*, Ithaca, NY: Cornell University Press.

Mukherjee, S. (2008) 'Senior Asian journalist at BBC denounces corporation's "patronising" white series', *Evening Standard*, 12 March, www.standard.co.uk/news/senior-asian-journalist-at-bbc-denounces-corporations-patronising-white-series-7281502.html, accessed 22 June 2016.

Murray, N. (1986) 'Anti-racists and other demons: the press and ideology in Thatcher's Britain', *Race and Class*, vol 27, no 3, pp 1–19.

Nayak, A. (2003) *Race, place and globalization: Youth cultures in a changing world*, Oxford: Berg.

Nayak, A. (2006) 'After race: ethnography, race and post-race theory', *Ethnic and Racial Studies*, vol 29, no 3, pp 411–30.

NERCJRRN (NE Race, Crime and Justice Regional Research Network) (2012) *A place called Townsville: Rural racism in a north east context*, https://www.dur.ac.uk/resources/sass/research/Rural_Racism_Report.pdf, accessed 26 April 2016.

Paul, K. (1997) *Whitewashing Britain: Race and citizenship in the post-war era*, Ithaca, NY: Cornell University Press.

Parekh, B. (2000) *The future of multi-ethnic Britain: The Parekh Report*, London: Profile Books.

Perry, P. (2001) 'White means never having to say you're ethnic: white youth and the construction of "cultureless" identities', *Journal of Contemporary Ethnography*, vol 30, no 1, pp 56–91.

Preston, J. (2009) *Whiteness and class in education*, Dordrecht: Springer.

Ramamurthy, A. (2013) *Black star: Britain's Asian youth movements*, London: Pluto Press.

Rawlinson, K. (2016) 'Jo Cox was working on report on anti-Muslim attacks before her death', *Guardian*, 20 June, https://www.theguardian.com/uk-news/2016/jun/20/jo-cox-was-working-on-report-into-anti-muslim-attacks-before-death, accessed 24 June 2016.

Rollock, N. and Gillborn, D. (2011) Critical race theory (CRT), British Educational Research Association online resource, https://www.bera.ac.uk/wp-content/uploads/2014/03/Critical-Race-Theory-CRT-.pdf, accessed 3 September 2016.

Rose, A. (2016) 'The Brexit debate has made Britain more racist: the idea of "getting our country back," once considered a crass empire throwback, is now causing ripples of bigoted glee', *Washington Post*, 22 June, https://www.washingtonpost.com/posteverything/wp/2016/06/22/the-brexit-debate-has-made-britain-more-racist/, accessed 26 June 2016.

Saeed, A. (2007) 'Northern racism: a pilot study of racism in Sunderland', in C. Ehland (ed), *Thinking Northern: Textures of identity in the north of England*, Amsterdam/New York: Rodopi Press, pp 163–89.

Saeed, A. (2008) 'My jihad: a personal reflection', in S. Davison and J. Rutherford (eds), *Race, identity and belonging*, London: Lawrence Wishart, pp 114–22.

Schwarz, B. (1996) '"The only white man in there": the re-racialisation of England 1956–1968', *Race and Class*, vol 38, no 1, pp 65–78.

Schwarz, B. (2011) *The white man's world: Memories of empire*, Oxford: Oxford University Press.

Sercombe, H. (2010) *Youth work ethics*, London: Sage.

Shire, G. (2008)'Introduction: race and racialisation in neo-liberal times', in S. Davison and J. Rutherford (eds), *Race, identity and belonging*, London: Lawrence Wishart, pp 7–18.

Skott-Myhre, H. and Skott-Myhre, K. (2007) 'Radical youth work: love and community', *Relational Child and Youth Care Practice*, vol 20, no 3, pp 48–57, www.cyc-net.org/Journals/rcycp/rcycp20–3.html#2, accessed 22 June 2016.

Sivanandan, A. (1982) 'From resistance to rebellion: Asian and Afro-Caribbean struggles in Britain', *Race and Class*, vol 24, no 2/3, pp 111–52.

Sunderland Echo (1998) 'I thought they were going to kill me', 28 August, www.sunderlandecho.com/news/i-thought-they-were-going-to-k-1–1083411, accessed 24 June 2016.

Syal, R. (2014) 'British towns being "swamped" by immigrants', says Michael Fallon', *Guardian*, 26 October, https://www.theguardian.com/uk-news/2014/oct/26/british-towns-swamped-immigrants-michael-fallon-eu, accessed 19 June 2016.

Thomas, P. (2009) 'Between two stools? The Government's preventing violent extremism agenda', *The Political Quarterly*, vol 80, no 2, pp 282–91.

Thomas, P. (2011) *Youth, multiculturalism and community cohesion*, Basingstoke: Palgrave Macmillan.

Thomas, P. (2012) *Responding to the threat of violent extremism: Failing to prevent*, London: Bloomsbury.

TSO (2010) *Equality Act* (c.15) London: The Stationery Office.

Twine, F.W. (2004) 'A white side of black Britain: the concept of racial literacy', *Ethnic and Racial Studies*, vol 27, no 6, pp 1–30.

Tyler, I. (2013) *Revolting subjects: Social abjection and resistance in neoliberal Britain*, London: Zed Books.

Unison (2016) *The damage: A future at risk*, London: Unison Centre, www.unison.org.uk/content/uploads/2016/08/23996.pdf, accessed 17 August 2016.

Versi, M. (2016) 'Why the British media is responsible for the rise in Islamophobia in Britain', *Independent*, 4 April, www.independent. co.uk/voices/why-the-british-media-is-responsible-for-the-rise-in-islamophobia-in-britain-a6967546.html, accessed 12 April 2016.

Venn, C. (2002) 'Refiguring subjectivity after modernity', in V. Walkerdine (ed), *Challenging subjects: Critical psychology for a new millennium*, Basingstoke: Palgrave, pp 51–71.

Withnall, A. (2013) 'Lib Dem MP Sarah Teather attacks "nakedly political" plot to make UK "hostile" to immigrants', *Independent*, 13 July, www.independent.co.uk/news/uk/politics/lib-dem-mp-sarah-teather-attacks-nakedly-political-plot-to-make-uk-hostile-to-immigrants-8707347.html, accessed 19 June 2016.

Žižek, S. (2008) *Violence: Six sideways reflections*, London: Profile Books.

Section Two
Building capacity with BME groups

Introduction

Gary Craig

This section describes a range of projects and programmes that aim to 'build capacity' with BME groups of different kinds, including long-settled minority populations, migrant workers and asylum seekers. Although I (and others) have been critical of the term 'capacity building' elsewhere as simply 'an old wine in a new bottle', its use seems appropriate here since all of the contributions, in differing ways, describe work to help build varying dimensions of capacity among the groups that community workers are helping to organise and support, whether knowledge, understanding, skills, organisational frameworks or abilities – for example, to access services or make them more culturally appropriate to the needs of minority users and, critically, do so in a 'bottom–up' manner. The contexts include work around health, mental health, arts and culture, the labour market and other forms of service provision.

Ware's Chapter Three (which also helpfully reviews some of the key literature around the concept of capacity building) describes a continuing struggle among BME VCS groups to obtain secure funding for a range of work where, on the one hand, those groups were viewed by major funders as being weakly organised, yet, at the same time, were allegedly the targets of funding streams that were unequally distributed, to their disadvantage. Without secure and autonomous organisations, the voice of BME groups remained largely silent or, at best, mediated through the advocacy of 'mainstream', that is white, organisations who were more concerned with their own survival.

In Chapter Four Smith and Moreno-Leguizamon focus on a particular organisational approach, Learning Alliance partnerships, as a way to help BME groups access health services provision in a most sensitive area, that of palliative care and end–of–life support. Critically, despite the fact that small BME groups with little experience of engagement in this work might well be overwhelmed by the institutional inertia and lack of sensitivity of professional statutory health organisations, the account demonstrates how it is possible for BME groups to insert their own needs and knowledge effectively, and to begin to exert some control over the development of culturally appropriate policy and practice.

The account of *sampad* in Chapter Five provides a wide-ranging set of examples of how BME groups can promote truly autonomous expressions of culture and artistic endeavour covering music, art, dance, performance, philosophy and heritage, thus underpinning key aspects of their identity. The project challenges the narrow hierarchical and exoticised notions of culture that have developed within much of the UK's (and no doubt other countries') multicultural discourse by concentrating on an approach that marries both unity and diversity and that is, in the words of the author, 'radical, iconoclastic, subversive'. Only if culture is encouraged to flourish in this way can we hope for 'the construction of an open, liberal, democratic society' in which minority cultures have an authentic voice, rather than being typecast within narrow stereotypes of 'dancing and drumming'.

Tang's Chapter Six focuses on a site of service provision, mental health services, which has characteristically been a site of contestation between differing cultural norms (as well, of course, as within 'mainstream service provision itself) and, of course, remains severely underfunded. Given the association of mental (ill–)health with social and economic inequalities, it is not surprising that minorities often have higher than normal levels of mental illness. The struggle is to develop services, and ways of accessing those services, that acknowledge that the recovery journeys of those suffering from mental illness need to focus not so much on the individual symptoms displayed by service users but on the structural factors that generate mental ill-health. One further important insight is to remind us of the heterogeneity of the Chinese population (also discussed by Hung and Fung in Chapter Seventeen), which may contain within it a variety of traditions and practices. The role of community development must be to challenge the exploitative and discriminatory policies and practices that generate mental distress.

Gregory's account in Chapter Seven – one that reflects many similar projects across the UK – describes work with Portuguese migrant workers working in, for European migrants, a typically economically depressed and isolated community, one that, again, is highly representative of many such communities within the UK over the last twenty years. Characteristically, such migrants are the victims of racial hostility, being blamed both for taking away native workers' jobs and for depressing wage levels in the local economy (claims that are challenged by most objective evidence). Traditional forms of community organisation have led to some gains, although the creation of organisations and groups continues to be undermined to some degree by both the transience of some migrants and their focus on economic goals. The key role, in the event, for the community development worker appears to be to act as a broker between migrants and host community, and particularly to challenge the myths that have been promoted by those on the political Right.

Finally in this section, in Chapter Eight Greenfields describes work done in a participatory action research (PAR) context with vulnerable minority women, including some seeking asylum. The values of PAR are similar to those of community development, emphasising participation by all those involved in the research, whether as formal 'researchers' or being 'researched'. The author describes a painstaking project that built on an understanding of the vulnerability of women from differing national origins coming to the UK as refugees or seeking asylum, and focused in particular on the health-related issues that often originated in traumatic experiences while fleeing, travelling and then coping with a hostile and gender-unfriendly asylum system. Appropriately, the writer concludes not by describing research findings as such but by outlining ways in which women became engaged in the policy process and practice development.

THREE

Capacity building with BME groups

Phil Ware

Background

This chapter aims to examine community capacity-building processes in relation to the UK BME VCS, using a specific project in Birmingham, the UK's second-largest city, as its focus. The project, Birmingham Skills Training Reaching Organisations and Neighbourhood Groups (using the acronym B.STRONG), ran from 1998 to 2011 and was evaluated at regular intervals. B.STRONG covered the whole of Birmingham, although at certain times it prioritised certain areas of the city due to limited funding sources, and employed between two and eight staff. The account uses information available from these evaluations and the author's knowledge of the project, gleaned over what was an unusually long period.

Specifically, the chapter looks at the experiences of BME community groups in their engagement with community capacity-building processes and the wider 'mainstream' VCS. BME groups have been identified as being widely excluded from capacity-building programmes (Afridi, 2007 and Chapter One in this volume).

Community development staff within Birmingham City Council had identified the need for extra developmental support for community groups, along with the availability of European and area-based initiative funding. Consequently, B.STRONG was developed as a local authority project. This chapter examines the benefits and challenges of this approach.

It also looks at the current situation for community capacity building for the BME VCS in the longer term, given the current context of recession, government austerity measures and the reduction of funding possibilities.[1] An analysis from the perspective of BME groups will be the subject of a future UK Third Sector Research Centre (TSRC) research paper.[2] The term BME as used in this chapter includes people not born in the UK and second and third generations, and therefore includes white European migrants.

The project's period of operation coincided with an increase in the diversity and superdiversity (Phillimore, 2011) of the population of Birmingham and of other similar areas of England. Between 2001 and 2011, the population of Birmingham with an ethnic background other than White British (the core 'host' ethnic group) grew from 29.8% to 42.1% (Office of National Statistics [ONS] 2012). McCabe (2002) found that 65% of the project's users in the period 2000–02 were from a BME background. Goodwin (2006), in a later evaluation report on a government-funded regeneration project, found that over 90% of management committee members were from a BME background. The project user groups also reflected the increasing populations from the Middle East and North and Central Africa living in Birmingham.

Community capacity building

The interpretation of the terms 'capacity building' and 'community capacity building' has been the subject of considerable debate (Simpson et al, 2003; Craig, 2005; Mowbray, 2005). It is not the intention of this piece to extend the debate, but to clarify the terms as they are used here. The Churches Community Work Alliance (CCWA, 2011) defined capacity building as a process by which organisations address their development needs from a self-defined starting point. In this context community capacity building widens the definition to include communities addressing their needs in this way. However, community capacity building has also been defined as 'Developing the capacity and skills of the members of a community ... to help meet their needs and to participate more fully in society' (Charity Commission, 2003). This refers to the development of communities, as opposed to organisations. It is closer to definitions of community development that involve the development of the skills and knowledge of individuals to be better able to engage with political processes and to respond to the needs of their community/communities. The B.STRONG programme was initially focused on the organisation development approach, but developed a community capacity-building element as the project refined its scope. The Take Part programme (Miller and Hatamian, 2011) was an example of a programme focused on individual and community, rather than organisational, capacity.

Taylor (2015, p 140), writing in relation to health promotion, identifies nine domains for capacity building and asserts that 'active community participation in decision-making to lead to social and political change is essential'. The domains identified are community participation, leadership, organisational structures, problem assessment, resource mobilisation, asking why, links with others, the role of outside agents and programme management. As Taylor argues, it is important to bear in mind *who* is building *whose* capacity.

There are problems with the ways in which capacity building can be seen as addressing a deficit model for communities and/or their organisations, as defined by those who are the guardians of power and resources. Those capacity-building programmes that are closest to the community development model would recognise this power relationship. They would seek to support communities in achieving their own aims, rather than those that meet the agendas of local and central government. This is discussed further in detail in Craig (2005) and is relevant to the discussion of the local authority-managed B.STRONG project, as its staff sought to develop a more community development-based approach. This is examined at greater length later below.

The development of capacity building programmes

The term capacity building was first used in the mid-1990s and was defined by the UN Commission on Sustainable Development in 1996 (Craig, 2007). Since then, a range of funding regimes have supported UK capacity-building programmes, including the European Social Fund (ESF), the Single Regeneration Budget (SRB), the BIG Lottery Fund (the main UK-wide lottery, much of which was invested into charitable work) and government programmes such as ChangeUp that provided substantial funds for building CVS organisations.

The priorities for funders have been varied. For example, the BIG Lottery was clear that two of its three priorities for capacity building were 'to ensure organisations are able to apply, receive and spend a BIG grant' and 'deliver agreed project outcomes' (IVAR, 2010, p 76). Early literature on capacity building identified that a key purpose of the process is to enable community organisations to participate in the regeneration process with statutory partners (Coventry and Warwickshire Partnerships Ltd, 1998).

However, programmes, including the BIG Lottery, also envisaged a more self-defined approach to capacity building. The third aim of BIG's funding was 'to support wider skills development within the voluntary and community sector' (IVAR, 2010, p 76). The ChangeUp programme's goals included 'Improve the quality and effectiveness of support for third sector organisations' and 'Influence funding policy and practice to ensure sustainable support to third sector organisations' (TSRC, 2009, p 6). The Joseph Rowntree's (JRF) Changing Neighbourhoods project worked with 20 neighbourhoods in England, Scotland and Wales to test out a 'light touch' approach to supporting community groups. While JRF does not refer to this as a capacity-building project, it has many of the features of one. It recognised that a strengths-based capacity-building approach requires those in power to identify their own needs when engaging with communities and community organisations to achieve effective outcomes (Taylor et al, 2007).

Capacity building and the BME CVS: 'lumping together' and marginalisation

This section will examine the experience of the BME CVS in relation to capacity building and specific capacity-building programmes, using their own evaluation literature. There was an expansion of programmes in the first decade of the new millennium, which has reduced in line both with recession and austerity measures since 2008.

Programmes such as the JRF's Neighbourhood Programme (JRF, 2007), Equal to the Occasion's Equal Support (ETTO, 2010) and ChangeUp (TSRC, 2009) operated at a national level. Common themes arose from their evaluations. Provision was fragmented, due to the fact that funding, while relatively generous, was time limited and unequally distributed both geographically and across communities of interest. Support needs were identified as access to more secure funding, management structure advice and an ability to have an influence on policy makers.

Barriers included the difficulty in developing voice and influence and the 'lumping together' of different communities with different needs, aspirations and resources. There was also a perceived requirement for BME agencies to work with individuals in their own communities, at the expense of undertaking development work and campaigning. A common theme was that BME groups did not necessarily have the experience and/or understanding of how the political system works and perceived their accountability to be to their users rather than, as funders expected, to them. The lack of critical mass was a particular barrier in rural areas, where the severity of race hate crime also affected priorities for BME groups. This required them to focus on individual needs, rather than to progress a wider campaigning and/or policy agenda.

Lessons from the JRF Neighbourhood Programme (JRF, 2007, p 3) included the importance of women as community leaders; the need to allow time for positive bonding within and between groups; and the need for service providers to be prepared to work with 'neighbourhood organisations representing diverse community interests'. The ChangeUp evaluation (TSRC, 2009) found that there had been a failure to embed BME projects in many consortia programmes. There was a difficulty in obtaining the core community development funding that was required by many of the BME groups involved. ETTO (2010, pp 5–6) identified that 'generalising about the BME voluntary sector masks significant differences between ethnic minority communities', with some ethnic groups in some areas being much more able to access funding than others. Current provision was seen as fragmented, and a 'tick box' approach was leading to funding being channelled to only one specific organisation in an area, irrespective of its need or ability to deliver.

Regional/sub-regional programmes in London and Birmingham, managed by the UK-wide Council of Ethnic Minority Voluntary Organisations (CEMVO) and Birmingham Voluntary Service Council (BVSC), respectively, developed localised programmes both funded by the central government Single Regeneration Budget (SRB). Both programme evaluations highlighted tensions between the BME voluntary sector and the 'mainstream' VCS structures. In the case of the CEMVO programme in London, it was an aim of the programme to challenge 'this inequality and marginalisation of certain groups from the process of mainstream society' (Ellis and Latif, 2006, p 4).

In Birmingham, BVSC's B:CAN programme was not specifically targeted at the BME VCS and the evaluation identified several areas where BME respondents were critical of the programme. On the other hand, it was alleged that the BME VCS had 'become disengaged', with some BME organisations choosing to seek support from the Scarman Trust, a BME infrastructure organisation in Birmingham (Garry et al, 2004, pp 59–60). It was argued by some, however, that a stronger relationship between BVSC and the BME VCS had been developed by B:CAN. These conflicting comments were echoed by participants in the author's research with community organisations elsewhere in both urban and rural areas (Ware, 2013, 2015).

Afridi (2007) researched 50 BME front-line organisations interviewed for brap's (see http://www.brap.org.uk/) Performance and Race Equality Project Research Report. Only 14 (28%) had received any performance improvement support, but 'the majority of respondents could point to specific issues that they would like assistance with ...' (Afridi, 2007, p 4). Barriers that the report identified included a lack of time and resources; negative perceptions by organisations about performance improvement; and 'more BME organisations seeking to operate in the mainstream' (Afridi, 2007, p 5).

In summary, it is apparent that BME community organisations have received inadequate capacity-building support. They have felt largely unsupported by the mainstream VCS and statutory bodies. Consequently the BME VCS has been predominantly uninvolved at a strategic level in the development and programming of capacity-building projects.

B.STRONG and BME community capacity building in Birmingham: progress and challenges

B.STRONG was a community capacity-building programme managed by the Youth, Community and Play service of Birmingham City Council. Throughout the 13-year period of its operation it was dependent on external funding, including European funding and UK government New Deal for Communities (NDC) and SRB funds. Although the council provided little direct funding, it was able to provide administrative, training and management services. It also underwrote any potential losses during periods when new funding was being sought. This gave the project an important element of continuity that was not necessarily available to comparable voluntary sector infrastructure projects. In total the project had over 500 member community groups across Birmingham. Preliminary investigation suggests that less than half of these are operational a few years on.[3]

Despite local authority management input, there were periods when funding was uncertain, leading to a loss of momentum and a reduction in impact, highlighted in an evaluation report (McCabe, 2002). This report demonstrated the irony of the situation, pointing out that 'whilst capacity building has moved to the centre of the policy stage and been recognised as a long-term process ... projects which support this process remain reliant on short term "stop-start" patterns of funding' (McCabe, 2002, p 19).

Initially the B.STRONG project was largely focused on formal and informal training, providing courses to respond to gaps in capacity, based on groups' perception of their ability to deliver services to and articulate the policy needs of their users. This used the initial ESF-funded work undertaken to identify needs and deliver a pilot training programme. An early evaluation of the project undertaken by International Organisation Development (IOD, 1999) found that while the training had a reputation for being of good quality and accessible, there was also a need to focus on providing individual group support, through workers who would work with groups on a one-to-one basis, in order to complement the wider training programme.

Project strengths identified by evaluation reports included the following.

- The project was able to 'reach its target audience', which included 267 individuals from 83 community groups accessing training, with a further 30 groups receiving more intensive support. Working 'effectively with refugee organisations and other communities of interest operating outside regeneration zones ...' was also seen as a significant strength (McCabe, 2002, p 21).
- In the same report it was found that B.STRONG was reaching those groups that had been identified as priorities in the previous evaluation undertaken by IOD– smaller, emerging BME organisations.
- The training provision was identified in the report as 'high quality ... with 65% of those attending from minority ethnic communities' (McCabe, 2002, p 23). McCabe also found that member groups valued the flexibility and quality of the organisation development support.
- A later report evaluating an SRB6-funded project in North-West Birmingham (Goodwin, 2006, p 11) found that the 12 organisations interviewed 'were very satisfied with the support on offer from the project'. It reported that they were 'better able to secure funds, run services and generally improve performance as a result of support from the project'. In total, 102 out of 115 members (89%) of the project groups were from a BME background.

Project weaknesses were also identified in the reports, particularly in relation to B.STRONG's strategic position. In 2002 McCabe identified weaknesses at strategic, operational and management levels.

- Strategically, there was a lack of partnerships and alliances, and the effectiveness of the system of referral to the project via geographically based local authority Community Development Officers was challenged. This system was seen as a strength by the local authority, in that it contributed to core objectives of the Youth, Community and Play service. However, it was also seen as unnecessary 'gate-keeping' and 'Local Authority patronage' by other statutory and voluntary sector agencies. In the longer term a system of self-referral was developed for the majority of the project's organisations.
- Operationally, the short-term nature of European funding raised issues of staff retention, and consequently the potential for

B.STRONG to take on longer-term commitments for its member groups, for example, business plan development. Other operational concerns were monitoring and evaluation systems, the quality of marketing materials and the lack of a coherent ICT strategy.

• Managerial weaknesses identified by McCabe included operating on two sites (later rectified), the lack of systematic 'learning for capacity building', with information being held by 'individuals rather than a shared resource' (McCabe, 2002, p 25) and complex management structures.

Goodwin (2006, p 32) found that there was a lack of clarity on the part of the group members interviewed about the capacity-building process in which they had participated, including the organisation health check. Goodwin identifies the dilemma of balancing '"light touch" initial support, which is encouraging and enabling, with more intensive development work which … may can be seen as intimidating and disempowering'.

The SRB6 project that Goodwin evaluated was short term, using funding available through a regeneration initiative. Increasingly, B.STRONG was dependent on funding from area-based initiatives (ABIs) in order to maintain the project, and further regeneration funding was accessed from other SRB and NDC programmes. Short-term funding did not allow long-term development support for BME groups, which by the latter period of the project comprised 80–90% of the overall member groups.

The later evaluation identified progress made in some areas, including operating from a single site and the newsletter that 'provides B.STRONG with a useful vehicle for communicating with members and sharing information and is well received' (Goodwin, 2006, p 33).

The demise of the ABIs and the prevailing narrative from certain funders that capacity building had 'been done' and that organisations should not need to continue to be supported (Cabinet Office, 2010), allied to the economic and political change from 2008 onwards, meant that funding to sustain capacity-building projects became extremely limited. New funding regimes such as BASIS[4] and Fair Shares were not available to B.STRONG as, essentially, a statutory provider. Following a Capacitybuilders project undertaken in partnership with the Digbeth Trust, with B.STRONG providing the organisation development support to groups, B.STRONG finished in 2011, due to a lack of funding opportunities. Additionally, it was no longer being seen as a priority for the city council, which was now faced with making departmental budget cuts of 30–40%, in the face of government austerity measures. The strategic Youth, Community and Play team was disbanded altogether in 2014.

The main impact of the project's closure was experienced by new and emerging BME community groups in Birmingham, given that there was no opportunity for other infrastructure organisations to provide comparable support, faced with their own budget reductions and a scarcity of new funding opportunities.

BME groups and the mainstream VCS: outside looking in?

Previous research by the author (Ware, 2013, 2015) examined the position of the BME community sector's voice and influence in both urban and rural areas of England. The findings were that voice and influence were extremely limited, particularly in rural areas, where the sector had never developed a strong presence, but also in urban areas, where there was a lack of strategic infrastructure and reduced funding. This led to groups having to focus on service provision to attract funding, at the expense of policy development and campaigning.

BME respondents to the research studies perceived a number of factors to have contributed to this situation, including the economic downturn and a lack of funding, the Equality Act 2010, the new government emphasis on localism[5] and racism at community and institutional levels. BME respondents perceived that the Equality Act had the effect of watering down the impact of previous legislation and reducing the resources available to BME communities in favour of other disadvantaged groups. Localism was seen to ignore the fact that BME communities may be thinly spread, particularly in rural areas, and therefore would not benefit from funding targeted at specific geographical areas. In rural settlements there were additional influential factors, including sparseness of population, the impact of superdiversity and an 'invisibility' that meant that the needs of rural BME communities were either ignored or 'lumped together'.

Interviewees in both urban and rural studies argued that there was a disconnect between the 'mainstream' and BME VCS sectors. One participant said that 'in relation to the VCS as a whole, the BME VCS is not significant' (Ware, 2013, p 20). Some identified a lack of trust between BME and mainstream VCS organisations, particularly where larger mainstream organisations were taking the credit for work done by BME groups. One respondent said that 'those organisations have used the BME organisations, as in used their membership, used their information, used their time, for the benefit of the CVS ... and have pulled down funding' (Ware, 2013, p 20). In a focus group for this research study participants argued that 'it's always the usual suspects who get the money' (Ware, 2013, p 21), referring to the larger mainstream VCS organisations.

The experience of the B.STRONG project supported these comments. The participating organisations were not strategically linked with the VCS overall and there was a lack of strategic bodies representing BME community groups at local, regional or national level. Respondents to the research studies shared this experience, arguing that 'mainstream organisations were taking on voice for BME groups and, through claiming representation, also taking advantage of funding opportunities' (Ware, 2015, p 14).

Community capacity building and BME community groups in Birmingham: an incomplete programme

Successive evaluations have found that the B.STRONG project was effective in meeting the capacity-building needs of its target audience, namely 'below the radar' community groups operating in disadvantaged areas and/or with disadvantaged communities. However, McCabe (2002, p 27) found that the project was 'not in a strategic position to develop via the opportunities presented by the modernising government agendas', particularly those in support of Neighbourhood Renewal strategies. Its position within a local authority department was therefore a strength in terms of delivery, but a weakness in terms of developing a strategic approach with potential VCS partners. Many in the Birmingham VCS felt that it was inappropriate for community capacity-building work to be delivered by the local authority. To develop strategy it would in any case have been advantageous to have been part of a central strategic department such as the Chief Executive's Department.

The irony was that the project had a good reputation with BME community groups, (confirmed by the later evaluation – Goodwin, 2006), many of whom trusted the work done, despite the local authority project management. This was helped by the fact that most of the project staff, including all three project managers, were from BME communities themselves. Most staff had experience of working in the voluntary sector in Birmingham. McCabe (2002, p 2) found that the project was able to offer 'tailored support in community languages, where appropriate'. This was valued by the member groups and was important in the effectiveness of the project by developing trust and working in a way valued by project users.

The difficulty for the BME member groups was that, following the conclusion of the project, there were (and remain) a limited number of organisations able to provide capacity-building support to BME community groups within Birmingham. Additionally, there were no specific initiatives, other than BASIS· to support capacity building, whether at a strategic or neighbourhood level.

Craig (2011) has argued that BME groups more generally had identified that government funding had been captured by mainstream third sector organisations and ignored BME organisations' development needs. The later study of BME community organisations' voice and influence (Ware, 2013) included seven Birmingham BME community groups. It found that BME groups had been particularly adversely affected by the fact that capacity building was under-resourced and 'out of favour'. While all community groups had capacity-building needs, many BME groups were newly formed and therefore had less experience and knowledge of developing and running a community group, especially in an unfamiliar social, economic and political environment. Established BME community groups in Birmingham were found to be facing severe challenges. Groups interviewed were faced with, for example:

• their coordinator being made redundant at the end of the week;,
• a staff reduction of over a third in the previous two years;
• providing services at weekends and in the evenings only (as previously paid staff had needed to find other work), and running the group's services to a newly arrived community on a voluntary basis.

There is a danger in considering the needs of one disadvantaged sector of the community as being more important than those of another, that the needs of one group can be diminished or ignored. This can lead to division between communities, whether white and BME communities, or between BME communities of different origin and length of settlement, especially when resources are limited. Taylor and Wilson (2015), in their report on changing communities, looked at the challenges faced by these communities. In particular they highlighted how existing groups might need to change in a restricted funding scenario, while understanding the newer communities and keeping the trust of those they have traditionally served. 'Lack of contact and understanding between communities may bring with it insecurity ... and, too often, this is fuelled by the media' (Taylor and Wilson, 2015, p 5).

Discussion

As identified earlier, community capacity building can be seen as a patronising approach operating on a deficit model, seeing disadvantaged communities as inherently in need of help and support. It can ignore the existing skills, knowledge and experience of the people who comprise these communities. Additionally, the funding, development and operation of projects is generally controlled by state organisations, which brings a range of other issues, highlighted above. Simpson et al (2003, p 283), in a case study in a rural Australian town, found that 'the nature of the community's participation was regulated by the government's agenda for the project' and that barriers to future development were created. Mowbray (2005, p 262) argued that a community-building programme in Victoria, Australia served to 'depoliticise social problems' and was 'meant to bolster the standing of the state government'. This echoes the experience of projects in the UK funded by governmental organisations.

BME groups that participated in the B.STRONG project and those that were part of the voice and influence research papers (Ware, 2013, 2015) shared this experience. While they were able to make short-term gains and develop skills, they were rarely able to engage at a strategic level or to have an impact on policy. Some respondents recognised that many white groups were equally under-recognised and underfunded. However, others saw that through historical connections or a sympathetic councillor or MP these groups were more likely to be able access scarce resources and have voice and influence.

This unequal situation is exacerbated for groups representing newly arrived communities that have had less opportunity to build up skills, knowledge and resources to engage in equal partnerships with funders and policy makers. These communities can be particularly affected by a lack of numbers, or 'critical mass', to enable them to develop activities and facilities and to be able to have a 'voice'. This was found to be especially true in rural areas, where distance and racism were also key factors (Ware, 2015).

Conclusions

Community capacity building has suffered an almost total lack of funding since 2010, due to the recession and subsequent austerity measures and a lack of evidence to funders that it worked (Cabinet Office, 2010). The 'Big Society' initiative, David Cameron's 'big idea' on becoming prime minister in 2010, has produced little extra activity and the initiative also failed to acknowledge the amount of existing voluntary work that was already taking place, largely unfunded, in disadvantaged communities (Abbas and Lachman, 2011; Mohan, 2012).

In many cases the stated aim of funders of capacity building was to produce better bidders, but in a very mechanistic way. While an organisation and its key players could be developed to produce effective bids, outlining their organisational competence, there was less clarity about the purpose of the activity and the impact and the quality of service delivered (see, for example, the quality-assurance system for small voluntary organisations: PQASSO, 1997).

At a strategic level a wide range of national community development organisations have been closed down, including the Community Development Foundation, Community Matters and the Community Development Exchange. BME strategic organisations, such as SIA and the Black Regeneration Network, were very short lived and were wound up at an earlier date. Thus, national infrastructure bodies sympathetic to the interests of BME communities and their development were virtually non-existent by 2015.

In Birmingham no capacity-building programme has been developed to replace B.STRONG and there have also been considerable reductions in the funding of both statutory and voluntary community provision, affecting all communities. Where third sector strategic organisations do exist, the work of projects such as B.STRONG has largely been replaced by IT-based capacity building, conducted online rather than face to face. While all disadvantaged communities have been adversely affected, BME community groups are facing more considerable and unmet need for the development of their groups and the support of members of their communities, who are facing the most social and economic disadvantage. Arguments that BME community groups need greater support of different kinds than other parts of the VCS have fallen on deaf ears, particularly as government has turned its back on issues of 'race' and racial disadvantage (Craig, 2013). What is particularly distressing is the fact that, despite a variety of schemes and funding opportunities, the same issues remain central to the development of the BME VCS as were apparent in the 1990s. Minorities continue to face a future of disadvantage and exclusion, with little formal organisational structure to defend their interests.

Notes

[1] Now aggravated by the UK's proposed withdrawal from the EU.

[2] See www.bham.ac.uk/tsrc.

3   This figure is derived by using groups interviewed for project evaluations from 2002 and 2006, and following up contact details through the internet.
4   BASIS was a programme funded by the BIG Lottery for projects run by voluntary and community organisations to increase their resources, knowledge, skills and influence.
5   A central government approach that stressed public service reform allied to increased devolution of powers to local government – this approach is highly compromised by central government cuts in funding.

References

Abbas, M-S. and Lachman, R. (2011) *The big society? The big divide?*, Bradford and Oxford: JUST West Yorkshire and Oxfam.

Afridi, A. (2007) *Performance and race equality project research report*, Birmingham: brap.

Cabinet Office (2010) *Making it easier to set up and run a charity, social enterprise, or voluntary organisation*, London: Cabinet Office.

Charity Commission (2003) *The promotion of community capacity-building*, Taunton: The Charity Commission.

Churches Community Work Alliance (CCWA) (2011) *What is community capacity building?* London: CCWA.

Coventry and Warwickshire Partnerships Ltd (1998) *Action checklists for capacity building*, Coventry: Adept Community Development Agency Ltd.

Craig, G. (2005) 'Community capacity building: definitions, scope, measurements and critiques', unpublished paper prepared for Organisation for European Cooperation and Development (OECD), Prague.

Craig, G. (2007) 'Community capacity-building: something old, something new …?', *Critical Social Policy*, vol 27, no 3, pp 335–59.

Craig, G. (2011) 'Forward to the past: can the UK black and minority ethnic third sector survive?', *Voluntary Sector Review*, vol 2, no 3, pp 367–89.

Craig, G. (2013) 'The invisibilisation of "race" in public policy', *Critical Social Policy*, vol 33, no 4, November, pp 712–20.

Ellis, J. and Latif, S. (2006) *Capacity building and minority ethnic voluntary and community organisations*, York: Joseph Rowntree Foundation.

Equal to the Occasion (ETTO) (2010) *Equal support. Do identity-based voluntary and community groups need identity-based organisational development?* London: ETTO for Big Lottery Fund.

Garry, K., Goodwin, P. and McCabe, A. (2004) *Review of collaboration and localisation strategies, Birmingham CAN programme evaluation*, Birmingham: Birmingham Voluntary Service Council.

Goodwin P. (2006) *Empowering for regeneration: Programme evaluation*, Birmingham: Merida Associates.

Institute for Voluntary Action Research (IVAR) (2010) *BIG and small: Capacity building, small organisations and the Big Lottery Fund*, London: IVAR for the Big Lottery Fund.

International Organisation Development (IOD) (1999) *One shoe doesn't fit all*, Birmingham: IOD.

JRF (Joseph Rowntree Foundation) (2007) *Lessons from the JRF Neighbourhood Programme; Diversity: a summary*, York: Joseph Rowntree Foundation.

McCabe, A. (2002) *Building strengths: An evaluation of B.STRONG 2000–2002*, Birmingham: Community Research and Training.

Miller, S. and Hatamian, A. (2011) *Take Part final report*, London: Community Development Foundation.

Mohan, J. (2012) 'Geographical foundations of the Big Society', *Environment and Planning A*, vol 44, no 5, pp 1121–9.

Mowbray, M. (2005) 'Community capacity building or state opportunism?', *Community Development Journal*, vol 40, no 3, pp 255–64.

ONS (2012) *Ethnicity and national identity in England and Wales 2011*, London: Office of National Statistics.

Phillimore, J. (2011) 'Approaches to health provision in the age of super-diversity: accessing the NHS in Britain's most diverse city', *Critical Social Policy*, vol 31, no 1, pp 5–29.

PQASSO (1997) *Practical assurance system for small organisations*, London: Charities Evaluation Services.

Simpson, L., Wood, L. and Daws, L. (2003) 'Community capacity building: starting with people not projects', *Community Development Journal*, vol 38, no 4, pp 277–86.

Taylor, J. (2015) *Working with communities*, Melbourne: Oxford University Press.

Taylor, M., Wilson, M., Purdue, D. and Wilde, P. (2007) *Changing neighbourhoods: The impact of 'light touch' support in 20 communities*, York: Joseph Rowntree Foundation.

Taylor, M. and Wilson, M. (2015) *Changing communities: Supporting voluntary organisations to adapt to local demographic and cultural change*, London: The Baring Foundation, London.

Third Sector Research Centre (TSRC) (2009) *Evaluation of ChangeUp 2004 to 2008: Summative evaluation report*, Birmingham: TSRC.

Ware, P. (2013) *'Very small, very quiet, a whisper …': Black and minority ethnic groups: voice and influence*, Working Paper 103, Birmingham: TSRC.

Ware, P. (2015) *'Black people don't drink tea ...': The experience of rural black and minority ethnic community groups in England*, Working Paper 130, Birmingham: TSRC.

FOUR

Learning alliance approaches to working with BME communities on healthcare innovation: a case study in palliative and end-of-life care services

David Smith and Carlos Moreno-Leguizamon

Introduction

In 2015 the Economist Intelligence Unit ranked the UK first in its 2015 Quality of Death Index, citing a combination of factors. These include comprehensive policies at the national level; the integration of palliative care into the National Health Service (NHS); subsidies that provide long-term funding for hospices and specialised units; the provision of educational and specialist courses; transparency; and a commitment to community engagement that, the report notes 'is central to the NHS model' (Economist Intelligence Unit, 2015, p 75). Despite the UK's ranking as the 'best place in the world to die', significant inequalities in accessing and using palliative and end-of-life (EoL) care services still remain, and promoting an 'equality led approach' and delivering 'equitable end of life care' has become an objective of health providers (Care Quality Commission, 2016, p 7). The increasing centrality of community engagement, alongside the contemporary concern with addressing inequalities in health service provision towards the end of life provides the background from which the project discussed in this chapter evolved. More specifically, the chapter will discuss and evaluate the use of a learning alliance (LA) as a methodology for community engagement and capacity building through a case study examining the use of, and attitudes towards, palliative and EoL care services among BME groups in North and Mid-Kent in the United Kingdom. The LA consisted of researchers from the University of Greenwich in South East London; local healthcare and palliative service providers; healthcare and specialist palliative and EoL care professionals; BME community groups and individual members from various BME groups.

The LA methodology emerged following increasing criticism of the limited application of much 'traditional' academic enquiry, with its hierarchical and sequential mode of knowledge creation and dissemination. Among the various definitions in the literature on LAs, is a common element: the centrality of inter-organisational learning and sharing of knowledge (Oliver and Kalish, 2012). Organisations are generally 'boundedly rational', utilising past experience and accumulated knowledge when making strategic decisions and developing policy (Yang et al, 2011). Clutterbuck (1998) argues that LAs are essentially vehicles for tapping into and sharing that accumulated knowledge and are characterised by their proactive nature and commitment to dissolving the gap between research and practice. Moreover, the term 'alliance' implies that participation will be beneficial for all parties through maximising joint capabilities and identifying new opportunities and perspectives. In the context of public services, LAs comprising multi-stakeholder networks represent an integrated approach to adapting to external changes and developing appropriate policy interventions. Indeed, building such linkages between theory, research and policy in the context of health practice 'may represent a new model of collaborative research that may be just as useful for developing theory and faculty as it is for educating managers and managing change' (Ghoshal et al, 1992, p 53). In the UK so far there are few experiences of implementing an LA methodology in healthcare research projects (Moreno-Leguizamon et al, 2015). This chapter is actually only the second to analyse and document the implementation of an LA in the south-east of England. The overarching policy context for this is the differential – and generally poor – quality of public services, including healthcare, experienced by BME groups as compared with their white counterparts (Craig et al, 2012).

The first section will summarise the key tenets of the LA methodology before summarising the project itself and the process of implementing the LA. The overarching background to the project is the convergence of two significant demographic trends: population ageing and an increase in the BME population. These both have far-reaching implications for healthcare, and policy makers have started to connect the two discussions and recognise that the future elderly population will be increasingly diverse ethnically (Lievesley, 2010). For the project reported here, a third trend is also relevant: the accelerated movement of BME groups out of London (and other urban areas) and into small towns (often at the centre of rural areas) and peri-urban areas in what can be called an 'internal economic displacement' of people due to the speculative trend in London's housing market (Simpson, 2012). For BME people of national origins relatively new to the UK, health and other service providers often lack the accumulated institutional knowledge concerning beliefs, practices and attitudes surrounding health, and there is a corresponding deficit of knowledge or experience concerning how to tailor interventions to meet the needs of those groups. This is particularly salient in sensitive areas such as palliative and EoL care, where the outcomes of limited knowledge or experience on the part of healthcare practitioners may be more acutely felt and with significantly more of a negative impact on BME service users (Koffman, 2014). It is against this background of demographic and social change and the challenges they pose for healthcare providers that the LAPCEL (Learning Alliance on Palliative Care and End of Life) project was developed. The final sections of the chapter will discuss the formation and evolution of LAPCEL, and consider what this approach added to the project in terms of inter-organisational learning, knowledge creation and dissemination.

The learning alliance methodology

The LA methodology emerged from the systems innovation literature as a way of exploring 'the relationship between science and technology and the economic performance of industrial countries', particularly in the context of so-called information/knowledge societies (Verhagen et al, 2008, p 118; Walshe et al, 2009). LAs represent a non-linear model of knowledge production comprised of 'multiple actors with multi-layered sources of knowledge to cope with the complexity of fostering continuous technological, social, and institutional innovations to respond to rapidly changing context and demands' (Gotrett et al, 2005, p 2). Further elements that complement this methodology are the search for common goals, sharing of material, human and financial resources around a research project and recognition of the learning (horizontal and vertical) that occurs and that may exceed the accomplishment of research outcomes.

The LA methodology therefore involves a series of connected multi-stakeholder platforms or networks (practitioners, researchers, policy makers, activists) at different institutional levels (local, national) involved in two basic tasks: knowledge innovation and its scaling up in time (sustainability) and space (coverage) (Butterworth et al, 2011; Moreno-Leguizamon et al, 2015, p 7). Researchers, working through a network of stakeholders, maximise the project's socioeconomic impact by including stakeholders in the project from the very beginning and by jointly developing practical solutions to research findings. LAs avoid the traditional dichotomy between research outcomes and processes by foregrounding documentation of the 'daily' aspects of a research project, which is where socioeconomic impact is gestated, and by adopting a reflexive approach to the research process. The most important tools of an LA are: stakeholder analysis, capacity building, action research, process documentation and dissemination and process monitoring according to particular context and needs (Locke, 2009; Moreno-Leguizamon et al, 2015). In order for an LA to work effectively, support, commitment, resources and leadership from all stakeholders are needed. Service users, practitioners and policy makers are key groups that are considered significant to include. For this reason the LA methodology works well in research concerned with service provision in general, and healthcare in particular.

The project: Learning Alliance on Palliative Care and End of Life

North and Mid-Kent, in the south-east corner of England, has experienced significant changes in its ethnic profile over the last ten years. While BME groups within the UK as a whole remain largely concentrated in urban areas, their rate of growth has been relatively highest in areas such as Kent, where they were fewest in 2001 (Jivraj, 2012). Kent's BME population grew by 103% between 2001 and 2011, with the highest populations in North East Kent: Dartford, Gravesham and Medway. The largest group are Asian/Asian British, followed by Mixed/Multiple Ethnicity and then Black African/Caribbean groups (KCC, 2011). Kent is also home to the country's largest Gypsy–Traveller population, with an estimated 12,000 (ITMB, 2013). This is likely to be an under-estimate, as it accounts only for those who declare their ethnicity and/or are known to reside on caravan or roadside sites, thus omitting the majority who are now living in conventional housing and the county's significant population of Roma migrants from East and Central Europe (Smith, 2014). Kent's population was projected to increase by 13% between 2007 and 2017, while its population of older people (50+) was projected to increase by over 16%, a growing proportion of whom would comprise BME groups. This increase would be especially notable in the county's larger and longer-established groups (for example, Irish and Asian/Asian British) (KCC, 2011).

Studies indicate significantly lower levels of referrals to palliative care services for BME groups (Fountain, 1999; Moreno-Leguizamon et al, forthcoming) and, despite, most members of BME groups expressing a preference for dying at home, they are more likely to die in hospital (Coupland et al, 2011). These findings stimulated research into the structure and organisation of palliative and EoL services and the experiences of healthcare practitioners in caring for different cultural groups at the end of life (Karim et al, 2000; Randhawa et al, 2003). Given the increasing ethnic diversity of the elderly population, healthcare providers have been trying to improve access to and the quality of palliative and EoL care. The NHS *End of Life Care Strategy* (DoH, 2008) noted significant disparities in access, with older, non-cancer, BME, disabled and rural patients being less likely to be referred, or to access, palliative services. The report continues that there is much unknown about BME experiences of palliative and EoL care and, although recommendations exist for improving the care provided to those groups, examples of best practice are less common. Calanzani et al (2013, p 13) note that

> Ethnic minority health is increasingly recognised as a crucial 'tracer' for measuring the success in achieving health and patient preferred outcomes for the population in general, and for palliative/end of life care in particular, where there is growing evidence that we are not all equal in death.

Policy recommendations stress the need for education and 'cultural competence' among practitioners (Ahmed et al, 2004). Evans et al (2011) note, however, that few concrete recommendations have been developed and such an approach can become a 'tick box' exercise. It was felt that these concerns could be addressed by forming an LA that would help to 'shape perspectives and to assist in identifying, defining and framing problems' (Ghoshal et al, 1992l, p 15). The aim was to address the contextual factors that shape decisions and preferences around terminal illness and the end of life in a manner that linked research, capacity building and networking among different levels of organisation.

The LAPCEL project was designed by initially creating a multi-stakeholder network across the North and Mid-Kent region. The main participants were Health Education Kent Surrey and Sussex (HEKSS), the research team from the Faculty of Education and Health at the University of Greenwich, Diversity House (Sittingbourne), Medway Older People's Partnership, the Medway Ethnic Minority Forum, Ellenor Lions Hospices and Medway Council. Other collaborations developed by the project were with Public Health England and the

Gypsy–Traveller support group One Voice 4 Travellers. LAPCEL was a one-year feasibility study funded by HEKSS to build the capacity and capability required within primary health and community services better to meet the palliative and EoL needs of BME members in the region (Smith et al, 2015). More specifically the project aimed to:

- document the palliative and EoL health needs of BME groups in North/Mid-Kent;
- document the EoL rituals, practices and customs of those groups;
- build the capacity of Kent community health services by making them part of the LA;
- monitor the process of networking and increase opportunities for working with different stakeholders; and
- disseminate the process of creating an LA to serve BME populations concerning palliative and EoL care.

LAPCEL's longer-term aims were to develop innovative models that would incorporate the partners' tacit knowledge into concrete knowledge through joint learning activities and by disseminating and debating findings with the LA network as they emerged at various stages of the project. This would include (i) incorporating new working practices regarding palliative and EoL care with BME communities; (ii) generating a sustainable learning network in North/Mid-Kent with a core focus on improving palliative and EoL care for BME communities; and (iii) informing the development of a multi-professional education pack for the palliative and EoL sector in the HEKSS region. Thus, following the LA methodology, LAPCEL implemented the following components: capacity building with both BME communities, NHS services and health professionals; research activities (focus groups and interviews with service providers and service users of different BME backgrounds); documentation and dissemination. These components were integrally implemented and discussed with the LAPCEL stakeholders during three major meetings throughout the project's life cycle (beginning, middle and end) and via an online platform that allowed for uploading of relevant documents and stakeholder feedback. It is important to note that ideally a full LA project should last a minimum of two years, although in this case there was an adaptation of the steps and components recommended in the literature to fit the project's one-year time-scale (Butterworth et al, 2011).

The formation of LAPCEL

Each organisation that participated in LAPCEL represented different institutional layers (for example, grassroots, local, regional, national) and came with its own perspectives, experiences and bodies of knowledge surrounding palliative and EoL care, which were delineated at the first LA meeting. It was agreed that cooperation at the local, regional and other levels of organisation would be achieved through establishing institutional arrangements and developing mutual knowledge among all stakeholders. The three BME grassroots organisations were also co-producers of the knowledge, collaborating in the research process in two main ways: first, through taking part in LA meetings and initially raising relevant topics and issues that were not identified in the literature review, and in later meetings providing insights and feedback regarding the shaping of the questions to be formulated in the data collection; and second, through using their contacts within local BME communities to organise focus groups and facilitate data collection.

The first LAPCEL meeting took place between the academic team, representatives of two local grassroots organisations, community members from various BME groups and health and palliative care personnel. The meeting was an eye-opening experience and highlighted the importance of recognising differing conceptualisations of death and the expectations of different communities regarding the 'disposal' of the body after death. For some Hindu and Muslim communities, immediate – sometimes within hours – cremation and/or burial of the body was important, while for some African Christian communities transportation of the body 'home' was a concern, mainly among first-generation immigrants. Similarly, gender roles around the process of death and dying emerged as another significant issue for almost all communities, with an abundance of details. The organisation of a will as a very mundane activity was considered in some communities as invoking or 'calling death' – explaining to a certain extent the lack of planning and organisation of those activities by some groups, and with clear implications concerning advance care planning.

As the project was centrally concerned with people's experiences, beliefs and perceptions of palliative and EoL care, the qualitative methodology was validated by the stakeholders at the first meeting. The sampling strategy was discussed and co-designed with LAPCEL stakeholders to represent some of the main minority groups in the North/Mid-Kent region and a combination of longer-established groups, for example, Asian/Asian British, Gypsy–Travellers and more recent – but numerically significant – arrivals such as Africans. The different methodological tools and approaches appropriate to cover issues such as access; participants' experiences, beliefs and practices surrounding the end of life and EoL care; understandings of the concepts of end-of-life and palliative care; experiences of accessing palliative care; identifying unmet needs; obstacles to effective care and how such care could be organised to better suit the participant's needs, were all discussed and agreed upon at the initial meeting.

During the first meeting a prominent role was played by the grassroots organisations, in particular with observations and questions that informed the prospective research process. The LA methodology, without being fully participatory, allowed for valuable co-learning in which the researchers could incorporate important observations, helping to refine the focus of the research, data collection and analysis. This is one element that an LA can offer to healthcare and services when they are conducting research with minority populations.

Mid-term meeting: validation of the findings

The first LAPCEL meeting was positively dominated by the community organisations. The mid-term meeting, by contrast, occurred after the first phase of data collection and was focused on validating research findings. Here it was the service providers who played the more central role. Present at the meeting were personnel from a local hospital care staff and specialists and representatives from a local support organisation for the elderly. The stakeholders present largely confirmed that the provision of palliative care services to BME communities was less than ideal, and the reasons for this were discussed at length. As an outcome of the meeting and in order better to understand the experiences of those service providers, a workshop on compassionate care was organised for hospice staff and conducted by two members of the academic research team. This was provided in exchange for a more in-depth and on-site exploration of some of the issues raised at the meeting. Following the compassionate care workshop a questionnaire was conducted with hospice staff that confirmed that BME groups made less use of their service, and there was a general consensus that many minority community members lacked knowledge of what palliative and EoL services were and how to access them. It was also observed that only after somebody had been referred did they get an opportunity to receive clarification about what those services entail.

Regarding validation of findings by the stakeholders the main issues to emerge from the focus groups varied in terms of specific concerns while also demonstrating commonalities. The African and Gypsy–Traveller groups were more likely to emphasise racism and discrimination as barriers to palliative care, reflecting the social structural location and status of these groups. However, how these factors were experienced, contextualised and subsequently shaped attitudes towards their own care at the end of life showed marked variation. Among the former African (largely female) focus groups many participants had worked or were working in the health and social care sector and experiences of workplace racism made them hesitant to use palliative care themselves. They were also critical of the impersonal nature of much formal care and had concerns around inadequate resources or staffing and poor standards of care towards elderly and frail patients, which made many afraid to enter such care themselves in later years. While the historical context of prejudice and discrimination can result in minority mistrust of the medical profession and was present in the African focus groups, it was more prominent among the Gypsy–Traveller participants. The three main interrelated themes were societal discrimination both generally and in the use of healthcare services more specifically, and how these cumulative experiences influenced perceptions of where they would prefer to die. Related to these concerns, many noted reluctance to disclose their ethnicity, with the consequence that any specific cultural needs were not acknowledged or recognised. A final theme was conflicts around customs and practices when a community member is close to the end of life in formal healthcare settings. For the South Asian participants, stigma surrounding illness and death was an important theme, meaning that communication with community and non-community members took on a special significance. Like the African women, many first-generation Asians also expressed a wish to either die or be buried in their country of birth, which again is important when considering advance care planning.

The mid-term meeting of the LAPCEL project allowed for an appreciation and awareness that the interpretation and validation of the findings encapsulated a different message for each stakeholder. For example, while it was obvious that the healthcare providers needed to know more about the nuanced practices of different BME groups, many of the members of those groups also needed to learn about palliative and EoL care outside the hospital and, in particular, the role and function of the hospice. Thus another element that an LA can offer to practical and policy-oriented research in healthcare and the provision of health services is a more effective and rapid use and appropriation of research outcomes.

Final meeting: dissemination of results

If the first and second meetings had, respectively, the grassroots organisations and service providers playing the central role, in the final meeting the academic team took centre stage, given its key responsibility for dissemination of the final results and to analyse the effectiveness of the LA methodology as a different way of conducting research. Regarding the latter, elements of the LA that were addressed as significant were: the types and application of learning that took place among the stakeholders; the process of networking and knowledge generation with different categories of stakeholders; and how to ensure the sustainability of LAPCEL and to further develop the networks established by collaborating on future projects. At the time of writing, one proposal has been submitted, developed by different LAPCEL stakeholders exploring issues of intersectionality in hospice settings, and a meeting with one of the community organisations to discuss future collaboration has been arranged. The value of knowledge sharing and generation through the LA methodology and the nurturing of sustainable networks is another significant element that LAs can offer as an advance on traditional hierarchical research relationships in healthcare and social care and when conducting research with BME populations.

Discussion

The LA, as a methodology to increase and improve the socioeconomic impacts of research, in particular community research projects, offers a variety of opportunities as demonstrated in this chapter. First, it narrows the gap between research and practice by facilitating knowledge sharing with different stakeholders (service users, service providers, policy makers) at various levels (local and national). By involving the service users as key stakeholders in the project, LAPCEL opened the floor for them to shape and complement the research with valuable information that in some cases was not identified in the literature. Second, the LA methodology not only contributes to the refinement of the data collected for a research project but also offers capacity-building opportunities to all stakeholders. Capacity building and early appropriation and use of research results by different stakeholders are, for example, concerns of new disciplines such as implementation and translational science. Third, the process of learning through a network of stakeholders and organisations allows for an appreciation that a research project can be more than the traditional linear process of research, report and publications. A research project can build the capacity of the stakeholders, disseminate and allow the appropriation of early research results, as well as document and reflect on what has worked well, and otherwise.

In terms of the research findings themselves, one of the main implications to emerge for palliative and EoL care service providers was the need for a more refined and nuanced picture of palliative care needs than that which is currently driving much policy in this area, where the possibility of ethnic stereotyping is apparent. The dangers of cultural/ethnic determinism became clear as patients' needs differ between groups as well as within them, intersecting most commonly with class, generation and gender (Craig et al, 2012; Gunaratnam, 2013). Koffman et al (2007) critically address the intersections of ethnicity and class in suggesting that lack of information and of access to services may be an outcome of socioeconomic status over ethnicity or culture. Certain ethnic minorities therefore face a 'dual disadvantage', being over-represented in areas of deprivation (as in the poorer electoral wards of Medway and Gravesham), and even within those areas have lower levels of service use than deprived White British residents (Evans et al, 2011).

A further important finding to emerge corresponds to Diver et al's (2003) argument that social scientists often neglect acculturation and change in BME individuals' orientation to the majority culture by failing to account for generational variants in attitudes and practices. Walshe et al (2009), for example, found different perceptions of hospice care between UK-born Chinese and those born in China, with the former more favourable towards palliative care. Similarly it was acknowledged in focus-group discussions with African and South Asian participants that generational differences existed, with the practices of British-born BME members converging more with the majority population and a corresponding decline in practices such as returning the person 'home' to die or burying the body in the deceased's birthplace. Imposing a false homogeneity on BME groups inevitably entails neglecting the diversity of individual needs within those groups. Identity and power, as two of the underpinning concepts of the intersectional approach, can be useful when framing policies that do not homogenise people based on their ethnic/cultural backgrounds yet recognise that these factors (along with gender, age, social class and sexuality and so on) play a significant role in shaping preferences, attitudes and beliefs towards palliative and EoL care.

Conclusion

The LA methodology offers several benefits when engaging in policy-oriented research with minority groups, due to the sharing of control over the priorities and aims of a piece of research and the convergence of theory, conceptual refinement, applied research and policy application. This approach assisted the LAPCEL project in facilitating inter-organisational learning, knowledge creation and dissemination. In addition, the LA methodology served to shape the research questions, data collection and analysis, yielding a richness of data from different vantage points, allowing for triangulation. Potential difficulties include establishing trust and a sense of shared purpose early on in the project's implementation phase. This is to overcome possible stakeholder misgivings over opportunism by other participants in the LA and to reduce any tensions that may exist. Ensuring the necessary levels of commitment and involvement by all stakeholders is another latent difficulty, although this is not specific to the LA methodology. Finally, although many strategic partnerships are short-term alliances designed to achieve a specific objective, sustainability should be a central objective of the LA. Ideally an LA should function for at least two years, unlike the case study reported here, to allow for the effective dissemination and consolidation of knowledge and for novel insights and policy solutions to evolve. For BME groups in particular, who are unused to engaging with health professionals as equals, two years would be the minimum period to enable their capacity to take on such roles in the future more effectively.

References

Ahmed, N., Bestall, J.E., Ahmedzai, S.H., Payne, S.A., Clark, D. and Noble, B. (2004) 'Systematic review of the problems and issues of accessing specialist palliative care by patients, carers and health and social care professionals', *Palliative Medicine*, vol 18, no 6, pp 525–42.

Butterworth, J., McIntyre, P. and da Silva Wells, C. (eds) (2011) *SWITCH in the city: Putting urban water management to the test*, The Hague: IRC International Water and Sanitation Centre, www.switchurbanwater.eu/outputs/pdfs/SWITCH_in_the_City.pdf.

Calanzani, N., Koffman, J. and Higginson, I.J. (2013) *Palliative and EoL care for black and minority ethnic groups in the UK*, London: Public Health England.

Care Quality Commission (2016) *A different ending: Addressing inequalities in end of life care*, Newcastle Upon Tyne: CQC

Clutterbuck, D. (1998) *Learning alliances: Tapping into talent*, London: Chartered Institute of Personnel and Development.

Coupland, V.H., Madden, P., Jack, R.H., Moller, H. and Davies, E.A. (2011) 'Does place of death from cancer vary between ethnic groups in South East England?' *Palliative Medicine*, vol 25, no 4, pp 314–22.

Craig, G., Atkin, K., Chattoo, S. and Flynn, R. (eds) (2012) *Understanding 'race' and ethnicity: Theory, history, policy, practice*, Bristol: Policy Press.

DoH (Department of Health) (2008) *NHS end of life care strategy*, London: Department of Health.

Diver, F., Molassiotis, A. and Weeks, L. (2003) 'The palliative care needs of ethnic minority patients attending a day-care centre: a qualitative study', *International Journal of Palliative Nursing*, vol 9, no 9, pp 389–96.

Economist Intelligence Unit (2015) *The 2015 Quality of Death Index: Country profiles*, https://www.eiuperspectives.economist.com/sites/default/files/images/2015%20Quality%20of%20Death%20Index%20Country%20Profiles_Oct%206%20FINAL.pdf, accessed 4 March 2017.

Evans, N., Menaca, A., Andrew, E.V., Koffman, J., Harding, J., Higginson, I.J., Pool, R. and Gysels, M. (2011) 'Systematic review of the primary research on minority ethnic groups and end-of-life care from the United Kingdom', *Journal of Pain Symptom Management*, vol 43, no 2, pp 261–86.

Fountain, A. (1999) 'Ethnic minorities and palliative care in Derby', *Palliative Medicine*, Vol 13, pp 161–2.

Ghoshal, S., Arnzen, B. and Brownfield, S. (1992) 'A learning alliance between businesses and business schools: executive education as a platform for partnership, *California Management Review*, vol 35, no 1, pp 13–36.

Gotrett, M.V., Lundy, M. and Ashby, J. (2005) *Learning alliances: An approach for building multistakeholder innovation systems*, ILAC Brief no 8, Rome: ILAC.

Gunaratnam, Y. (2013) *Death and the migrant: Bodies, borders and care*, London: Bloomsbury.

ITMB (2013) *Gypsy and Traveller population in England and the 2011 census*, London: Irish Traveller Movement in Britain.

Jivraj, S. (2012) *How has ethnic diversity grown 1991–2001–2011?* York: Joseph Rowntree Foundation.

Karim, K., Bailey, M. and Tunna, K. (2000) 'Nonwhite ethnicity and the provision of specialist palliative care services: factors affecting doctors' referral patterns', *Palliative Medicine*, vol 14, no 6, pp 471–8.

KCC (2011) *Ethnicity in Kent and Medway*, Maidstone: Kent County Council.

Koffman, J., Burke, G., Dias, A., Raval, B., Byrne, J., Gonzales, J. and Daniels, C. (2007) 'Demographic factors and awareness of palliative care and related services', *Palliative Medicine*, vol 21, no 2, pp 145–53.

Koffman, J. (2014) 'Servicing multi-cultural needs at the end of life', *Journal of Renal Care*, 40 (Suppl 1), pp 6–15.

Leivesley, N. (2010) *The future ageing of the EM population of England and Wales*, London: Runnymede Trust/Centre for Policy on Ageing.

Locke, C. (2009) 'Community cohesion and black and ethnic minority communities' health inequalities: A learning alliance experience in Kent', unpublished master's thesis, Coventry: Coventry University.

Moreno-Leguizamon, C., Smith, D. and Spigner, C. (2017) 'Positive aging, positive dying: Intersectional and daily communicational issues surrounding palliative and end of life care services in minority groups', in R.E. Docking and J. Stock (eds) *International Handbook of Positive Aging*, Abingdon: Routledge International Handbook.

Moreno-Leguizamon, C., Tovar-Restrepo, M., Irazábal, C. and Locke, C. (2015) 'Learning alliance methodology: Contributions and challenges for multicultural planning in health service provision: A case study in Kent, UK', *Planning Theory & Practice*, DOI: 10.1080/14649357.2014.990403

Oliver, A.L. and Kalish, Y. (2012) 'Interorganizational learning in alliances and networks', in T.K. Das (ed), *Strategic alliances for value creation*, Charlotte, NC: Information Age Publishing Inc.

Randhawa, G., Owens, A., Fitches, R. and Khan, Z. (2003) 'Communication in the development of culturally competent palliative care services in the UK: a case study', *International Journal of Palliative Nursing*, vol 9, no 1, pp 24–31.

Simpson, L. (2012) *More segregation or more mixing?*, York: Joseph Rowntree Foundation.

Smith, D. (2014) *Local engagement Roma integration project: UK feasibility report*, Brussels: Fundamental Rights Agency.

Smith, D., Moreno-Leguizamon, C. and Grohmann, S. (2015) *End of life practices and palliative care among black and minority (BME) ethnic groups*, Greenwich: Health Education Kent, Surrey and Sussex: University of Greenwich.

Verhagen, J., Butterworth, J. and Morris, M. (2008) 'Learning alliances for integrated and sustainable innovations in urban water management', *Waterlines*, vol 27, no 2, http://wedc.lboro.ac.uk/resources/conference/33/Verhagen_J.pdf.

Walshe, C., Todd, C., Caress, A. and Chew-Graham, C. (2009) 'Patterns of access to community palliative care services: a literature review', *Journal of Pain Symptom Management*, vol 37, no 5, pp 884–912.

Yang, H., Zhiang, L. and Peng, M.W. (2011) 'Behind acquisitions of alliance partners: exploratory learning and network embeddedness', *Academy of Management Journal*, vol 54, no 5, pp 1069–80.

FIVE

sampad: working with arts and culture

Ranjit Sondhi

Introduction

sampad is a South Asian arts and heritage organisation based at the Midlands Arts Centre (mac) in Birmingham, UK that develops high-quality dance, music, drama, literature, poetry, crafts performances and events based on traditions drawn from the countries of the Indian subcontinent to engage in a creative intercultural dialogue with all sections of Britain's increasingly diverse society. It deploys skills in community education and community development to reach a great variety of audiences. Through the language of art, it explores the relationship between traditional and emerging identities, between established and popular art forms, within and between different religious, cultural and social groupings and between settled communities and new migrants to create the basis for a wider and more informed debate in wider civil society about the construction of community and identity in the modern era. This chapter explores the extent to which *sampad* has met its aims and objectives. *sampad*'s formal mission statement now is to connect people and communities with British Asian arts and heritage and to play a pro-active role in the creative economy.

The thinking

Twenty-first-century identities are fluid and dynamic. Any attempt to fix them in time and space by using anthropology, geography, mythology or religion freezes identity and turns it into a caricature of itself. However, the paradox is that without reference to these markers, discourse about 'identity' and 'community' cannot begin. There has to be a full stop at the end of a sentence for it to mean something.

We need boundaries across which we can create a dialogue. These boundaries are real and palpable. But they are also fictional and not there forever; there is nothing absolute about them. They are artefacts, not nature-facts. In essence, they are primarily constructions of the mind and can therefore be deconstructed. This applies particularly in relation to cultural boundaries. There is a saying in India, 'culture does not make people, people make culture'. And what is made can be unmade.

It is instructive to note how the cultural debate has been incorporated into the UK psyche (as it has in so many other 'receiving' countries of the West) since the arrival of migrant workers and their families in the immediate aftermath of the Second World War, when colonial workers were sucked in from the hinterlands of an empire in decline and relocated in the twilight areas of labour-hungry conurbations at the very heart of the 'mother country'.

The new migrants were, foremost, perceived as 'units of production', confined initially to the public and industrial sectors. The realisation that they were citizens too, operating in the wider social and cultural spheres, dawned on government many years after their arrival. Since then, there have been several well-meaning attempts to construct policies and practices that could more fully integrate the migrant settlers into the cultural and social life of neighbourhoods and cities.

It was within this economic and social milieu that the concept and consequent policy development of multiculturalism took shape in post-war Britain. The new migrants were 'made visible' by colour, religion and cultures that were markedly different from those of the indigenous population. People from the Caribbean, Africa and, in particular, the Indian sub-continent were exoticised. And it was their culture – their language, food, dress, festivals, family structures and rituals – that exercised the national imagination but troubled the national psyche.

That was the base on which multiculturalism was built – designed to achieve better 'race and community relations' through a greater understanding of the cultural expression and behaviour of the 'new arrivals', in the hope that cultural differences could not only be understood and tolerated but even celebrated. One of the central strategies of multiculturalism was to put on public display the cultural wares of migrant settlers. So, from the 1960s onwards there were cultural and religious festivals and celebrations in schools and town halls, and on radio and television broadcasts. This was followed by the burgeoning of folk and classical music and dance performances in pubs, clubs and community centres, and the emergence of distinctive music styles and cultural expression. It was the 'bhangra-balti-rap' era of 'saris, samosas and steelbands'.

But a more sober, critical review of multiculturalism revealed its limitations and drawbacks. Multiculturalism was based on the belief that the many different minority cultures should be tolerated and even encouraged to flourish in society and that services and facilities such as health, education, broadcasting and the arts should be delivered in a way that embodied and promoted this belief. However, the problem was that it focused primarily on difference. It failed to provide a framework for inter- and intra-cultural understanding, sharing and exchange. It encouraged identity politics but was silent on social injustice and economic inequalities. And most crucially, it failed to recognise the unintended consequence of creating fixed ethnic enclaves, both physical and mental.

In many respects, migrant communities internalised these truncated images of themselves. There was, in some cases, no option other than to play out the roles prescribed for them. At first minorities had been 'racialised'; now they were to be 'ethnicised'. A whole ethnic industry sprang up, particularly in the heart of inner cities. There were balti houses, taxi services, corner shops, minority language programmes, wedding video companies, saree warehouses, sweat shops, tropical fruit and vegetable sellers and spice stalls. Black became, first, Black and Asian, and then, Black, Asian and Minority Ethnic (BAME). Within just a small area of inner-city Birmingham, local and central government funding was made available for Harambee Housing Association, the Asian Resource Centre, the Sith Youth Service, the Pakistan Welfare Association, the Bangladeshi Youth Forum and the Irish Community Centre, each with its own circumscribed clientele and area of cultural activity, its own workers and its own management committees. Often these groups found themselves competing for the same resources, occasionally striking oppositional stands against each other.

But even as diverse Britain began to fragment into its ethnic components, some community development initiatives began to generate a strong belief that strategies based on culture and heritage possessed the power to *transform*, as well as to *replicate*, to experiment as well as to preserve, to question as well as to accept. This approach was built on a controversial and contested concept that while people may be immersed in culture, they are not saturated in it.

When expressed in this way, culture became radical, iconoclastic, subversive. It also became the prerequisite for the construction of an open, liberal, democratic society. But it would take a degree of commitment, conviction and courage to enter into this brave new cultural terrain.

The doing

sampad is one such South Asian arts organisation that has gradually evolved its cultural policy and practice over the last twenty-five years along these lines. It takes its inspiration from ancient music, dance and the performing arts and reinterprets them within the context of a modern diverse Britain. It keeps pace with the changing social, political, economic, cultural and technological landscape. Its performances pay respect to traditions but are no longer straight-jacketed by them.

sampad performances are based on the principles of interculturalism. First, it must be made clear what the *sampad* concept is not. It is not a simple aggregate of the discrete cultural traditions of India, Pakistan and Bangladesh. It is not put together as a device to attract government funding, it is not a marriage of convenience between the 'West and the Rest' in which, under the surface, there is a minimal amount of emotional, intellectual and physical exchange and interaction between dominant and subjugated cultural traditions.

What the *sampad* experiment proposes is a significant departure from going on doing things in the way in which they have always been done. It goes to the very heart of why and how an intercultural society might be conceived and constructed. In the past, out of a perfectly understandable and well-intentioned but somewhat misguided liberalism we have tinkered with the idea of multiculturalism as a composite, a simple arithmetic sum, of self-contained cultures existing side by side in parallel worlds. But the depressing point about parallel worlds is that they never meet. *sampad* believes with a quiet conviction that the future must lie in creative connections and crossovers. However, before this critical debate about both defining and breaching cultural boundaries can take place there has to be a much greater understanding of the richness and complexity of minority cultural traditions that should take their place alongside western cultural forms.

In general, the public, both majority and minority, remains deeply uninformed about the long, highly complex and refined traditions of South Asian music and dance, the key texts, poets and novelists, the great civilisations and the extraordinarily varied cultural history of the Indian sub-continent. This knowledge remains beyond the reach of even the well-educated.

Therefore, as we have asserted, the contest is between two distinct ideological positions – the traditional stance of the arts as a temple, and a newer one of the arts as a forum. As temple, art plays a 'timeless and universal function involving the use of a structured sample of reality, not just as a reference but as an objective model against which to compare individual perceptions' (Cameron, 1971, p 71), In contrast, as a forum, art is a place for 'confrontation, experimentation, and debate' (Cameron, 1971, p 71).

sampad performances, installations, exhibitions and events emphasise that cultural identity is neither fixed and unalterable, nor is it wholly fluid and subjected to unlimited reconstruction. Those of us who are brought up in non-Western cultures marked by dualism do not find it impossible to reconcile the *ha* and *tha*, the *ying* and *yang* of life and meaning. So, as an increasingly significant community arts project, the role of *sampad* is both to reflect minority and majority cultural identities and to transcend them. This means finding novel ways of balancing the demands for both unity and diversity within the world of arts and heritage.

But since both are important, each limits the other. We do not wish to strive for a unity that is so extensive that it leaves no space for diversity, nor should we tolerate so wide a diversity that our communities remain fragmented and cannot effectively pursue a common interest. Unity should not be formal, abstract and devoid of energy, but should possess great moral, political and cultural depth. Diversity should not be passive, mute and ghettoised but expansive, interactive and capable of creating a rich and plural collective culture.

Part of this purpose is achieved by programmes and programming. But it is also fulfilled through spatial configurations – bricks and mortar, glass and steel; together with performance, spaces provide practical solutions for our intellectual and aesthetic demands. Hence our active participation in the activities and development of the mac. We want distinctive spaces, clearly signposted across boundaries, fixed and movable, that are like semi-permeable membranes. We want to ensure that our fragile Asian ethnicities are neither obliterated, erased from memory, nor doomed to survive forever, locked away, shut up, sectioned off, hermetically sealed off from other cultures.

We hope that the following selection of what *sampad* has curated in the last decade bears testimony to our approach to arts, culture and heritage. As a preface, we would like to restate the mission and values of *sampad*.

Mission and values

sampad exists to develop a deep and distinctive structure of South Asian arts in Birmingham and Britain and beyond through production, promotion, advocacy, education and outreach activity. *sampad* aims to be inclusive in all its practices and will be as concerned with the pursuit of *excellence* as it will be with widening *access*.

The mission statement is underpinned by the following core values:

• provide a rich, complex and deeply satisfying experience of true intercultural practice;
• maintain a special sensitivity to serving those South Asian groups whose cultural aspirations and contributions remain unrecognised and under-represented;
• reflect the socio-cultural and identity issues affecting communities of the British and South Asian diaspora;
• develop and maintain a commitment to working inclusively with all sections of the community;
• ensure that education and life-long learning is at the heart of all *sampad*'s work.

The projects, representative of the range of our work, are presented in the following sections.

Tribhangi Dance Theatre

Based in Johannesburg, South Africa, and working in partnership with *sampad*, Tribhangi has toured extensively throughout the world. Its striking, high-energy performances combine the strong physicality of African dance with the grace of classical Indian Bharatanatyam, incorporating colourful Afro-fusion and contemporary styles into the mix for an exhilarating dance experience that can be enjoyed by people of all ages and from different cultural and social backgrounds.

For *sampad*, Tribhangi represents a fearlessly innovative approach to creating a dialogue between the diverse cultural groups of the new South Africa. It is a showcase for the creative energy that exists between cultural art forms that have traditionally remained, or have been kept, separate from each other. It is a powerful example of the creative energy that exists at the boundaries between countries.

Mandala

Mandala was an outdoor performance event that took place in Birmingham's Chamberlain Square and Nottingham's Old Market Square in 2012.

Directed by Kully Thiarai, with choreography by Aakash Odedra and artistic direction by Piali Ray, it presented South Asian dance and music in a fresh and exciting new way.

Mandala united exciting British Asian dancers Aakash Odedra and Devika Rao, and hip-hop/streetdance collective Bboy's Attic, mixing the subtle, evocative forms of classical Asian dance with edgy, urban attitude.

The striking dance sequences were set to a powerful soundtrack that featured the music of world-class artists Anoushka Shankar and Zakir Hussain, and the performance culminated with an uplifting live appearance by an award-winning tabla artist, Talvin Singh.

The façades of Town Hall Birmingham and Nottingham Council House formed an interactive backdrop to the shows, and the structures came to life with stunning visual effects and 3D digital light projections triggered by the live South Asian music and dance.

A 'mandala' is a circular symbol that represents the universe in some Eastern religions. The performance reflected on our journeys through life and how we are all shaped by our experiences. The mandala shape formed by the projections symbolised the idea that the past, present and future are all part of a never-ending life cycle, as well as representing our intertwined histories and cultural heritage.

Mandala aimed to awaken a mood of joy and celebration by inspiring audiences to salute past achievements and renew collective hopes for the future. Its ultimate achievement was the creation of an immersive and memorable experience enjoyed by more than 12,000 people in the UK.

My Route

This was *sampad*'s major community heritage project, which researched and documented the changing fortunes of the radial Stratford Road in Birmingham in the period after the Second World War.

Around 25,000 Birmingham residents took part in activities exploring the historical evolution of Stratford Road as one of Birmingham's busiest and best-known thoroughfares.

Working with local people between Sparkbrook and Hall Green, My Route identified changes in the population, landscape and culture from the 1940s to the present day, with the settlement and migration of new communities along the road.

It began with a wide-ranging investigation that looked at how the different demographics, faiths, trades, food, languages and architecture of the area have evolved and merged together to create a vibrant and diverse city quarter. In partnership with Birmingham Archives, it went on to equip volunteers with new heritage research skills, using oral histories, factual data collection and public donations to uncover the unique history of the road.

A series of lively arts and culture activities gave people of all ages a chance to learn more about the story of the area. A 1970s-styled taxi took passengers on a trip down memory lane, using props, sound recordings and storytelling to immerse them in the sights, sounds and memories of the Road. Elsewhere, students from South and City College explored the history of faith in the area, using photography to examine symbolic architecture, while foodies got a taste of Stratford Road as *sampad* hosted culinary workshops at three of the most popular restaurants in the area.

One of the principal highlights of the project was the My Route Exhibition Trail, an outdoor exhibition that featured large-scale photographs of 11 everyday people who live and work around Stratford Road – drawing attention and commentary from passers-by. The portraits, by internationally respected photographer Vanley Burke, were accompanied by personal memories from each person in the form of audio clips that were accessed by members of the public via 'sound pods' designed by pioneering artist Brian Duffy.

In total, nearly 25,000 people connected with the My Route experience, whether as exhibition visitors, participants or volunteers. Fifty-one volunteers from 13 different ethnic groups clocked up 450 hours as they brought the project to life by recording interviews with residents, collecting statistics, carrying out research and compiling Wikipedia articles about the local history. My Route leaves a legacy of several permanent resources for future generations, including a new public archive of local memories. *sampad* also joined forces with local film-maker Sam Lockyer of Iconic Productions to produce a documentary film featuring interviews with the project's contributors, participants and volunteers.

A screening of the My Route documentary at the University of Birmingham's Arts and Science Festival provided members of the public with another opportunity to view a selection of portraits featured in the My Route Exhibition Trail and to chat to Vanley Burke, Tas Bashir (curator of the Exhibition Trail) and members of the My Route project team.

Inspired by Gandhi

Mahatma Gandhi was one of the most influential thinkers of the 20th century and his philosophy of non-violence, belief in the equal worth of all human beings and struggle for independence continue to inspire many modern political leaders. *sampad*'s third international writing competition in its 'Inspired By ...' series, on Gandhi, provided an opportunity for aspiring writers from across the globe to connect with the influential thinker and leader and express their personal responses through creative writing.

The main objectives for delivering 'Inspired by Gandhi 2015' were to:

- encourage interest in Gandhi's life and philosophy
- motivate people of all ages (8 upwards) to express themselves through creative writing;
- inform new generations about Gandhi's thought and actions.

The writing competition had an international appeal and revealed how people with very different histories and cultures could unite through the enduring universal values espoused by great thought leaders.

Moving Earth

One of *sampad*'s biggest and most ambitious dance productions to date, Moving Earth, took place in summer 2012 as part of Dancing for the Games, which celebrated the countdown to London 2012 by encouraging people across the West Midlands to get dancing.

Our vision for Moving Earth was to capture the celebratory spirit and international collaboration of London (Olympics) 2012 by showcasing the dazzling array of dance styles practised in the West Midlands, including Bollywood, Bhangra, Indian folk dance, hip-hop and contemporary African and UK dance forms.

Taking our cue from the vitality and strength of the natural elements, 240 dancers (20 groups of 12) came together thematically to represent Space, Earth, Fire, Water and Air. The groups came from diverse locations across the region and we were privileged to have an opportunity to broaden our activities by exploring some of their repertoire of contemporary dance styles, while also reinforcing our existing working relationships with leading South Asian dance groups and connecting with talented new dancers not previously within our compass.

In return, the Moving Earth dancers had a unique opportunity to join the celebrations for London 2012 by taking part in a large-scale intercultural dance project and developing their confidence and artistic practice by working with other dance groups and internationally respected choreographers such as Santosh Kumar Nair. Under his direction, the groups developed new dance routines inspired by Moving Earth's central theme of ecology. A Dance Leaders in the Community course was developed alongside the choreographic activity in order to embed leadership skills within the groups for future development.

Radius 5

This was an innovative volunteering project for young people aged 16–24, providing opportunities to work at high-profile cultural and music events in and around Birmingham.

Cultural volunteers researched and digitally mapped the cultural activity taking place among young people within a five-mile radius of *sampad*'s base at mac. These young participants produced a unique and interactive cultural map that showcased the wealth of creativity happening locally. This was an initiative based on a growing recognition of the critical importance of social media in young people's lives and the contribution that technology makes to the creative industries. It was also a means of including the younger generation, structurally deprived of power, to influence the direction of cultural development.

Conclusion

This selection of projects underlines that *sampad* exists to educate and entertain, to inform and to challenge. Through its focus on the arts and heritage, *sampad* creates powerful mechanisms to affect social change that are both transactional and transformational. It underscores the fundamental principle of self-determination – the right for people to choose to participate in the cultural enterprises of their particular group. It fosters both independence and interdependence. When constructed in this way, artistic endeavour adds a valuable aesthetic dimension to our lives and obliges us to engage in a process of critical self-analysis in the presence of the Other. It encourages a growing reflexivity about the constructed and contestable nature of the process by which some people acquire the authority to 'write the culture of others'. It questions who should control the power to represent, and who has the authority to represent the culture of others. It redefines notions of community and identity. And it gradually and inexorably places the lives, the memories and the traditions of the newer members of our society alongside the hegemonic presence of the great and the good. The inclusion of cultures 'from below' has shifted and democratised our conception of value: of what is and is not worth preserving. Arts projects like *sampad* become a powerful mechanism for decentring power and democratising the nation

We hope that our programming demonstrates our belief in the construction of an intercultural space – mental and physical – where inter- and intra-group tensions are constantly being played out between black and white art forms, between South Asian and Caribbean groups, between Punjabi and Bengali traditions, between bourgeois and proletarian cultures, between folk and classical dance, between tradition and modernity, between preservation and experimentation. Interculturalism is not just another exercise in mental gymnastics – it is creative, dynamic, yet elusive, and it defies a precise definition. But it is deeply symbolic of a new way of reimagining and rethinking contemporary Britain. It is physically demanding, intellectually challenging, deeply satisfying. But that, after all, is what good art is all about.

Reference
Cameron, D. (1971) 'The museum: a temple or the forum', *Museum Journal*, vol 14, pp 11–24.

SIX

Community development with Chinese mental health service users in the UK

Lynn Tang

Introduction

The aim of community development is to change social conditions so that people can develop their capabilities and flourish. In mental health, tackling social determinants that contribute to (mental) ill-health is now an agenda of the World Health Organisation. For ethnic minorities, evidence has shown that (mental) health has been closely linked to social and economic inequalities (Nazroo, 2014). Based on my research, this chapter focuses on Chinese mental health service users in the UK and aims to illustrate how structural inequalities shape their recovery journeys. It starts with a discussion of the Recovery Approach with which the research critically engaged. Then, the diversity within the Chinese community in the UK will be introduced. Two stories from the research were selected to shed light on how, for UK Chinese people, inequalities such as class, gender and ethnicity intersect at national and transnational levels and impact on the way recovery journeys unfold. Such inequalities contribute to their distress and ill-health in the first place and could hinder their recovery. The implications for community development work with Chinese communities will then be discussed.[1]

Mental health recovery

The Recovery Approach is being mainstreamed in mental health policies in countries such as the UK. Against a prognosis of pessimistic chronicity, or an emphasis on cure and complete removal of symptoms of illness, advocates of the Recovery Approach argue that recovery should be considered as a way of living a meaningful life with or without the limitations caused by distress and mental ill-health (Anthony, 1993). Recovery is both personal and social. It is personal in its assertion of the rights of mental health service users to control their own lives, and in an understanding that recovery is a personal process unique to each individual, with self-defined routes and goals (Deegan, 1998). It is social in that its emphasis is to ensure that service users have equal opportunities and that their ability to live fully as part of a community is not compromised (Davidson and Roe, 2007).

Yet, there are criticisms of the way recovery and social inclusion discourses are being mainstreamed in government policies across the world. Spandler and Calton (2009) argue that in the UK in particular these discourses assume that service users fit the dominant norms of health and ill-health, without critical reflection on dominant ideas about what the person is recovering from, nor about the environment in which people are expected to be included. Mental health systems still generally most readily adopt an emphasis on individualistic biomedical treatment of the symptoms of illness, rather than tackling structural determinants; this has become more the case under the current economic policies of austerity (Mattheys, 2015). The social environment in which service users are expected to be included could be strongly influenced by factors that cause their mental ill-health in the first place. For ethnic minorities, one such prominent factor would be racial discrimination (Nazroo, 2014). Thus Carpenter and Raj (2012) have called for a community development approach in order to shift the focus away from seeing mental health problems as lying within the individual and towards rectifying the problems of power inequalities, exclusion and social and economic injustice.

The research reported here was a bottom-up exploration of the social conditions for recovery for Chinese mental health service users through collecting their experiences and perceptions of their recovery journeys. Pilgrim (2008) argues that recovery can mean recovery from (i) illness, that is, a focus on symptom treatment; (ii) impairment, that is, rehabilitating social skills; as well as (iii) invalidation, that is, tackling social exclusion and invalidation in the mental health system and the community. The mental health system in the UK is more ready to incorporate (i) and (ii) rather than (iii), which requires structural changes. Service users they may aspire to one or all three meanings of recovery. In the research, life-history interviews were carried out with 22 Chinese users in 2009–10 to solicit their perceptions and experiences of recovery journeys.[2] These journeys were contextualised in their wider social history so as to explore how social inequalities contribute to the social exclusion and invalidation they experienced (Elder et al, 2003).

Chinese people as a heterogeneous community in the UK

UK Chinese people form a heterogeneous community with diverse needs: people generally labelled as Chinese may have differing national origins, having immigrated over the past 100+ years from Hong Kong, the People's Republic of China, Taiwan, Singapore, Vietnam and the Philippines, for example. Chan and Yu (2001) argue that UK Chinese people faced social exclusion both from mainstream society and within their own community. For their survival, the Chinese catering business (based on the ubiquitous 'takeaway') was a common economic strategy. Yet the business owners saw each other as rivals and so the catering business was dispersed across the country in order to minimise competition with each other[3] (Tong et al, 2014). Huang and Spurgeon (2006) found that psychological distress was common among this 'community'. Workers with limited English skills worked in the catering sector and faced long working hours and isolation; and while those with better educational qualifications and language skills were able to seek jobs in the mainstream labour market, they still experienced a cultural gap between themselves and British colleagues.

Apart from class and language ability, gender and generation are other factors contributing to diversity within the Chinese community. Lee et al (2002) documented the gendered migration trajectories of Chinese women. Bringing with them different cultural and social capitals, some were able to improve their social position on coming to the UK, while others were vulnerable due to isolation, the burden of domestic work and their emotional and financial dependence on their spouse and family-in-law. They would be further marginalised when they reached old age because of the lack of retirement protection, linguistic barriers and the generation gap with their children, who had become generally more Europeanised in their attitudes and behaviours (Lane et al, 2010). For this young generation of British-born Chinese, most of whom did not face language barriers, issues concerning identities and positioning in a multicultural society were more easily addressed than was the case for their parents and grandparents. For example, some sought to explore and express their racialised identities through arenas such as the internet (Parker and Song, 2006). Yeung et al (2012) suggested that with the marginalisation found in this dispersed community, and often a lack of knowledge of mental health services, mental health professionals needed proactively to identify and work with resources within the community to facilitate members' access to appropriate services.

Given the diversity of this community, intersectionality analysis was used to explore how different inequalities such as class, gender and ethnicity mutually shaped each other in producing the different social locations in which participants lived (Walby, 2007). For ethnic minorities, Anthias has proposed a framework of 'translocational positionality' (Anthias, 2006). Inequalities can intersect to constitute hierarchical opportunity structures at the national and transnational levels in a globalised world, as evidenced in different migration trajectories, diasporic experiences and subsequent differential life chances. In contrast to a stereotypical view that people from the same ethnic background must aspire to the same traditional cultural practices, the idea of positioning also sheds light on the fluid ways in which individuals relate to cultural practices and develop cultural identities.

The following stories reflect two of the social locations in which UK Chinese people positioned themselves, and consequently what mattered to them in terms of personal recovery. The narratives below show how inequalities such as class, ethnicity and gender intersect in a myriad ways at the national and transnational levels for Chinese mental health service users.

Some case histories

Lai-ming and Wu-wei were on long-term medication and had been hospitalised. While they both experienced relatively stable mental health at the time of the interview, their stories confirmed that a recovery meaningful to them as service users would entail recovery from social exclusion and invalidation. Lai-ming's story reflects the detrimental working conditions of the Chinese catering sector and the barriers for UK Chinese people in gaining a foothold in the mainstream labour market. Wu-wei's story illustrates the predicament of 'overseas brides' with limited cultural and social capital during immigration. After presenting their stories, we discuss how the macro-social inequalities shape their recovery journeys.

Story 1: Lai-ming

The main theme of Lai-ming's story is about recovery from an ethnically divided labour market in the UK. The social exclusion that he experienced is an intersection of class and ethnicity, later overlaid with mental health discrimination and ageism. Lai-ming immigrated to the UK with his family in the 1960s. Before migration, as a young person in Hong Kong he sacrificed his place at university and chose to work as a civil servant for job security to support his working–class family. Coming to the UK in his 20s, he started working in the Chinese catering business, as many other new Chinese immigrants would do in his generation. Not long after migration, he experienced a mental health crisis that led to hospitalisation.

Lai-ming attributed his mental ill-health to the exploitative working conditions in the Chinese catering sector. Long working hours were common. Working till after midnight, he hardly got enough sleep, and then needed to get up early in the morning to prepare for the next day's work: 'I worked like a dog. Then I got this mental illness.' It was a hierarchical workplace. Waiters are at the receiving ends of people's anger in the restaurant:

> Many got nervous breakdown being a waiter. I am not the only one ... People in the kitchen shout at you. The boss shouts at you. The customers shout at you.

He observed other waiters suffering from nervous breakdown:

> It's hard work. Won't you get fatigue from working like this? It's a reason why people have nervous breakdowns. It's one factor. A latent factor. Breakdown does not happen suddenly. The mental illness has been latent for a while. When it's time to manifest, it will manifest. You will know.

Yet, mental health was a topic never being talked about; often the only strategy to protect workers against these working conditions was resignation.

After the crisis, Lai-ming avoided the kind of Chinese catering work in which he had fallen ill in the first place. He could speak English and thus tried to find a job in the mainstream labour market. But this was difficult:

> First, we have 'yellow face'. They don't want foreigners. Racial discrimination. Compared to other interviewees, we will score lower. Second, we have had nervous breakdowns. They would prefer to hire someone normal.

Lai-ming was trapped in the margins of the labour market. He was honest about his mental ill-health to potential employers when looking for jobs. He felt that if he did not disclose it, employers would enquire about the gaps in his CV anyway. He tried to take on further study in order to gain some better qualifications. But he was unable to finish the course, as he found it stressful and this might trigger another breakdown. Once he got a low-skilled job that was again plagued with poor working conditions. He worked in a printing workshop where he was not provided with adequate occupational protection. He suffered from ear problems from the noise of the machines, which led to him being unable to go to work. He was sacked.

After this, he was unable to find another mainstream job. At the time of the interview he was in his 60s. In more than 30 years of unemployment he had persevered and kept going to job centre. Now at the age of retirement, despite trying to improve himself by taking English language tests, he knew that his chances were now even more slim than ever. He tried hard to improve his skills so as to be 'included' in society. Yet, the lack of opportunities in the labour market meant that he remained excluded. This was a cause of psychological harm that was detrimental to his pride and well-being:

> I can work. After the nervous breakdown, sometimes I would feel sad. A sense of loss.

Over the years his livelihood was supported by welfare benefits such as the Disability Living Allowance. Yet he felt the pressure to prove to himself and others that he was not a 'benefit scrounger', that he 'really' was disabled.

> I always admit that I have a disability. I know it. I have actually been in hospital. I was on benefit. I was on medical treatment and I did not cheat the government for money ... You lost your ability to work and the low pay you got. That's why they give you the money. I am not those who cheat, lie about their sickness.

The disciplinary effect of the 'benefit scrounger' discourse generated by right-wing politicians and the media was disempowering, as evidenced by the way in which Lai-ming justified his disability and proved that he was not lazy.

Despite his persistent attempt to find jobs and improve his 'employability', Lai-ming's journey is a story of deskilling. While he could maintain relatively stable mental health, his social positioning could not be recovered. This brought about a sense of loss and demoralisation that was detrimental to his mental well-being.

Story 2: Wu-wei

The main theme of Wu-wei's story is one of recovery from the hidden impacts of gender and class discrimination at a transnational level. At the time of interview Wu-wei was in her 30s and had been hospitalised several times. In the late 1990s she migrated to the UK to join her husband, whom she had met through a parental arrangement in China. The move was considered a 'marrying up', as her husband was a university graduate and her in-laws were richer than her parental family. Coming from a poor family, having a low level of qualifications and not being able to speak fluent English, she worried that people in her home town would gossip, accusing her for marrying for money. She later discovered, through counselling, that her low self-esteem originated from a sexual assault that had happened in childhood. The aftermath of this became apparent when she married, as she felt the pressure of gender ideology because she had not 'preserved' her virginity for her husband. This added to the status gap she felt between her own family and her husband's family in the UK.

After migration, Wu-wei's mental health worsened under the weight of generalised social class hierarchy, the stress of migration and integrating into the family-in-law, with whom she lived. Her mother-in-law lectured her about filial piety. At home she was expected to do all the housework. Wu-wei wanted to set up a home of her own, but felt guilty about not doing enough for the in-laws. The following quote reflects her dilemma and the way she positioned herself in regard to the traditional expectation of filial piety:

> My mother-in-law gave me a lot of pressure. She wanted me to live with them until they died, take care of them. In my heart I wanted to live with them too. I struggled. I wanted a home of my own, instead of coming home being shouted at. When I got home I had to rush through my meal and then do things for them, worrying that they would shout at me. I kept crying. I blamed myself for not doing enough. I always condemned myself. I know my mother-in-law is good to me.

There were other reasons, however, for feeling trapped. On the one hand, Wu-wei's parental family in China received financial help from her in-laws, so they told her to respect the in-laws. On the other hand, she had a constant fear that she would not be able to survive in the UK if her husband were to abandon her for another woman who matched his class background. This fear had a structural origin underpinned by knowledge of a common scenario: marriage as a perceived secure future for women who 'married up' to the UK might not be delivered in reality. The fear was also linked to her isolation:

> I am the least educated person in the house. I didn't graduate from the school. I knew nothing when I came here. Just crying.

Wu-wei's mental health deteriorated as a result after her migration.

The turning point of her recovery journey was related to these more hidden injuries and fears. She received counselling through the local Chinese community centre to help her heal the childhood trauma. Through counselling, she was able to look back on her history and express her grievances and emotions for the first time in her life. The counsellor taught her ways, such as meditation, to cope with sometimes fluctuating symptoms and skills. Most importantly, she learned to put self-care first. In addition, Wu-wei's part-time work in an old people's care home contributes to her self-worth:

> I feel a sense of satisfaction that I can help others while earning money. Working makes me feel that I can contribute to society. I want to prove that I am a useful person.

The positive self-image that she gained through work helped Wu-wei to recover from the shame she felt from belonging in a lower-class group. The income gave her a sense of security about the future. Eventually she set up her own home with her husband, away from the in-laws. It was not an easy decision but the move, into her own space, made her 'feel so free'. She no longer felt that going home was a burden. This helped her to maintain a healthy distance from and relationship with the in-laws, as well as yo develop mental well-being to prevent any relapse.

Although developing a sense of self-esteem and economic empowerment was important to Wu-wei's recovery from the hidden injuries of class and gender, there were other lingering aspects of recovery that she needed to grapple with. She felt embarrassed by her behaviour during her relapse and worried about being discriminated against by neighbours. Such worry could be traced back to her experience in her home town:

> I think not many Chinese people, initially at least, would want to admit they have a mental illness. Because 'crazy' and 'mad' are in the vocabulary used to insult people. Also in my home town, some girls who were said to be 'mad' were being locked up or being forced to work for others. So this is what I came into contact in the past. I still would ask myself why I had this illness … Sometimes I accept it, sometimes I don't.

While she considered that medication could help her, she was ambivalent about taking medication for the long term, as it kept reminding her that, in her words, 'I am a mental patient', which she wanted not to associate with herself. The weight of perceived discrimination and 'patienthood' was something she needed to recover from in order to achieve personhood.

Discussion and implications

These two stories illustrate how the recovery journeys of Chinese mental health service users in the UK are shaped by an intersection of inequalities. They confirm Nazroo's (2014) argument that ethnicity intersects with class inequality, giving rise to the structural constraints that ethnic minority groups face. The stories further show how, for Chinese people, other power relations such as those associated with gender play an important role in contributing to their distress and ill-health. The intersection of these inequalities can be *national*, as shown in the example of the segmented labour market that Lai-ming experienced. It can also even be *transnational*, as demonstrated in the example of complex family networks between the UK and country of origin, as well as the ethnic and gender ideology behind the marriage institution, in Wu-wei's story. Such national and transnational intersections of inequalities shape the social conditions in which Chinese service users live. We do not claim that these are the only ways that inequalities shape the recovery journeys of Chinese service users. Rather, what is shown through these two stories is the need to recover from structural inequalities in order to achieve meaningful recovery. This is apparent in the following ways.

First, their recovery journeys were shaped by the social conditions that had contributed to their distress and ill-health in the first place. Thus it is necessary to tackle these detrimental social conditions in order for recovery to take place. For UK Chinese people, the catering business is the predominant source of job opportunities in a segmented labour market. Yet Lai-ming's story reflects that the harsh working conditions in this sector could contribute to restaurant workers' mental ill-health. When looking for jobs after his crisis Lai-ming, who could speak fluent English, avoided this sector in order to maintain his mental health. For service users who speak limited English, they might have no choice but return to such work environments for a living. This could make it difficult for them to recover. Even though Lai-ming did not face language barriers, his relatively low qualifications meant that he could find only manual work that again ignored impacts on his health. Thus it is the segmented labour market and exploitative working conditions that need to be tackled in order to achieve recovery and social inclusion.

For Wu-wei, her recovery was linked to gendered migration and marriage pathways with upward social class mobility. For this group of women, gender ideology in the guise of 'filial piety' may be used to justify their subordination to husband and family. This ideology becomes what they have to recover from. Counselling helped Wu-wei to develop her self-esteem and coping skills in order to take care of herself. Employment contributed to her sense of self-worth. Together, these improved her status at home and empowered her. This shows the importance of empowering women to cope with and negotiate in marriage and family institutions.

Second, along their recovery journeys, they both encountered new barriers due to mental health discrimination, ableism and ageism. These could intersect with class, gender and ethnic inequalities to make it difficult for service users to achieve their valued ways of living. Lai-ming perceived that it was difficult to secure a job, due to racial and mental health discrimination. Despite his efforts to improve his employability, he found that few opportunities opened up for him. He was further disadvantaged in the labour market as he grew older. Prolonged unemployment brings negative psychological effects. Furthermore, under the ableist discourse of 'benefit scrounger', the felt need to prove himself as a 'useful' member of society was dispiriting and hindered the development of a positive self-identity. For Wu-wei, she was worried about the possibility of discrimination by others. Her ambivalent feeling towards medication reflected her wish to recover from patienthood in order to achieve personhood.

What does this mean for community development?

Some implications can be drawn from this in relation to community development practice for UK Chinese service users. To facilitate recovery, community workers should go beyond a focus on individualistic biomedical intervention and tackle the inequalities contributing to mental ill-health and that hinder recovery. Workers should understand the various ways that class, gender and ethnic inequalities could shape the social conditions in which service users live at national and transnational levels. Such knowledge of their structural predicament could be included in cultural competency training so as to avoid pigeonholing or stereotyping the diverse needs within this heterogeneous community (Dein and Bhui, 2013). Understanding the social conditions in terms of power inequalities could ensure appropriate empowering practices. For example, for Wu-wei, her well-being and recovery were closely linked to her improved self-esteem in face of gender ideology, the institution of marriage and economic empowerment. Moreover, some social conditions require collective efforts to challenge and tackle them. The segmented labour market that Chinese service users face limits their life chances; this entails a transformative community development approach to radically challenge exploitative working conditions within and beyond Chinese communities. Anti-discrimination practices in relation to mental health and ethnicity need to be implemented (Tang, 2016).

Through exploring the micro-life histories of Chines service users, we argue for tackling macro-social inequalities in order to achieve personal and social recovery. Workers need to understand that, for this community, social conditions detrimental to mental health and recovery are linked to national and transnational social inequalities. The need for collective change through community development in order to remove these barriers to recovery is evident. Many Chinese community associations tend to be inward looking, focusing on narrow and specific cultural concerns of the Chinese community. These associations, and new ones that need to be formed, should develop an outward perspective, building links with other minority organisations to understand and combat the common experiences of discrimination that are disempowering and oppressive. This will not be easy because of the dispersed nature of the Chinese community/ ies and it will require other minority groups actively to reach out to build alliances with Chinese groups. Currently in the UK, it appears that the Chinese population is the minority suffering the greatest, although hidden, levels of 'race' hate crime (Tong et al, 2014). This may be the most promising area in which to start building these links. It also requires policy makers and politicians to free themselves from current myths about the Chinese-origin population, that is, that they are economically successful (whereas many are very poor), that they are well integrated (whereas in fact they have difficulty accessing basic services), that Chinese girls in particular do well (but they disappear off the radar after they leave school), and to acknowledge that this is probably one of the most deprived minorities overall within the UK. It also requires substantial investment in capacity building of one kind or another to ensure that Chinese people can articulate voices of their own at the levels of policy making and service delivery.

Notes

[1] For a full discussion on barriers to recovery, capability development and community development, see Tang (2016).

[2] The author would like to thank the Birmingham Chinese Community Centre, Wai Yin Chinese Women Society, Chinese Mental Health Association and, most importantly, the participants for their help and participation in this research. The study was funded by the Overseas Research Students Award, Warwick Postgraduate Research Scholarship, and the Phil Strong Memorial Prize.

[3] Chinese-origin people represent the only minority ethnic group in the UK to be found in every local authority area, including the most remote and rural areas.

References

Anthias, F. (2006) 'Belongings in a globalising and unequal world: rethinking translocations', in N. Yuval-Davis, K. Kannabirān and U. Vieten (eds), *The situated politics of belonging*, London: Sage, pp 17–31.

Anthony, W.A. (1993) 'Recovery from mental illness: the guiding vision of the mental health service system in the 1990s', *Psychosocial Rehabilitation Journal*, vol 16, no 4, pp 11–23.

Carpenter, M. and Raj, T. (2012) 'Editorial introduction: towards a paradigm shift from community care to community development in mental health', *Community Development Journal*, vol 47, no 4, pp 457–72.

Chau, R. and Yu, S. (2001) 'Social exclusion of Chinese people in Britain', *Critical Social Policy*, vol 21, no 1, pp 103–25.

Davidson, L. and Roe, D. (2007) 'Recovery from versus recovery in serious mental illness: one strategy for lessening confusion plaguing recovery', *Journal of Mental Health*, vol 16, no 4, pp 459–70.

Deegan, P.E. (1998) 'Recovery: the lived experience of rehabilitation', *Psychiatric Rehabilitation Journal*, vol 19, no 3, pp 91–7.

Dein, S. and Bhui, K.S. (2013) 'At the crossroads of anthropology and epidemiology: current research in cultural psychiatry in the UK', *Transcultural Psychiatry*, vol 50, no 6, pp 769–91.

Elder, G.H., Johnson, M.K. and Crosnoe, R. (2003) 'The emergence and development of life course theory', in J.T. Mortimer and M.J. Shanahan (eds), *Handbook of the life course*, New York: Springer, pp 3–19.

Huang, S.L. and Spurgeon, A. (2006) 'The mental health of Chinese immigrants in Birmingham, UK', *Ethnicity & Health*, vol 11, no 4, pp 365–87.

Lane, P., Tribe, R. and Hui, R. (2010) 'Intersectionality and the mental health of elderly Chinese women living in the UK', *International Journal of Migration, Health and Social Care*, vol 6, no 4, pp 34–41.

Lee, M., Chan, A., Bradby, H. et al (2002) 'Chinese migrant women and families in Britain', *Women's Studies International Forum*, vol 25, no 6, pp 607–18.

Mattheys, K. (2015) 'The Coalition, austerity and mental health', *Disability & Society*, vol 30, no 3, pp 475–8.

Nazroo, J.Y. (2014) 'Ethnic inequalities in health: addressing a significant gap in current evidence and policy', in British Academy (ed), *'If you could do one thing …' Nine local actions to reduce health inequalities*, London: British Academy, pp 91–101.

Parker, D. and Song, M. (2007) 'Inclusion, participation and the emergence of British Chinese websites', *Journal of Ethnic and Migration Studies*, vol 33, no 7, pp 1043–61.

Pilgrim, D. (2008) '"Recovery" and current mental health policy', *Chronic Illness*, vol 4, no 4, pp 295–304.

Spandler, H. and Calton, T. (2009) 'Psychosis and human rights: conflicts in mental health policy and practice', *Social Policy & Society*, vol 8, no 2, pp 245–56.

Tang, L. (2016) 'Barriers to recovery for Chinese mental health service-users in the UK: a case for community development', *Community Development Journal*, doi:10.1093/cdj/bsw025.

Tong, Y., Craig, G. and O'Neill, M. (2014) *The Chinese population in North East England*, Durham: North East 'Race' Crime and Justice Regional Research Network.

Walby, S. (2007) 'Complexity theory, systems theory, and multiple intersecting social inequalities', *Philosophy of the Social Sciences*, vol 37, no 4, pp 449–70.

Yeung, E.Y.W., Irvine F., Ng, S.M. et al (2012) 'Role of social networks in the help-seeking experiences among Chinese suffering from severe mental illness in England: a qualitative study', *British Journal of Social Work*, vol 43, no 3, pp 486–503.

SEVEN

Construindo comunidades: community building with Portuguese migrant workers on the east coast of England

Robert Gregory

Introduction

> I tell you there is no sense of community here. The people, they think about themselves, not each other. It is why no one cares about the association. They all talk in the cafes and say 'the association should do this and that' and 'when are we going to have another party?' but no one wants to get involved unless they can make money.

This quote is taken from an interview in 2007 with a founding member of the Portuguese Community Association in Great Yarmouth. I use it as a starting point. The rhetoric of the New Labour Government of the time emphasised the importance of community engagement to support the integration of a new wave of migrant workers arriving to the UK. In Great Yarmouth, a medium-size seaside town surrounded by agricultural land where many migrants found employment, a community development response was subsequently interpreted as one in which robust community infrastructures such as the community association referenced above needed to be built. This was to ensure that Portuguese workers were empowered to overcome issues of exploitation, discrimination and disadvantage and were able to integrate more fully into local life.

I don't offer a conclusive account of the migrant worker experience in Great Yarmouth in this chapter but, rather, reflect on how community development responses over 10 years have evolved in a deprived coastal town in eastern England. I started working with newly arrived Portuguese-speaking migrants in the early 2000s as a community development worker for a local charity. I have since worked as a neighbourhood manager and then as a commissioner for community development employed through the local council. I have built a range of professional relationships and friendships with migrants over that time. While I possess strong local knowledge and an experiential insight into the migrant worker context in a particular coastal town, I am also mindful of the limits of my own objectivity. So too am I aware of my (in)ability to reflect these experiences, not as a migrant worker but as a White British male, from my own culturally crafted perspective.

Locating Portuguese migration

Great Yarmouth lies on the easterly tip of Norfolk, England. Its heyday as a popular summer tourist destination has long gone and it remains an urban conurbation on the edge of rural East Anglia where agricultural and food-processing industries dominate the low-skilled, low-paid employment sector.

The town suffers one of the highest unemployment rates in England and Wales, at 3.4% compared to a UK average of 1.6% (Great Yarmouth Borough Council, 2016). Yet conversely, over a number of years, many agricultural businesses have directly recruited contract workers from Portugal as labour has become harder to source locally and demands for production have increased. Upon recruitment, workers are typically provided with accommodation and contracted hours at a designated site. Much of this accommodation has been sourced in Great Yarmouth, making use of redundant and semi-derelict guesthouses, often provided as housing for those on low incomes. Nestled behind the seafront's 'golden mile' (the seaside attractions of arcades, restaurants and shops), this is classed as one of the most deprived neighbourhoods in the East of England. In the Census of 2001, 3% of Great Yarmouth's population classed itself as non-White British. While no official comprehensive contemporary data on migrants exists,[1] the 2011 Census notes the non-White British population of this particular ward had grown to 22% (Great Yarmouth Borough Council, 2014, p 11). The rapid arrival of so many workers of a different culture and ethnicity therefore had a notable impact.

There were outward signs of hostility from the existing population, manifested predominantly through outpourings in the largely irresponsible local press, fuelling a misconception that these workers were refugees or asylum seekers, were taking local jobs and homes and were generally creating neighbourhood tensions. I have come into contact with these views many times over the years. Such views have been further exacerbated by the on-going impact of the global recession on weak, peripheral coastal economies like Great Yarmouth and by the growth of extreme nationalist politics as reflected in the rise of the anti-EU UK Independence Party (UKIP). UKIP secured one-third of the seats on the borough council in the 2014 local elections. In the 2016 EU referendum in Britain, Great Yarmouth ranked as the fifth most Eurosceptic place in the country, with 71.5% of voters opting to leave the EU (www.telegraph.co.uk), clearly motivated by the national anti-immigration sentiment of the time.

In my early years as a community development worker my role focused on the promotion of social justice for those most marginalised. I eagerly facilitated the formation of collective groups to address shared issues of inequality and concern. The opening of the first Portuguese-run café, Arroz Doce, in 2003 gave me a suitable gateway to meet new arrivals. I made an initial approach to the café's owner, who responded positively and invited me to return to talk to some friends of hers. Coincidentally they had been discussing doing something to help new arrivals in the town. We swiftly set up a range of meetings with those interested. I spent much of this time listening, observing and attempting to understand the ways in which newly arrived migrant workers made sense of their arrival in Great Yarmouth. I substantiated this by conducting informal interviews and recording a series of life histories as part of a research project.

Portuguese migration is not a new European phenomenon. Since the late 19th century Portugal has seen significant emigration, due to over-population, taxation and economic crisis (Cole, 1991, p 23) and since the Second World War it has fed labour into Northern Europe (Brettell, 2003, p 2). Brettell and Klint both conducted ethnographic fieldwork with Portuguese migrants in France and Germany. Brettell suggests that the 'emigrant' carries a core symbol of meaning in Portugal (Brettell, 2003, p 16). He or she becomes a vehicle for an imagined community (Brettell, 2003, p 9) where emigration is seen as an opportunity in which one betters oneself through both social and economic mobility (Klint, 1989, p 61) but maintains an ideological tie to a Portuguese homeland (Brettell, 2003, p xvii).

Klint and Brettell both noted a deep 'ideology of return' evident among migrants, who deemed their time abroad as merely a temporary transition. Brettell noted a difference, however, between the 'goal of return' and the 'act of return'. The goal is based on the ideology, the act on the economics (Brettell, 2003, p 59). In the case of Great Yarmouth I found that a common perception in the local public services was that the Portuguese migrants were only temporary residents and would return to Portugal. This assumption was based on the turnover of staff at factories, particularly as companies became more efficient in their offering of short-term contracts to meet peaks in production demand. However, my fieldwork tended to contradict this assumption. Many migrants were actually moving to other parts of the town due to better job opportunities and housing conditions. They were not necessarily moving back to Portugal. Some suggested that this was because they could not afford to save, but others suggested that they had no immediate desire to return. There were also, as I experienced, migrants who returned to Portugal and who then returned to Great Yarmouth some months or years later.

The political and ideological climate of wider society maintains a particular relevance to forging the migrant experience. The New Labour Government of the early 2000s promoted a policy of integration. In Great Yarmouth (and indeed in many other similar deprived areas) it was clear that migration had a notable positive economic impact on the surrounding communities. Boarded-up properties were being let for accommodation. A street of redundant shops had been revived with Portuguese cafes and markets. An increased population, with limited means of mobility, meant that more money was being spent in the town centre, where businesses were struggling. This also had a spatial impact, as housing stock and local cafes were concentrated in one particular part of the town. New forms of food, entertainment and arts were also emerging. This was celebrated by some. The Portuguese migrants were filling not only an economic niche but also a spatial and cultural one. For many of the existing population, however, this fuelled resentment, hostility and outright racism. The perception – underpinned often by media myths – that newcomers were taking scarce resources, including jobs and housing, from a struggling area was strong. This perception has been fuelled further particularly over the last two decades by the rise of right-wing nationalism and political campaigns focused on immigration and national sovereignty, and a policy shift towards the demonisation of migrants, including those from within the EU.

Initial responses from local agencies promoted the fostering of community cohesion as the solution, looking at ways to facilitate the integration of migrant workers into the wider social fabric of the town. This was very much the direction I received in my role as a community development worker. The state and non-governmental organisations had based their responses on a number of assumptions about 'an ethnic community'. However, these interpretations failed to invite migrants to articulate their own sense of place and identity.

A critique of early responses

The most prevailing assumption resonating throughout the discourse of agencies and institutions in Great Yarmouth was that there was 'a well-established Portuguese community' (Great Yarmouth Local Strategic Partnership, 2007, p 2). The concept of 'community' was central to the New Labour Government's policy during the late 1990s and early 2000s, although it was only barely defined (Craig, 2007a, p 336). Indeed it continued to resonate during the following Conservative/Liberal Democrat Coalition from 2010–15 through the failed 'Big Society' agenda, with the notion of 'communities' doing more and government doing less in terms of providing services to local communities. As Creed explained: 'whether we see it as the nostalgic desire for a lost past or the creative reformulation of a post-modern society, the focus of community has become ubiquitous in the way we talk and think about life in the twenty-first century' (Creed, 2006, p 3).

The general label of a 'Portuguese community' in Great Yarmouth has been a problematic one. I use it cautiously as an umbrella term for those associated with Portuguese migration to Great Yarmouth. There are significant numbers of migrant workers living in Great Yarmouth who are not Portuguese, including those from East Timor, Mozambique and Brazil, all Portuguese speaking, yet from different countries of origin. Various rights to work exist for such individuals, but this was largely disregarded by public agencies. Portuguese-speaking migrants were referred to as a homogeneous group, defining their identity solely by a common language. It reflected the communitarian vision of the New Labour Government, believing that a healthy society needs people to act together (Taylor, 2003, p 38). An essentialist notion of a bounded ethnic community helped to reinforce this view.

Captured in this discourse was a strong reference to ethnicity and 'race'. Bauman describes how the term 'ethnic community' has often been used by government in a positive sense, depicting an ethnic group that is not associated with the nation-state making a positive contribution to the local society (Bauman, 1996, p 137). Craig describes how British migration policy remains essentially racist, offering connotations of the civilising white man managing an ethnically inferior group that refuses to integrate (Craig, 2007b, p 620). Feldman has termed this the 'migration apparatus' of the state, a set of controlling devices deployed to manage migrants (2012, p 8).

While such narratives helped to place the Portuguese migrants as a homogeneous 'ethnic community', they also informed a particular approach to community work. The approach I was expected to adopt was to engage migrants into an existing 'community empowerment' infrastructure. During my initial outreach in emerging Portuguese social spaces I was under significant pressure to quantify the community work I was doing. I had to monitor the number of groups I was working with and the individuals representing particular sections of the population on decision-making bodies. There was a very conscious drive to support and develop a group representing the 'Portuguese community'. It was almost inevitable, therefore, that after my initial outreach a core group of Portuguese activists began to emerge and I would guide them into forming a community association. This proceeded with the formation of Herois do Mar (Heroes of the Sea), its name taken from the title of the Portuguese national anthem. A steering group came together to organise a launch event, and coined the strap-line 'Feel closer to Portugal'. It had been envisioned as a way of celebrating Portuguese culture, with food, fado (a music genre) and dance.

While the event was hugely successful, with over 1,000 people attending, on-going support for the formal incorporation of the association was not so evident. The association launched a newspaper and an employment project, yet struggled to sustain either, with very few people wanting to get involved in running the association on a voluntary basis. Many people approached me individually with ideas for personal business ventures, for which they were seeking funding, but very few people were willing to be part of the association's committee. On reflection, there were several reasons for this. The quote at the beginning of this chapter comes from one of the founders of the association. Her suggestion was that the primary motive for migration among her compatriots was economic gain, or to better oneself. Forming an association for the *common* good was not of immediate economic benefit to the individuals involved, particularly when such an effort required longer-term planning and community mobilisation. In addition, the lives of most migrant workers were clearly transient and often lacked the permanence associated with the building of neighbourhood institutions. Housing conditions often meant that tenancies in private sector housing were short term. During the 1990s, while working with Brazilian migrant workers in New York, Margolis noted that 'the lack of community ethos and community associations was one of the most striking, and for a time most puzzling features of the Brazilian migrant scene' due to mistrust, the desire for economic gain and a lack of permanence (Margolis, 1994, p 195).

The community association did continue, but largely became the preserve of one individual community leader, who mixed business and political interests with a range of projects for community benefit.

Over the following years other groups emerged, including a network for Portuguese speakers organising language support and running campaigns, a community association representing migrants from East Timor and a range of dance, cultural and sporting groups. In a briefing for the UK Community Development Foundation, Mullen outlined some of the challenges facing development workers working with such communities, noting issues with the lack of long-term settlement in one place, language difficulties and issues of cohesion (Mullen, 2009, p 1). These issues presented themselves in the Great Yarmouth context, with some initiatives being particularly short lived and limited. This process also saw the emergence of other community leaders building a strong presence in local civil society.

Identification and negotiation

During early fieldwork I was keen to explore relationships between new arrivals. Did they feel a sense of connection to each other and to this new place they had arrived in? A particular response that emerged was one of unease.

A: [...] Again, I am going to talk about the Portuguese community in Yarmouth, because there are different things that happen when people work abroad, but in this instance they all work [together], there is not a very big difference in their status, you know what I mean?

R: Yeah.

A: And because they are always trying to show each other that they are in much better positions, in their private lives. So what my experience is, is that when people get together in groups and then they will make gossip about whoever comes into the coffee shop ...

A: [...] You know two friends, one has a nice house and they both have nice cars. One asked the other one to go and check the balance on her bankcard, to show off because she has got money. And what happened, he saw her bank balance and went off and said to people, 'You know she's got £10,000 in the bank?' It's showing off all the time.

In this transcript taken from an early interview, the respondent outlined a competitive attempt to attain status and prestige among other migrants. She explained that this was due to people from a range of backgrounds being stripped of their former identity or status and then banded together on a factory production line. Eriksen notes that immigrants often have come from a majority group in their country of origin and then become a minority group in the host society (Eriksen, 1993, p 131). This inevitably has an impact upon how migrant workers view themselves and their position in a new community. A Portuguese friend explained to me a common expression: 'In Portugal I was a King/Queen!', used to refer to people who would boast about (exaggerated) recollections of former lives in a position of high status.

These occurrences were very common, most of all in positions of community leadership. Community groups became platforms for status and social positioning for some self-appointed leaders. Rumours circulated throughout wider communities about community leaders embezzling grant monies for their own benefit, or receiving privileges from the local council. Many of these were unfounded, but there was an underlying unease around the motivations of some individuals and mistrust as a consequence. The power of word of mouth and coffee-shop conversations cannot be overstated in this context. There was also an uneasy affiliation with local political parties for some of the groups. Some leaders established a strong link with the local Labour Party, their activities becoming overtly political. For some this was to assume individual social standing. One leader even abandoned the Labour Party after a disagreement and, bizarrely, joined UKIP, standing as a candidate in local elections. This event alone caused significant ructions within the migrant communities, with local police expecting those tensions to escalate into violence and criminal damage. As a consequence the leader stepped down from the community group, abandoning a committee that was left to fend off further speculation and accusations from those it was trying to help.

Migrant workers were also not just victims of racism and discrimination from the wider population. Discrimination also existed within such communities. There were clear demarcations between Portuguese-speakers of Black African heritage and White European heritage. This was reflected in the types of café where people would drink, the social circles in which individuals would operate and, indeed, in the different community groups responding to such notions of identity. The very title of the community association Heroes of the Sea had a strong historical reference to the Portuguese Empire and undoubtedly had different connotations for those migrants who were not from Portugal.

In her 2009 briefing, Mullen explained how 'settled migrant communities often display antagonism to new migrants' as both start to compete for jobs and resources. This became a key theme in Great Yarmouth after the joining of accession states such as Poland and Lithuania to the EU in 2004. The following years saw a new wave of migrants begin to arrive on the east coast of England. Factories and farms started actively to recruit these new migrants as they were deemed to be hard working, partly because initial benefit restrictions limited access to out-of-work welfare for these migrants. Portuguese-speaking migrants talked about being seen less favourably because they were deemed to be less hard-working and were more likely to assert their rights. Some also referenced different values and life styles, suggesting that Eastern European migrants were less likely to make a positive contribution to the town's wider social and cultural life.

Over the years of working with such communities I have learned to appreciate the complexity of the migrant worker experience. To suggest that there was one Portuguese-speaking community was naïve, and suggest that it was unified was equally ill conceived. However, there were shared symbols of identity, shared experiences, a shared language and a shared physical space that created a sense of relatedness. These became a rallying call for positive community action, such as anti-discrimination work and raising awareness about employment rights, driven by some of these groups.

Brettell suggests that the Portuguese state carefully reinforces the concept of an imagined Portuguese community through its assertion of images and traditions that reflect a proud nation of explorers (Brettell, 2003, p 9). There are numerous examples of affinity to a 'homeland', evident in self-organised events and parties to celebrate saints' days and cultural occasions. Assigning the community association the title Heroes of the Sea linked a strong ideological tie to a patriotic symbol depicting proud explorers of the modern world. There was a close relationship to a shared cultural heritage, but it was clear that a collective identity was imagined differently. The younger people I worked with tended to hold less regard for Portuguese traditions. One person suggested during interviews, 'I like Portugal. I was born there. My family is still there, but there is more for me here. I would like my children to grow up British.'

While it is true that migrant workers have been regarded as an 'ethnic group' fulfilling a particular economic function, it is important not to view them simply as marginal, operating outside of the mainstream social system (Roy and Alsayyad, 2004, p 9). In Great Yarmouth at a neighbourhood level, the intersection between migrants and the wider population becomes more complex as interaction increases, whether through daily activities such as taking children to school or through work. Migrants, many of whom are young and have subsequently had families, have established friendships and relationships with members of the wider population. Mixed-heritage families are becoming more and more common; a sense of migrant identity therefore becomes more complex and certainly more distant for some.

Evolving practice

Since the arrival of Portuguese migrants in the early 2000s there has been rapid change. The flexibility and insecurity of job contracts, combined with a spirit of entrepreneurship, has seen a high turnover of migrants in the local food-processing industry. Many have gone on to pursue other low-skilled occupations in the local tourism and retail sectors. Many have attempted to establish their own businesses and some have upskilled and moved away or returned to Portugal. The original concentration of migrants in Great Yarmouth is no longer so stark and geographically defined.

Community development practice has continued to evolve and respond to these changes. Practitioners have built a stronger cultural appreciation of some of these particular issues and advocate more nuanced approaches. Positively, we see a range of migrant groupings represented and helping to shape the annual South Yarmouth Neighbourhood Fair. The fact that there are numerous collectives of people from migrant communities wanting to develop activities and initiatives for social good, over a number of years, goes some way to suggest that migrant workers are clearly settling and investing time in building neighbourhood institutions.

The rigid monitoring constraints required by funders of community development work have become more outcomes focused and have been supplemented by a range of qualitative measures. Success is certainly not measured by the permanence of some of these organisations. In my early days of working with migrant workers I went above and beyond my basic role to support the stability of the first community association, running training sessions, prompting communications campaigns and mediating between individuals. I was anxious that we needed to prove that community development could work for migrant workers. As we've appreciated the context of the migrant worker experience, the volatility of relationships and the lack of permanence based on jobs and housing, we've become more at ease with the longevity of particular initiatives, accepting that some of these served a purpose for a set moment in time for a specific group of people, but in doing so have established stronger bonds and networks of association. Gilchrist and Taylor argue the strength of informal community networks as alternatives to formalised structured associations. 'It is these (*informal ties*), rather than any particular project or organisation, which are the real basis for the construction and maintenance of bonds of "community", "solidarity" and "collective empowerment"' (Gilchrist and Taylor, 1997, p 173, emphasis in original).

Specific considerations continue for work with such communities. Language remains a limiting factor for facilitating the involvement of some, who may have little or no grasp of English. Translation resources are scarce, as the expectation for migrants to learn English or 'return home' dominates current public policy. There are also clear cultural issues that continue to need unpacking. The legislative framework for voluntary associations will undoubtedly differ, based on past experiences and expectations in migrants' countries of origin. Considerable time has been spent working with new and existing community groups on developing understanding of good governance, particularly in relation to funding and reporting, but also in terms of participatory democracy and broader issues of equality, human rights and social justice.[2]

As efforts continue in Great Yarmouth, a greater sense of appreciation continues to need to be built, even within the voluntary sector. Well-meaning social welfare organisations continue to reference migrant workers in funding bids and targeted programmes. These continue to play to notions of homogeneity and continue to present as somewhat tokenistic in their approach. When the funding ends, these programmes disappear. This will be resolved only when funders and commissioners work together to support genuine and longer-term community development efforts.

There are a number of further challenges for community development, going forward. Questions around power, gender, equalities and broader social justice need to continue to be explored through development work, both directly within migrant communities and in their relationships with others. The hostility to migrants in places like Great Yarmouth that was exemplified during the EU referendum and the resultant anxiety within migrant communities post-Brexit will provide further challenges as migrants attempt to demonstrate a positive contribution to British society amid a less-than-certain and potentially hostile future. Good-quality support will therefore be vital.

I suggest that there is not a formulaic approach to such community development efforts. The interplay and exchanges between individuals are constantly evolving, and as this conceptualisation of identity develops so too does the realisation of community. What becomes clear is that community development needs to be intuitive. Practitioners embedding themselves within social networks and undertaking a range of informal conversations is perhaps more important than structured surveys depicting community needs and aspirations. Practitioners now reflect in 'conversation books' to capture these nuances. It is through these interactions and those with non-Portuguese migrants that one can best understand situational relationships. This does not necessarily need to be the depicted 'communitarian' vision of community conveyed by successive British governments. 'Community' as public policy has defined it does not need to be evident for community development to happen.

Conclusion: community development at the forefront

In this chapter I have outlined how the Portuguese migrant experience in Great Yarmouth is culturally specific but not unique or homogeneous. Often it is assumed that a community exists that merely needs to be empowered. I have suggested that the process of migration is a complex one, underpinned by a range of meta-narratives about 'race' and ethnicity and past and present experiences. A wide interplay of identification and association creates idioms of relatedness that do not posit migrant workers in an imagined homeland, nor as harmoniously integrated into a new, host society. This, I believe, is part of a continual process of negotiation between migrant workers and with others. The challenge for community development is to be at the forefront of these issues by appreciating these ever-evolving global–local relationships and responding accordingly.

Notes
[1]   The Workers Registration Scheme, a very good source of data, was terminated a few years ago. National Insurance numbers can be used to plot residential data, but not the places where migrants work.
[2]   It is also worth reporting that Portuguese migrants, along with those from Eastern Europe, have often fallen into situations of forced labour, that is, modern slavery. These are the most difficult to identify and support back into society (Scott et al, 2013).

References

Bauman, Z. (1996) *Contesting culture: Discourses of identity in multi-ethnic London*, Cambridge: Cambridge University Press.

Brettell, C. (2003) *Anthropology and migration: Essays on transnationalism, ethnicity and identity*, New York: Alta Mira Press.

Cole, S. (1991) *Women of the Praia: Work and lives in a Portuguese coastal community*, Princeton: Princeton University Press.

Craig, G. (2007a) 'Community capacity building, something old, something new?', *Critical Social Policy*, vol 27, no 4, pp 335–59.

Craig, G. (2007b) '"Cunning, unprincipled, loathsome": the racist tail wags the welfare dog', *Journal of Social Policy*, vol 36, no 4, pp 605–23.

Creed, G. (2006) *The seductions of community: Emancipations, oppressions, quandries*, Oxford: James Curry.

Eriksen, T. (1993) *Ethnicity and nationalism: Anthropological perspectives*, London: Pluto Press.

Feldman, G. (2012) *The migration apparatus: Security, labor and policymaking in the European Union*, Stanford: Stanford University Press.

Gilchrist, A. and Taylor, M. (1997) 'Community networking: developing strength through diversity', in P. Hoggett (ed), *Contested communities: Experiences, struggles, policies*, Bristol: The Policy Press.

Great Yarmouth Borough Council (2016) *February employment briefing*, Great Yarmouth: Great Yarmouth Borough Council.

Great Yarmouth Borough Council (2014) *Borough profile*, Great Yarmouth: Great Yarmouth Borough Council.

Great Yarmouth Local Strategic Partnership (2007) *Community cohesion report*, Great Yarmouth: Great Yarmouth Borough Council.

Klint, A. (1989) 'Returning "Home": Portuguese migrant notions of temporariness, permanence and commitment', *New German Critique*, vol 46, pp 46–70.

Margolis, M. (1994) *Little Brazil: An ethnography of Brazilian immigrants in New York City*, Chichester: Princeton University Press.

Mullen, H. (2009) *Briefing. Migration and community cohesion: community development responses*, London: Community Development Foundation.

Roy, A. and Alsayyad, N. (2004) *Urban informality: Transnational perspectives from the Middle East, Latin America and South Asia*, London: Lexington.

Scott, S., Craig, G. and Geddes, A. (2013) *Forced labour in the United Kingdom*, York: Joseph Rowntree Foundation.

Taylor, M. (2003) *Public policy in the community*, Houndmills: Palgrave Macmillan.

www.telegraph.co.uk/news/2016/06/24/revealed-the-most-eurosceptic-and-europhilic-areas-in-the-uk/ accessed 28 June 2016.

EIGHT

Participatory action research with refugee and asylum-seeking women

Margaret Greenfields

Introduction

This chapter discusses the methods, processes and outcomes of a Comic Relief[1]-funded three-year community development and advocacy programme undertaken with Refugee and Asylum-Seeking Women (RASW) in London. It focuses on how the use of participatory action research and training delivered *by* RASW can challenge and inform the way in which 'professionals' deliver health and legal services to vulnerable communities. The project, undertaken during 2012–15 by Independent Academic Research Services (IARS[2]), a London-based charity, was co-designed with participant beneficiaries with the explicit aim of generating institutional change and increased gender sensitivity in the treatment of RASW, both through harnessing research findings to drive policy and practice change and by allowing women themselves to articulate the problems they currently face in terms of accessing appropriate support.

IARS (now renamed as the IARS International Institute) specialises in utilising community development methods in its work with young people at risk of exclusion, and other vulnerable groups, aiming to bring about policy change while enhancing participants' knowledge and skills base. The three-year RASW project (entitled Abused No More) was carried out in partnership with Buckinghamshire New University/Institute for Diversity Research, Inclusivity, Communities and Society (IDRICS).

The context to the Abused No More project

Prior to examining the community development processes used within this project and the findings and practice-focused outcomes and recommendations, we commence with a short discussion on existing legislation, literature and research relevant to this work. These materials demonstrate that while legal advice and health services available to refugees and asylum seekers are typically regarded as gender blind and politically neutral, and thus perceived of as adding to the 'public good', in practice, underlying presumptions and common professional models of engagement can increase harm to women who are already vulnerable, hence creating a cycle of re-victimisation (Singh, 2010; Tate, 2015).

The UK asylum system (operationalised by the UK Border Agency [UKBA]) is governed by a complex mixture of international law (that is, United Nations Conventions and Protocols, and European rulings and guidance) as well as individual legislative enactments by states that are signatories to the United Nations 1951 Convention relating to the Status of Refugees.[3] Although under the Convention rules persecution due to gender is not *explicitly* recognised as grounds on which a person can be recognised as a refugee, any individual who has suffered gender-related persecution may seek statutory protection on the grounds of being a member of a Particular Social Group (PSG) who is unable or, owing to a well-founded fear, unwilling to avail themselves of the protection of the country of which they are a national (or if they are a 'third country' national residing outside of their former place of habitual residence, to which they cannot return or are unwilling to return, as a result of such fear). Thus, under international law it is not enough for a woman seeking protection as a refugee to demonstrate that she has good reason for fearing persecution as an individual, but she must *also* demonstrate that her own country is unable or unwilling to protect her from threatened or experienced harm (Crawley, nd).

Accordingly, a woman who has a well-founded fear of persecution from family or community members (non-state actors), often as a result of stepping outside of the bounds of conventional gendered, cultural or religious behaviour within the private sphere (perhaps as a result of sexual orientation, political activities, experience of stigmatised sexual violence or because she has entered into relationship that is not sanctioned by her family[4]), should be entitled to protection under Convention rights if state protection is not available to her in her own country as a result of widespread agreement (including by public authorities) that a transgression of gendered practices or cultural norms that she is perceived to have breached warrants punishment amounting to persecution. However, as we demonstrate, the barriers that a woman is required to surmount in order to achieve refugee status may be considerably exacerbated by virtue of her gender, and compounded by the difficulties in accessing support services or proving that she has suffered gender-based violence or persecution. It has been persuasively argued that the concept of a refugee that emerged after the Second World War, and developed further in the context of people displaced or seeking asylum during the 1950s, came to be equated with male political activists who were persecuted by Communist states as a result of dissent opinions, while women were largely framed in terms of their assumed dependent status on such claimants (Asylum Aid, 2011). Not only does such a model deny women's agency, with their own motivations to flee persecution or independent grounds for claiming asylum potentially being subsumed under a 'household' or androcentric narrative, but the circumstances that specifically impact on women asylum seekers (for example, experiences of systematic sexual violence perpetrated as war crimes in Daesh-controlled areas of Syria and Iraq; or abuse that occurs on a more individual basis as a way of 'shaming' a political rival through assaults on female kin) are frequently excluded from the documentation of their asylum claims.

In recent decades strenuous attempts have been made by the UN High Commission for Refugees (UNHCR) to encourage more gender-sensitive interpretation of the 1951 Refugee Convention (for example in 1991,[5] updated with additional emphasis in 2002[6]), with the Commission producing guidelines on determining asylum claims containing a gendered element. The precise mechanisms by which gendered claims for asylum are interpreted are, however, subject to considerable national variation (Freedman, 2009). Following extensive lobbying by a range of non-governmental organisations (NGOs), the UK Border Agency (UKBA) adopted an Asylum Instruction in 2004 (updated in 2010) that provided information for case workers on 'Gender issues in the asylum claim' (Home Office, 2010), for example referring to the situation in a number of countries with particular human rights challenges and highlighting risks to trafficked women. The Instruction also made explicit (Home Office, 2010, p 2) that gender-specific duties exist under the 1986 Convention on the Elimination of All Forms of Discrimination against Women, the Human Rights Act 1998 and the Equality Act 2006. Particularly pertinent, given the findings from our project that indicated that women's narratives were often side-lined or dismissed when their husband was a primary claimant, it was emphasised that adult dependants should be reminded that they are entitled to make their own claim for asylum.

Despite the implementation of the Instruction, and the introduction of the UK's New Asylum Model in 2007, which sought to speed up the asylum process and ensure greater sensitivity and flexibility in the process, concerns were repeatedly raised in the next decade by NGOs (Ceneda and Palmer, 2006) pertaining to the pressured time frame and associated culture of 'tick-boxing' within the UKBA. Indeed the third UNHCR Quality Initiative Project Report found evidence that gender-sensitivity guidelines were routinely broken in the UK, with women who had experienced rape, forced marriage or domestic violence overwhelmingly being interviewed by male officers – circumstances that could impact significantly on the quality of evidence provided to support a claim.[7] Given that the Home Office/ UKBA's own guidance (Home Office, 2010) requires case managers to take into account the type of persecution and discrimination someone might face on account of their gender, it is clear that there is a policy implementation mismatch in terms of the stated intent of guiding regulations and the impact of such practices on vulnerable female asylum claimants.

In the last decade abundant evidence indicates that there is a systemic failure in the way in which asylum claims are assessed both by case officers and at the Tribunal stage, increasing the trauma of vulnerable women and effectively re-victimising them within the asylum process. To flag up but a small sample of research evidence, the Refugee Council (2005a)[8] report on asylum-seeking women with special needs (both physical and mental health-related) and its strategy document *Making women visible* (Refugee Council, 2005b) both stressed that the substantive difference in the way that women experience persecution is overwhelmingly not taken into account at interview; while interviewing officers frequently were found to utilise their discretionary decision-making authority in a manner that greatly exacerbates the hardship of both women and children who are party to asylum processes. Indeed, the latter of these documents highlighted the extreme levels of deprivation, on-going hardship and fear that asylum-seeking women often experience after entering the UK, while the research report (Refugee Council, 2005a) clearly evidenced how the accommodation conditions and sense of insecurity experienced by asylum-seeking women frequently exacerbated trauma or existing health conditions.

Asylum Aid (2012) research on women's experience of claiming asylum damningly noted that both refugee and asylum-seeking women and their legal representatives reported a lack of confidence in the asylum system, noting that inappropriate questioning at interview was common and that failures to develop or implement gender-specific guidance or follow House of Lords judgments at Immigration and Asylum Tribunals have resulted in a 'discriminatory approach to the determination of asylum claims based on gender-based particular social groups' (Asylum Aid, 2012, p 2). Women for Refugee Women (2015) explored the in-depth narratives of women detainees at Yarl's Wood Detention Centre, finding concerning evidence of the negative impacts on mental health of both detention and an atmosphere described repeatedly as lacking in privacy and that felt threatening, particularly as male guards were routinely in charge of and were reported to 'watch' women detainees while they were showering, using the lavatory or changing.

Moreover, recent cut-backs in legal aid, the loss of specialist NGOs following reductions in funding and the financial disincentives for solicitors to take on asylum appeals, coupled with the impacts of dispersal policies that can disrupt on-going contact with existing lawyers or that lead to RASW being dispersed to areas with only limited specialist legal practitioners (Hobson et al, 2008; Muggeridge and Maman, 2011) can greatly enhance the risk of appearing at appeal without representation, or of women's finding that they cannot access legal advocates. Asylum Aid (2007) reported its disquiet over the facts that women in detention at Yarl's Wood were frequently seen by male legal representatives, which made it difficult to disclose supporting evidence pertaining to gender-based violence and sexual assault, and that legal advice was often obtained only after an applicant had experienced their substantive interview, potentially leading to fast-track detention where relevant information had not been taken into account. Indeed, prior to the July 2015 landmark legal ruling[9] that overturned and suspended the streamlined Detained Fast Track (DFT) routing decision (that allowed certain categories of asylum seekers to be sent to detention centres on the basis of a short initial interview before the claimant was able to present evidence to support their claim, or indeed without having had adequate legal representation), repeated recommendations had been made in policy/research reports (Cutler, 2007; Human Rights Watch, 2010; Cheikh et al, 2012) that the DFT process was highly inappropriate for women experiencing gender-based victimisation.

Given the emphasis on mental health impacts of both detention and the well-recognised long-term psychological effects of suffering sexual violence, it is of concern that there seems to be relatively limited research and policy interest in the health experiences of RASW in the UK (and those studies that do exist overwhelmingly focus on reproductive health: for example, Harper Bulman and McCourt, 2002; Feldman, 2013; De Lomba and Murray, 2014). Moreover, many of the reports cited above flag up (almost as a subsidiary if persistent theme) both the poor mental health status and traumatising experiences of women asylum claimants and the barriers they face to accessing appropriate services when they do seek help through front-line GP services (Ahmed, 1996; Burnett and Peel, 2001; Bhatia and Wallace, 2007; Aspinall and Watters, 2010). Dumper (2004) emphasised both the lack of cultural competence of many healthcare staff and that cultural restrictions that may significantly exacerbate women's lack of appropriate access to physical and psychological treatment, while Johnson (2003) noted that dispersal practices could impact on continuity of care or access to specialist support for refugees.

There is thus abundant evidence to suggest that not only is the asylum process routinely failing RASW but there is also an embedded potential for institutional neglect and re-victimisation of women at all stages of the asylum system as case officers, legal advocates and health professionals fail to engage appropriately with vulnerable asylum claimants. This in turn impacts negatively on the potential success of women's cases.

The philosophy behind the Abused No More project was not only to uncover more evidence to add to the weight of the research findings detailed above, but in so doing also to seek to gain further policy traction in support of RASW. Importantly, we also sought to enhance the knowledge and skills-set of the women so as to empower participants collectively and individually, and thus enable recognition of their agency and role as experts by experience. Accordingly, Abused No More was conceived from the first in a manner that incorporated collaboratively co-designed[10] community development practice that was sensitive to being nuanced and calibrated so as to meet the anticipated needs of RASW who were survivors of trauma (Craig and Lovell, 2005; Westoby, 2008) while utilising participatory action research (PAR) methods[11] to support the gathering of information on the experiences of RASW in contact with key services post-migration to the UK.

Aims, objectives and methods

The main project aim, as noted, consisted of developing skills and capacity among RASW as they undertook training and developed as action researchers, enabling them to act as community-empowerment catalysts and drivers of change through intra- and cross-community dissemination of information to other RASW with regard to good practice, legal rights and knowledge of what could be reasonably expected or asked of service providers.

The secondary aim of the project was to enable a (self–identified) sub-group of the women to operationalise these newly acquired skills by bringing their knowledge to bear upon professional practice (with particular emphasis on targeting lawyers and medical practitioners) through the co-production of training materials that RASW would deliver to attendees in order to increase awareness of the impacts of professional behaviours and attitudes on vulnerable RASW and of the risk of secondary victimisation through thoughtless behaviours or lack of cultural competence. In addition (see further below), short downloadable podcasts were made available via YouTube[12] to enable a wider audience freely to access materials contained in longer and more interactive format within the 'experts by experience' training days targeted at health and legal professionals.

Methods

In line with best practice models of PAR (Baldwin, 2012), we set out explicitly to transform lives through co-produced emancipatory activity. The project was guided from the earliest planning stage by a multi-stage process of investigation that triangulated existing literature pertaining to the impact of gender-related violence on the experiences of refugee and asylum-seeking women, coupled with empirical community-driven research phases. The policy officer employed at IARS at the point in time when the project was under initial discussion (prior to the development of the funding application in 2012) had completed a post-graduate dissertation into the experiences of RASW while working as a volunteer with NGOs supporting vulnerable women.[13] As such, she was aware of persistent anecdotal reports about the numerous barriers faced by women claiming asylum. During preliminary planning discussions the team was thus able to identify a range of issues that included accommodation, poverty and poor-quality legal and medical services. This practice-based learning was embedded into the identification of initial themes, forming the basis of phases one and two of the research. In the first instance, a desk-based literature review was undertaken that then informed a scoping exercise into the lacunae in provision experienced by RASW and the key 'crisis points' at which point women's experiences could be compounded by multiple exclusion or failure of policy and existing services. To support this scoping exercise, consultations were carried out (by electronic methods, face-to-face interviews and informal discussion groups) with 42 professionals from civil society organisations working with RASW across the UK. The results of this scoping exercise indicated a focus on two key areas of work: those of access to legal services (specifically solicitors specialising in immigration law) and GP and front-line primary healthcare. We identified that the importance of these professionals in acting as gatekeepers to other services and specialist advice teams frequently compounded the difficulties experienced by RASW in urgent need of support both pre and post asylum interview.

At the same time as the scoping exercise was taking place, a process of recruitment was undertaken to identify and recruit refugee and asylum-seeking women appropriate to participate in the peer-led PAR interviews that explored the challenges faced by RASW. The use of peer-interviewers was chosen for two reasons: for the explicit focus on PAR (and hence developing the skills-set and knowledge of RASW to support a trickle-down effect of both knowledge and role-modelling) and in order to ensure commonality of experience between interviews and participants (Greenfields and Ryder, 2012) so as to build empathy and encourage open discussions. In total, after screening for vulnerability, migration status, language skills and prior experience of the asylum system, 12 community interviewers from a range of African and Middle-Eastern countries were recruited with the assistance of a number of civil society organisations working with refugees and asylum-seekers. The women, who were of diverse Christian and Muslim denominations and had a range of roles including parent, carer, spouse and student, varied in age from early 20s (a former child migrant) to late 30s and had been resident in the UK for periods ranging from 15 to 2 years.

All interviewees undertook a series of six training sessions prior to commencing interviews, as well as participating in on-going peer support and having access to a dedicated mentor via project/IARS link staff. Training (based on the handbook of good practice prepared for the programme by Greenfields, 2013) consisted of in-depth sessions exploring the processes of PAR, ethical issues and reporting requirements, 'self-protection' (emotional and physical) during interviews, referral services and the provision of emotional support to interviewees, and practical interviewing skills. As part of the training sessions the team members also collaboratively co-produced the questionnaire to be used with participants, with the RASW leading on the design of the tools and providing input into the analysis process that would subsequently be undertaken. Pilot interviews were carried out by peer researchers under the initial supervision of an IARS staff member; subsequently (for the main sample) they interviewed in pairs with a trained non-RASW volunteer present or available to provide support.

The sample of 46 refugee or asylum-seeking women interviewed were accessed using a combination of snowballing (accessed via earlier waves of interviewees) and convenience sampling, with the first tranche of interviewees having been recruited with the assistance of a number of civil society organisations working with RASW who supported the project. All organisations active in recruiting interviewees were sent advance information on the nature of the project and had access to the questionnaire so as to enable familiarity with the survey content. Potential interviewees were pre-screened to assess for language-skills competency and to enable the identification of mental or physical health conditions. Particular attention was paid to the prevalence of depression, anxiety and post-traumatic stress disorder (PTSD) among the sample. Following pre-interview screening, interviewees (all aged 18 or over) were carefully matched with peer researchers to ensure, as far as possible, a match with country of origin, migration route, language, culture and faith. Prior to their interviews, participants were read (or read for themselves) an information sheet and provided informed consent to participate, with the clear understanding that they could stop the interview at any point. Peer researchers were provided with guidelines pertaining to the well-being of interviewees (see above) and it was stressed that reporting lines existed and guidance must be followed in relation to concerns over vulnerable adult participants.

The interview consisted of a series of questions on basic demographic issues such as country of origin, immigration status, number of years in the UK and number of children (both resident and non-resident with the interviewee). This section of the interview was then followed up by a semi-structured interview that considered the experiences of RASW in relation to access to and satisfaction with GP and legal services, as well as barriers to the receipt of service and the impacts of dispersal on service provision. In total, of the 46 (recorded) interviews undertaken, 21 were conducted using diverse community languages or supported by interpreters.

Following completion and translation/transcription of all interviews, group and individual debriefing sessions occurred with the peer interviewers to enable discussion of the core themes identified during the process. This thematic analysis framework was then applied to the data by the IARS project worker and findings (including key quotations) were entered into a spreadsheet. Subsequent meetings with the peer interviewers enabled validity checking of themes and topics.

Key findings

While this chapter does not focus on the findings of the research, all of which are discussed in depth in Challenger (2013), it is worth flagging up that the vast majority of the women interviewed reported suffering from poor mental health, with 75% stating that they had depression, 83% experiencing stress and anxiety and 40% having been diagnosed with PTSD. Overwhelmingly, the women attributed their poor mental health to trauma experienced in their country of origin or during the migration journey, exacerbated by anxiety over their asylum claims, dispersal and living conditions. Although 90% of women had not been dispersed outside of London, rapid, repeated movement within London was common, as were narratives of appalling housing conditions, reliance on friends and family for short-term accommodation (sofa-surfing) and living 'out of suitcases' in bed-and-breakfast accommodation. Experiences of rapid change of address were common to those housed by the UKBA, via local authorities or resident in other forms of accommodation. This also impacted on the ability of RASW to access medical care, with women frequently noting that they had difficulties in registering with a GP without documentary proof of address. Other core concerns reported included difficulties in building trust in GPs, so as to enable RASW to disclose sexual and gender violence, problems with translation services (and understanding information supplied by doctors or pharmacists in relation to medication), as well as the re-victimisation process inherent in needing to repeatedly recount their personal stories (for example, related to gynaecological problems following gang rape) when seeing serial medical personnel. In terms of legal advice, while some women reported receiving a good and consistent service, more common by far was the experience of dealing with different lawyers on each occasion (or failing to access advice prior to interview), a process that was difficult in terms of both building trust and, moreover, that disrupted the process of obtaining legal representation if they were unable to access legal aid solicitors with experience of the asylum process when they were moved. In common with reported experiences of disrupted legal access, receiving advice of variable quality, lack of communication from lawyers, short and truncated interviews, language barriers and the necessity of having children present at interviews could all prove distracting or a barrier to full disclosure of experiences of gendered or sexual violence.

Outcomes of the project

In addition to the delivery of the project report and the core aim of increasing confidence and skills through the training of peer interviewers identified during post-project evaluation,[14] secondary outcomes of the programme consisted of the production of free-to-view YouTube films and podcasts that raise awareness and enhance knowledge of good practice (including through trust building and overcoming administrative barriers) among health and legal services personnel as well as members of the general public.

Within the film and podcasts, RASW peer interviewers both speak to camera about their own experiences and role-play good and bad practice scenarios in relation to healthcare and legal professionals' engagement with them (for example, vignettes of interactions in doctors' surgeries in which the scenario is based on the text of interviews). Elements of the podcasts also incorporate advice on where to seek assistance if women are dissatisfied or are unclear as to their right to access a specific service. The advice booklet by Greenfields (2013) on good practice in undertaking research with RASW, based on both the findings from the project and intensive discussions with peer researchers, is also freely available from the IARS website to support researchers and service providers in engaging ethically and sensitively with RASW.

In the final phase of the project (2014–15) refugee and asylum-seeking women involved in the project, working in partnership with IARS staff (and following consultation on preferred content with professionals working the 'refugee sector'), have delivered a series of tailored half-day face-to-face continuing professional development-accredited training sessions for legal and healthcare practitioners who work with this particularly vulnerable group. The training sessions (delivered in total to over 80 organisations/individual practitioners) have involved multi-method interactive learning techniques and focused on delivering findings from the project as well as explaining the impact of professionals' attitudes, practices and cultural awareness on enhancing both hard (improved numbers of successful asylum claims) and soft (women feeling listened to, empowered to discuss experiences, moving through the processes of overcoming trauma and achieving medical care for long-standing conditions) outcomes. In tandem with the training sessions led by RASW, a formal online training programme and associated manual[15] were developed and are available on a pay-to-download basis via the IARS website. The manual, which was designed for use by any professional or agency in contact with vulnerable

RASW, aims to raise awareness of the prevalence of violence against women and girls in refugee communities as well as providing links to additional resources, while the training programme concentrates on delivering practical information on ways to support RASW through the application of relevant communication and interviewing techniques. By late 2015, a total of 2,132 individuals had attended training sessions or accessed the online programme, in addition to other to whom the findings were disseminated via conference presentations to health practitioners and academics working in the field of refugee studies.

Further, the community researchers have developed a peer support network for RASW and former RASW involved in the project, and in 2015 engaged in an end-of-project showcase event and fundraiser to pay for childcare costs for women participating in the ongoing linked activities listed above.[16] As a further spin-off, the project has led to the formation of an IARS gender advisory group led by peer researchers from the project, who have helped to develop follow-up applications and programmes.[17]

The policy and practice implications of the project

As detailed above, Abused No More has a strong emphasis on influencing practice through enabling professionals to gain a new perspective on their role and the impacts of their activities on the well-being and outcomes experienced by RASW. It can be argued that the success of the project represents a new strategic approach to the development and delivery of training by triangulating action research, theoretical and practice-based findings, combined with the community development elements of the programme.

In policy terms, the emphasis has been on input to practical policy development, operationalised through strategic interactions with legal, medical and political actors. For example, sending briefings and initiating contact on policy recommendations with the (then) Home Secretary, Theresa May, in 2013 and providing input to the 2013 Government Action Plan, *Call for End to Violence against Women and Girls*, which included a pledge to 'work to ensure that the asylum system is as gender-sensitive as possible'. While many of our activities are 'slow burners', policy activities and contact with policing, probation, legal and medical professionals remain core to the outputs of this project, while the practice-based dissemination and community development activities (outlined above) remain embedded within IARS's strategic plan. These continue to evolve and impact on the lives of refugee and asylum-seeking women on a consistent, everyday basis.

Notes

[1] Comic Relief is a national UK charity distributing funds raised by TV appeals.

[2] The IARS dedicated project web page can be accessed here: www.iars.org.uk/content/AbusedNoMore.

[3] 1951 UN Convention relating to the Status of Refugees and Article 1(A) of the attached 1967 Protocol.

[4] For a comprehensive discussion of the various grounds on which women may claim asylum and the emergence of legal awareness on the interplay of human rights and asylum law (for example, pertaining to successful claims for asylum related to female genital mutilation, LGBT identity, arranged marriages and so on), see Arbel et al (2014).

[5] UNHCR (1991) *Guidelines on the protection of Refugee Women*, Geneva: UNHCR, www.unhcr.org/3d4f915e4.html.

[6] UNHCR (2002) *Guidelines on International Protection* no 1: *Gender-Related Persecution*, Geneva: UNHCR, www.unhcr.org/3d58ddef4.pdf.

[7] Refugee Council briefing (2007) on the New Asylum Model, at p 9, www.refugeecouncil.org.uk/assets/0001/5834/New_Asylum_Model_Aug_07.

[8] Refugee Council (2005a), *A study of asylum seekers with special needs*, This found that 30% of women interviewed had experienced sexual violence and 64% physical torture; while 82% of respondents reported they suffered from ongoing mental health issues.

[9] For a summary of the lengthy legal proceedings that ended this system, undertaken by Detention Action NGO/legal charity see further: http://detentionaction.org.uk/campaigns/end-the-fast-track-to-despair/legal-challenge.

[10] The processes of co-design are outlined below under the methods section of this chapter, but throughout this project we sought at all times to ensure that the RASW fully participated in all elements of the decision-making process and the identification of their training needs and content of the project in meaningful manner, thus ensuring the development of research skills among participants as well as increasing confidence and agency and delivering outputs that were validated by the women who took part in the project. See further Beebeejaun et al (2015).

[11] For the current purposes PAR is defined as a method of research *with* (rather than *on*) communities that emphasises collective practices of enquiry, developed in partnership with community members, and that draws upon shared, non-hierarchical understanding of social meaning, histories and experience with the intent of bringing about transformative community development through a process of action-focused research. Reason and Bradbury (2008) refer to PAR as a process through which 'communities of inquiry and action evolve and address questions and issues that are significant for those who participate as co-researchers'.

[12] See the IARS website for access to the Abused No More podcasts/films in which a number of RASW enact scenarios using text drawn from interviews in which women discuss good and bad practice they have encountered in the UK; www.iars.org.uk/content/AbusedNoMore.

[13] See the work of Holly Challenger, who in 2013, shortly after moving to work for a refugee charity, completed the IARS project report *Abused no more* (Challenger, 2013), which detailed the early stages of the programme.

[14] In the post-project evaluation a total of 24 women who had participated as peer interviewers and/or interviewees reported that after taking part in the programme they had improved self-esteem and confidence; or had an enhanced ability to

disclose sensitive information pertaining to their asylum claim/experiences of gender violence; or that felt better able to engage with their lives and daily circumstances.

15 Both authored by Natalia Paszkiewicz, the Abused No More/RASW project coordinator 2013–16; www.iars.org.uk/content/online-training-gender#voices

16 IARS, press release, 9 March 2015, www.iars.org.uk/content/HelpWomen.

17 For example, the on-going (at time of writing) Abused No More – Safeguarding Young Migrants project, concerned with enhancing legal literacy for vulnerable youth, www.iars.org.uk/content/ErasmusAnM; and the Gender and Justice Empowerment Project, www.iars.org.uk/node/1924, which aims to assist vulnerable RASW affected by crime through delivering training on RASW's legal rights in relation to the incorporation and implementation of the 2015 Victim's Directive. Both projects also incorporate opportunities for participants engage with policy makers, the judiciary and political representatives through workshops, conferences and involvement in lobbying opportunities.

References

Ahmed, M. (1996) *Refugee women in East Sussex*, London: Refugee Action.

Arbel, E., Dauvergne, C. and Millbank, J. (2014) *Gender in refugee law: From the margins to the centre*, Abingdon: Routledge.

Aspinall, P. and Watters, C. (2010) *Research report 52 – Refugees and asylum seekers: a review from an equality and human rights perspective*, project report, Manchester: Equality and Human Rights Commission.

Asylum Aid (2007) *Legal Services Commission detention advice specification: Response to LSC consultation by Asylum Aid*, London: Asylum Aid, www.asylumaid.org.uk/response-to-the-legal-services-commission-consultation-on-the-draft-legal-services-commission-detention-advice-specification-v-4/ accessed 9 April 2014.

Asylum Aid (2011) *Unsustainable: The quality of initial decision-making in women's asylum claims*, London: Asylum Aid, p 11.

Asylum Aid (2012) *'I feel like as a woman I'm not welcome': A gender analysis of UK asylum law, policy and practice*, executive summary, London: Asylum Aid, at: http://d2t68d2r9artlv.cloudfront.net/wp-content/uploads/2013/02/Ifeelasawoman_EXEC_SUM_WEB.pdf accessed 18-7-16.

Baldwin, M. (2012) 'Participatory Action Research', in Gray, M., Midgley, J. and Webb, S. (eds), *Social work handbook*, London; Sage.

Beebeejaun, Y., Durose, C., Rees, J., Richardson, J. and Richardson, L. (2015) 'Public harm or public value? Towards coproduction in research with communities', *Environment and Planning C: Government and Policy*, vol 33, pp 552–65.

Bhatia, R. and Wallace, P. (2007) 'Experiences of refugees and asylum seekers in general practice: a qualitative study', *BMC Family Practice*, vol 8, p 48.

Burnett, A. and Peel, M. (2001) 'Health needs of asylum seekers and refugees'. *BMJ*, vol 322, pp 544–7.

Ceneda, S. and Palmer, C. (2006) *The Home Office gender guidance and women's asylum claims in the UK*, Refugee Women's Resource Project, London: Asylum Aid.

Challenger, H. (2013) *Abused no more: The voices of refugee and asylum-seeking women*, London: IARS.

Cheikh Ali, H., Querton, C. and Soulard, E. (2012) *Gender-related asylum claims in Europe: a comparative analysis of law, policies and practice focusing on women in nine EU member states*, Brussels: European Commission and European Refugee Fund.

Craig, G. and Lovell, H. (2005) 'Editorial introduction', *Community Development Journal*, vol 40, no 2, pp 131–6.

Crawley, H. (nd, circa 2015) *Gender related persecution and women's claims to asylum*, International Refugee Rights Initiative: rights in exile programme, online guidance, www.unfpa.org/publications/managing-gender-based-violence-programmes-emergencies, accessed 19 September 2016.

Cutler, S. (2007) *'Refusal Factory': Women's experiences of the detained fast-track asylum process at Yarl's Wood Immigration Removal Centre*, London: Bail for Immigration Detainees.

De Lomba, S. and Murray, N. (2014) *Women and children first? Refused asylum seekers' access to and experiences of maternity care in Glasgow*, Glasgow: Scottish Refugee Council, www.scottishrefugeecouncil.org.uk/what_we_do/policy_and_research/research_reports, accessed 5 October 2016.

Dumper, H. (2004) *Missed opportunities: A skills audit of refugee women in London from the teaching, nursing and medical professions*, London: IoE.

Feldman, R. (2013) *When maternity doesn't matter: Dispersing pregnant women seeking asylum*, London Maternity Action and Refugee Council, www.researchasylum.org.uk/when-maternity-doesnt-matter-dispersing-pregnant-women-seeking-asylum, accessed 14 August 2016.

Freedman, J. (2009) 'Protecting women asylum seekers and refugees: from international norms to national protection?' *International Migration*, vol 48, no 1, pp 175–98.

Greenfields, M. (2013) *Action research with refugee women: Good practice and solutions to community participation*, London: IARS, https://www.scribd.com/document/125286265/Action-Research-With-Refugee-Women-Good-Practice-and-Solutions-to-Community-Participation.

Greenfields, M. and Ryder, A. (2012) 'Research "with" and "for" Gypsies and Travellers', in J. Richardson and A. Ryder (eds), *Gypsies and Travellers: Accommodation, empowerment and inclusion in British Society*, Bristol: Policy Press.

Harper Bulman, K. and McCourt, C. (2002) 'Somali refugee women's experiences of maternity care in west London: a case study', *Critical Public Health*, vol 12, no 4, pp 365–80, www.researchasylum.org.uk/somali-refugee-womens-experiences-maternity-care-west-london, accessed 9 October 2016.

Hobson, C., Cox, J. and Sagovsky, N. (2008) *Deserving dignity*, London: Independent Asylum Commission.

Home Office (2010) *Gender issues in the asylum claim*, London: Home Office, https://www.gov.uk/government/uploads/system/uploads/attachment_data/file/257386/gender-issue-in-the-asylum.pdf.

Human Rights Watch (2010) *Fast tracked unfairness*, London: Human Rights Watch.

Johnson, M. (2003) *Asylum seekers in dispersal: Healthcare issues*, London: Home Office.

Muggeridge, H. and Maman, C. (2011) *Unsustainable: The quality of initial decision making in women's asylum claims*, London: Asylum Aid.

Reason, H. and Bradbury, J. (eds) (2008) *The Sage handbook of action research: Participative inquiry and practice*, California: Sage.

Refugee Council (2005a) *A study of asylum seekers with special needs*, London: Refugee Council, www.refugeecouncil.org.uk/assets/0002/8820/AsylumseekersspecialneedsApril2005.pdf (accessed 5 June 2016).

Refugee Council (2005b) *Making women visible: Strategies for a more woman-centred asylum and refugee support system*, London: Refugee Council Aid, https://www.refugeecouncil.org.uk/assets/0001/5592/WomenstrategyMarch2005.pdf, accessed 15 August 2016.

Singh, R. (2010) 'In between the system and the margins: community organizations, mandatory charging and immigrant victims of abuse', *Canadian Journal of Sociology*, vol 35, no 1, pp 31–62.

Tate, F. (2015) 'Impunity, peacekeepers, gender and sexual violence in post-conflict landscapes: a challenge for the international human rights agenda', *Law, Crime and History*, vol 5, no 2, pp 69–96.

Westoby, P. (2008) 'Developing a community-development approach through engaging resettling Southern Sudanese refugees within Australia', *Community Development Journal*, vol 43, no 4, pp 483–95.

Women for Refugee Women (2015) *I am human: Refugee women's experiences of detention in the UK*, London: WRW, www.refugeewomen. co.uk/2016/wp-content/uploads/2016/07/WRW_IamHuman_ report-for-web.pdf, accessed 2 October 2016.

Section Three
Working with Roma communities

Introduction

Gary Craig

This small section (and I should also point to Chapter Twelve, on work with Roma youth from Romania, in the following section) quite deliberately focuses on community development work of different kinds with Roma, Gypsy and Traveller groups as a contribution to redressing the imbalance whereby these most deprived groups – by any measure and within every European country – have been the most profoundly 'invisibilised' (a term I used in relation to the treatment of the issue of 'race' in UK public policy) by governments throughout their 400 or 500-year history in the Continent, only finally emerging into public view as the subjects of victimisation, discrimination and genocide, most of all during Hitler's 'final solution'. The three accounts here – two from Scotland, one from England – will give the reader some idea of the profound levels of discrimination still faced by these groups whether, as in the case of Gypsies and Travellers, largely non-sedentary, living both on caravan sites and on the move, or, as in the case of the many thousands of Roma who have moved to the UK from East and Central European countries following the enlargements of the European Union in 2004 and 2007, living in the most deprived and unhealthy housing areas of towns and cities across the UK.[1] They also give some idea of the size of the task facing community development workers, both because of the levels of deprivation they suffer, the mistrust of gorgas (white people) as a consequence of the hundreds of years of discrimination and abuse they have suffered, and the more general hostility they face from local settled communities. As a result of these challenging conditions, community workers often have to be satisfied with what might seem, in other contexts, relatively minor gains.

In Chapter Nine, Hashagen and his collaborators' work with Roma moving to Glasgow, Scotland's largest and most multi-ethnic city (in terms of numbers and diversity), situates work with Roma within a long tradition of community development in the city, including with minorities of different kinds. The account here, covering 10 years, allows us to see how the work moved from building links and organisational responses to ensure that this deprived population was able effectively to access a range of basic services, through advocacy, to more structured forms of organisation. Work with Roma has been set within a neighbourhood approach informed substantially by Alinsky's pluralist but conflict-based approach, ensuring that the Roma could take their rightful place within the wider work on race relations emerging across the city.

Small – and conditional – gains are very much the theme of Notcutt's account of community development work with Gypsy and Traveller women in the East of England, in Chapter Ten. Critically, she reinforces the need to listen and learn carefully from people whose experience has for so long been dismissed or overridden by authority. She demonstrates how an understanding of local power structures can often be the key to gaining access to communities, with a single male spokesperson providing the means for building service responses involving all of the women and children of a community. This, however, contains the seeds of a significant contradiction, as, in effectively allying herself with dominant patriarchal power exercised in this community, she soon comes up against the clash of values between what that represents and the values she holds herself as a community worker operating in a framework of, not least of all, gender inequality. This contradiction will be resolved, amid considerable internal struggle, only over a long period of time, one suspects. In the meantime, these gains are important: health access is improved, services are more available (including some that had wrongfully been denied), confidence and educational levels are increased and the ability to negotiate both with the holders of power and other oppressed minorities is enhanced.

Finally, in Chapter Eleven, Clark analyses the role of mediation, a process involving trained Romani workers acting as a bridge between Romani communities and public institutions, often the source of profound racism and discrimination against Romani communities. Although there have been some gains for Romani individuals and groups, and European institutions have invested fairly heavily in a series of programmes, the structural barriers faced by mediators, some of them reflected in the programmes themselves (such as the facts that they pay mediators very poorly and remain short term in their scope), mean that Clark's analysis is inevitably fairly critical of the programmes. Echoing Belton's comments later in this book, his major criticism is that

> the underlying 'social inclusion' model that still views Roma communities as largely dependent and lacking in both agency and ability to articulate need and represent collective, democratic thinking and governance ... is a redundant, neocolonial model ... that needs to be stripped of power, control and influence.

Note

[1] Ironically, many of these Roma tried to enter the UK as refugees seeking asylum in the late 1990s and were refused entry, often facing hostile mobs at the English ports at which they arrived. Following EU enlargement, they had a right to enter the UK as migrant workers as long as they satisfied basic work-registration conditions. There are around 200,000 Roma now living in the UK, making them one of the largest – and fastest-growing – minority groups in the UK.

NINE

Cultural identity, migration and community development in Glasgow

Stuart Hashagen with Mick Doyle and Brian Keenan

This chapter examines two linked stories of community work and migration in Glasgow. One is of the work taken forward by the Scottish Refugee Council with refugees and asylum seekers across the city, the other is of the neighbourhood-level work of Crossroads, a long-established youth and community association in the Govanhill area of the city. It is set within the shifting context of community work in the city over the years.

Community work and minorities in Glasgow

Through the 1980s and 1990s a strong commitment to community development was established by Scottish local authorities, especially the more strategic Regional Councils (until their abolition in 1996), embracing its values and approaches as a cornerstone of social, educational and economic development.[1] However, by the time the local government reorganisation of 1996 had bedded in, many of the new and smaller councils had abandoned or severely reduced their commitment to community development.

Since then there has been a curious, somewhat contradictory path for community development. In many ways it is seen to be strongly embedded in Scottish thinking and culture. The non-governmental organisation (NGO) Community Development Alliance Scotland has over 100 national organisations in its membership, each of which sees community development as a key part of its purpose. Yet, on the ground, very few organisations (either public or third sector) are to be found doing the basic neighbourhood or community work that is at the core of community development.

Working with migrant communities is one of the few areas in which community development and neighbourhood work have remained in place in Glasgow. In this chapter we look at some of the work done in recent years, trying to assess its impact.

Glasgow has been a destination city for migrants for at least 150 years. People from the Scottish Highlands, Ireland, Italy, the Punjab, Uganda, Eastern Europe and many other places have arrived and settled. In the last ten years migration to Glasgow has been predominantly from two main groups: refugees and asylum seekers, mainly from Africa or the Middle East; and people from Central and Eastern Europe, in particular Slovakia and Romania, including a significant number of Roma. For many of these, the neighbourhood of arrival has been Govanhill. An area of 19th-century tenements less than two miles south of the city centre, Govanhill avoided the wholesale demolition and rebuilding that characterised most similar communities in the city, many of its tenements having been adopted and refurbished by the active community-based Govanhill Housing Association. Other tenements have remained in the rented sector and it is here that migrants find relatively cheap if substandard and overcrowded accommodation, as well as contact with others with similar origins. Of the refugees and asylum seekers who arrived since 2000, most were placed in high-rise local authority housing stock in other, less central parts of the city. Here, we discuss the community-work approaches adopted with each of these groups.

It is estimated that during 2001–10 between 18,000 and 40,000 asylum seekers were dispersed to Glasgow. This amounts to 10% of total UK dispersals, to a city containing substantially less than 2% of the total UK population. In 2010 there were 2,800 refugees and 3,500 asylum seekers in the city, and a further 1,500 'legacy case' households (that is those with indeterminate status) on human rights grounds. Between 1991 and 2011 the size of the ethnic minority population in Glasgow increased by 13%, to 21% of the total population.[2] The non-white population increased from 24,700 to 68,700, an increase from 4% to 12% of the total population. Nationalities coming to Glasgow particularly included people from Sri Lanka, Somalia, Afghanistan, Iraq, Iran and the Democratic Republic of the Congo.

The general issues confronting refugees include the operation of the Westminster-led asylum system, which is seen as unjust and stigmatising, and limiting life-chances within a generally hostile political climate. Refugees and other migrants are confronted with inadequate housing in the poorest high-rise stock; health issues, and especially trauma and mental ill-health, with, as elsewhere, very poor levels of mental health services; racism, harassment and violence, especially experienced by women; together with complexities in accessing education and employment. For all, there are significant transitions in their status, life-chances and quality of life.

The Scottish Refugee Council strategy

Glasgow has a long tradition of community development work, carried out by the local authorities throughout the 1980–90s and more recently adopted by a mix of voluntary and community organisations, housing associations and health projects. The Scottish Refugee Council (SRC) adopted a clear community development strategy, working in partnership with the residual Glasgow City Council community development team.

This work was, and remains, underpinned by an understanding of the structural oppression of asylum seekers and a belief that community development methods could support multiculturalism and greater understanding between migrant groups and the existing communities. There was also a social learning element, raising awareness of the push and pull factors associated with migration, seeking to displace myths with 'better truths', thus enhancing the skills and confidence of community representatives and community workers as well as of asylum seekers and refugees themselves.

Based on these principles, SRC's community development aims were established as being to:

- build dialogue between refugees, receiving communities and local and national agencies;
- ensure refugee participation in local community life and encourage solidarity;
- develop involvement in the planning and delivery of services;
- facilitate development of local and national forums;
- develop autonomous independent refugee community organisations, usually around common bonds of nationality but including federated activity;
- enable refugees to organise practical responses and influence policy; and
- promote long-term integration.

At neighbourhood level, these aims were realised through establishing or supporting a network of refugee organisations across Scotland, and Integration Networks and Framework for Dialogue groups in Glasgow. The Integration Networks are a key component in the strategy; there are currently seven in the city. These are groups of local agencies, community groups and volunteers who plan and deliver services to asylum seekers and refugees in their area. Services may include information and advice, English classes, drop-in services, activities for children and adults, cultural programmes and emotional and practical support. These services are not confined to refugees and asylum seekers, but serve to promote integration and cultural diversity. The South East Integration Network area covers Govanhill; Crossroads is a member of this network.

Although refugees and asylum seekers are clearly in the most hostile circumstances, many of the challenges are also typical of the experience of European migrants, albeit in a less extreme way. For Govanhill, in a growing local population of over 15,000, more than a third of local people are from ethnic minorities, and over 50 languages are spoken in the area and in local schools. Due to the high availability of cheap private rented accommodation, Govanhill has traditionally been an area of settlement for new migrants – people living in the area include 'white Scottish', Scottish Asians (mostly from a Pakistani background), overseas students, people seeking asylum, refugees, Irish people and European migrants. More recently, people from Poland, the Czech Republic and Romania have moved in – many of whom are Roma in origin – with between 3,000 and 4,000 Roma now living in the area.

There are many issues faced in common by people living in the area, including poverty, unemployment, discrimination and racism between groups in the community and from public bodies, negotiating the asylum system, destitution, exploitation by rogue landlords and below-tolerable housing, social isolation, mental and physical health issues, domestic violence and severe overcrowding. Migrant workers are frequently exploited, and often victims of serious organised crime, such as human trafficking.

Communication and relationships between different communities in the area are challenging. Many people living in the community are isolated, particularly those with young children. Some children have limited opportunities to participate in cooperative and developmental play activities. There have been conflicts between people of different ethnicities and cultural backgrounds living in the area. Many people lack knowledge of and are misinformed about other ethnic identities, resulting in barriers and bad feeling between groups.

Poverty is a major issue. Many residents are not entitled to the full range of welfare benefits, while others are openly discriminated against in the application process, which can delay their applications for up to a year (sometimes more than this), leaving them in deep poverty. Five of the 12 census data zones in Govanhill are in the bottom 15% in the Scottish Index of Multiple Deprivation, with one data zone in the bottom 5%. Overall, 26% of adults are income deprived, 23% are employment deprived, while in some smaller areas 42% are income deprived and 32% are employment deprived.

Within the 'white Scottish' community, male life expectancy is 70 years (4 years less than the Scottish average), and female life expectancy is 76 years (also 4 years less than the average). But for the Roma community, life expectancy is 54 years for males and 58 years for females. Coronary heart disease and stroke are the leading causes of death in Roma populations. There is a higher than average use of alcohol and drugs in the area and there are infestations of mice, rats and bedbugs. Many of the flats in the area are in very poor condition, recent reports highlighting serious infestations of cockroaches, and rogue landlords collecting abandoned mattresses from the street and using them to furnish rooms to let.[3]

In terms of housing, many are living in below-tolerable-standard housing that is overcrowded – the poverty faced by many migrant residents results in people pooling resources to share overcrowded accommodation. All of Govanhill's housing falls within the bottom 10% of data zones in the Scottish Index of Multiple Deprivation, with four data zones falling into the bottom 1%. Thirty-one per cent of households in the area are overcrowded, 163% above the Scottish average. Some two-bedroom properties have as many as 18 people living in them. Unscrupulous landlords and employers exploit people who may have limited options. Some people are employed illegally and paid at rates significantly below the minimum wage. Many people who come to settle in Scotland have limited information, and often misinformation, on the realities of migrating to another country.

Social issues have an impact on the physical and mental health of people living in the area. An area that is home to people from so many different ethnic and cultural backgrounds presents a challenge when it comes to integration and the promotion of understanding between different groups. The fact that many people living in the area do not speak English as their first language creates barriers in their day-to-day lives. Language barriers, lack of knowledge, insecurity and isolation can often mean that people don't access, and often don't know about, the services that can provide them with support.

Despite the serious social and financial issues described, a vibrant and cross-cultural arts scene is developing in the area, and there is an impressive array of community groups, organisations and public sector projects active locally. There are a diverse range of shops, cafes and pubs, and a growing sense of solidarity and mutuality, particularly between younger people. A 2010 report[4] mapping the various assets of the neighbourhood suggests that, despite the deficits, there are many human and organisational strengths in the area that can be built on, including groups and organisations active across the whole range of cultural, care, recreation and rights issues.

The work of Crossroads

Crossroads Youth and Community Association, a community-led NGO, has been working in the area since 1968. The ethos behind community work in Govanhill is to provide opportunities for the integration of the communities. This work is done in a number of ways – by working with groups, providing safe places where people from different backgrounds can come together and participate in community and awareness-raising activities; by providing one-to-one support to people who are more vulnerable; organising community awareness-raising events around International Women's Day, Refugee Week and Sixteen Days of Action Against Gender Violence; and working in close partnership with other local organisations. The focus is on local neighbourhood work, taking a structural perspective. This emphasises that social problems are inherent in the ways in which society is organised, looking at social structures and the ways in which these maintain oppression and privilege. While radical social change (for example, redistribution of wealth and resources) is needed, it is also essential to attend to the immediate needs of those who are being marginalised, exploited and harmed. The work is therefore informed by an analysis of structural power and oppression, reflected in an approach that focuses on building community organisations, resistance and direct action, but starting with the immediate requirement to focus on bringing different groups together to build solidarity and a sense of cohesion on which more challenging actions can be built.

Crossroads' work with the Roma community commenced in 2007. At that time a considerable number of Slovak and Czech Roma had migrated to Govanhill. The arrival of this new migrant population created suspicion, fear and alarm among the existing population. In response, Crossroads collaborated with National Health Service health visitors to offer practical help and support to Roma people and to find out more about these new migrants and their needs. This service offered clothes, food and one-to-one support to those in need and was quickly overwhelmed by demand. After a few months it became evident that this ad hoc approach to support was insufficient, and although the direct provision of food and clothes was invaluable, a more structured and formalised support system was needed.

The overall aim of this was to facilitate the integration of local Roma residents into the wider community in Govanhill. The underlying objectives were to:

- engage with the Roma population in Govanhill;
- support it to interact with the existing community; and
- provide safe spaces for the Roma community to meet and build solidarity, using the principles and practices of community development.

Based on these aims, Crossroads established an advocacy project in June 2007. The advocacy project employed two Slovak-speaking staff who provided an intensive support service to Slovak and Czech Roma individuals and families. This project was successful, and the first of its kind in Glasgow. It continued for five years until its closure in June 2012 due to the withdrawal of funding. This service was crucial in terms of making Roma people's migration socially and economically sustainable, but four years after its closure, the need for a strong advocacy service is as acute as ever.

From 2010 onwards Crossroads delivered locally a migrational and cultural awareness programme, called Understanding Each Other, a project established by the Integration Network as one arm of the SRC's work. This programme was, and still is, rolled out in primary schools locally and its aim is to raise awareness and develop an appreciation of the history and reasons for migration leading to cultural diversity among the pupils. The project involves volunteers from the various ethnic and cultural groups living locally telling their stories and discussing their experiences with the children. Given that there are over 3,000 Roma people living in Govanhill, and that Govanhill is the most culturally diverse community in Scotland, the impact of this programme in terms of awareness raising and the exchange of knowledge between Roma and other cultures has been considerable.

In 2011, the Tuesday Evening Drop-In was established, specifically to provide a safe environment for Slovak and Czech Roma to meet. It provides them with an opportunity to build friendships and networks with each other and serves as a catalyst for the participants to discuss and work together on issues or concerns of common interest. The drop-in also hosts a number of specialist agencies that provide information and advice on a weekly basis. Initially, one of the key challenges was the language barrier, so in September 2012 a Slovak community worker was recruited to work with the group. This shaped the focus of the group significantly. The drop-in continues to run, with an increased focus on community engagement, empowerment and community development. This has resulted in members of the Roma community working collectively as a group, being less reliant on direct service provision and more focused on directly addressing the issues that they face.

In 2013 a new collaboration with the Slovakian Ministry of the Interior was established. This focused on the issue of human trafficking from Slovakia to the UK, a phenomenon that affects many Roma people from Slovakia. Crossroads staff were involved in both desk-based and local research on the topic, and this made a significant contribution in terms of raising awareness of the issue and identifying the signs of human trafficking.[5]

The year 2013 also saw the development of a Roma Streetwork project in Govanhill. The purpose of this is two-fold – to enhance engagement with a wider section of the Roma community in Govanhill; and to identify the needs of the Roma community, as well as identifying some of the assets within the community that could potentially feed into an asset-based approach to the work. Since it started, workers have made contact with over 200 people from the Slovak and Czech Roma community, and this has yielded much valuable information that will be used to shape future work and influence policy at a wider political level. A partnership has been established with the Minority Ethnic Employment and Training project of the West of Scotland Regional Equality Council to support a number of Roma towards employability.

Alongside these projects, Crossroads has been actively involved locally in supporting and facilitating participation in Refugee Festival Scotland, Sixteen Days of Action Against Domestic Violence, International Women's Day and International Roma Day. There have also been partnership projects, for example to establish a local Roma Heritage and Music project that ran four shows in Glasgow to create an awareness of Roma and Scottish heritage through the medium of music.[6] The music group formed during this project, E Karika Djal (Moving Wheel) now performs on a regular basis in Glasgow and beyond.

Choosing an appropriate strategy

The experience of community development work with migrants in Govanhill has highlighted a number of questions. The profile of the people who make up the migrant community is not static. While the longer-established Scottish and Asian communities are predominantly settled, the area has a more transient population than many other areas of Glasgow. This is a function of having a high proportion of cheap private-let housing (Govanhill is reputed to have the highest number of registered landlords in Glasgow). As a consequence, the turnover of tenants is high and the community is constantly changing. An important question therefore is how to balance a focus between building 'bonding' social capital, bringing together oppressed and marginalised people in groups and networks and supporting their collective needs, and building 'bridging' social capital, allowing different groups to share and exchange information, ideas and innovation and building consensus between the groups representing diverse interests. The ability to address both the bonding and bridging strands is central to a credible community development approach, and also the foundation on which 'linking' social capital is based, enabling appropriate services to be designed and policy to be established. The important, problematic challenge is to achieve the level of self-organisation and inter-community solidarity to do this, without deepening divisions.

This leads on to questions of the balance between advocacy and community organising. Crossroads' approach to community work has always been to focus on local neighbourhood work, to have a structural perspective and analysis of power and powerlessness, to build community organisations and to adopt resistance and direct action where necessary. The central ethos behind more recent work has been on integration – to facilitate people from different backgrounds in the community coming together through groups and by providing one-to-one support and advocacy to the most vulnerable people. So, while there is a primary need to tackle the most immediate and serious problems confronting people, especially new arrivals, and to create environments where mutuality and solidarity can be built, there also comes a point where this strategy can create dependency and become static, rather than moving to a position where critical issues are identified, around which collective action can be initiated and supported in the interests of the most vulnerable. The key may well be to try to identify common issues that have an impact on all communities, or to find opportunities to engage people from across the neighbourhood in shared interests or activities.

As well as seeking a balance between advocacy and organising, there are challenging questions about what is likely to be the most effective approach to community work. The origins of community work for Crossroads were strongly influenced by the issue-based organising model associated with Alinsky (1971) and written up by early Crossroads workers (Bryant and Bryant, 1982). This was coupled with a neighbourhood-based information, advice and advocacy service that played an important role in identifying the community issues on which organisation and action could be based. Even at that time there were difficulties in finding the right balance between the endless stream of callers to the information centres with financial, benefits, legal or housing problems, and the capacity to work to establish and support community organisations working on those same issues. Fast-forward to the present day, and many of the dilemmas remain. When Crossroads had the funds required to operate an advocacy service primarily for Roma it was necessary to introduce severe restrictions on the times at which the service would operate, not least to ensure that staff were not themselves exploited or unreasonably stressed. At the same time, the drop-in sessions, streetwork and research were under way, but it has proved difficult to draw on these activities to formulate a more community-wide response to any of the intractable issues in the area. It may be the case that there is little experience of collective organisation among Roma and other East European migrants, or that the provision of drop-in opportunities needs to be more firmly embedded before such action can be considered. Many migrants are also transient, which can mean difficulties in establishing and sustaining longer-term community groups and networks.

Conclusions about the impact of the work can be found in reports and evaluations conducted at various times. In a 2009 evaluation, the work of the SRC was found to have been effective in encouraging many more individuals and community groups to become involved in race equality work in Glasgow's neighbourhoods than ever before, with local race equality programmes being planned, resourced and delivered across Glasgow. These programmes are no longer solely focused on the asylum seeker and refugee population. They address the needs of local BME populations as a whole. The work is increasingly owned by local people – including the majority white population, the community projects they run and the local services that serve them. This is a significant development within race equality work, which has been historically driven by city-wide or national partners mainly from the BME voluntary sector, which had difficulty generating local impact. New refugee communities have a significant stake in this work because meaningful consultative structures exist through the SRC-supported Framework for Dialogue groups and refugee community organisations that allow refugee voices to be heard, while local communities are securing dedicated resources for this work. Most local networks employ their own support workers and have much greater influence over how various resources to promote cohesion and positive race relations are deployed.

Crossroads reports positive outcomes from its work, particularly for individuals who have been supported to navigate complex services due to reasons such as cultural difference, low self-esteem or mental health problems. People involved in the various groups greatly value the way problems are dealt with or new relationships are built. Quotes from group members illustrate the value they place on these connections and mutual support:

"I have been just everywhere, and they always send me somewhere else or don't have an interpreter and I don't understand. I am so glad I came here."

"What would I do, without you folks? I can have a chat here, relax from all of it. And children have a great play every time."

"I started attending this group just half a year ago. I had breast cancer two years ago and underwent heavy treatment. I felt depressed and didn't want to leave the house. Right now I am on a pill, which makes you to put on weight around your waist so my GP has recommended me this class … it is so much more than exercise; I wish I would have known about you earlier."

This chapter has sought to explore the connections between community work at a city-wide level with refugees and asylum-seekers and the community work done at neighbourhood level in a very diverse area with a large number of Roma migrants. The methods adopted by both are similar, involving what could be described as community social work providing support, information and advocacy to those in need of this, alongside community work actions to promote connection and understanding between different groups of origin, including the more settled groups. The work at both levels has had a significant impact in supporting the migrant communities as well as bridging between the different groups and the more settled residents.

Figure 9.1: International Roma Day, Glasgow (photo provided by Crossroads Youth and Community Association)

Notes

[1] Strathclyde Regional Council (1982) *Social strategy for the eighties*, Glasgow: SRC.
[2] Glasgow has, absolutely and relatively, the largest ethnic minority population of any Scottish city.
[3] www.bbc.co.uk/news/uk-scotland-glasgow-west-37169170.
[4] www.scdc.org.uk/media/resources/assets-alliance/Govanhill%20community%20assets%20and%20ownership%20small%20(2)%20(2).pdf.
[5] Human trafficking may be for the purposes of either sexual activity or forced labour, or even both. The UK has acknowledged the seriousness of this issue by passing the Modern Slavery Act 2015; Scotland, which has its own legislative framework, has also passed a parallel Act, the Human Trafficking and Exploitation (Scotland) Act 2015.
[6] See https://www.facebook.com/ekarikaedjal/.

References

Alinsky, S. (1971) *Rules for radicals*, New York: Random House.
Bryant, R. and Bryant, B. (1982) *Change and conflict*, Aberdeen: Aberdeen University Press.

TEN

Gypsy, Roma and Traveller women: how community work can both challenge and contribute to gender inequalities

Holly Notcutt

This case study provides an insight into the experiences of applied community development work with Gypsy, Roma and Traveller (GRT) communities at a specific site in the East of England from 2010–16. It summarises a range of observations, reflections and questions gathered throughout this prolonged period of practice, with a view to informing the work of others working with GRT people, regarded as the most disadvantaged minority communities in the UK.

Situated on the margins of a large urban settlement and nestled between motorways, an industrial estate and sizeable swathes of unsightly marshland, lies a 27-pitch local authority caravan site. Practically unnoticeable to passers-by in their cars, trucks and lorries, it is home to families and individuals belonging to GRT communities in the region of East Anglia.

In parts of this region there has been a variable scattering of community work over the last 15–20 years, focusing on communities living within areas categorised as having multiple deprivations. Limited employment opportunities, above-average health inequalities and low educational attainment have led to a range of neighbourhood-level initiatives, framed by community development principles, all with the general aim of working with local people to address their priorities. Community development work featured as a key underlying component in various urban regeneration-focused initiatives instigated by the UK government from the late 1990s, representing a more general drive to address issues of inequality and social injustice faced by people living in these areas of multiple deprivation.

During 2009, new Neighbourhood Management initiatives were developed in East Anglia, in one of which the author was employed as a community development worker. These initiatives were built around a partnership of local community leaders, statutory services and voluntary and community sector (VCS) representatives, centred on small local communities – often no bigger than one or two electoral wards[1] – and were embedded in community development principles. It was not unexpected that the newly established programme, driven by a mandate to coordinate service delivery to improve quality-of-life outcomes in the locality and, importantly, to ensure that delivery was informed by and, in turn, focused on people who needed support the most, would seek to engage with people from the GRT community.

I have used the collective of Gypsy, Roma and Traveller, or GRT for short, in an attempt to encapsulate the diversity of the Gypsy and Traveller communities of the UK, plus the wide range of Roma communities originating from Eastern Europe. This is clearly not intended to be an exhaustive description of these communities.[2] Rather, it is more an introductory gesture towards the wealth of comprehensive and historical accounts of GRT people in the UK, further exploration of which is encouraged. It is important to note that the three groups have very significant issues in common, but there are also equally significant differences between them in terms of culture, history and patterns of settlement.

For the last six years, GRT people have been protected as racial and ethnic groups within the UK, featuring as a distinctive grouping in the Equality Act 2010, the UK's primary anti-discrimination legislation. Despite appearing in accounts of British societal history for some 500 years (Okely, 1983), Gypsies and Travellers (although notably not Roma) were for the first time recognised and featured specifically in the 2011 UK National Census. This population was subsequently listed as 58,000 in number, or 0.1% of the total population of England and Wales, constituting the smallest ethnic group (of those provided with a distinctive box to tick in the census form). Later, in 2015, caravans were counted in England across a range of authorised and unofficial caravan sites (DCLG, 2015), with results suggesting the existence of 21,084 caravans, providing a little extra formal information on the communities.[3]

From my early days in community work, the singular terms 'Gypsies' or 'Travellers' were commonly used interchangeably to refer to GRT people. In many ways this continues today, although, as noted above, the differences within this grouping need continually to be acknowledged. From working in both the voluntary and the public sectors over a 10-year period, I have seen a growing use of the collective term, representing a small but positive progression in terms of recognition. GRT people collectively are now widely regarded by agencies within the social sector, such as local government, healthcare trusts, police forces and voluntary sector organisations, as a marginalised group, relatively small in number but vulnerable to low socioeconomic outcomes, particularly concerning health, employment and education (ONS, 2011) – for example, as having the highest proportion of people of any ethnic group with no formal qualifications at all (ONS, 2011). As a result of this people's being recognised as a minority, marginalised community, service providers are increasingly conscious of their obligations proactively to work to support GRT people.

During 2009 the community development workers from our Neighbourhood Management programme in East Anglia were approached by a local National Health Service (NHS) community nurse and a Traveller education officer from the local authority with a community project ambition. They were among the few practitioners engaged with people on the site, driven initially by GRT-specific work remits that had ultimately been reinforced by a compelling sense of responsibility to challenge the inequalities and discrimination they had witnessed while working within the communities.

These practitioners provided us with a brief history of the site, based on their own experience and a collection of stories and anecdotes derived from former colleagues, other officers and the people living there. Historically, many local authorities had catalogued sites within their Environmental Health departments (along with the management of noise nuisance, hygiene regulation and pest control), and in doing so had acted as contributors, whether knowingly or otherwise, in creating and maintaining a significant focus on the order and regulation of sites, but with little inclination to initiate any socially focused work beyond what was driven by statutory obligations.

While the community nurse and Traveller education officer had achieved many successes in supporting the local GRT community – most notably an increase in nursery and school attendance, and improved uptake of childhood immunisations and maternal health checks – they had registered difficulties in their ability to support people with wider needs and individual challenges. Additionally, the officers – both women – had managed to develop all their relationships on site with GRT women only (notably, dominant gendered roles were attached to their lines of work, focusing largely on maternal health, child immunisations, primary school attendance and attainment, all falling within the traditional sphere of 'women's work'). They shared with us stories and anecdotes that they had gathered from the GRT women, highlighting the challenges and discrimination they felt as individuals and as a community. This included how taxis would charge more to pick up from the site, how they were billed on a commercial rather than a domestic rate for waste collection services, how mobile hairdressers would suddenly become unavailable when the address of the site was given and how they could leave and arrive at the site safely with their children only by car, due to a total absence any infrastructure of pavements and pedestrian crossings in the surrounding industrial estate.

Hostility, negligence and discriminatory behaviours towards GRT people, in the UK and beyond, is nothing new. Regularly seen by settled communities as a racialised group existing on the periphery of modern society (Okely, 1983), they are routinely envisioned as outcasts not bound by wider societal norms. They are still maintained as the 'other' in contemporary British society (Taylor, 2011), and modern media portrayals fixate on an inaccurate depiction of outlandish behaviours and customs, such as those seen in the now infamous television programme *My Big Fat Gypsy Wedding*, while the press reinforce and perpetuate negativities by presenting anti-social narratives of lawlessness, evictions and invasions (Acton et al, 2014; Richardson, 2014). Challenging the commonly held preconceptions that GRT people 'do not pay taxes', that 'they thieve' and that 'they are unhygienic', the editor of the *Travellers' Times* has recently called for an end to what has been frequently referred to as 'the last acceptable racism', citing such prejudices manifested in the daily structural and societal discriminations experienced by GRT communities (Doherty, 2016).

Theories of the 'underclass' (Wacquant, 1996; Murray, 2001) have been helpful in further understanding the dominant negative perceptions of GRT people in Britain. The theories describe the advent of the underclass; people who are seen as outcasts and barely recognised as citizens. The underclasses are separate from wider society, both physically, living in ghetto-like communities (Wilson, 1991), and morally, due to a particular characteristic or trait that presents them as undeserving, parasitic and deviant. The emergence of this socially excluded population, often within or in close proximity to the urban core, has become known as 'advanced marginality' (Wacquant, 1996; Musterd, 2008). In the context of GRT communities, this concept has been helpful understanding the connection between the relatively prosperous and developed status of many UK towns and cities and the increased inequality generated through the suppression of lower working classes or minority ethnic groups such as GRT people. The separation and social isolation produced by the way these 'underclasses' are viewed has been identified as a key reason for their continued marginalisation (Massey and Denton, 1993), reflecting a process done *to* them rather than, as the myths outlined above suggest, created *by* them.

The GRT women on the site had also described the difficulties of not having a community area among their on-site facilities, which denied them a physical space to come together outside of their individual caravans and, in particular, prevented their children from having a space in which to play and socialise. Less overtly, they also referenced the limits on their own free time, due to being women, and provided complex and busied detailed accounts of the dawn-to-dusk daily routines within the home, while the men spent their time out at work.

The reproductive role, traditionally performed by women around the world, centres on the maintenance of the family. For these GRT women, this involved managing childcare, caring for elders, cooking for men and children and cleaning – cleaning to a meticulous standard in line with pollution and contamination taboos (Okely, 1983; Casey, 2014). These gendered traditions are of course not normalised just within GRT communities. Gender hierarchy, affirmed within wider social structures, while perhaps benefiting from considerable progress, still favours male superiority and the maintenance of female subordination (MacKinnon, 1989). It was, however, far more pronounced on the site, as every woman performed the same roles, with no deviation. In exploring gender inequality, the notion of 'reproduction' is central (Duffy, 2007): the child rearing, the cooking, the cleaning and the caring that allow for the maintenance of the labour force (perpetually men and older boys), and how work traditionally tied to women is devalued (and consequently unpaid) within the paid labour market, yet is critical to its existence. It appeared that the day-to-day lives of the women were impacted on by both latent and blatant discriminations toward GRT communities, but that these were further compounded by their position as women within the community itself.

By looking at multiple dimensions of social identity (race and class, plus gender), commonly known as 'intersectionality' (Crenshaw, 1991), we had an additional lens when developing community-based work on the site; in particular, we were able to take into account everyday experiences and social relationships. While there is generally a growing body of literature on the intersectionality of race, class and gender, the experiences of women from a low socioeconomic background, and who are also GRT, have only recently been formally and distinctly acknowledged, and are still notably absent in many published accounts (Casey, 2014). When I researched both gender and intersectionality with regard to GRT women I was surprised to find a limited focus on them, or, at best, references largely obscured by discourses centred on race, ethnicity and inequality between what were characterised as homogeneous communities – large groups of alike and indistinguishable people; for example, between the collective 'them' and the 'other', between GRT and 'settled' communities. GRT communities were referenced as 'one', without no regard paid to the variance, difference, uniqueness and inequalities that exist within the broad GRT classification. This, perhaps unwittingly, contributes to the veiling of intra-group discriminations and oppressions (Shachar, 2000). So, while protective and anti-discriminatory legislation exists for GRT communities, protections do not necessarily manifest for individuals within communities, and particularly in relation to those issues concerning women.

These initial observations captured our attention and drove our early work on site. In addition, the sparsity of published material on the overlapping nature of the identities and social characterisations of race, class and gender within GRT communities reinforced our initial concerns, and so became the focus of our community development work at one site in East Anglia in 2009.

First we met Coilin. He was both the general manager and the site's undisputed patriarch. Our health and education colleagues arranged for an informal introduction, gently recommending that by first initiating a relationship with Coilin the metaphorical gate would be opened to us, making any subsequent activity on site easier to instigate. Coilin was a natural frontman; polite and authoritative, tall, heavy set, with a thick Irish accent spoken at breakneck speed. Upon noting that we were linked to the council he presented a frank and unequivocal case regarding what he saw as the main priority for people on the site. We spent that initial 'meeting' (outdoors, leaning against the wall in a sunny spot at the entrance to the site) discussing an unfair refuse collection arrangement with the council. The site, for as long as he had been manager, was charged a commercial rate for weekly collections, rather than a domestic rate for the fortnightly service provided to every other household in the district. Disappointed to learn about this apparent inequality of service delivery received by people living at the site, we assured him that we would help to call the issue into question by facilitating a dialogue between the relevant council officers and associated service providers. Coilin was happy with this outcome of our impromptu meeting and subsequently, knowing that we were interested in exploring community project ideas, introduced us to Margaret, his wife. This was the first revelation of gendered dimensions within the community, although arguably not necessarily dissimilar to male-dominated households in non-GRT communities the world over.

Margaret was the site's matriarch, a status seemingly assumed by default through her role as Coilin's wife. Margaret and other prominent women in the social hierarchy had already been engaged in a dialogue with our colleagues regarding the idea of installing 'a community cabin'. Our aim to build relationships primarily with women on the site notwithstanding, we found that it was mainly the women who were interested in talking with us (incidentally, yet not deliberately, all of the practitioners were also women). We noticed that the men were either reluctant or just not particularly interested in discussing 'community things' and uniformly referred us to their wives. Conversations with the women developed gradually, circling around the detail of the on-going domestic duties that each of them undertook continuously throughout the day. This gendered reproductive role was expected to be entirely undertaken by women and girls, understood as 'the way things are' (Bourdieu, 1984) and normal, endorsed rather than tolerated. None of the women spoke negatively about these domestic duties. In fact, some became more animated in discussing their daily routines. Many GRT women display a sense of pride and identity in upholding and solely undertaking the reproductive role (Okely, 1983; Casey, 2014). This was difficult to react to. Being familiar with the rapidly growing wider societal progress towards the removal of fixed gendered roles, it seemed to me to be something of a time-warp that the women should accept this as their lot, and even less so that they were proud of it. Although we masked our opinions, our initial feelings towards this were blurred; an impulse to challenge this gendered inequality was countered by a observed responsibility not to impart our own views. This was problematic, and the first of several obstacles to developing our work. Our question to ourselves was whether to accept something that we understood to be discriminatory, leaving it unchallenged and unaddressed in order to preserve relations and to show respect to what the other person holds as a proud tradition and their substantive purpose in life. Was that right and, even if so, was it our place? Would that be an imposition? But would it be wrong to ignore something that we believed to be socially unjust? After much deliberation, we just kept on with the conversations so as to develop a mutual sense of familiarity and respect with the women.

The community cabin idea had originally stemmed from many of the women, who had a desire to develop a community space, and their priority for it to be for the children to go and do their homework and play together when the weather was bad, on the site and outside of the caravans and trailer homes. A series of informal conversations therefore continued on site, via all of the practitioners, during the following weeks. Despite the mixture of remits held by practitioners on the site, we quickly recognised the community development focus that we all had, and a collective view of the need to support a community to become stronger. Together, we used our work circles to raise the profile of the site and its community, and the lack of community facilities accessible to them. It was interesting that during this time some colleagues with a wider remit who had never visited the site, let alone those who had not even known that it existed, became increasingly interested and aware of their broader responsibility to the GRT community. Some colleagues did not get this far, and reacted with challenges based on the prejudices common in wider society. However, after months of careful promotion, negotiation and persuasion we finally harnessed the necessary resources to acquire a disused mobile classroom that was due for disposal from a nearby school.

The cabin was an instant hit. Once installed in a vacant lot on the site, it became the real entry point for developing community work. It provided the much-needed social and recreational space, but also supplied us with a physical focal point and a centre for conversations and informal meetings. With the agreement of the women on site, it also became the preferred place for the nurse to hold one-to-one appointments, and where the education officer could start to run sessions with the children.

Maintaining our focus on the women, conversations started to shift towards them, their ideas, desires and ambitions for themselves. We listened, and began asking questions about what they would most like to do with free time, if it were suddenly available via a gap in their daily domestic routines. And how could the cabin could be used to those ends? Without exception, the number one response was to have provision on site focused on hair and beauty. A hairdresser's. A beauty salon. A nail bar. All the women were interested – for many of them their physical appearance, the embodiment of an exaggerated femininity (which at the time was being projected in a disrespectful way through television programmes), seemed to be of the utmost importance.

Exploring this back at the office we were excited about having reached a point in the relationships where ideas and interests were being shared. There was suddenly scope to nurture new ideas, a potential new project coming from the women themselves, that they could plan, shape and deliver and that would benefit them directly. Leading a self-driven project would be an exercise within their power to break the routine and make changes to their lives on the domestic treadmill. It represented an inadvertent challenge to the gendered roles to which they were tied. And there was even a community cabin in which to do it all.

Within weeks we had made arrangements with the women about the sessions and what they would focus on. Finding a convenient time was tricky; not early mornings because of the children and the school run, not late mornings because of cleaning, not lunch times because of cooking and caring for elders, not mid-afternoon because of post-lunch cleaning and the school run, not late afternoon or evening because of cooking and the husbands and the children. After eventually identifying an hour in the early afternoon, we got in touch with contacts at the local college. Upon hearing the history of our collective work on the site they were immediately supportive of exploring how they might contribute to the initiative. This surprised me. I had been convinced that it was going to be a hard job to persuade them, following previous insights into the latent prejudices that had been displayed by some officers working in statutory services. It was reassuring to experience this positivity, suggesting a shift away from prejudices, 'othering' and perceptions of an underclass, which had not long ago been extremely commonplace.

The college staff created a proposal, which we discussed together with the women on site. Once a week, for a six-week trial period, they could deliver 'taster' versions of their entry-level hair and beauty courses, directly at the cabin. To ensure outcomes in line with their broader targets as an educational institution, they wove entry-level learning into the sessions, such as reading, writing, verbal communication, team working and so on, wrapped up in the practical sessions. Once agreed, we set a date and spread the word. The sessions were well attended. Weekly, the women and girls crammed into the cabin, emerging an hour later with newly buffed nails, styled hai, or a full face of make-up.

With the GRT women working in pairs, the activities promoted relationship building and challenged intra-group discrimination. The one Roma woman who was living on the site at that time had experienced hostility from some of the site's many Irish Travellers, with her children experiencing similar unfriendliness on the site's playground. However, over the weeks and through the intimacy of the activities (for example, holding someone's hand and painting their nails), we saw the tensions settle and positive fledgling relationships form. The college staff struck up such a rapport with them, that two of the women arranged to meet the staff at the college to talk about options for a formal course. The sessions also became an informal space for building relationships with other services. The effects of this included improved relationships with the local Police Community

Support Officer, who would pop in each week just to say 'hi'; new connections with health services and increased contraceptive take-up; increased sign-up to nursery and early years provision, and so on. Supported by the feedback from the women and other practitioners on site, we declared the sessions a success. We were proud to be able to report back to our managers on the wide array of positive benefits and knock-on effects that had occurred, purely through creatively utilising the women's interests in hair and beauty.

Focus on the physical appearance of women and girls, their (our) attractiveness, their body shape, their weight, their hair, their faces, is a shared and relatively unchallenged cultural norm. The manufactured beauty and body ideals projected through the media have not only defined this cultural norm but have dominated it and persisted. This is beyond GRT cultures, beyond just Britain or other Western countries, extending to the global level (Banyard, 2010). However, these ideals create objectification: possibly the most unfaltering and dominating force imposed upon women and girls today, viewing women and girls as objects rather than as human beings (Banyard, 2010). As with objects, inert and lifeless things to be looked at, judged, criticised, used, consumed and disposed of, the concept of objectification demonstrates how women and girls are viewed and ultimately devalued in society, a circumstance that is informed and compounded by the perpetual and extreme beauty ideal. We realised, amid our joy at the project's 'success', that this was our second problematic stumbling block. In our attempt to somehow tackle and confront the devalued and unequal gendered roles of the women at the site, we had inadvertently contributed to them.

The question we went on to ask was, was it worth it? In many ways, this could always be debated. Looking back, I still see that period of time and the success of the project as something that brought about both nuanced and tangible benefits to the women who participated; everything from improved friendships on the site, through to first-time reports to the police of domestic violence. From something that we eventually came to recognise as conceptually problematic, actually came many good things.

Seven years on, and community work is still a strong and productive feature on the site, testament to the need for long-term approaches, particularly in communities where marginalisation and inequality are still rife. The cabin is still there and has been at the centre of the community for the people who have come and gone from the site over the last few years, helping to establish friendships among children and support networks among women.

The current team visit weekly and facilitate sessions with the children and young people from the families currently living on the site – homework club, arts and crafts, storytelling. It has particularly resulted in outcomes for girls, who have grown in confidence and self-esteem, while still being proud members of their community. As a result of working with the children, who all flock to the cabin as soon as they hear the community worker's car on the gravel driveway, new, productive relationships have been formed with the mothers. This includes helping one woman to access money advice services, after she confided in one community worker about her mounting debt due to her low literacy level. This in turn led to her and others engaging with basic skills sessions and introductions to reading and writing, delivered in the community cabin. Additionally, in 2015 the original issue of refuse collection, introduced to us by Coilin and other residents on the site, was finally resolved. The commercial arrangement and associated charges imposed on the site were reviewed and reinstated under a domestic arrangement and rate. This took five years, from the initial meeting at the entrance to the site. The time it took to get to this point also signifies the long-game nature of much community work and the sustainable communities agenda. This also flies in the face of much formal UK government-sponsored community development that seems to suggest that communities, and particularly the most deprived and marginalised ones, can be 'developed' in a matter of a year or two, whereas in reality it may take many years to retrieve communities.

From my experience of working in the UK social sector, long-term community development approaches to working in GRT communities are few and far between, appearing too minor, too challenging or too difficult to fund. There is, thankfully, a growing research and practice focusing interest in GRT communities, informing decision makers and challenging widespread perceptions and attitudes. But, while these are to be welcomed, there must be more careful consideration given to the entanglement of traditions, norms, expectations and fundamental inequalities that exist within the community life of GRT people. Without this, we are at risk of regression just as much as we are in a position to make progress.

Notes

[1]   Covering typically a few thousand households at most.
[2]   See, for example, for a background picture of political and policy developments regarding these communities in the last few decades, www.peer-review-social-inclusion.eu/network-of-independent-experts/2011/promoting-the-social-inclusion-of-roma.

[3] A proportion of the Gypsy/Traveller groups and most of the Roma groups recently migrating to the UK are sedentary. Some live in caravans; others, however, live in private or state-provided fixed housing, so the caravan count is only part of the demographic picture for GRT communities. In terms of data about these groups, in 2010 the outgoing New Labour Government published a report on economic equalities that noted that the GRT group was the single minority grouping for which virtually no robust research then existed (Hills, 2010). Given that most caravans are occupied by more than four people, this already gives an idea of the difficulties of counting this population.

References

Acton, T., Cemlyn, S. and Ryder, A. (2014) *Hearing the voices of Gypsy, Roma and Traveller communities: Inclusive community development*, Bristol: Policy Press.

Banyard, K. (2010) *The equality illusion: The truth about women and men today*, London: Faber and Faber.

Bourdieu, P. (1984) *Distinction: A social critique of the judgement of taste*, London: Routledge.

Casey, R. (2014) '"Caravan wives" and "decent girls": Gypsy–Traveller women's perceptions of gender, culture and morality in the North of England', *Culture, Health and Sexuality*, vol 16, no 7, pp 806–19.

Crenshaw, K. (1991) 'Mapping the margins: intersectionality, identity politics, and violence against women of color', *Stanford Law Review*, vol 43, no 6, pp 1241–99.

DCLG (2015) *Housing statistical release, count of Traveller caravans, July*, London: Department for Communities and Local Government.

Doherty, M. (2016) 'It's time to end "the last acceptable racism" – against Gypsies and Travellers', *Guardian*, 15 January, https://www.theguardian.com/commentisfree/2016/jan/15/acceptable-racism-gypsies-travellers-prejudice.

Duffy, M. (2007) 'Doing the dirty work: gender, race, and reproductive labor in historical perspective', *Gender and Society*, vol 21, pp 313–36.

Hills, J. (chair) (2010) *An anatomy of economic inequality in the UK*, London: National Equality Panel.

MacKinnon, C. (1989) *Towards a feminist theory of the state*, Cambridge, MA: Harvard University Press.

Massey, D. and Denton, N. (1993) *American apartheid*, Cambridge, MA: Harvard University Press.

Murray, C. (2001) *Underclass +10; Charles Murray and the British underclass 1990–2000*, London: CIVITAS.

Musterd, S. (2008) 'Banlieues, the hyperghetto and advanced marginality: a symposium on Loic Wacquant's urban outcasts', *City*, vol 12, no 1, pp 107–14.

Okely, J. (1983) *The Traveller–Gypsies*, Cambridge: Cambridge University Press.

ONS (2011) *Census analysis: What does the 2011 Census tell us about the characteristics of Gypsy or Irish travellers in England and Wales?*, London: Office for National Statistics.

Richardson, J. (2014) 'Roma in the news: an examination of media and political discourse and what needs to change', *People, Place and Policy*, vol 8, no 1, pp 51–64.

Shachar, A. (2000) 'On citizenship and multicultural vulnerability', *Political Theory*, vol 28, no 1, pp 64–89.

Taylor, B. (2011) 'Britain's Gypsy Travellers: a people on the outside, *History Today*, vol 61, no 6, pp 17–19.

Wacquant, L. (1996) 'The rise of advanced marginality: notes on its nature and implications', *Acta Sociologica*, vol 39, pp 121–39.

Wilson, W. (1991) 'Studying inner city social dislocations: the challenge of public agenda research',1990 Presidential address, *American Sociological Review*, vol 56, pp 1–14.

ELEVEN

Romani activism and community development: are mediators the way forward?

Colin Clark

Introduction

> Our ambition goes beyond mediation. As long as Roma face human conditions far worse than the rest of the Europeans, we cannot be fully satisfied with the results of our work. We cannot be satisfied as long as Roma people live in ghettos, as long as children attend segregated schools and as long as there are groups who *de facto* cannot vote. *We cannot be satisfied as long as the injustice towards Roma people persists. The programme is only one important element of a complex change. The result needs to be reinforced further with other elements of democratic participation.* This means creating opportunities for the involvement of the Roma in decision-making processes. This means enabling Roma to assume responsibility for their own future.[1] (Thornjørn Jagland, Secretary General of the Council of Europe (emphasis added)

This chapter examines a particular example of 'democratic participation' within the diverse and heterogeneous Roma communities across Europe – the role of community and cultural mediators.[2] To what extent have various mediation training programmes helped or hindered Romani empowerment and emancipation across the member states of the EU? To address this question requires some critical thinking about an array of strategic and policy-orientated work; the on-going policy/educational activities around mentors can help to shed light on structural initiatives arising out of this significant developmental work (for example, within health promotion as well as in improving access to educational opportunities). In the last ten years there has been significant growth in European funding to promote Roma mediation via the training and employment of Romani mediators in more than

20 member states. Much funding has come from the Council of Europe and its ROMED programmes, which started operation in July 2011.[3] The main areas of attention for such efforts have been employment (Messing, 2014, pp 6–10), health (Open Society Foundations, 2011, pp 37–44) and education (Friedman, 2013, pp 11–12). Mediators, largely coming from a Roma background themselves, now numbering well over 1,000 people across the EU, are employed by public authorities to act as a 'bridge' between the wider Roma communities and state agencies and institutions, with a view to promoting 'culturally appropriate' engagement with public services. ROMED1 has moved into a second phase, ROMED2, and this is working in tandem with another initiative, the Council of Europe and European Commission joint project ROMACT.[4] The purpose of such projects is to increase *participation* in democratic governance processes by Roma from largely disenfranchised communities, as well as to encourage local-level political commitment to Roma inclusion from mainly *gadzhe* (non-Roma) elected officials and politicians.

This chapter asks the following key question: what have been the successes and challenges of these mediation schemes, to date, and what impact have they had on grassroots Romani activism across Eastern and Central Europe? It will be argued, based on the available evidence, that although mediation is having a positive impact in some communities, for certain individuals, it is not *in and of itself* an appropriate or suitable vehicle for wider grassroots campaigning and political activism, especially on issues of *structural* poverty, disadvantage and racist discrimination. Indeed, it could be argued that Roma mediation schemes are acting as something of a deflection or even a barrier to more demanding, structural campaigns for justice, equality and liberty, especially in translating national policies to local practices (Popkostadinova, 2011). To progress, the chapter first details some thoughts on mediation, specifically commenting on community and peer mediation, and then moves on to an examination of ROMED in its various guises, charting its successes and challenges.

Mediation in theory and practice

As a system and process, mediation is primarily evaluative and is viewed as a usually confidential means to resolve conflict in a structured and proactive manner (Georgakopoulos, 2017). A range of skills are often deployed to encourage parties to interact via measured communication and focused dialogue. Mediation happens in a range of environments, such as family centres, legal chambers, workplaces, diplomatic offices and commercial settings. The focus of mediation lies with the parties involved in the conflict and the role of the neutral mediator is to try to constructively find 'common ground' among the often competing interests, needs, rights and priorities of the individuals directly involved (Moore, 2014). The goal, essentially, is to facilitate an acceptable solution to the issue(s) causing concern, distress or conflict. In terms of possible outcomes, these often rely on the training and skills of the mediator involved – a skill set that is becoming increasingly validated via a range of courses and training programmes – and their ability to facilitate meaningful dialogue is regarded as critical to the success or failure of the mediation process (Winslade and Monk, 2000). Two specific forms of mediation are discussed here: community mediation and peer mediation.

Community mediation, as the name implies, tends to involve specific neighbourhoods of a town or city where trained individuals, usually themselves living in the area, act as informal mediators (Bradley and Smith, 2000). This is particularly relevant to the situation of those communities residing in Roma districts across Eastern and Central Europe as often there is reluctance to get involved in *gadzhe* courts, due to issues of trust, confidentiality and finance. Peer mediation is also relevant here, as with this form of mediation the individuals involved as mediators tend to share a similar ethnicity or nationality (or, indeed, age, class, gender, disability, sexuality and so on) to those individuals whom they are working with and for. As an example, such peer mediation practices are often found in schools and other educational establishments (for example, in attempts to combat and challenge bullying). Peer mediation has been shown to be effective in terms of tackling anti-social behaviour, promoting self-esteem and encouraging leadership skills (Zuure, 2014). Having introduced the general practice of mediation, we will now examine the systems and practices of Roma mediation, especially how this has been operationalised via an on-going programme of work, ROMED, initiated via the European Union and Council of Europe (Liégeois, 2013).

Roma mediation as community development

The formalisation and bringing together of scattered Roma mediation initiatives dates back to 2010, when the Strasbourg Declaration on Roma committed signatory states to the following article (No. 46) whereby they would:

> agree to set up a European Training Programme for Roma Mediators with the aim to streamline, codify and consolidate the existing training programmes for and about Mediators for Roma, through the most effective use of existing Council of Europe resources, standards, methodology, networks and infrastructure, notably the European Youth Centres in Strasbourg and Budapest, in close co-operation with national and local authorities. (Liégeois, 2013, p 43)

This formal commitment led to the ROMED1 programme being implemented, which started in 2011 with the specific aim of creating a training network of Roma mediators across Europe. The underlying rationale for the Council of Europe and European Union embracing mediation as a way forward for Roma social inclusion was a recognition that such practices can, when working effectively, ease communication and relationships between public institutions, such as local authorities, hospitals and schools, and the communities they serve, such as Roma minorities. This commitment on the part of the Committee of Ministers of the Council of Europe to mediation as a means of securing Roma human rights, was further strengthened in 2012 by the adoption of Recommendation CM/REC (2012)9 (the Strasbourg Declaration on Roma; Council of Europe, 2012). This Recommendation noted the 'important benefits' to be gained from the training and employment of Roma mediators, especially in terms of allowing for:

> improved school attendance and access to quality education, improved access to healthcare and other public services, along with better communication between members of Roma communities and public institutions. (Council of Europe, 2012, np)

The 2012 Recommendation captured the essence of what the overall aims of ROMED1 were: to assist better communication and cooperation and articulation of needs across a number of related social policy areas between Roma communities and member state public officials and institutions. Similarly, there was explicit mention in the objectives of adopting a 'rights-based' approach to 'intercultural' and cooperative mediation work as well as providing resources to allow activities to be transparent and empowering and emphasising the accountability of public authorities and bodies (Liégeois, 2013). In adopting and underlining the need for an explicitly rights-based approach to processes of mediation, the Council of Europe was issuing a challenge of sorts to hesitant or evasive public bodies that were regarded as asserting and employing rather paternalistic and condescending attitudes and policies towards marginalised and disadvantaged Roma communities. In stressing a rights-based agenda via an intercultural approach, the Council of Europe has, from the programme's inception, sought to challenge the denial of fundamental human rights and to move away from systems that seemed to view Roma communities as 'deviant' and untrustworthy, as well as occupying a socioeconomic position that deemed them to be 'dependent' on the state or charities in the long term (O'Nions, 2016). From the outset, the explicit aim of ROMED1 was to get to a position whereby the training of Roma mediators would allow for the direct and sustainable employment of empowered Roma people to assist in facilitating dialogue between public bodies and local Roma communities to address issues of access to, take-up and delivery of, initially, healthcare, employment and education services.[5]

After ROMED1, which ran from 2011 to 2013, came ROMED2, which started in April 2013 and was completed in February 2017. The overall stated goal of this second ROMED programme, which is formally entitled Democratic Governance and Roma Community Participation through Mediation, is to increase the participation of members of Roma communities in decisions that have an impact on their lives and livelihoods at the local level. To date, 11 different countries have been involved in ROMED2: Bosnia/Herzegovina, Bulgaria, Germany, Greece, Hungary, Italy, Portugal, Romania, the Slovak Republic, the former Yugoslav Republic of Macedonia (FYRoM) and Ukraine. To this end, ROMED2 expands on mediation as a personalised system and process and looks towards broader, collective participation – that is, decision-making processes – at the local community level. It is more about the active participation of Roma citizens, as well as about how local bodies react and respond to demands for greater democratic governance and participation in local affairs. Such an ambition could be realised only through the creation of Community Action Groups (CAGs), whereby Roma communities were encouraged to be self-organised and to channel their articulation of the collective interests and priorities of the local community (Council of Europe, 2013).[6]

The overall approach of ROMED2 is also an interesting development as compared to ROMED1, in the sense that the language used is quite explicit in its recognition of structural power imbalances and the inequities of European forms of neoliberalism – for example, the documentation talks of 'unequal and unfair distribution of community resources' (Council of Europe, 2013). Such language is revealing and marks a departure from usually quite conservative commentary when it comes to such EU matters. Further, ROMED2 acknowledges that some previous EU initiatives have lacked appropriate and representative consultation with Roma communities, even where such mechanisms do formally exist. It could be argued that cultures of tokenism, paternalism, distrust and superficial discussion have hindered rather than supported Roma empowerment and emancipation. Indeed, this is nothing new: the involvement of only a few Roma people invited to *gadzhe*-dominated meetings to 'represent Roma' and then being ignored or silenced is something that has been written about elsewhere (Craig, 2016). As a way forward, ROMED2 concedes that more is to be done in terms of building trust and promoting 'active citizenship' that positions Roma community needs in the foreground: as the document suggests, this means 'moving from dependency and paternalism to empowerment and recognition' (Council of Europe, 2012, np). However, are good governance and participatory democracy the answer? Do they help to address a fundamental issue that many Roma activists are increasingly raising, which could best be summarised via the powerful slogan 'Nothing about us without us!'[7] This issue will be assessed in the next section, which examines the relative successes and failures of the two ROMED programmes and in what way lessons can be learned to empower Roma via community development and anti-racist activism.

Roma mediation – success or failure?

Although the Council of Europe has noted various successes during the period 2010–16 via ROMED1 and ROMED2,[8] such as (1) the production of various reference and training documents, (2) influence on member state policies and (3) impact on the training/practice of mediators, there have been several notable criticisms of the claimed 'success' of such activities. It is worth considering each 'success' in turn and then examining a critique of these claims by outside agencies and other bodies, such as independent evaluators, Roma activists and academics. First, with regard to reference documents, this includes the production and distribution of a training curriculum for mediators as well as a code of ethics to establish 'core principles' to enhance service quality. As noted earlier, the adoption of Recommendation CM/Rec (2012)9 (Council of Europe, 2012) is also highlighted as being of significance due to its recognition that mediation without a wider climate of human rights and social inclusion was ineffective. In terms of the second noted success, influence on member states, the Council of Europe contends that the incorporation of mediation as an interventionist tool via member state National Strategies for Roma Integration (NSfRI) is a positive step and one that will secure greater involvement of Roma in decision-making processes about their lives.[9] Likewise, it was noted that mediation systems were being introduced in a range of countries both within and outside of the EU, including, for example, Ukraine, Romania, Bulgaria and Kosovo. Finally, with regard to the third claimed success, that mediators themselves are benefiting from their involvement in mediation work and that they are having an impact on the ground, the Council of Europe notes the numbers involved in the mediation training events and their professional certification: over 1,500 mediators in more than 25 countries, with the majority of these coming from Roma backgrounds (Council of Europe, 2012). Further, the Council of Europe highlights the 'perception and awareness' of mediators in terms of their roles and functions, and the fact this has gained some ground even among reluctant public bodies that were increasingly witnessing the positive work they were engaging in, bridging the divide between Roma communities and health services, schools and local authorities. Finally, with the relative success of the training programmes, a new generation of Roma mediators were staying on and being trained as trainers themselves, often delivering sessions in various dialects of Romanes, the Romani language.

However, as noted above, there have been several criticisms of the ROMED1 and ROMED2 mediator programmes and these are worth exploring in order to generate further discussion and to assist in future planning, should a ROMED3 be announced at some point by the EU and the Council of Europe. As an example of some of the criticisms, in an article examining instances of 'best practice' in Roma mediation, the Roma sociologist Hristo Kyuchukov argues that there are many challenges for Roma individuals who find themselves at the sharp end of such mediation work. It is worth quoting him in full and then assessing this valuable contribution:

> Mediation has often led to significant improvements, but its effectiveness is frequently challenged by issues such as the low status of mediators and precarious employment conditions, dependency (on the head of the institution, political influence or community leaders) or the assignment of additional minor tasks, which are sometimes not included in the job profile. *In addition, mediators might be used as an excuse to avoid direct contact with the community, or they*

are expected to shoulder full responsibility for solving problems.
Their work can be day-to-day, reactive, with little or no
planning, inconsistent evaluation and lack of support in
performing their job. Such factors mean that success is
strongly dependent on the mediator's personal qualities
and on the personal attitudes of the staff of the institutions
the mediator works with. (Kyuchukov, 2012, pp 375–6;
emphasis added)

What is valuable about Kyuchukov's intervention is his emphasis on
both the emotional labour and personal characteristics required to
be able to work effectively as a Roma mediator. The challenging
employment environments that workers face mean that much depends
on the nature of the relationships formed – almost always political and
contested – with the public bodies they are working *with* and the Roma
communities they are working *for*. Additional tasks that go beyond
mere contractual 'job descriptions' are noted, as well as an important
point about Roma mediators being used, in a sense, as 'buffer zones'
between often intransigent public authorities and Roma communities
who may resent such 'forced' interventions on their behalf. Indeed,
many of Kyuchukov's concerns are also noted by a team from the
Open Society Foundation (OSF) that undertook work to evaluate the
'successes and challenges' of the work of Roma health mediators (Open
Society Foundations, 2011). In this research, six different countries –
Bulgaria, Macedonia, Romania, Serbia, Slovakia and Ukraine – were
assessed with regard to the impact of mediation work in healthcare
settings. Although progress was evident in terms of general health
education awareness, accessing necessary insurance and identification
documentation, increased vaccination rates and healthcare provider
knowledge, it was also highlighted that many challenges still prevailed.
For example, the OSF team noted that mediators were generally
low paid, located in insecure working environments and had limited
opportunities for professional development and promotion. A lack
of support and supervision was also highlighted, as well as general
isolation from other parts of the wider healthcare system, this reflecting
Kyuchukov's point about Roma mediators being, in a sense, caught
between 'two worlds' and taking on too much responsibility to try to
tackle every problem. More recently, the World Health Organization
(WHO), in a report also looking at Roma health mediation work, but
this time in Romania, noted that:

Among the challenges encountered during programme implementation have been insufficient initial training, modest remuneration of the mediators, difficult working conditions and changes brought about by the decentralization. *The programme has often been criticized for shortcomings in the supervision of health mediators (use of formal and quantitative templates for activity reporting, no empirical verification of the reports and lack of feedback) and the insufficient use of data collected by mediators in the communities.* Lack of transparency in programme funding and limited opportunities for continuous training of mediators have also attracted criticism. (WHO, 2013, p viii; emphasis added)

Looking deeper into these issues, with a comparative perspective in mind, it is evident that the experience in Romania noted by the WHO team is replicated across other parts of Europe. The implementation of ROMED programmes has invariably been accompanied by substantive issues regarding a lack of training, poor wages and working conditions and the willingness of *gadzhe* medical staff to work in collaboration with Roma mediators. The demanding nature of the mediation role in public institutions requires a set of technical and communication skills that cannot possibly be covered in three-day introductory training sessions. Detailed policy, legislative and topic knowledge is often required and much of this is lacking in the documentation. There is a noted lack of concern with personal and professional development issues as well as a lack of incentives and prospects for career advancement. As an example from the WHO (2013, p 16) study, a Roma health mediator in Romania could expect to earn just €133 per month, and work-related expenses were generally paid for by the workers themselves. This financial barrier, as well as the use of temporary, fixed-term contracts, has obvious consequences for the recruitment and retention of mediators. A further major challenge for mediation across Eastern and Central European territories has been the creeping decentralisation of health and education systems. Such processes have led to reported issues with authorities employing mediators, due to budget constraints, as well as problems with fixed-term contracts, personnel changes and discrimination of treatment (Arora et al, 2016). In addition, there have also been criticisms of both monitoring and evaluation processes regarding the work of Roma mediators – this relates back to a point made earlier about insufficient monitoring – as well as concerns regarding the limited use by public bodies of the actual data and reports gathered by mediators.

Discussion and conclusion

In reviewing the Roma mediator programmes it is evident that much of the claimed success is contested and can be subjected to critical scrutiny. What success has been achieved has come about via a personal commitment on the part of local mediators and their professional relationships with individuals working for local authorities and other public bodies such as healthcare providers and schools. Further, the interest and engagement of wider Roma communities in processes of mediation and collective governance and participation is crucial and relies on clear and visible advantages and benefits from such involvement via improved social policy services across a number of areas. Arguably, the shift from ROMED1 to ROMED2 and the use of CAGs is a visible sign of a trans-European Roma community development process in action (Acton et al, 2014).

Driving change is never easy, but some immediate lessons are apparent. For example, determined, transparent efforts on the part of local authorities and service providers fully to involve themselves in matters too often regarded as being just 'Roma issues' is urgently required. There needs to be a fundamental change of viewpoint and paradigm, whereby *gadzhe* educationalists or health professionals no longer regard themselves as 'experts' on 'Roma issues' – instead, Roma people themselves are 'experts by experience'. This also applies to non-Roma mediators who lay claim to 'knowing what the community needs' (Lane et al, 2014). For this to happen requires heads of services and their equivalents to make a personal and professional commitment to this vision and to bring about energetic change.

Additionally, this chapter has noted that meaningful dialogue and exchanges can occur between civil society, mediators and local authorities only once trust has developed. Partnership working, in an effective and sustainable sense, takes time to develop and requires action plans that are bought into by all involved, including younger people who are emerging as future activists and engaging via the ROMED2 CAGs.[10]

A further aspect that the chapter has explored is the acknowledgement that such community development via Roma mediators is hard work and has to be viewed as a long-term strategy. Empowerment is not something that magically occurs after a three-day training session in Strasbourg or Brussels. To be sure, it is a complex issue, and the more so when working in isolated rural villages where endemic, structural poverty and racialised discrimination are the harsh reality. With CAGs, ROMED2 is seen to be working best when the groups are mixed and have, as a regular membership, Roma community members as well as local authority officials from across the social policy areas, such as education, health and housing. To help drive and focus this developmental work the mediator is expected by the Council of Europe to play a leading role but, as noted, this is hard to ask when contracts are temporary, wages are low and career-development opportunities are negligible. Success stories are also seen as worthwhile to share, via media, TV and radio programmes, especially where best practice may translate across national borders from one CAG to another.[11] In addition to the Roma mediators requiring training, it also needs to be acknowledged that the capacity of local officials working in key social policy areas needs to be improved via meaningful and realistic cultural awareness sessions and training in how to engage with Roma issues and local communities in order to challenge (often racialised) stereotypes.

Finally, as indicated earlier, there are also much broader, structural forces in play that impact on the work of the ROMED programmes and these need to be acknowledged. With challenging socioeconomic conditions in many of the Eastern, Central and Southern European countries involved in Roma mediation, it is to be expected that limited financial input will lead to limited policy and practice output. Government and local authority funding cannot be assumed as an on-going reality and other avenues have urgently to be explored, including other EU funding schemes and donations from international non-governmental organisations and charitable bodies (which of course bring their own risks and rewards).

In closing, it is worth remembering that in announcing the Roma mediators programme back in 2010, Thornjørn Jagland suggested that 'our ambition goes beyond mediation'. Has this ambition been realised and will these programmes of work go some way to unsettling years of *antiziganism* and 'Romaphobia' (McGarry, 2017)? This chapter has examined Roma mediation in the context of the EU and Council of Europe ROMED programmes and wider concerns with community development and capacity building. Although it was seen as a bold move back in 2010 and 2011, progress has been stilted and subject to criticism. Final evaluations of the ROMED2 project, which completed its cycle in February 2017, are awaited and, looking to the future, it remains to be seen whether a ROMED3 Roma mediation programme will be desired or funded. There are several positives to be acknowledged from the Roma mediators' work – the production of various reference and training documents, the influence on member state policies and an impact on the training/practice of mediators – but even these 'gains' are illustrative of a *gadzhe* 'social inclusion' model that still views Roma communities as largely dependent and lacking in both agency and ability to articulate need and represent collective, democratic thinking and governance. This is a redundant, neocolonial model in the 21st century and one that needs to be stripped of power, control and influence.

Notes

[1] See Council of Europe ROMED website, http://coe-romed.org/romed1/testimonies .

[2] Within this chapter the term 'Roma' is recognised as a contested and politicised 'umbrella' term and one that in EU documentation tends to include groups such as Manouches, Ashkali, Sinti, Travellers, Gypsies and Boyash and so on. For more on definitions, especially from a socio-legal point of view, see Farget (2012).

[3] For further details about the background to ROMED, see: http://romed.coe-romact.org/content/roma-mediators .

[4] For reasons of space, a discussion of ROMACT is not possible here, but for more information see: http://coe-romact.org/.

[5] As an example, a guide for Roma mediators working in schools was published and circulated in 2009 by the Council of Europe: www.coe.int/t/dg4/education/roma/Source/Guide_EN.PDF .

[6] An impressive example of work conducted under ROMED2 is from Portugal, where Roma citizens came together as CAGs, forming relationships with local authorities and presenting their priorities in a participative manner. The film *Experiencing ROMED2* beautifully captures processes of change and personal as well as collective empowerment: https://www.youtube.com/watch?v=jyoJH_mu-ZM.

[7] See the 2015 special issue of the *Roma Rights* journal, published by the European Roma Rights Centre (ERRC), based in Budapest, www.errc.org/cms/upload/file/roma-rights-2-2015-nothing-about-us-without-us.pdf .

[8] Further information about the on-going ROMED2 programme (2013–17) can be found at http://coe-romed.org/romed2/about .

[9] For further information about the European Commission-led National Strategies for Roma Integration see: http://ec.europa.eu/justice/discrimination/roma/index_en.htm .

[10] As an example, see the very encouraging final report of the 2014 OSCE conference on 'Activism, Participation and Security among Roma and Sinti Youth', Belgrade, 8–9 December 2014, www.osce.org/odihr/187861?download=true .

[11] Once such 'success story' is from the municipality of Ilida, Greece. See: http://coe-romed.org/content/romed2-pioneer-integration-roma-according-local-greek-newspaper .

References

Acton, T., Rostas, I. and Ryder, A. (2014) 'The Roma in Europe: the debate over the possibilities for empowerment to seek social justice', in A. Ryder, S. Cemlyn and T. Acton (eds), *Hearing the voices of Gypsy, Roma and Traveller communities: Inclusive community development*, Bristol: Policy Press.

Arora, V.S., Kühlbrandt, C. and McKee, M. (2016) 'An examination of unmet health needs as perceived by Roma in Central and Eastern Europe', *European Journal of Public Health*, vol 26, no 5, pp 737–42, doi: https://doi.org/10.1093/eurpub/ckw004.

Bradley, S. and Smith, M. (2000) 'Community mediation: reflections on a quarter century of practice', *Mediation Quarterly*, vol 17, no 4, pp 315–20.

Council of Europe (2012) *Recommendation CM/Rec(2012)9 of the Committee of Ministers to member States on mediation as an effective tool for promoting respect for human rights and social inclusion of Roma*, Strasbourg: European Union and the Council of Europe, https://search.coe.int/cm/Pages/result_details.aspx?ObjectID=09000016805c9f3e, accessed 26 January 2017.

Council of Europe (2013) *Democratic governance and community participation through mediation*, Strasbourg: European Union and the Council of Europe, http://coe-romact.org/sites/default/files/leaflets/ROMED2%20-%20ENGLISH.pdf , accessed 26 January 2017.

Craig, H. (2016) 'Roma integration in Glasgow: real or fake', an interview with Eva Kourova, *The Govanhill Voice*, 15 February, https://govanhillvoice.wordpress.com/2016/02/15/roma-integration-in-glasgow-reality-or-a-fake/, accessed 26 January 2017.

Farget, D. (2012) 'Defining Roma identity in the European Court of Human Rights', *International Journal on Minority and Group Rights*, vol 19, pp 291–316.

Friedman, E. (2013) *Education in Member State Submissions Under the EU Framework For National Roma Integration Strategies*, ECMI Working Paper, no 73, December 2013, www.ecmi.de/uploads/tx_lfpubdb/WP_73.pdf, accessed 13 December 2014.

Georgakopoulos, A. (2017) *The mediation handbook: Research, theory and practice*, London: Routledge.

Kyuchukov, H. (2012) 'Roma mediators in Europe: a new Council of Europe programme', *Intercultural Education*, vol 23, no 4, pp 375–78.

Lane, P., Spencer, S. and Jones, A. (2014) *Gypsy, Traveller and Roma: Experts by experience reviewing UK progress on the European Union Framework for national Roma integration strategies*, York: Joseph Rowntree Foundation.

Liégeois, J.-P. (2013) *Developments in mediation: Current challenges and the role of ROMED*, Strasbourg: Council of Europe Publishing.

McGarry, A. (2017) *Romaphobia: The last acceptable form of racism.* London: Zed Books.

Messing, V. (2014) *Patterns of Roma employment in Europe*, NEUJOBS Policy Briefing, no D19.4, www.neujobs.eu/sites/default/files/publication/2014/04/D19.4_policybrief_review%20%281%29.pdf, accessed 13 December 2014.

Moore, C.W. (2014) *The mediation process: Practical strategies for resolving conflict*, London: John Wiley and Sons.

O'Nions, H. (2016) *Minority rights protection in international law: The Roma of Europe*, London: Routledge.

Open Society Foundations (2011) *Roma health mediators: Successes and challenges*, New York: Open Society Foundations, www.opensocietyfoundations.org/sites/default/files/roma-health-mediators-20111022.pdf, 13 December 2014.

Popkostadinova, N. (2011) 'Little to celebrate halfway through Europe's 'Roma decade'', *Balkan Insight*, 8 July, www.balkaninsight.com/en/article/little-to-celebrate-halfway-through-europe-s-roma-decade, accessed 14 December 2014.

WHO (World Health Organization) (2013) *Roma health mediation in Romania*, Denmark: WHO, www.euro.who.int/__data/assets/pdf_file/0016/235141/e96931.pdf, accessed 26 January 2017.

Winslade, J. and Monk, G.D. (2000) *Narrative mediation: A new approach to conflict resolution*, London: John Wiley and Sons.

Zuure, D.N. (2014) 'Peer mediation as a mechanism for resolution of inter-personal conflicts among students', *Journal of Education and Practice*, vol 5, no 39, pp 35–9.

Section Four
Global experience

Introduction

Gary Craig

This section contains six accounts drawn from different corners of the world – Romania, the US, Canada, Australia and Hong Kong (with a seventh, New Zealand, appearing in Section Five) – of community development with BME groups: these include such disparate groups as young Roma, First Nations peoples, those seeking asylum and migrant workers. The contexts for this work include empowering work, building leadership, using arts and culture as a means of building confidence, addressing racism and discrimination and promoting integration. This selection of accounts is not, of course, presented as being representative of all such work across the world: the intention of including this section was merely to demonstrate that the challenges facing community development workers addressing issues of racism across the world were similar, despite the differences in local history, culture, social, economic and political context and the varying forms of approach used. These accounts are a selection from a wider range of those offered following an international call for contributions made by the editor as the book was gestating. The selection here was made on the basis that the contributions provided a good range of accounts in different policy contexts and from significantly differing parts of the world but offered the possibility of contrasting and complementary experience vis-à-vis the accounts from the UK. The only more unique contributions here in terms of context are those that deal with the experience of working with First Nations people in Australia and New Zealand/Aotearoa.

In Chapter Twelve Cocris reports on work with Hungarian youth in Romania, a country emerging from a political and welfare regime that was highly structured, autocratic and hierarchical, contrasting almost entirely with the kinds of values reflected in community development work. Here the focus is on a white ethnic minority dominated by a white majority. The Hungarian minority, a product of the country's turbulent history and changing borders, has long been regarded with suspicion and hostility by native Romanians. The existence of a YouthBank, a grant-giving mechanism that itself was autonomous, provided both community groups and groups of young people with the autonomy to develop intercultural projects in an atmosphere of acceptance rather than 'invitation' where the minority felt beholden to the majority. This obviously raises the issue of community workers using money as a lever for change – an issue that might provoke differing views – but it is clear in this case that the impacts were largely benign; in any case, this might be seen in the context that community workers bring, directly and indirectly (as with the community cabin described by Notcutt in Chapter Ten), all kinds of resources to their work for the benefit of groups with which they work, of which money might simply be the most concrete and obvious.

Chapter Thirteen, the first of the two contributions from Australia, describes work with an Aboriginal community group using an approach described as structural community development (based on an analysis developed by one of the authors), a 'bottom-up, citizen-led and -owned approach that seeks to challenge racism at its source in systems, laws and policies based on white privilege' – the same unremarked privilege described earlier in the book by Bowler (Chapter Two). Because the Benarrawa group owned this approach, the authors argue that it provides an excellent example of how grounded practice by community groups can inform the theorising of community development. The work of the group involved a range of activities, including workshops, cultural events, commemorative gatherings and social activities, all designed to affirm the ownership of land by Aboriginal groups and strengthen their determination to assert that ownership against the depredations of the Australian state.

The second Australian contribution, Chapter Fourteen, recounts the work of the Australian Refugee Council to provide support for the many asylum-seeking refugees arriving at the shores of Australia, a story that has echoes in many other countries, all them now governed by states explicitly hostile to refugees that are attempting to erect hostile and punitive ideological, material and financial barriers to those seeking refuge. The chapter outlines the strategic shift of the organisation towards a community development strategy that, while constrained to some degree by its charter, allowed a much more group-based practice to emerge from its casework. The way in which community development emerged depended on local conditions in the various offices, but basing work on the notion of connectedness among and between asylum seekers helped to establish a sense of community that was fundamental to the work and, most of all, intelligible to asylum seekers themselves.

Beckford, a black community worker in highly multiracial Toronto operating across a range of diverse communities that, as he notes, all have their own needs and priorities, reflects in Chapter Fifteen on the question of whiteness and white privilege, again from the perspective of one who has achieved a substantial leadership position, acknowledged most of all by his co-ethnics (broadly people of Black African and Afro-Caribbean origins), but less so by people of Asian origin and, seemingly, hardly if at all by his white peers. One of the major indicators of racism is the collection of stereotypes used to demean and undermine minorities (see frontispiece to this volume). Meeting with white peers to discuss a range of strategic policy issues, Beckford might just as well sometimes have been the caretaker of the building as far as they were concerned, so certain were they that someone of his ethnic origin could not possibly be in a leadership position. Beckford also offers other significant insights for working in multiracial communities, notably that such communities, being heterogeneous, have within them a range of differing and sometimes contradictory sets of values, norms and practices: being a community worker requires knowing when to challenge patriarchal practices, for example, echoing Notcutt's observations in Chapter Ten – a balancing act indeed.

In Chapter Five, Sondhi described how community development approaches to arts and culture helped to build the capacity of disparate minority groups in the English West Midlands. In Chapter Sixteen Gutierrez and her colleagues return to this theme in an American context, outlining a series of initiatives, in urban settings with a variety of minorities and over a considerable period of time, through which various aspects of arts and cultural work – including photography, dance and community publishing – were used within an asset-based community development process to help give voice to differing minority interests.

Finally, in Chapter Seventeen Hung and Fung remind us again that even within apparently homogeneous minorities there will be differences – of culture, language, history, hopes and expectations – of which the community worker must take account. Their account examines the difficulties of promoting integration of Chinese minorities (migrant workers from mainland China – the People's Republic of

China or PRC) within a Chinese majority – long-standing residents within some Hong Kong neighbourhoods. It is well-understood that this movement of people from the PRC is part of a deliberate strategy to China-ise Hong Kong in the face of a strengthening call for democratic rights within Hong Kong and a continuing large degree of separation from the PRC (the tensions between the PRC and Hong Kong's democratic movement are emerging more into public view as this book is being completed). This underlying fact brings other tensions with it, but the process of integration is also impeded by some very central cultural and linguistic differences. Community workers here were also engaged in what Beckford (Chapter Fifteen) called 'the balancing act': in some areas (for example, discussion about families), tensions were minimised, but some of the attitudes and values brought by PRC migrants – for example towards work – were relatively progressive and thus the cause of some hostility in Hong Kong communities. Strategically, community workers tended to work on areas where commonalities could be observed, perhaps driven by an understanding that they were moving with the tide of convergence that was slowly blurring cultural distinctions. However, they still needed to be culturally sensitive to both groups, as a process of integration, if properly understood as a mutual undertaking rather than one of cultural imperialism, requires shifts by both parties.

TWELVE

Youth participation among ethnic minorities in Romania

Louisa Cocris

Introduction

YouthBank is an international, youth-led initiative to engage in community development with young people, aimed at encouraging their empowerment and through grant making. There are YouthBanks operating in over 24 countries worldwide, including Scotland and Romania. I was particularly well placed to conduct a study on YouthBanks in these two European locations, having a very good knowledge of both countries as well as recent experience on a placement with YouthBank Scotland. Part of the remit of the placement was, by drawing on my previous in-depth knowledge of the Romanian language and country, to develop links between the two YouthBanks at national level. Currently in Romania there is no accredited qualification at degree level for youth or community workers, and the term 'youth work' has no equivalent in the Romanian language (Mitulescu, 2014). The Romanian Youth Council, the CTR, is a non-governmental organisation established to act for the 'promotion and protection of youth rights' in Romania (CTR, 2016). It also seeks to encourage training opportunities in non-formal education. This commitment at a non-governmental level is also evident in recent EU policy: 'Non-formal education is important to promote social and democratic participation of young people' (EC, 2015). Within this context, I was curious to explore and illuminate the differences and similarities of YouthBank across these two sites, in a project that encourages the 'transformative participation' of young people and the communities in which they live. First suggested by White (1996) and then further by Tisdall (2013), the concept of 'transformative participation', in terms of both personal and societal possibilities, was of particular interest to me.

I had experienced 'transformative participation' at first hand as an outcome through engagement with a YouthBank project in Scotland

and was curious to explore the potential in contrasting contexts that would be provided by my chosen research sites. I have spent, and continue to spend, a considerable amount of time in Romania since the regime change in 1989 and have personally experienced the constraints and controls imposed on young people in particular in this society over the past two decades. I was, therefore, especially interested to have the opportunity to explore to what extent things had changed for the generation that has followed that which I first knew in Romania. I felt that I could draw on my own experience of Romania and those of the diverse contacts I have there to enable me to carry out an interesting and informative comparative study. The extraordinary events of 1989 and their subsequent impact on Romanians, had a profound effect on me as a young graduate and first-hand witness. The jubilant enthusiasm and optimism of that time was infectious and exciting; however, it was quickly tempered by a realisation that real change would be a slow and painful process and that democratic participation and social justice were still a long way off.

Although there has been a study on one YouthBank in Scotland (McCulloch, 2007), no comparative study has been carried out on YouthBanks in Scotland and Romania. In the UK there is a long tradition of youth work, starting from the idea of providing opportunities for the betterment of the lives of young people living in deprived conditions (Tett, 2010). Early manifestations of youth work sought to encourage and enable recreation, education and religion (Tett, 2010). In the 19th century, forms of youth work came out of national and international organisations such as the Scouts movement for boys and, subsequently, the Guides movement, founded to provide a similar experience for girls. Additionally, youth work took place in churches and local clubs. However, despite its existence in such varied settings, youth work in Scotland has been underpinned by several core features that distinguish it from other forms of education and approaches to working with young people. Youth work has always relied on the voluntary participation of young people and this immediately creates and defines a very unique approach (Jeffs and Smith, 2010). The purpose of early youth work was centred on the aspiration to improve the character and civic responsibility of, initially, young men, particularly with the creation in 1844 of the Young Men's Christian Association.

There are a number of different traditions in youth work, from the social and leisure provision found in youth clubs that starts from the premise that young people meet and take part in activities that are fun and enable them to develop skills at the same time in an atmosphere conducive to such development (Smith, 1998), through to what Smith refers to as 'professionalized youth work'. This refers to later developments in the field of youth work where the policy emphasis is closely aligned to the employability discourse. The role of the youth worker has arguably shifted to reflect this. In the main, however, the objective of youth work is still seen as giving young people opportunity to to shape their own futures by acquiring the necessary skills and enabling them to be integrated and included in society (Coussee, 2010).

In Romania, youth work has followed a very different path from that of its counterpart in Scotland – unsurprisingly, given the vastly differing social and political contexts and history. Until December 1989, when the totalitarian regime presided over by Nicolae Ceaucescu was overthrown, the historical roots of Romanian youth work were fixed firmly in the uniformed, non-voluntary junior organisations attached to the governing Communist Party. Engagement in such organisations was mandatory, with severe retribution commonplace if compliance was refused (Pantea, 2014). From the 1950s onwards, Romania was a Stalinist-oriented communist state and the ideology of the Communist Party permeated every part of society and civil life (Howard, 2003). Ensuring that young people were brought into the youth associations of the Party was essential for the successful and continuing enforcement of the ideology, so the role of the youth worker, or instructor as they were known then, was that of enforcer, in contrast to their Scottish counterparts at this time. Young people were given 'the mission of building the bright communist future' (Wallace and Kovacheva, 1998). Despite the fact that they were forced into participation in youth associations, individuals had very limited opportunities to influence any activities in these organisations and were given no responsibilities (Williamson, 2008). That there are significant differences in the contexts of the two research sites is undisputable; however, there were some interesting and worthwhile comparisons to note. Both in Romania and inScotland, the projects were focused on developing leadership in young people and working collectively to improve their situations and the position of young people in the wider society. In Scotland, at a macro level, youth participation has been addressed through establishing the Scottish Youth Parliament in 1999, a national organisation that seeks to represent the voice of young people across Scotland. In Romania there was no equivalent national youth platform that was driven by and for young people. YouthBank, which works at a local level, has been able to encourage and engage young people from diverse backgrounds to be actively involved in their communities in a meaningful way.

Following the collapse of communist systems throughout Eastern Europe in 1989, the situation in Romania changed entirely. The dismantling of state-run institutions and infrastructure took place rapidly, leaving young people in a fragile position. Where there had been some investment in infrastructure and, with this investment, a degree of security for young people, there was now a climate of uncertainty and apprehension regarding the future. Exacerbating this situation were the increasing tensions between minority ethnic groups and the majority Romanians, which had been forcibly contained by measures employed by the police state introduced by Ceaucescu. One of these groups, the Hungarian minority, who live principally in Transylvania, the western region of Romania, provides the focus for this case study.

In order to set the context for this study, a brief outline of Romania's history is necessary. For centuries Romania was dominated by powerful empires, Hapsburg, Ottoman and Czarist, all competing for territorial gains. Mungiu-Pippidi attributes this to the prominent 'irredentism'[1]of these empires (Mungiu-Pippidi, 2015). The result is a country whose imposed borders do not coincide with ethnic borders. The Treaty of Trianon (1920), which concluded the First World War, had a far-reaching impact on Hungary. This former kingdom was created as a new Hungarian state, but in the process lost approximately two-thirds of its territory, including Transylvania and Banat, which were taken over by Romania. From the 11th century, Transylvania had been part of Romania, but it was lost to the Habsburg Empire in the 17th century. The Hungarian population of these regions, by and large, chose to remain living in Romania rather than to repatriate to Hungary. At present there are approximately 1.5 million ethnic Hungarians living in western Romania (Veres, 2014). Their relationship with their fellow Romanians and the ruling government has fluctuated over the years, and during the latter part of Ceaucescu's leadership and the period immediately following his removal from power inter-ethnic conflict was a very real possibility in the region. During the early communist years, minority groups were allowed a degree of self-determination. However, as Ceaucescu tightened his grip in Romania politically, socially and economically, ethnic minority groups became increasingly forced to accept his nationalist policies. It was no coincidence that the political uprising that ultimately led to Ceaucescu's violent deposition started in Timisoara, a city on the western border of Romania with Serbia, instigated in part by the charismatic Hungarian priest Laszlo Tokes.

In 1990 civil unrest erupted violently between some of the ethnic Hungarians and Romanians, with rioting and demonstrations on the streets of Targu Mures, a town with a significant Hungarian minority. This situation caused widespread alarm across the political parties in Romania at the time and was dealt with by the newly installed government of Ion Illiescu, through questionable strategies (Stroschein, 2012). Mungiu-Pippidi (2010) describes how nationalism was used by ex-communist parties in Eastern and Central European countries at this time, primarily in Romania and Serbia, 'where demands voiced by assertive minorities seemed to pose a threat to the state'. This of course has been a strategy used by political leaders throughout time and across the world. This disturbance led to a devastating civil war in Serbia but not, fortunately, in Romania; but it was nevertheless a very challenging time for the minority groups. The capital of Transylvania, Cluj-Napoca, the second-largest city in Romania and the site for this research study, saw the dominance of Georghe Funar, a nationalist politician, as mayor. Funar was unashamedly and publicly anti-Hungarian. His presence and policies were often deliberately antagonistic and provocative to the 23% of the population of the city who were ethnic Hungarians. One of his actions was the renaming of the vast stone statue of Matthias Corvinus (Matthias Rex Hungarorum), which dominates the central square, to simply Matthias Rex (dropping the Hungarian part and rewriting history). Another policy was to paint the city benches, bins and streets red, yellow and blue, the colours of the Romanian national flag. Despite these often inflammatory policies, Funar remained in power until 2004. This situation was not exclusive to Cluj-Napoca but gives a clear picture of the lack of voice and inability to participate in decision-making structures and processes that was experienced by the minorities living in Romania.

Amid this potentially explosive situation, the Project on Ethnic Relations (PER) a non-governmental American organisation, was formed. Through dialogue and high-level intervention approaches, PER worked across the political spectrum from 1991 until the project in Romania was wound up in 2012. There were notable successes as a result of its intervention, particularly the coalition government that emerged from the 2000 elections in which the ruling PDSR and the Hungarian minority political party, UDMR, joined forces. The new-found legitimacy that this coalition gave to the role of minority political parties is undisputed but it would be overly optimistic to say that there was an immediate end to ethnic tensions (PER, 2001). The electoral success of the ultra-nationalist party, Greater Romania, which enjoyed significant success in the regions of Banat and Transylvania where the majority of the Hungarian population live, emphasises the fact that caution must continue to be observed when considering the legacy of the coalition government.

Political will and aspiration at national level does not always translate to the local level. A strong degree of separation between Hungarians and Romanians still exists in some parts of Romania. In certain areas of Transylvania, road signs are in Hungarian and little or no Romanian is spoken in the villages. Hungarian-speaking schools exist where instruction is solely in Hungarian and the desire for a state-funded Hungarian university is an on-going, albeit highly controversial, debate.

The Romanian research site, the city of Cluj–Napoca, is a vibrant cultural centre with a large student population. The first YouthBank in Romania began there in 2006, and since then the concept has become a very successful project, with 13 YouthBanks operating in towns and cities across Romania. The concept of YouthBank is straightforward: young people are involved in grant-making in their communities, with programmes achieving two distinct outcomes that are not mutually exclusive. The first outcome is the immediate impact on the communities that benefit financially from a YouthBank grant, and the second is the more personal impact on the lives of the young people who are directly involved as grant makers and grant recipients (Grantcraft, 2014). The project is youth led, with an adult coordinator in each YouthBank whose role is to advise and support the young people. Each YouthBank must adhere to the Golden Rules, which ensure inclusion, fairness and transparency and underpin the ethos of YouthBank. When talking about YouthBank, a number of keywords and phrases are often repeated: youth led, community, financial literacies, young people as decision makers and self-development.

Throughout the research process in Cluj, where there is actually a diverse ethnic mix with significant numbers of ethnic minorities (beyond ethnic Romanians and Hungarians) living together, I was consistently told by young people how they had been encouraged to work together with young people from different communities through their involvement with YouthBank. They recognised that through doing so they had learned a new tolerance and respect for these groups. One respondent, a young woman aged 19, described how she had become firm friends with a Hungarian young person after working with her on a project and how, prior to being involved with the project, she 'did not really like Hungarian people'. These attitudes are relatively widespread in Romania at present, including, maybe surprisingly, within the younger generation (European Social Survey, 2006.). Even in modern-day Romania, the Hungarian minority is still marginalised and it is a common perception that they feel less entitled within decision-making structures, despite the organised and effective presence of the Hungarian political party, UDMR, at government level (Mungiu-Pippidi, 2007). What became apparent through my study was the success of YouthBank in tackling this alienation and lack of egalitarianism and in providing an open platform for all young people, regardless of their ethnic origin. A clear focus for the coordinator in the project was the establishment of a culture of inclusion in YouthBank to ensure that the environment was fit to challenge these prejudices. However, she highlighted the difficulties in achieving this, particularly among the young Hungarian population living in Romania, as they often do not speak Romanian and feel that YouthBank is primarily a Romanian project and therefore not accessible to them.

Through a process of actively engaging young Hungarians in YouthBank, both by means of membership and also through encouraging Hungarian youth-led projects in the city to apply to the local YouthBank for a grant, this project was able to fulfil its obligations to uphold the Golden Rules and achieve a varied membership profile in the project. The complexities surrounding 'safe spaces' for participation are well documented by Cornwall (2008). There is a feeling of inevitability in the development of hierarchical structures wherever groups of people are operating together, but what was apparent as both surprising and exciting in equal measure was that, in YouthBank's case, this power imbalance was wholly lacking. Throughout the interviews in Cluj I was told how YouthBank had developed skills such as leadership and confidence and the ability to make decisions, sometimes difficult ones, in a collective environment. In order for young Hungarians to feel included and respected, the YouthBank setting had to move from an 'invited space' to an open, accessible space where everyone felt a sense of ownership and belonging. A YouthBank provides a framework for participation but, crucially, the space itself is occupied by young people who choose to be there and share a common purpose.

When asked what she considered to be the transformative effect of YouthBank on young people in their communities, the adult coordinator responded that she felt that she personally had learned to empathise with people from ethnic minorities and that this had led to her being able to develop a deeper understanding of the different cultures existing in the city. It was evident from interviews and conversations with young participants in the YouthBank that this progressive attitude had permeated through to and was shared by them. The coordinator also drew on the opportunities provided by YouthBank at national level to break down barriers and cited an example of a recent training opportunity organised by YouthBank

Romania that had brought together young people from three geographical areas of Romania, including Roma, Hungarians and Romanians whose default common language was English. As she said, 'We were brought together through YouthBank and the bottom line was that we had to be more tolerant and find solutions to work together.' Through the shared interest and common purpose provided by YouthBank, barriers that have existed for generations between these groups were broken down. Self-development is often cited as one of the key factors associated with being part of a YouthBank.

There has been some research on current levels of participation across post-communist Eastern Europe that has highlighted the low levels of participation in civil society (Wallace et al, 2012). While participation in formal structures, such as school councils, may have been more common, for many young people, and particularly those from minority groups, having a voice and a platform to express it is a new experience. Nevertheless, youth participation in general is sporadic and in decline. In the area of political participation, the situation is similar to that of many Western democracies, with dwindling numbers of young people taking part in formal political activities. The Youth Partnership, a joint venture formed in 2005 between the European Commission and the Council of Europe, commissioned a wider country study on young people in Romania. The study, carried out in 2007, explored young people's attitudes to politics. Only 1.5% of the respondents aged between 15 and 24 described themselves as very interested in politics and, interestingly, the same respondents, when questioned about their attitude to the government, revealed that, on a scale of satisfaction from 1 to 10 (1 being extremely dissatisfied), the majority response was a mere 3.4 (European Social Survey Data, 2008).

One of the potential factors contributing to this disengagement in Romania is the current political system, widely seen as corrupt and elitist (Robertson, 2009). This viewpoint has been supported more recently by Maria Pantea, an lecturer working in Babes-Bolyai University in Cluj-Napoca, with whom I made contact through my research. In a conversation in Cluj in June 2014, Pantea suggested that this extreme dissatisfaction and disillusionment with the government could be attributed to blatant corruption, cronyism and a growing sense of disappointment among the population, young and old, at the lack of improvement in their circumstances and opportunities. It is undeniable that there is a deep sense of disillusionment with the current situation, exacerbated further by the recent trials and imprisonment of high-ranking politicians on grounds of fraud and corruption.

Furthermore, under the communist regime, people were forced to participate in communist-run leisure and sport programmes, so is it the case, as has been suggested by Howard, that they are consciously exercising their newly acquired rights by not participating (Howard, 2003)? The participants in this study are too young to have been affected directly by the communist regime but they will undoubtedly be influenced by the attitudes of parents and teachers who were[2] Howard suggests that, over time, the influence of the communist legacy will be replaced and participation patterns, both political and informal, will more closely relate to those in established democracies. Wallace and others (2012), using data from the World Values Survey, found a dramatic decrease in participation in Romania between the years 1995 and 2008, due largely to a decline in church attendance. However, in an example of the 'Westernisation' of the region, there has been a marked increase in Eastern Europeans in general choosing some types of voluntary associations more similar to those found in the West. My research indicates that, in terms of informal participation, the YouthBank experience in Romania supports the findings of their study.

Conclusion

It is important to acknowledge from the outset that this research was based on a very small-scale study (see also Youth Partnership, 2008) and there are, therefore, limitations to the conclusions that can be drawn from the findings. The research took place over a short space of time and in one only project in Romania and I was therefore constrained by time and other limits. Although some research has been carried out into youth participation across post-communist Eastern Europe, there is little specific research based in Romania, so I was not able to draw on others' findings. This said, I believe that, within the parameters of the study, the findings I outline are significant and pose some interesting and important questions for future research and, in turn, for those working with young people to empower them. I would suggest that future research might focus further on the ability of YouthBank to achieve integration with minority groups, and, where I have concentrated on the Hungarian minority, there is rich material from a closer analysis of some of the other 12 YouthBank projects working across Romania and involving a number of other minority groups, for example, the Roma.

It is crucial to ask how YouthBank succeeds in bringing together groups of young people from different ethnic minorities, with centuries of enmity and distrust behind them, and fostering an environment where they are willing and able to develop trusting and productive relationships. While there is a framework and a structure dictated by the Golden Rules, each YouthBank is autonomous and I believe that this is one of the project's key strengths. Because of this autonomy, each project, effectively working along community development principles, can develop its own local and individual identity. This identity is formed by its members, so they have the advantages that structure brings, as well as the freedom to make it their own. Additionally, they are given responsibility not in a tokenised manner but in a real financial way to decide how to spend the monies raised, and frequently the money is raised through their own fundraising endeavours. Consequently, as stakeholders, they are fully invested in the project and want to see it work and succeed.

The Paris Declaration of Education Ministers of 17 March 2015 called for 'actions at all levels to reinforce the role of education in promoting citizenship and the common values of freedom and helping young people become responsible, open-minded and active members of our diverse and inclusive society' (EC, 2015). It is clear from this that policy makers are committed at least in principle to the importance of developing the skills and giving young people the opportunities to participate, to exercise tolerance and non-discrimination and to strengthen social cohesion within their communities. Perhaps even more so now, in this climate of uncertainty, lessons should be learned from a project that seeks to overcome ethnic tensions and that celebrates instead diversity and inclusion. If the model can work in Romania, with its long and troubled history of ethnic division, there seems to be no reason in principle why it could not work in other countries.

Notes

[1] Irridentism refers to the desire of nations to (re)claim territory over which they assert some historical connection.

[2] On the other hand, of course, this historical context does not obtain in Scotland and other Western European democracies where there is, nevertheless, a huge democratic deficit in terms of young people's political participation.

References

Cornwall, A. (2008) 'Unpacking "participation": models, meanings, and practices', *Community Development Journal*, vol 43, no 3, pp 269–83.

Coussee, F. (2010) 'The history of youth work – re-socialising the youth question?', in F. Coussee et al (eds), *The history of youth work in Europe*, vol 2, *Relevance for today's youth work policy*, Strasbourg: Council of Europe Publishing.

CTR (Romanian Youth Council) (2016), www.ctr.ro, accessed 18 June 2016.

EC (European Commission) (2015) *EU Youth report*. European Commission: Brussels. Available at http://ec.europa.eu/assets/eac/youth/library/reports/youth-report-2015_en.pdf

European Social Survey Data (2006), www.europeansocialsurvey.org/docs/findings/ESS1_5 – select-findings.pdf, accessed 24 May 2016.

European Social Survey Data (2008) www.europeansocialsurvey.org/data, accessed 28 May 2014.

Grantcraft (2014) 'YouthBank model has global appeal', www.grantcraft.org, accessed 30 June 2014.

Howard, M. (2003) *The weakness of civil society in post-communist Europe*, Cambridge: Cambridge University Press.

Jeffs, T. and Smith, M.K. (2010) *Youth work practice*, Basingstoke: Macmillan.

Mungiu-Pippidi, A (2007) 'The influence of EU accession on minorities' status in East Central Europe', *Romanian Journal of Political Science*, vol 7, no 1, p 58.

Mungiu-Pippidi, A. (2010) 'Twenty years of postcommunism, the other transition', *Journal of Democracy*, vol 21, no 1, pp 120–7.

Mungiu-Pippidi, A. (2015) 'The splintering of postcommunist Europe', *Journal of Democracy*, vol 26, no 1, pp 88–100.

McCulloch, K. (2007) 'Democratic participation or surveillance? Structures and practices for young people's decision-making', *Scottish Youth Issues Journal*, vol 9, pp 9–22.

Mitulescu, S. (2014) 'History of youth work in Romania', in M. Taru, F. Coussee and H. Williamson (eds), *The history of youth work in Europe, relevance for today's youth work policy*, vol 4, Strasbourg: Council of Europe Publishing.

Pantea, M. (2014) 'Handle with care', in M. Pantea, R. Diroescu and M. Podlasek-Ziegler (eds) *Young people, entrepreneurship and non-formal learning: A work in progress*, Brussels: SALTO – Youth Participation Centre.

PER (Project on Ethnic Relations) (2001) *Political will: Romania's path to ethnic accommodation*, www.per-usa.org, accessed 2 May 2016.

Robertson, F. (2009) 'A study of youth political participation in Poland and Romania', unpublished PhD thesis, School of Slavonic and East European Studies, University College London.

Smith, M.K. (1998) *Developing youth work*, Milton Keynes: Open University Press.

Stroschein, S. (2012) *Ethnic struggle, coexistence, and democratization in Eastern Europe*, Cambridge: Cambridge University Press.

Tett, L. (2010) *Community education, learning and development*, Edinburgh: Dunedin.

Tisdall, K. (2013) 'The transformation of participation? Exploring the potential of "transformative participation" for theory and practice around children and young people's participation', *Global Studies of Children*, vol 3, no 2, pp 183–93.

Veres, V. (2014) 'Identity discourses on national belonging: the Hungarian minority in Romania' (Report), *Romanian Journal of Political Science*, vol 14, no 1, p 61–86.

Wallace, C. and Kovacheva, S. (1998) *Youth in society. The construction and deconstruction of youth in East and West Europe*, London: Macmillan.

Wallace, C., Pichler, F. and Haerpfer, C. (2012) 'Changing patterns of civil society in Europe and America 1995–2005: is Eastern Europe different?', *East European Politics and Societies*, vol 26, no 1, pp 3–19.

White, S. (1996) 'Depoliticising development: the uses and abuses of participation', *Development in Practice*, vol 6, no 1, pp 6–15.

Williamson, H. (2008) *Supporting young people in Europe: Volume 2*, Strasbourg: Council of Europe Publishing.

Youth Partnership (2008) Information sheet on living conditions in Romania, www.youth-partnership.net, accessed 3 May 2014.

THIRTEEN

Benarrawa Aboriginal and Torres Strait Islander Solidarity Group: working to reduce the deleterious effects of racism through structural community development

Athena Lathouras and Dyann Ross[1]

Introduction

In the late 1990s members of the Benarrawa Solidarity Group in Brisbane, Australia came together to explore issues of racism and learn more about Aboriginal and Torres Strait Islander (ATSI) histories and culture. The Solidarity Group, comprising Indigenous and non-Indigenous community members, has demonstrated a long-term commitment to community development actions to promote justice and understanding between all people. The multifaceted nature of their relationships and work significantly contributed to one of the author's research studies and to theorising about structural community development (SCD) (Lathouras, 2012a; 2013). SCD is a bottom-up, citizen-led and -owned approach that seeks to challenge racism at its source in systems, laws and policies based on white privilege (Pease, 2010). This chapter seeks to acknowledge the path-breaking community development work of the Benarrawa Solidarity Group by providing an account of how many aspects of its initiatives can be understood as SCD. In this way academic theorising is deeply informed by bottom-up community activism (Lathouras, 2016) where there is a mutual learning and sharing from the exchanges that form the basis of the ideas presented here.

There is a pressing need to retheorise community development, to strengthen its ability to address racism caused by structural disadvantage. This structural disadvantage takes the form of the undermining long-term effects of colonisation and neoliberalism that have resulted in intergenerational oppression for many of Australia's First Peoples[2]

(Hollinsworth, 2006). Government interventions in Indigenous communities, often employing top-down, service-oriented strategies, have compounded the institutional bases of racism in Australia (Cox, 2014).

The theorising related to SCD will show how Benarrawa's work over time can be seen as a form of politically aware practice aimed at reducing the deleterious effects of racism in two ways. First, racism is challenged through the adoption of a multifaceted structural analysis of the root causes of oppression that seeks to address the issues at their source. Second, racism is shown to be challenged by the adoption of a three-fold practice framework focuses relationship building linked to a power analysis and collective action beyond the purely local geographical level. The structural analysis 'frames' the practice framework such that both are crucial to effecting structural change.

The Australian racial context

The Indigenous people of Australia are members of the oldest continuous culture in the world, historically comprising around 600 cultural groups and languages. White settlement in the 18th century literally shipped in white supremacy (hooks, 1995) and a British form of legally enforced colonialism (Huggins, 1998; Hollinsworth, 2006) that has persisted until the present time. Some commentators write about white settlement as an invasion and the history of colonialism in Australia as nothing short of cultural genocide. For example, the government legally authorised practices such as the forcible removal of children from their families (Holt, 2012; see also the film *Rabbit-proof fence*) in what has been referred to as the Stolen Generation. The *Bringing them home report* on the Stolen Generation (Human Rights and Equal Opportunity Commission [HREOC], 1997) described this as 'the Australian holocaust ... an Australian ethnic cleansing'. The evidence for institutional racism, as the main expression of state-sanctioned colonialism, shows in the continuing removal of Indigenous children from their families – and often their communities – at a greater rate than in the period referred to in the report (Pilger, 2014). This colonialist practice is one of a range of equally damning examples, and others include: the Northern Territory Emergency Response (NTER) to child sexual abuse (Korff, 2016a); paperless arrests Giles, 2016; black deaths in custody (Korff, 2016b); the closing of Aboriginal remote communities (Pilger, 2015); and the failure of the Closing the Gap initiatives (Cox, 2014). These issues sit in tension with, and far outweigh the gains from, hard-won struggles for social justice

(Anderson, 2014) and the continuing struggle to protect traditional land rights.

Neoliberalism as a dominant discourse in Australian politics (Baum, 2014) and public debate is premised on racism that hides, and in hiding further increases, the power of white privilege. White privilege is unearned advantage by virtue of a set of characteristics that are valued at the cost of non-white social groups who are defined as 'other' (Pease, 2010). Referring to the dominant racial imagery of white people in the media, Dyer writes:

> There is no more powerful position than that of being 'just' human. The claim to power is the claim to speak for the commonality of humanity. Raced people can't do that – they can only speak for their race. But non-raced people can, for they don't represent the interests of a race. (Dyer, 2005, p 10)

Racism has a functional value that serves some people – namely those powerful groups of white people who gain from the status quo (Hollinsworth, 2006; Holt, 2012). State power is sanctioned by neoliberal discourses such as the rightness of rule of (white) laws and policies (Barns, 2016), and simultaneously this state power is reinforced by regressive legislation (such as the paperless arrests: Giles, 2016) or by ignoring legislation (such as the Racial Discrimination Act 1975, in enforcing the NTER).

Community development theory needs to guide practitioners in how to address this issue of white privilege and the consequent power inequalities (Thompson, 2011) and the inter-sectionality of oppressions (Watts, 2015) that these inequalities create. It is suggested that community development funded by the state will not be able robustly to critique and challenge the status quo (Campbell et al, 2007). A different order of engagement with and sharing of power with Australia's First Peoples is required to stop the harm and loss caused by white privilege.

There is a form of community development in Australia that is seen as a growing 'alternative' sphere of practice beyond the apparatus of the state. This alternative community development can be found in areas such as co-housing, peace and non-violence work, permaculture and social enterprises (Boulet, 2010). Practice in these contexts is based on the idea of 'claimed spaces' where opportunities are created for people to debate, discuss and resist, outside of institutionalised policy arenas (Gaventa, 2011, p 16).

Burkett (2011) provides a hopeful response for organising within a robust neoliberal context when she argues that resistance against dominant structures can take many forms. One form, she argues, is to engage with the system to create change. The Benarrawa Solidarity Group is a good example of a claimed space that is working to reduce the deleterious effects of racism as it critically analyses, visions and takes practical steps to bring that vision into reality.

Introducing the Benarrawa Aboriginal and Torres Strait Islander Solidarity Group

Benarrawa is flowing.

We dream that the people will listen to the land and to each other.

(Benarrawa Dreaming Statement)

Hinds, a community development practitioner, writes that the Benarrawa Community Development Association took the name Benarrawa after consultations and permission given by the Jagera Elders and the Brisbane Council of Elders (Benarrawa Community Development Association, 2000). 'Benarrawa' is the Jagera name for Oxley Creek and surrounds, near where the organisation is located. Not being an Aboriginal organisation per se, members of the organisation were aware that the non-Indigenous histories of the Benarrawa area were completely silent about its Indigenous past. Their hope in forming the Solidarity Group was to reclaim community consciousness of the Aboriginal history of their local area. Their local history project found surviving historical records and stories that revealed a level of overt racism and cruelty towards local Indigenous people that was very distressing for members. The project made members more aware of the historical lack of recognition of, and the importance of, Australia's First Peoples' cultures and heritage.

One important outcome of this work has been the building of strong ties with the Indigenous community. The Benarrawa Solidarity Group informs itself and the wider community about issues affecting the lives of Indigenous peoples through regular gatherings and actions. They are working from the principle of 'multiple pathways in' (Lathouras, 2010, p 19), providing a range of opportunities for people to connect with others, build relationships and work together.

Benarrawa's actions include the following.

- An *Annual Sorry Day Ceremony*, providing the opportunity for local community members, both Indigenous and non-Indigenous, teachers and pupils from primary and secondary schools, youth groups, clergy and local churches members, and politicians to join in the ceremony. This is a key annual event for the Solidarity Group to listen to the history of the 'stolen children' and its intergenerational effect on their lives and those of their families.
- On *Survival Day* (26 January) each year, a gathering of members meets to honour the strength and resilience of the First Peoples and the opportunity to reflect on the 18th-century invasion by the British and consequent changes to their lives. The 26 January, formally known as Australia Day, is Australia's national day that marks the anniversary of the 1788 arrival of the first fleet of British ships.
- The annual *Mabo Day Celebration* acknowledges the significance of 'terra nullius',[3] Torres Strait Islander Eddie Koiki Mabo's disbelief that his people's land was not legally theirs, and subsequent action that eventually led to the granting of Native Title legislation.
- A *Biennial ATSI Art Show and Cultural Festival* is an event providing the wider public an opportunity for developing relationships with Indigenous peoples and opportunities for learning about each other's lives, culture, traditions and art.
- *ATSI Awareness Workshops* conducted by Indigenous cultural workers are occasions where people share stories, histories, culture, knowledge and protocols with the Solidarity Group and members of the wider community.
- Regular *Elders' Lunches* enable the space to meet, talk, share, learn from each other and to honour Elders and cultural workers of the Solidarity Group and their friends in a less formal environment.
- A *Back-to-Country Funeral Fund* provides a small donation towards assisting families to take their deceased loved ones home, or travel back to their own country themselves.

This brief introduction to the Benarrawa Solidarity Group does not convey how the community development ideas and strategy linkages that the group employs combine to address racism. The next sections of the chapter outline how SCD is one thinking frame and related practice framework that can describe its vision and work.

Benarrawa and an SCD thinking frame

Contemporary community development is prone to 'ideological elasticity' (Shaw, 2007, p 34). This is where ideas of 'community' have been 'appropriated' to legitimate or justify a wide range of political positions, a phenomenon known as the 'politics of community' (Shaw, 2007, p 24). Shaw (2003, p 45) quotes Craig, who argues that 'community work is too often drawn into the latest fashions of government policy agendas because that is where funding is, rather than developing a clear analysis to inform action. Practice is dominated by the policy and political context rather than creating it.' Within this context the Benarrawa Solidarity Group is informed by a clear multifaceted structural analysis that shapes a strong framework of practice that informs its anti-racism work.

Research conducted by Lathouras (2012a) suggests that community development needs a multifaceted theory to understand *the structural*, or the elements of a structural analysis, for our contemporary times. She explains structural analysis as:

1. looking for the *root causes of oppression and disadvantage*, and seeking to *address them at their source* (Ledwith, 2011);
2. undertaking *the act of structuring*, that is, purposeful action is undertaken, particularly as it relates to forming a base from which action is structured beyond the local level; and
3. viewing the issue from the standpoint of *the structured*, that is, the type of structures developed and maintained to hold community development work while it is in process.

Lathouras's (2012; 2013) research developed a three-fold practice framework for enacting this structural analysis after she found that many community development practitioners were not acting to change issues at their source. One exception was the work of the Benarrawa Solidarity Group, which was able to confirm the value of the ideas through its own practice. The SCD three-fold practice framework has the following components:

1. *structural connecting*, which seeks to form developmental relationships and create a community analysis that leads to collective action;
2. *structural shaping*, which seeks to develop a nuanced understanding of power and looks for incremental change across systems; and
3. *structural politicking*, which relates to processes that seek democratic equality.

SCD involves the on-going use of a structural analysis while employing the practice framework. The work of the Benarrawa Solidarity Group will be described to explain the nature of the SCD approach in its practice, seeking to challenge systemic racism in Australia.

Benarrawa Solidarity Group and the SCD practice framework

Structural connecting

Practice situated within the framework *structural connecting* seeks to form developmental relationships and create a community analysis that leads to collective action. Developmental practice privileges bottom–up work (Lathouras, 2010, p 18). This is where practitioners share power and work with 'community members', 'constituents' or 'citizens' who set the agenda; and make decisions about the way the work will be undertaken and issues that affect them and their communities.

As a community of interest for anti–racism work, the Solidarity Group is connecting structurally through dialogic practice. Theorised by Owen and Westoby (2012, p 3), this type of practice employs particular communication skills helpful in forming 'purposeful developmental relationships' that lay the platform for community processes. Developmental relationships, they argue, are those that involve 'sustaining connection' with people through an approach that has the dual aims of developing *mutual relationships* and also *strategic outcomes* (Owen and Westoby, 2012, p 3; emphasis added). The term 'mutuality' is focused on the humanising dimension of communication and relationship making (Owen and Westoby, 2012, p 3). It is featured in Benarrawa's structural analysis where safe spaces are created to reduce the effects of isolation and stigma resulting from such discrimination. Drawing on Buber's (1937) philosophy of dialogue, White (2008) discusses his conception of dialogue as a valorisation of communication as *communion* where, through dialogue, a bond is formed. These conceptions of dialogue, White (2008) argues, emphasise an accommodation of otherness, a commitment to ethical processes and the potential to produce profound personal and social transformations.

The Solidarity Group's Elders' Lunches are a good example of this work, creating spaces for personal sharing through dialogue, where members educate each other to the realities of racism and disadvantage and where a culture of self-interest is sacrificed for common interest. Hinds explains that the lunches are held in non-formal spaces, such as Elders' own homes or community spaces. They foster respectful and egalitarian relationships, and although very sensitive sharing occurs, these are happy occasions with storytelling and humour, creating a sense that people are on common ground.

From this base of developmental relationships, strategic outcomes are sought. Importantly mandates are not disingenuous processes done *to* members in the guise of community capacity building. The current governmental community development policy context in Australia emphasises capacity building and social capital, and uses the language of social relationships but tends to ignore the operation of power within those relationships (Craig, 2007; Rawsthorne and Howard, 2011, p 91). Benarrawa's processes foster a genuine mandate for community development that seeks outcomes and processes fostering solidarity and instilling a sense of hopefulness that members' private concerns can be addressed.

Structural shaping

Community development situated within the framework *structural shaping* develops a nuanced understanding of power and looks for incremental change across systems. Having the ability to analyse power, which may include who holds power and how that power is exercised, is an important component of community development. Processes to analyse power can be viewed as consciousness–raising processes, or conscientisation. The term *conscientisation* refers to learning to perceive social, political and economic contradictions and to take action against the oppressive element of these realities (Freire, 1970, p 85). Processes that raise the consciousness of a group regarding arbitrarily applied social policies that overshadow their particular circumstances can be empowering for group members, especially when they make decisions to act against such oppression.

The starting place for this analysis is with people's stories. A vast array of social realities and their associated power inequalities are discussed at the Solidarity Group's meetings in areas such as health, housing, education, income, employment, culture and the impact of racism and violence on family and community life, identity and gender. This conscientisation process can be viewed as analysis constituted by a matrix of lenses (Lathouras, 2012a) to examine social realities and disadvantage based on race, gender, class, geographical living situation and other indicators of structural disadvantage (Thompson, 2011). Ledwith (2011) argues that, in our contemporary globalised world where structural inequalities persist, it is necessary that much greater attention be paid to developing theory and skills to address these issues. This critical approach to power analysis that the Solidarity

Group employs is in tension with more post-modern understandings of power. Gaventa (2001, p 6) argues that there is more than one way of understanding power because its meanings are diverse and contentious. Powerful structures can be viewed as constructs that can be both deconstructed and reconstructed. This kind of analysis understands that dynamic sets of relationships exist across a system and that structures are both 'made and makeable' (Joas and Knöble, 2009, p 289), that is, through dialectical processes and webs of relations, participants can co-create new realities.

Significantly, developing these webs of relations means that the Solidarity Group makes connections with non-Indigenous and Indigenous people beyond their locality by forming bridges with people in society who also have an interest in Indigenous affairs. This indicates that the Group has an analysis that there need to be connections with groups and organisations outside its immediate sphere, perhaps to assist the Solidarity Group to further its own aims, or for the Group to be an influence within those spheres. In this regard, Benarrawa's story shows that community members are exposed to and gain experience in this aspect of structuring community development work, that is, bridging with organisations and institutions in society. It does this when, for example, members of the Solidarity Group have opportunities to talk and build relationships with government bureaucrats, academics and others who represent diverse groups within the wider community. It is working both horizontally and vertically within that system, and also creating webs of connections within that system.

Although the Solidarity Group has developed a range of actions, pathways into the Group are not just task or action oriented. It aims to keep creating connections with newcomers and place emphasis on education and building strong relationships. This suggests that the Group is open enough to include new people and their ideas, however sophisticated or developed the Solidarity Group's actions have become. This is also a strategy for keeping the Group energised and enhancing its ability to sustain itself over time, as new people and new energy have a replenishing effect on the Group and its actions.

Gaventa (2011, p 23) argues that transformative, fundamental change happens when social actors are able to work effectively across dimensions simultaneously, in terms of both analysis and strategy. 'The process of change is constantly dynamic and changing', requiring strategies that allow for constant reflection on how power relations are changing and the agility to move across shifting spaces, levels and forms of power (Gaventa, 2011, p 44). Viewing practice in terms of forms of power and their interaction is one key dimension. Having the agility to move across shifting spaces requires the structural dimension of systems thinking.

Wheatley suggests that if one sees a problem with one part of the system, one must also see the dynamics existing between that part and the whole system. She also claims (Wheatley, 2006, p 145) that 'the system is capable of solving its own problems'. If a system is in trouble, the solutions, she states, are found from within the system and the mechanism for creating health is to connect the system to *more of itself* (Wheatley, 2006, p 145; emphasis added). The kinds of connecting to which Wheatley refers are 'critical connections' where, through webs of relations, participants co-create new realities.

What seems evident in the Solidarity Group's story is that the quality of the relationships across the system is characterised by mutuality and reciprocity, where all participants are valued for the range of gifts, talents, skills and knowledge they bring to the table. Participation is key to the Group's strategy because it is seeking to educate a broad range of participants, including those who develop social policy in the area of ATSI affairs, regarding the deleterious effects of policies on community members. For example, through its Sorry Day Ceremonies it has developed relationships with local government, the lord mayor, local councillors and the council's community development officers, all of whom now hold different kinds of responsibilities and contribute to this significant event. Other critical connections involve the Solidary Group's work with younger people. Its current new work is with the local primary school to embed traditional knowledges into the curriculum when Elders share stories in the Bush Tucker[4] section of Benarrawa's community garden. Moreover, in its planning and strategising the Group also develops critical understandings about why things have worked as its practice has moved from the 'tacit' – that is, doing what just comes naturally – to the 'explicit'. This type of critical reflection is helping the Group to know if and how its practice is making a difference.

Structural politicking

Community development practice needs to be viewed as a form of political action and the final framework, *structural politicking*, is a framework that views practice as a space for citizens to participate in processes for democratic equality. Dryzek and Dunleavy (2009, p 334) assert that, despite global democratisation in which, for the first time in history, the majority of people live in more or less liberal democracies, there has been a failure to acknowledge that a deeper expression of democracy is needed. Because liberal democracies have failed to live up to their ideals, reform agendas associated with democratic renewal seek more authentic democracy. Authenticity of democracy, they argue, is 'the degree to which popular control is substantive rather than symbolic, engaged by critical, reflective and competent citizens' (Dryzek and Dunleavy (2009, p 209).

Alinsky's early seminal community organising text *Rules for radicals* called for a 'reformation', the process where masses of people reach a point of disillusionment with past ways and values and then, together, organise, build power and change the system from within (Alinsky, 1971, p 114). Discussing the importance of democracy, Alinsky was 'desperately concerned' that masses of people, through lack of interest or opportunity, are resigned to live lives determined by others. He argued that,

> The spirit of democracy is the idea of importance and worth in the individual, and faith in the kind of world where the individual can achieve as much of his [sic] potential as possible.... Separation of the people from the routine daily functions of citizenship is heartbreak in a democracy. (Alinsky, 1971, p 115)

The Solidarity Group is rethinking dominant attitudes and silencing techniques brought about because of hegemony. Hegemony is 'the way that a dominant group asserts control over other social groups' (Ledwith and Springett, 2010, p 159), and the subtle way in which dominant attitudes become common sense or internalised. Ledwith and Springett (2010, p 160) argue that these attitudes assert 'control over knowledge and culture, affirming the dominant culture and marginalising and silencing others'. For example, its Biennial Indigenous Art Show and Cultural Festival, held in an English language–intensive secondary school, is an example of the Solidarity Group's strategic action. It provides newly-arrived students from language backgrounds other than English and the wider public an opportunity for developing relationships with Indigenous peoples that is different to the often negative stereotyping and images portrayed of Indigenous peoples.

Within this framework, social change goals have a more socially transformative essence, aiming for democratic equality. The Solidarity Group's analysis about racism and the historical oppression of Australia's First Peoples is providing a vehicle through which they are enacting their rights as citizens. In this regard community development can be seen as a form of citizenship making, where citizen participation and engagement provide members with a voice for achieving democratic equality. These are the kind of politics in which people are not empowered by leaders, but empower themselves when they develop skills and habits of collaborative action (Boyte, 2008). This allows them to change institutions and systems, making them more supportive of civic agency.

Conclusion

The Benarrawa Aboriginal and Torres Strait Islander Solidarity Group is engaging in significant work to reduce the deleterious effects of racism within a pernicious neoliberal environment that continues to colonise Indigenous people and perpetuate structural disadvantage. Through the framework of SCD, the Solidarity Group's various activities and its critical–relational approach to community development can be seen as developing personal connections between people from many parts of the community and breaking down barriers across a range of historical divides. The work is a good example of activism where people based in local communities and people based across institutions in society are forming relationships founded on mutuality and reciprocity, and together are working towards justice and equality for Australia's First Peoples.

Notes

[1] In collaboration with the Benarrawa Aboriginal and Torres Strait Islander Solidarity Group.
[2] First Peoples is a term used across the world to indicate those people who originally lived in or settled territories, including, for example, the San in Botswana, Sami in Northern Scandinavia, Maori in New Zealand (Aeoteroa) and American Indians in North America.
[3] Literally, 'the land with nothing', i.e. a land where no-one existed. The political 'invisibilisation' of the Indigenous people allowed European settlers to claim the 'empty' land for themselves.
[4] Traditional foodstuffs, collected in 'the bush'.

References

Alinsky, S. (1971) *Rules for radicals*, New York: Random House.
Anderson, M. (2014) 'First Nation's sovereignty new way', https://www.youtube.com/watch?v=ZBz7GLP0vs8, accessed 24 June 2016.
Barns, G. (2016) 'COAG rule of law takes (another) back step', www.abc.net.au/news/2016–04–04/barns-coag:-rule-of-law-takes-(another)-back-step/7297852, accessed 24 June 2016.

Baum, F. (2014) *The new public health* (3rd edn), South Melbourne: Oxford University Press.

Benarrawa Community Development Association (2000) *Sharing our local Aboriginal history: Chelmer to Oxley*, Brisbane: BCDA..

Boulet, J. (2010) 'Editorial', *New Community Quarterly*, vol 8, no 4, pp 1–2.

Boyte, H.C. (2008) 'Civic driven change and developmental democracy', in A. Fowler and K. Biekart (eds), *Civic driven change: Citizen's imagination in action*, The Hague: Institute of Social Studies.

Buber, M. (1937) *I and thou*, New York: Charles Scribner's Sons.

Burkett, I. (2011) 'Organizing in the new marketplace: contradictions and opportunities for community development organisations in the ashes of neoliberalism', *Community Development Journal*, vol 46, no s2, pp ii111–ii127.

Campbell, D., Wunungmurra, P. and Nyomba, H. (2007) 'Starting where the people are: lessons on community development from a remote Aboriginal Australian setting', *Community Development Journal*, vol 42, no 2, pp 151–66.

Cox, E. (2014) *Closing the gap: We know what works, so why don't we do it?* http://theconversation.com/closing-the-gap-we-know-what-works-so-why-dont-we-do-it-23243, accessed 11 May 2014.

Craig, G. (2007) 'Something old, something new …?', *Critical Social Policy*, vol 27, no 3, August, pp 335–59.

Dryzek, J. and Dunleavy, P. (2009) *Theories of the democratic state*, Basingstoke: Palgrave Macmillan.

Dyer, R. (2005) 'The matter of whiteness', in P. Rothenburg (ed.) *White privilege: Essential readings on the other side of race*, New York: Worth Publishers.

Freire, P. (1970) *Pedagogy of the oppressed*, Harmondsworth: Penguin.

Gaventa, J. (2011) *Power pack: Understanding power for social change*, Brighton: Institute for Developmental Studies.

Giles, A. (2016) 'Paperless arrests remove trouble makers', http://chiefminister.nt.gov.au/news/paperless-arrests-remove-trouble-makers, accessed 24 June 2016.

Hollinsworth, D. (2006) *Race and racism in Australia* (3rd edn), South Melbourne: Thomson Social Science Press.

Holt, A. (2012) *Forcibly removed* (2nd edn), Fiji: Quality Print Ltd..

hooks, b. (1995) *Killing rage: Ending racism*, New York: Routledge.

Huggins, J. (1998) *Sister girl: The writings of Aboriginal activist and historian Jackie Huggins*, St Lucia: University of Queensland Press.

HREOC (Human Rights and Equal Opportunity Commission) (1997) *Bringing them home report: National inquiry into the separation of Aboriginal and Torres Straight Islander children from their families*, Canberra: Australian Government Printing Service.

Joas, H. and Knöble, W. (2009) *Social theory: Twenty introductory lectures*, Cambridge: Cambridge University Press.

Korff, J. (2016a) 'NTER – the intervention', www.creativespirits.info/aboriginalculture/politics/northern-territory-emergency-response-intervention#axzz4CSK1APra, accessed 24 June 2016.

Korff, J. (2016b) 'Royal Commission into Aboriginal deaths in custody', www.creativespirits.info/aboriginalculture/law/royal-commission-into-aboriginal-deaths-in-custody#axzz4CSK1APra, accessed 24 June 2016

Lathouras, A. (2010) 'Developmental community work – a method', in A. Ingamells, A. Lathouras, R. Wiseman, P. Westoby and F. Caniglia (eds), *Community development practice: Stories, method and meaning*, Melbourne: Common Ground Publishing Pty Ltd, Melbourne, pp 11–28.

Lathouras, A. (2012) 'An exploration of the relationship between structure and community development practice: towards a theory of structural community development', unpublished PhD thesis, Brisbane: University of Queensland.

Lathouras, A. (2013) 'The power of structural community development to unlock citizen-led change', *New Community*, vol 11, no 4, pp 15–26.

Lathouras, A. (2016) 'A critical approach to citizen-led social work: putting the political back into community development practice', *Social Alternatives* (forthcoming).

Ledwith, M. (2011) *Community development: A critical approach* (2nd edn), Bristol: The Policy Press.

Ledwith, M. and Springett, J. (2010) *Participatory practice: Community-based action for transformative change*, Bristol: The Policy Press.

Owen, J.R. and Westoby, P. (2012) 'The structure of dialogic practice within developmental work', *Community Development*, vol 43, no 3, pp 306–19.

Pease, B. (2010) *Undoing privilege: Unearned advantage in a divided world*, London: Zed Books.

Pilger, J. (2014) 'Festival of dangerous ideas: John Pilger – breaking Australia's silence', https://www.youtube.com/watch?v=0g73A-QHvao, accessed 24 June 2016.

Pilger, J. (2015) 'Evicting Indigenous Australians from their homelands is a declaration of war', *Guardian*, 22 April, https://www.google.com. au/?client=firefox-b#q=Evicting+Indigenous+Australians+from+their+homelands+is+a+declaration+of+war%E2%80%99&gfe_rd=cr, accessed 24 June 2016.

Rawsthorne, M. and Howard, A. (2011) *Working with communities: Critical perspectives*, Illinois: Common Ground Publishing.

Shaw, M. (2003) *Community work: Policy, politics and practice – working papers in social sciences and policy*, Hull: Social Policy Universities of Hull and Edinburgh.

Shaw, M. (2007) 'Community development and the politics of community', *Community Development Journal*, vol 43, no 1, pp 24–36.

Thompson, N. (2011) *Promoting equality: Working with diversity and difference* (3rd edn), London: Palgrave Macmillan.

Watts, J. (2015) *Gender, health and healthcare*, Farnham: Ashgate.

Wheatley, M. (2006) *Leadership and the new science: Discovering order in a chaotic world*, San Francisco, CA: Berrett-Koehler Publishers.

White, W.J. (2008) 'The interlocutor's dilemma: the place of strategy in dialogic theory', *Communication Theory*, vol 18, pp 5–28.

FOURTEEN

Building strengths in asylum-seeker communities in Australia

Lis de Vries, Mohita Roman and Linda Briskman

Introduction

An asylum seeker receiving individual casework said of her experience:

> "The only hope for people like me is Red Cross. I thank first to God. Second to the Australian Government because I feel safe. And third Red Cross." (Briskman, 2014a, p 60)

Australian Red Cross (Red Cross) has for many years delivered high-quality, strengths-based individualised casework services. In the last few years, our experience, on-going consultation with asylum seekers and a rapidly growing number of clients[1] drove Red Cross to consider a broader, more adaptive and more inclusive community development model. Such a model would encourage resilience and self-reliance, would recognise the role of the community in supporting dignity, health, well-being and social inclusion and would bring clients in as their own experts. However, in determining this change, Red Cross was faced with the challenge of implementing a community development model in a large, formal organisation with a group often considered by the broader Australian community as 'outsiders', and without access to many mainstream services and opportunities.

This chapter discusses how Red Cross, through its vast experience of casework with people seeking asylum, adapted and changed the service delivery model from individual casework to a community development approach. This approach recognises the essential role of community in resilience and well-being, and holds much potential. However, implementation is also fraught with ethical and practical tensions, largely arising from the external policy environment. Red Cross, as an impartial, humanitarian organisation mandated to provide assistance based on need, has had to consider the implications and develop responses when working as a contractor to government, where the scope of the service-provider role is clearly defined within government policy.

We draw on insider and outsider expertise of Red Cross. Two of the authors have had many years of experience working in asylum-seeker programmes within Red Cross. The third is an academic with research expertise in the area of asylum seeking, who conducted an evaluation of the Red Cross Casework Model at the time when the organisation was transitioning toward community development. In order to provide context for the chapter, we first provide an overview of asylum seeking in Australia, then describe Red Cross work in this domain. We then turn to the entry of Red Cross into the community development field, probing the benefits and limitations.

Asylum seekers in Australia

There are around 65 million displaced people in the world, more than 21 million of whom are refugees or asylum seekers (UNHCR, 2015). A refugee, according to the common United Nations definition, is a person who has left his or her country of origin and cannot return, due to a well-founded fear of persecution for reasons of race, religion, nationality, membership of a particular social group or political opinion. An asylum seeker has arrived directly to a country, applied for protection and is awaiting an assessment of his or her application. Refugees have had claims for asylum accepted, either after a government has considered the claim or, in a relatively few cases, by virtue of being members of a defined group, as in the case of the UN Gateway Programme.

Since the introduction of mandatory immigration detention in 1992, asylum seekers who arrive by boat have been subject to Australian government policies that have become increasingly punitive, focusing on deterrence and the security of Australia's borders. Although numbers of people arriving by boat are small on a global scale, successive Australian governments have focused on this mode of arrival, declaring that people seeking asylum and arriving by air have used a legitimate means of arrival (arriving with a visa) as opposed to those arriving by boat, who are usually availing themselves of people smugglers (arriving without a visa). The government describes people arriving by boat as 'unlawful non-citizens' or 'illegal maritime arrivals', despite the fact that they have a right to seek asylum under international law and not to be penalised for their mode of entry. For people seeking asylum, this stigma creates a further level of stress and vulnerability that has become a hallmark for their entry into life in Australia

People arriving by boat are detained in detention facilities in urban, regional and remote Australia. Detention time periods can be lengthy; as at March 2015, of the 2,512 people in detention, 40.1% had been detained for over two years (DIBP, 2015). Release from detention is generally dependent on being granted a temporary visa or leaving Australia to return to the country of origin. The temporary visa allows a person to stay in Australia while their application for protection is being assessed. The government is able to place any conditions on visas, including a length of time, reporting conditions and the right to work. Furthermore, the Department of Immigration and Border Protection (DIBP) requires people seeking asylum in the community to sign a Code of Behaviour that requires them to agree to abide by the laws of Australia (to which they are already subject) and not to engage in 'anti-social' or 'disruptive' behaviour. Breaching the Code may be grounds for cancelling a visa and re-detention.

Community support

For the past 20 years, Red Cross has supported thousands of people through a range of services for asylum seekers in the Australian community, funded by internal and external sources and run by staff and volunteers. During the period 2010–14, Red Cross supported 25,000 asylum seekers coming into the community from detention facilities (ARC, 2015, p 2). This took place under the now named Status Resolution Support Services (SRSS), funded by DIBP. SRSS provides casework and support services to clients, who are referred by DIBP into a 'band' based on their level of vulnerability, specified needs and other criteria that may be determined by the government. The SRSS contract became a vehicle to implement the community development approach.

SRSS clients are people seeking asylum and living in the community while their application for asylum is being resolved. This is a slow process that can take many years, creating prolonged uncertainty for people seeking asylum in the community. As of the policy changes in 2014/15, if found to be refugees they will be eligible for non-permanent visas; if not, as noted, they will be required to return to their country of origin.

The effect of living with this uncertainty creates a situation for people seeking asylum where they are living in limbo (ARC, 2013, p 12), as 'outcasts' who do not know whether their situation is temporary or permanent (Bauman, 2004). This is compounded by living on incomes less than the lowest social assistance payment (for most, this is 89% of the relevant 'normal' payment). Due to the temporary nature of their visas, asylum seekers find it difficult to obtain work and to secure stable housing (RCOA, 2015, pp 8–10) and are not eligible for a range of services and concessions to which Australian citizens are entitled.

Implementing an approach to community development that is sustainable is delicate for asylum seekers who are in a suspended environment that is temporary and transitional. This environment is not only a result of their asylum-seeker status, but from being exposed to a complicated range of government policies that may change over time.

Red Cross and asylum seekers

The situation facing asylum seekers awaiting a decision is difficult, is desperate and is often without hope. The framework for Red Cross work with asylum seekers is guided by seven Fundamental Principles of the international Red Cross and Red Crescent Movement: humanity; impartiality; neutrality; independence; voluntary service; unity; and universality.[2] The work with asylum seekers is primarily grounded in humanity and from a position of impartiality, or, colloquially, providing assistance based on need, not legal status, mode of arrival or nationality.

The Red Cross Movement has a long history and core commitment to working with migrants, and the parameters of that work in Australia are quite clear. For example, Red Cross does not support on-going detention of asylum-seekers and therefore provides services only to asylum seekers in the community, not in immigration detention facilities in Australia or Australian-funded offshore centres. It should be noted, however, that Red Cross does monitor these detention facilities. Red Cross does not support long-term detention. Its policy on migration states:

> While governments may determine that immigration detention is necessary for initial health and security checks, Australian Red Cross believes that it should otherwise only be used as a last resort and always for the shortest practicable time. We believe that families with children and unaccompanied minors should not be held in immigration detention facilities. (ARC, 2012)

The work of Red Cross in providing services to asylum seekers in the community is a strong message about the importance of alternatives to detention and is also consistent with the asylum seeker advocacy movement, which has long called for community-based alternatives to immigration detention.[3]

Red Cross has been providing casework support for asylum seekers since 1993; this work is funded by DIBP and has grown and developed significantly over time. With increasing government funding commensurate with increasing asylum seeker numbers, the SRSS programme was created and, through a competitive tendering process, SRSS services are now delivered throughout Australia by 10 organisations, including Red Cross. As often occurs in the privatisation process, this has created competitive tension and, ultimately, new forms of cooperation between the non-governmental organisations selected to deliver the services.

From casework to community development

In 2012 Red Cross formally implemented the strengths–based Casework Model, alongside a set of Good Practice Guides to support caseworkers. The Casework Model, supported by the Red Cross Fundamental Principles, outlines a casework practice based on the strengths and capabilities of clients and driven by the client as the expert. The model was used by Red Cross caseworkers consistently across the country, with casework tasks defined as undertaking client needs assessments, providing information, making appropriate referrals and seeking to ensure continuity of care.

By 2014, the numbers of asylum seekers living the community and supported by Red Cross were growing rapidly, and peaked at just over 10,000 clients. It became apparent that with this large number of clients, many with similar issues, support could be offered differently from the traditional casework approach. Red Cross therefore undertook a review of the strengths–based Casework Model (Briskman, 2014a) in 2014 and found that while the model was sustainable, and based on sound principles, benchmarks and literature sources, the organisation also needed to be able to balance support for individual clients with engagement with communities and with the need to be agile in a complex and dynamic environment.

It was at this time that Red Cross turned to community development to search for alternative responses. Fundamental to the approach of Red Cross is the intersection of casework and community development, which are seen as complementary (Palmer, 2014, p 5). The underpinnings of the Red Cross approach to community development are that it is community led, participatory and strengths based. The

Community Development Framework, as policy and practice guidance, is based on principles such as communities deciding on their own priorities and how to act on them, supporting communities to navigate and engage with systems, supporting culturally preferred practices and identifying skills and knowledge as well as what tools and resources they require. The aim is to build empowered and resilient communities.

With many Red Cross staff having qualifications in social work or cognate disciplines, a range of theoretical principles further underlined ways of working, including anti-oppressive practice and empowerment, among 'practice theories that can help with understanding and responding to complex human issues' (Connolly and Healy, 2013, pp 19–33). In drawing on well-established principles of community development, it was recognised by Red Cross architects that the term 'community development' is not fixed and that its application varies according to context (Ife, 2013).

A key concept within any community development model is defining the 'community'; this posed some difficulties in the consideration of asylum seekers as a community. Communities are complex and dynamic and it is often not possible for an outsider to define what is or is not a community. A good practice in defining a community would be to '[let] people define who they are, then [bring] them together' (Bloomfield, 2006). In this sense, the idea of 'community' slid between 'community of origin' (home location) or 'community of interest' (asylum seeker community), both inadequate in defining the meaning of community.

> "[I have no interest in connecting with the Iranian community] I am an Iranian Arab ... I speak Arabic at home and I live with an Iraqi Arab." (ARC, 2013, p 14)

Asylum seekers are by no means a homogeneous group. While some may have a common ethnicity, for example the Kurdish or Hazara, they may have lived in different countries. A group may have a common country of origin but have different languages and ethnicities, for example the Rohingyan and Kareni from Myanmar. Within ethnic communities there are sometimes divisions between those who are newly arrived and those who are settled. There are 'community' limitations arising from language, religion and also gender. Ife (2010) sees mobility as one of the causes of loss of community, and similarly Agier (2008) sees displacement resulting in 'the loss of a geographical place in which were attached attributes of identity, relationship and memory'.

Interestingly, a common bond or perhaps 'community' is often formed during the journey fleeing from their country of origin, which is extremely significant for asylum seekers. Many identify strongly with those they journeyed with to Australia, and this reinforced by the Australian government, which identifies asylum- arriving by boat by a boat number that becomes an identifier. Furthermore, for many the experience of detention can be one of bonding with fellow asylum seekers, particularly for those who have spent years in hot, dusty detention facilities in remote parts of Australia. Although they are a source of emotional support, these networks cannot provide the orientation, advice, practical and financial support that asylum seekers need from their community (ARC, 2013, p 14).

On entering the Australian community an asylum seeker may or may not become part of a common ethnic community. This could depend on the community and their view of asylum seekers, or an asylum seeker may isolate themselves by choice. In identifying asylum seekers as a community, Red Cross was aware from the outset that a community exists only to the extent that it is self-identified.

The community development approach was introduced based on a needs assessment of each individual client. If a client was deemed to have high needs, or to be experiencing complex vulnerabilities, they were allocated a caseworker who continued to work with them in accordance with the Casework Model. Individual casework remained an essential component of the service model, given the high risks, including high levels of mental health issues, facing this client group. For those clients assessed as having medium or low-level needs there was the capacity for clients to identify common areas of concern, to learn and work together and to support each other. Although this was initially facilitated at an individual level through client/worker interactions, programmes developed in a collaborative way in the implementation process, as discussed below.

Although there was good will to implement a community development approach, the architects and implementers of the approach were acutely aware that there were constraints, including government policies and funding. A Red Cross-specific community development approach was required that would work within constraints, would be consistent with the Red Cross ethos and would adher as closely as the context would allow to normative community development principles.

Implementing the community development model

The community development approach was conceptually introduced to clients and initially communicated as a new model of receiving services within a context of a 'Hub' within the office they usually attended. The Hubs were designed as resource centres where asylum seekers receive on-the-spot help for a range of issues. The introduction of the Hub was a first phase in moving towards the community development model, in itself a service and referral site, but with the potential to facilitate community development practices.

Importantly, the community development model would work only when local offices owned the approach. There were significant local variations in client demographics, and particularly in numbers of clients. The larger offices in Sydney, Melbourne and Perth had multiple service-delivery sites, compared to single city-based sites for those with fewer than 100 clients. Some Red Cross offices were refurbished to create an amenable Hub space, while others made only minor modifications.

Red Cross implemented a new staffing structure to support the move to the community development model. Through a careful reorganisation process, staff were placed into caseworker or support worker streams, with support workers reoriented to undertake Hub work alongside community development work. The human resource, training and team development process took approximately six months.

Red Cross commenced the implementation of the community development model with the introduction of the Hub and organisational changes; however, it was integral to the model that asylum seekers were engaged in the process in order for them to be empowered to make decisions into the future about what they needed and how services should be delivered. All local offices were asked to establish client consultative committees.

Case study 1: Client consultative committee

In the Tasmanian office, staff set up a Client Consultative Group. The staff recognised that while they consulted stakeholders broadly, they did not have a space for the key stakeholder, the client. They set up a group that met regularly and provided feedback on work of the organisation that was taken up by staff, identified referral services and took action on issues identified. For example, the need for legal support led to the establishment of a pro bono legal response from a network of local lawyers.

Red Cross actively worked on the principles of co-design rather than a client feedback model. Co-design was about learning from the clients, bringing them into the planning of services and making sure that services were delivered in a way that met the needs of the asylum seekers.

Case study 2: Co-design

The Red Cross Sydney office staff consulted with Afghan community leaders and a key Afghan community organisation, Human Care Welfare, in order to develop a better understanding of the issues facing Red Cross asylum seeker clients from an Afghani background. Red Cross and Human Care Welfare identified major challenges for asylum seekers in the process of transition into the Australian community – specifically, concerns related to orientation, linking with services and promoting connectedness and integration. A project to address these issues was developed and delivered through Human Care Welfare, not Red Cross. Through its community embeddedness and cultural sensitivity, Human Care Welfare was better able to locate, reach out and engage directly with asylum seekers. Demonstrating good community development practice, Red Cross works in the background with Human Care Welfare to provide advice, support and resources.

Local Red Cross staff worked with and facilitated groups of asylum-seeker clients to come together to plan their own activities. In this way asylum seekers identified their own areas of concern and planned responses. This might mean activities with gender or age segregation or activities within a particular ethnic community. Activities would need to be supported by Red Cross and in accordance with the Fundamental Principles; for example, this would exclude activities that might be considered too political as these would go against the principle of impartiality.

Case study 3: Community-driven activities

In Perth a leadership group including four members from asylum-seeker ethnic communities was developed to undertake community development activities locally. The group described its aim as 'improving settlement and community integration and participation with the local community'. One activity that resulted was a Women's Morning Tea to address the social isolation of vulnerable new female migrants; the group meets once a month in two separate locations, children are welcome and activities include craft, healthcare, English-language development and guest speakers.

An initiative in Melbourne is a Hub Harvest Program where a community gardening programme is run in two locations and asylum seekers generally are welcome to attend the gardening spaces. This includes an eight-week programme on composting, permaculture, seed propagating and other gardening skills. Participants are assisted in setting up their own home gardens.

In Adelaide, Multicultural Community Dinners were identified by the community as a project to address social interaction, skill development and alleviation of stress and anxiety. A committee was formed to plan the monthly events. The committee received food safety training and undertook all event planning including site, catering, advertising and financial management. The dinners were so successful that the committee explored social enterprise options.

The community development model, associated introduction of the Hubs and local area work is in very early stages. A first evaluation is being undertaken and the result of that will move the model from a more reactive phase into a more coordinated approach, with co-design at the centre.

Practice learnings and reflections

Red Cross took a very considered position in moving to a community development model in working with asylum seekers, and through this process there continue to be many hurdles, learnings and practice implications.

First, and perhaps most obviously, a community development approach could not be homogeneous. The national Red Cross developed a Community Development Framework (ARC, 2014) for the implementation of a practice model, alongside an organisational and staffing structure to implement this approach. However, a community development approach could work only if local offices of Red Cross took ownership, involved asylum seekers, were adaptive and dynamic and allowed the unexpected to emerge.

This 'top-down' organisational approach could be seen as the antithesis of community development. A true community development approach would, arguably, begin with asylum seekers themselves identifying their own strengths and capacities and deciding on their own priorities. It would also work to reduce power differentials and to value process rather than outcome; these are difficult aspirations within a formal organisation delivering a government contract.

This further calls into question the genuine collaboration between a formal organisation and people seeking asylum in the design and delivery of programmes. While local offices established client committees to work together to co-design the scope and delivery of programmes, this was generally facilitated by Red Cross and often led by Red Cross. However, the activities that emerged from this process were delivered much more successfully and sustainably through a community development process.

The defining of a community proved to be less problematic. People seeking asylum themselves demonstrate elements of community connectedness. They may have common shared experiences of their journey to Australia, or of their new life in Australia. They are bound by their 'outsider' status in being in situations of prolonged uncertainty while they wait for the government to determine the outcome of their claim for refugee status. These complexities, while present in many community development debates, are perhaps accentuated here and reinforce the importance of allowing asylum seekers to self-identify their own community membership. In many cases, of course, refugee communities may develop within a transnational context, with connections made between groups dispersed to different countries.

A practice conundrum present for Red Cross throughout its work in both casework and community development is the usefulness of a strengths-based approach for a group of people who, while seeking asylum, have control removed from many aspects of their lives. Asylum seekers usually arrive with very few material possessions and are resource poor. Asylum seekers are able to work only if permitted by government, are unable to study once they have reached adulthood, face challenges in accessing housing in an expensive market, have multiple health and mental health issues and are often alone or with few social supports. The evaluation of the casework model referred to above found that Red Cross practitioners grappled with the notion of strengths because of the vulnerability of asylum seekers. Responses from staff were that previous 'institutionalisation' (detention) compounded asylum seekers' difficulties. Others referred to mental health issues and said it was difficult to work from a 'strengths' position when there was a sense of hopelessness or 'risk' such as suicide ideation. Nonetheless, most referred to strengths and resilience inherent in all humankind, and specifically within the asylum seekers, who have faced persecution, trauma and often an unimaginable journey of escape. For Red Cross, it was apparent that, given appropriate resources, support and acknowledgement, all communities have strengths and assets that can create a climate for change (Briskman, 2014b).

For Red Cross there is also a question of sharing power in the community development context. Community development theory, while acknowledging the tension, generally holds a view that there should be shared power, or at the very least a shift in the relationships between the individual and the person in power, so that a community can take a more significant part in an issue that affects their lives. In this context, people seeking asylum have very little power and, organisationally, Red Cross possesses a wealth of power in many arenas, such as language, local knowledge, the capacity to refer to other services and financial resources derived from a government contract. This tension, while acknowledged, remains.

Finally, and importantly, Red Cross is delivering services to asylum seekers in the context of the SRSS contract with the government. Clients are referred by DIBP and allocated to a particular 'band' that stipulates the types of services that clients are entitled to. In applying the community development model Red Cross was required to evidence to DIBP that it was meeting the terms of the contract. There are a number of reporting requirements within the government contract, and while requirements related to reporting issues to DIBP are made clear to the client in the worker–client context, this potentially compromises the relationship between the organisation and the person seeking asylum. A client will potentially be guarded in both a casework and community development context if they are aware that issues could be reported to the very statutory authority that will determine the visa outcome for the client.

Enacting principles of community development is difficult in this complex environment. The community development model is client centred, allowing individuals and communities to decide on their own priorities and choose how to act on them. It also recognises agency, rather than positioning vulnerable groups solely as victims. It overcomes critiques of capacity building that can be interpreted as referring to a personal deficit. The Red Cross model allows communities to identify what skills and knowledge they would like to develop, as well as the resources they require. In this way, the approach is consistent with Ife's (2010) notion of community development that validates knowledge and expertise from the communities themselves and allowing them control of processes. The difficulty for Red Cross is that these community development principles can translate only into programmes and activities that are sympathetic to Red Cross as an organisation and meet the contract arrangements with DIBP.

Conclusion

Red Cross has systematically worked to develop and implement a Community Development Framework in its work with asylum seekers in Australia. This has been undertaken as a move from a fixed casework model to applying a more flexible service delivery model depending on the needs and vulnerabilities of clients.

People seeking asylum in Australia are highly disempowered, in a context of an acrimonious debate where the very act of seeking asylum is deemed illegal by many, and having to live in a situation of prolonged uncertainty awaiting the outcome of their application for asylum. Applying a strengths–based community development model in this context has faced multiple challenges.

Red Cross has successfully initiated a community development model with people seeking asylum; however, there is some way to go. Applying community development principles is challenging in an environment of complex issues facing people seeking asylum, delivered in the context of a government contract and by a formal organisation.

Notes

[1] The terms 'people seeking asylum', 'asylum seekers' and 'clients' are used interchangeably.

[2] For more information on the seven Fundamental Principles, see: www.redcross. int/en/.

[3] See, for example, International Detention Coalition, http://idcoalition.org.

References

Agier, M. (2008) *On the margins of the world: The refugee experience today*, Cambridge: Polity Press.

ARC (Australian Red Cross) (2012) *Policy statement on migration*, Melbourne: Australian Red Cross, www.redcross.org.au/files/ Policy_on_Migration.pdf, accessed 15 September 2016.

ARC (2013) *Inaugural Vulnerability Report, Inside the process of seeking asylum in Australia*, Melbourne: Australian Red Cross, www.redcross. org.au/files/ARC_VulnerabilityReport_LR.PDF, accessed 15 September 2016.

ARC (2014) *Community development framework, migration support programs*, Melbourne: Australian Red Cross.

ARC (2015) *Reflection report, Community Migration Program 2010–2014*, Melbourne: Australian Red Cross.

Bauman, Z. (2004) *Wasted lives: Modernity and its outcasts*, Cambridge: Polity Press.

Bloomfield, J. (2006) 'Making the most of diversity: profile of intercultural innovators. Bradford: Comedia', in A. Palmer (ed) (2014), *Community development with migrants in transition: A review of international best practice*, internal report, Melbourne: Australian Red Cross.

Briskman, L. (2014a) *Migration support programs (MSP) casework model: An evaluation*, Melbourne: Swinburne University of Technology.

Briskman, L. (2014b) *Social work with Indigenous communities: A human rights approach*, Melbourne: Federation Press.

Connolly, M. and Healy, K. (2013) 'Social work practice theories and frameworks', in M. Connolly, and L. Harms (eds) *Social work contexts and practice*, Melbourne: Oxford University Press, pp 19–33.

DIBP (Department of Immigration and Border Protection) (2015) *Immigration detention and community statistics summary*, Canberra: Australian Government.

Ife, J. (2010) 'Capacity building and human development', in S. Kenny and M. Clarke (eds), *Challenges to capacity building: Comparative perspectives*, Basingstoke: Macmillan, pp 67–84.

Ife, J. (2013) *Community development in an uncertain world: Vision, analysis and practice*, Melbourne: Cambridge University Press.

Palmer, A. (ed) (2014) *Community development with migrants in transition: A review of international best practice*, Melbourne: Australian Red Cross.

RCOA (Refugee Council of Australia) (2015) *Eroding our identity as a generous nation*, www.refugeecouncil.org.au/wp-content/uploads/2015/12/1512-Asylum.pdf, accessed 15 September 2016.

UNHCR (United Nations High Commission on Refugees) (2015) 'Global trends 2015', *Statistical Yearbook*, www.unhcr.org/figures-at-a-glance.html, accessed 15 September 2016.

FIFTEEN

The balancing act: community agency leadership in multi-ethnic/ multiracial communities

Morris Beckford

Toronto has become one of the most diverse cities in North America, and certainly the most diverse in Canada. In 2004 Toronto had the second-largest number of foreign-born residents of any major world city (UNDP, 2004). By 2011, nearly 50% of the total population were ethnic/visible minorities, with the top five visible minorities quickly becoming the 'visible majority'; these included South Asians, making up 12.3% of the population; Chinese, 10.8%; Black, 8.5%; Filipino, 5.1%; and Arab/West Asian/Afghan (that is, Assyrian and Iranian), 3.1% (Statistics Canada, 2011). In such an ethnically diverse environment, challenges are inevitable. Since ethnicity is a contested term with varying ontological and epistemological challenges I will borrow Varshney's definition to nail down how I intend to relate to the term. By ethnicity I mean a 'term which designates a sense of collective belonging, which could be based on common descent, language, history, culture, race, or religion (or combination of these)' (Varshney, 2007, p 277).

The communities on which this chapter focuses are nestled within two of the most diverse federal political boundaries in Canada – York West and York South Weston – in Northwest Toronto. In York West, over 72% of the population is non-white, while in York South Weston over 50% of the population is non-white. In York West, the top three ethnic groups proportionately are White (27.5%), Black (22.4%),and South Asian (16.0%). In York South Weston the top three groups are White (44.9%), Black (21.1%) and Latin American (9.0%) (City of Toronto, 2011). Within each of these political boundaries are three communities, whose real names have been altered, which we will call Days, Chalks and Falls. Days is ethnically dominated by South Asians; Falls comprises predominantly Somalis and Black/Afrodisaporic Caribbean peoples; and Chalks comprises predominantly Spanish-speaking peoples. This categorisation of course begs the question as to whether or not Somalis are Black and requires deeper analysis than I can provide here.[1] This classification is based solely on self-segregation of peoples in the communities. Although the primary focus of the chapter will be on my work with these communities, I will draw on community work in other communities in Toronto, as I have similar experiences throughout.

These communities are part of, or very close to, communities identified by the city of Toronto as Neighbourhood Improvement Areas (NIA), classified as such because of the lack of resources and levels of poverty. The unemployment rate, a key indicator and root cause of poverty, is higher than the city average. In one neighbourhood the unemployment rate was more than 5% above the city average (City of Toronto, 2011). In this milieu of rapidly increasing diversity and dwindling resources come additional tensions and inter-ethnic and interracial conflicts (Cantle, 2005). It is in this context that community development practitioners like myself find ourselves in leadership positions within local organisations. The intersections of race, gender, sexuality, age, religion and so on are infused in daily life, which leads to the identification of varied and competing concerns and requires a balancing act for community development leaders. This chapter will look at the balancing act that community development agency leaders must perform when working with different ethnic and racial/racialised groups, often with competing priorities and multiple differing opinions and needs.

'Race', a divisive trait that plays a significant role in the balancing act, has led to some of the most acrimonious tensions and abuses in human history. Yet many people in our society continue to hold the erroneous belief that there is something biologically significant about it. There is a perception that because two people share a skin colour they must be alike biologically. In fact, biologically speaking, there is nothing further from the truth. 'Race' is a sociocultural construct, a disturbing means by which we label people based on the colour of their skin and treat them the way we think they ought to be treated or have been taught to treat them, because of that label (Pincus, 2006). Schools and other publicly funded institutions in many of these communities often have long-held absurd beliefs, many of which are hold-overs from colonialism, that they attribute to or associate with 'race'. Although these institutions may not themselves have or perpetuate belief systems, they are operated by people who create ideologies and systems of oppression, many of which utilise the concepts of 'race' and ethnicity. For example, I cannot play basketball to save my life. All I wanted to play in high school was hockey. I remember going home once and telling my mother that one of my high school teachers wanted me to try out for the basketball team. My mother took me into the kitchen, looked me squarely in the eye and told me to tell my teacher that she didn't need me auditioning for a part I already had. I later realised that she was not talking about the part on the team. She was talking about the idea that since I was already visibly black I did not need to play into the ridiculous stereotype that all black people could play basketball. She too, much earlier than myself, understood the underlying racist stereotypes that continue to plague many people of colour. As Pincus wrote (2006, p 32), 'it's safe to say that most blacks like most whites have only average ability in these [basketball and football] two sports'.

There are also certain perceptions that people have of black leaders. It was not long after taking on my first non-profit executive role. I walked into a room full of other non-profit executives and leaders. We started talking about the challenges of doing non-profit work, and before I knew it one of the other executives chimed in and congratulated 'people like you' who were on the front lines of 'youth work'. Of course until then I had never met him and had not done any significant pieces of youth work, certainly nothing that would have made me known to the general public. Much of my work had actually been with seniors and adults. On another occasion, I was asked if I was still doing 'youth work'. Referring to one of the only black people in a group of leaders as a youth worker is problematic for a number of reasons. First, it's an assumption that one is not in a management or leadership role and, worse, should not possibly be even in a room full of leaders. Second, in the non-profit sector, youth work is entry level and among the lowest-paid positions. To assume that one of the only black people in a room that is supposed to be a meeting of leaders and managers is among the lowest-paid groups of the sector is offensive. These are of course those underlying systemic, micro-aggressive statements that sometimes get tossed out by people who may not even know that they being aggressive or dismissive (HR Council for the Nonprofit Sector, 2012b). Still, many of these perceptions make it difficult to navigate the daily systems of oppressions that leaders of colour often face. I distinctly remember a number of separate occasions that reminded me of this fact. There are, however, more significant and dangerous assumptions that people make about black people in our society.

The idea that blacks are innately inferior continues to fuel grossly exaggerated and racist stereotypes that breed ideas about criminality, ineptness, lack of intellectual ability and so on, which makes leading effectively even more precarious. These stereotypes breed a sense of fear of blacks among many members of our communities. These stereotypes are not new. They have been perpetuated since the days of slavery and the years following. In analysing *Birth of a nation*, a disturbing film, Reynolds and Robson (2016) notes that the film perpetuated the stereotype that blacks, especially black men, were to be feared because they are perceived as violent brutes who pose a risk to public safety and white purity. He also notes that this film played a pivotal role in the negative portrayal of blacks in the media that continues through to today.

Toronto has not been immune to or innocent of the spreading of these stereotypes. Desmond Cole, a Toronto journalist, made history with his exposé on what it is like growing up black in Toronto (Cole, 2015). Cole noted that he has been interrogated by police some 50 times because he is black.[2] This gross, race-based violation of a people's civil rights is common across the city of Toronto, as noted by the *Toronto Star*. Cantle (2005, p 101) notes that 'the "stop and search" debate about policing methods has become part of the mythology surrounding notions of inferiority of Blacks ...'. A 2004 report by Corrections Canada found that 'although they account for about 2% of the population in Canada, Blacks make up 6% of offenders incarcerated in federal correctional facilities and 7% of those serving time in the community' (Trevethan and Rastin, 2004). Many of these stereotypes then get perpetuated by the media, and then become the norm. They add to other stereotypes and get compounded. The perpetual bombardment then allows little space for reason. As a result, when I walk into these communities I am immediately perceived the way the media and others have defined me. Admittedly, there are steps between the mythology of inferiority and over-representation in the criminal justice system. However, what is more important here is the mythology of inferiority and the level of balancing that is needed when a black leader is forced to engage with the communities that at times subscribe to their leadership.

Much of my time as a community agency leader has been spent trying to fight these stereotypes, all the while trying to work from an antiracist perspective. I realised early that not only was I feared, I was also afraid. My blackness and living under constant oppression did not make me immune to the fear of those whom I perceived to be different from me. I too was being inundated by stereotypes about individuals. Many of us are taught, ever so subtly, through social service agencies, schools, media and a range of 'race'-based stereotypes – including that Asians are better at maths. Having taught maths for many years I can tell you that that is not true. I had to fight the urge to become complacent because I had an Asian finance manager. I had to remember that she, like all other finance managers, can make mistakes. I had to remember that a stereotype was no replacement for sound external financial advice and strong fiscal management.

When I worked in black communities there were certain expectations of me; this was probably because they see so few black leaders in the non-profit sector. The non-profit sector is a powerhouse in both the United States and Canada. It provides a considerable social safety net and helps to ensure that the unmet social, political and emotional needs of individuals often living in impoverished communities are catered for (Quarter et al, 2002). In Canada, there are over 85,000 non-profit organisations with charitable status, employing over two million workers. The sector adds nearly CAN$76 billion to the GDP, accounting for 8.5% of the nation's economic activity (Quarter et al, 2002). In the US there are over 1.4 million non-profits registered with the Internal Revenue Services. Together they contribute over [US]$900 billion to the American economy and account for 5.4% of the GDP (McKeever, 2015). So Canadian non-profits contribute more economic activity in relative terms.

Although the majority of these organisations aim to help poor and poorly served communities, staffing, especially at the leadership level, does not reflect the diverse nature of those communities. A recent study by Canada's Human Resources Council for the Non-profit Sector on non-profit executive leaders showed that over 90% of non-profit leaders are white and an alarming mere 2% are black (HR Council for the Nonprofit Sector, 2012a). In the US, the figures are even more disturbing. Studies show that among foundations, only 8% of leaders are people of colour (Gross, 2015). To a great extent, the black male social 'location' in Canada and the US has been one of either servitude or second-class status. The fact is that one of the largest sectors in both countries – ironically one that aims to help communities in need – has leadership staffing typically not representative of many of the communities it aims to help.

Being black brought me considerable cultural capital in the Black and Caribbean community, which made it infinitely easier for me to navigate the daily challenges of working in already challenging environments. Our shared class status allowed for a common understanding of oppression that made communication easier. A certain level of understanding is developed when two people share similar understanding and experience of systemic oppression. This makes it easier to create meaningful relationships. It also makes it easier for community agency leaders to discern situations accurately (Ehrenaus,

1983). This allows for easier navigation in and around topics that can sometimes be very difficult. During my time leading the agency a common challenge was around the area of the spanking of children. Spanking is a generally accepted disciplinary technique in many Black Caribbean homes. In my Caribbean–Canadian home it was almost like a rite of passage. Had I not been able to navigate my way through this, almost every parent in one of the communities would have had a file at the local Children's Aid Society (CAS) office.

In different cultural contexts, however, the relationship building and general engagement was not as easy. There were not only issues of 'race', as outlined above, and the challenges that come with them, there were issues of cultural context and communication. There were times when communication was not as effective because I was communicating using the expertise I had acquired from years of growing up among people of similar backgrounds and the person to whom I was communicating was deciphering my communications in terms of what they had learned from their upbringing (Ehrenaus, 1983, p 267). One summer I had a potentially explosive conflict with a parent in the largely South Asian community. I can't remember the reason why he was angry. I do remember that the communication between us slowly went off the rails because we were not able to speak to each other in a manner that we could each understand, even though we were both communicating in English. I finally decided to get one of our staff who was South Asian to act as a bridge to allow us to communicate effectively with each other. One of my great challenges is being careful not to run the risk of being radically reductionist when engaging with matters of 'race' and ethnicity. However, this too plays a significant role in the balancing act, as not every challenge is linked to matters of 'race'. There are times when I wonder whether or not a situation occurred because of my 'race' or ethnicity, or even my gender or some intersection of the three.

Although not as much as my 'race', but still to a significant extent, the balancing act also included my gender. I was taught that managing from the ground is a good management strategy, and so I have always striven to ensure that I know the agency I work for from the ground up. To that end I decided one day that I would join our kitchen staff and cut up fruit for our after-school programme. While I was in the kitchen I struck up a conversation with a female teacher. We started talking about the disrespect that people have for the social services sector and how sports players get paid more for doing far less. I started analysing why that was. She stopped me dead in my tracks and said 'It's because it's seen as woman's work'. We have a society that perpetuates the idea that men are dominant and women are subordinate (Pincus, 2006). As far as I was concerned, the agency was actively perpetuating this stereotype by having me as a man leading a team of female staff.

In working in these communities I had to be careful about balancing being male working in a patriarchal society and being the leader of a social service agency dominated by female workers, working to eliminate those barriers. In all three communities – Days, Chalks and Falls – community events showcased a clear segregation between men and women. In the South Asian community I would attend events where men and women seemed segregated, the men sitting on one site and the women sitting on the other. In the Caribbean community men would be sitting or talking outside while women engaged with each other inside. As an agency leader I had to make sure to spend an appropriate amount of time engaging with both groups while paying attention to the community's gender ideologies, making sure not to engage in activities that would reduce my cultural capital with either group. I realised early that it was perhaps not a good idea to try to serve food or wash dishes in such large groups. In the Caribbean community, residents were active in voicing their opinion about me not being in the kitchen because that was not where the men are supposed to be. Although these may seem like opportunities where challenging the stereotype would seem appropriate, a part of the balancing act is knowing when there is enough space to do so without exploiting any perceived power imbalance.

The ideal when doing community development work is to engage from an antiracist framework. A variety of writers identify antiracism as a 'call for a critical examination of how dynamics of social difference ("race", class, gender, sexual orientation, physical ability, language, and religion, country of origin) influence daily experiences often through institutions and inequitable access to resources and power and the historical, social, and political processes that have institutionalized and continue to maintain such unequal power' (Sankaran, 2011, p 65). Since I believe that I have moved closer to a place of antiracist discourse, I am confident that at the time I was merely trying to be more culturally competent in that I was working to operate in different cultures by trying to comprehend the challenges of those communities effectively. To this end I attended as many programmes and events as I could, and worked with community leaders better to integrate and immerse myself into everyday practices – understanding, of course, that it all amounted to merely dipping my toe into an ocean.

Days, which had the majority South Asian population, had a very popular seniors group that met weekly. It was a well-attended, vibrant group that I attended as regularly as I could. When I could not attend I would visit to at least say hello. After a few weeks of my attending, these seniors, all South Asian women, started to talk to me about what they needed in the community and what they needed for their group. A few months later they were making and offering me tea. I knew that things were different when they started referring to me as grandson and brought me tea. Cultural communication is a two-way street that also plays a significant role in the balancing act that community agency leaders play. It is not a linear, one-way action (Adler, 1991). Although spending time with me may have reduced and perhaps eliminated some of their stereotypes, where there are no specific benchmarks or indicators of what classifies a shift in perception from negative stereotyping to culturally competent or antiracist communication, one can never be sure. What I do know, however, is that some of the stereotypes I had heard about South Asian women were shattered. These women talked about issues important to them that bordered on radical feminism. One of them, who was not married and in fact had no interest in being married, loved being single and regularly sang parts of Beyoncé's 'single ladies' hit.

One of the biggest challenges of leading was dealing with competing priorities. This was particularly evident in Falls. The community has a mix of high-rise and single-family homes. The Somalis and Caribbean peoples largely lived in the high-rises and the Italians largely lived in the single-family homes. The agency for which I worked at the time did not have the resources to hire a staff member from each of these communities and so we relied heavily on the expertise of so-called 'community leaders' to help us engage with the communities. Each year we planned a community event and each year there were constant battles. As we planned the summer event, we were constantly trying to manage the opinions of the Italians present, who didn't think that the Somalian peoples should get any support for specific Somali activities. When the Italians didn't come to the meetings, the Caribbean peoples didn't think they should even be invited because they lived in the houses and were not considered a part of the community. When the Caribbean peoples didn't come to the meetings, the Somalian peoples thought that the Caribbean peoples shouldn't get anything else because they had a staff person who worked for the agency. It was difficult for many of them to see that they were all facing or had faced the same challenges. Even though their social and geographic locations were similar, their culturally, ethnically and raciallydefined walls were up, and had limited permeability.

Different ethnic and racialised groups have different priorities. These priorities are sometimes not in line with the priorities of other members of the community. While one ethnic group may think it pertinent to have a prayer room in their community, another group may think it a total waste of space. These competing priorities can lead to challenges ranging from violence, such as fights and racial slurs, to forms of conflict ranging from micro-insults to group avoidance and self-segregation (Walker, 2005). Maintaining stability and organisational neutrality is often difficult in communities with mixed ethnicities, especially when I am visibly linked to one of those communities. In Falls, there were perceptions that because I was of Caribbean descent I ought to side with the Caribbean peoples on issues important to them. So the same cultural capital that worked for me has in some instances worked against me. Many of these communities have already lost significant resources, and so any opportunity to make sure that they get a chance to become power brokers is explored thoroughly because they know that having control will allow them the capacity to mobilise resources to help their children or the children who look and, as far as they are concerned, think, act and do like them (Walton, 1971).

Race, ethnicity, antiracism, competing priorities, colonialist thought, underlying issues of gender around masculinity and femininity, ontological and epistemological origins and underlying discourse of who is right and whose knowledge is best, who should get and should not get resources are all their own tightrope on which community agency leaders must attempt to do their work well. Perceptions of blackness and male blackness are laced with everything from blatant racist comments to racist ambiguities that often affect black leaders in ways that I do not think many are even able to truly unpack, as there is the duality that we are supposed to be stronger than the rest because we have been through the experiences of racism and hate, but are simultaneously considered weak and inferior. There are, however, moments of light, those moments when someone tosses you a stick to help with the balancing, those moments when you are working with communities that have similar lived experiences and understand those challenges plaguing the hidden spaces between the seen and the unseen. There are also those moments when there seems to be an adoption of the leaders' otherness, genuine or otherwise, that if left out of the realm of immediate critical analysis may also lead to the chance to further engage with communities on a level that can lead to real growth and development for both the leader and the community. Torontonians continue to come from all across the country, and so we will continue our diversity streak. They will continue to have different, competing needs. This means that leaders will continue to perform the balancing act, and so we will need to continue to dialogue with each other in order to find those moments where we can engage with multi-ethnic communities effectively.

Notes

[1] See the Introduction to this volume for a discussion on terminology.

[2] A common phenomenon in most multicultural societies. For example, John Sentamu, a black Ugandan refugee, later to become the second most senior prelate in the Church of England in the UK, was frequently stopped by police when working as a parish priest in East London, on the basis, he suspected, of owning a reasonably priced car.

References

Adler, N. (1991) *International dimensions of organisational behaviour* (2nd edn), Boston, MA: PWS-KENT Publishing Company: esp. pp 63-91.

Cantle, T. (2005) *Community cohesion: A framework for race and diversity*, London: Palgrave Macmillan.

City of Toronto (2011) *Neighbourhood Demographic Estimates: 24, Black Creek*, Toronto: City of Toronto.

Cole, D. (2015) 'The skin I'm in: I've been interrogated by police more than 50 times – all because I'm black', http://torontolife.com/city/life/skin-im-ive-interrogated-police-50-times-im-black/.

Ehrenaus, P. (1983) 'Culture and the attribution process: barriers to effective communication', in W.B. Gudykunst (ed), *Intercultural communication theory: Current perspectives*, Beverly Hills, CA: Sage.

Gross, A. (2015) *The state of diversity in the nonprofit sector*, http://communitywealth.com/the-state-of-diversity-in-the-nonprofit-sector/

HR Council for the Nonprofit Sector (2012a) *Driving change: A national study of Canadian nonprofit executive leaders*, www.hrcouncil.ca/documents/driving_change.pdf.

HR Council for the Nonprofit Sector (2012b) *Recruitment and retention of new immigrants and members of visible minorities in the nonprofit sector's workforce*, www.hrcouncil.ca/documents/recruitment_newimmigrants.pdf.

Landis, D (2004) 'Developing intercultural sensitivity: an approach to global and domestic diversity', in D. Landis, J.M. Bennett, and M. Bennett (eds), *Handbook of intercultural training* (3rd edn), Thousand Oaks, CA: Sage.

McKeever, B.S. (2015) *The nonprofit sector in brief 2015: Public charities, giving, and volunteering*, www.urban.org/sites/default/files/alfresco/publication-pdfs/2000497-The-Nonprofit-Sector-in-Brief-2015-Public-Charities-Giving-and-Volunteering.pdf.

Pincus, F.L. (2006) *Understanding diversity: An introduction to class, race, gender and sexual orientation*, London: Lynne Rienner Publishers.

Quarter, J., Mook, J. and Richmond, B.J. (2002) *What counts: Social accounting for non-profits and co-operatives*, New Jersey: Prentice Hall.

Reynolds, G. and Robson, W. (2016) *Viola Desmond's Canada: A history of blacks and racial segregation in the promised land*, Halifax: Fernwood Publishing.

Sankaran, S. (2011) *Addressing health inequities for racialized groups: A resource guide*, Toronto: Health Nexus and Health Equity Council.

Statistics Canada (2011) *National Household Survey profile, National Household Survey year 2011*, Catalogue No. 99-004-XWE, Canada: Government of Canada.

Trevethan, S. and Rastin, C.J. (2004) *A profile of visible minority offenders in the federal Canadian correctional system*, Canada: Correctional Services of Canada.

UNDP (United Nations Development Programme) (2004) *Human Development Report, 2004: Cultural liberty in today's diverse world*, New York: UNDP.

Varshney, A. (2007) 'Ethnicity and ethnic conflict', *Oxford handbook of comparative politics*, http://ashutoshvarshney.net/wp-content/files_mf/varshneyethnicityandethnicconflict.pdf.

Walker, A. (2005) *Effective leadership in multi-ethnic schools: Part I: Priorities, strategies and challenges*, London: National College for School Leadership.

Walton, J. (1971) 'The vertical axis of community organizing and the structure of power', in C.M. Bonjeean, T.N. Clark and R.L. Lineberry (eds), *Community politics: A behavioural approach*, United States: The Free Press, pp 188–96.

SIXTEEN

Using arts and culture for community development in the United States

Lorraine Gutiérrez, Larry M. Gant and Shane Brady

The United States (US) is a settler nation, populated over the past five centuries by settlers from throughout the globe who displaced and dispossessed much of the original indigenous populations. This history of conquest and conflict, with voluntary and involuntary populations settling our country, has shaped the current state of race and ethnic relations in the United States. Our census statistics tell us that the population of the US is becoming increasingly complex and diverse. The US Census Bureau projects that through to 2050 the proportions of all racial and ethnic minority groups (Asian, Hispanic, African American, American Indian) will increase, while the proportion of Non-Hispanic White people will decrease as a result of fertility, immigration and age-distribution patterns (US Census Bureau, 2010). These trends challenge community development projects to implement methods and approaches that will be effective in a more diverse landscape that engages with increasing cultural complexity. We need to create and develop methods that are grounded within specific cultural contexts and that can contribute to community methods, that can bridge differences in race, culture, religion and identity (Thompson et al, 2011; Deepak et al, 2015).

Although this chapter is focused on community practice in the United States, growing cultural diversity and conflict is a global phenomenon. The globalisation of capital, environmental threats, political conflicts, economic contractions and religious conflicts have contributed to large population shifts across borders (Parrott, 2009). Recent events involving significant migration from the Middle East, northern Africa, and southern Europe into the European Union (EU) and other more stable and economically viable regions is only one example of the ways in which many societies are becoming more racially and culturally diverse.

We argue here that the arts and other cultural resources can be powerful tools for community development work in this multicultural and multiracial context. However, work with arts and cultural institutions must be intentional and mindful of potential differences and conflicts. We begin with an overview of arts-based community development, present our perspectives on considerations when doing this work and provide examples of different ways in which we have carried out this work with communities in the United States.

Arts-based community development

Community development is a major undertaking and focus of many different disciplines, including social work, urban planning, community psychology and public health. Community development can take on many different forms and encompass a variety of activities (Defilippis and Saegert, 2012). According to Thomas et al (2011), collaborative community practice values inclusivity, social participation from diverse groups, localised decision making at the neighborhood level and working with existing assets and strengths to address needs or deficits in the community. Community practice that lies within the collaborative paradigm takes root in the empowerment-oriented community work popularised by Addams (1910), Piven and Cloward (1977), Gutierrez and Lewis (1994), Checkoway (1995) and Reisch (2008). Community development from within the collaborative paradigm seeks to utilise local knowledge, assets and skills in order to bring about social change that is driven by community members' participation and vision (Brady and O'Connor, 2014).

In addition to being rooted in the paradigm of collaborative practice, our perspective on arts-based community development is rooted in the Asset-Based Community Development (ABCD) approach, with the use of culture and arts as mediums and mechanisms for bringing together diverse communities. ABCD was developed in North America by Kretzmann and McKnight (1993) as a practical guide for community-practice professionals and local organisers to build community capacity through utilising an asset-informed perspective, as opposed to the deficit or needs-based perspectives popularised by many community development and social planning entities (1993). ABCD is complementary to empowerment theories and practices that emphasise collaboration, respect for diversity and difference, and building collective power (Piven and Cloward, 1977; Gutierrez and Lewis, 1994). It seeks to first understand what is working well in a community, what unique skills and qualities and what forms of cultural and social capital exist among its members, in order to understand how to strengthen and build capacity in the community (Kretzmann and McKnight, 1993).

ABCD is best envisioned as an approach to community development that is targeted at both professionals and local community workers/leaders. It is based on the overarching theme that communities are rich, diverse places with many different assets or strengths that must be identified, appreciated and leveraged in order to address local needs (Checkoway, 1995). While many top–down approaches to community development begin interventions with collecting data on needs, privilege professional expert perspectives over localised standpoints and often ignore assets related to diverse cultures and associated arts-rooted strengths, ABCD emphasises beginning any community-based enquiry with community-building efforts that promote inclusivity from diverse groups, highlight the strengths within all sectors of the community and involve all members of the community (Kretzmann and McKnight, 1993).

Additionally, ABCD categorises assets as relating to: individuals, associations, institutions, physical spaces and connections. Individual assets are the inherent strengths, skills and knowledge that every person possesses and can bring forth to benefit the community. In ABCD, associations provide important and often localised networks of already-involved community members for new initiatives. Institutional assets include formal organisations, local businesses, social service agencies and others. For the purpose of ABCD, anchor institutions are of particular interest, as these institutions are the most embraced and frequented by community members as a result of their inclusive spaces, resources and opportunities (Delgado and Staples, 2008). Physical assets in ABCD are vacant buildings, green spaces, open land, footways/sidewalks, bike paths, water, gardens and other resources currently used by community members or that hold potential usefulness to community development efforts. Finally, connections as assets involve the larger social and professional networks that people belong to by virtue of their job, family and friends. The three cases discussed below in this chapter are all rooted in a collaborative paradigm, empowerment theory and an ABCD approach to community development.

The ABCD approach can be particularly appropriate for use within and between different cultural and racial groups because the arts and cultural resources (for example, libraries, museums, theatres, cultural centres) can be spaces for engaging and enriching communities. Arts and culture have great significance in many different racial and ethnic groups and, as a result, they can provide an excellent starting point for community building (Krajewski-Jaime et al, 2010). While many higher-need communities can become separated by racial, ethnic, cultural and religious differences, by coming to appreciate and learn from the cultural strengths that each group brings to the community it is possible to bridge differences through building connections across diverse community groups (Minkler and Wallerstein, 2011). The arts, as a vital component of diverse cultural groups, are an important and often overlooked asset in community development that must be considered when utilising an ABCD approach. Through realising and appreciating the cultural and arts-based assets of a community, the cases represented here were able to bring communities together and bridge difference.

Despite the popularity of ABCD in community development efforts, including those represented in the case studies presented here, it is important to point out that scholars and organisers have made several critiques of the ABCD approach. Many of the critiques of ABCD relate to the origins of the approach, which emerged during the rise of neoliberalism in the 1980s when conservative policies and approaches to community development sought to defund community organisations that emphasised critical models of community organising and social action in the US (Emejulu, 2015). As critical organising models became less fiscally viable and unpopular, community practitioners sought new ways to package community development initiatives and practices, which led to the popularity of approaches such as ABCD (Fisher, 1994). As a result of its neoliberal roots, ABCD has been criticised for not acknowledging power differentials and inequality between and within groups and populations residing in communities. Additionally, ABCD provides little guidance regarding how organisers and community leaders should address injustice in the context of community practice, which is also a critique of most community development approaches (Brady et al, 2014). Finally, critics of ABCD have questioned whether the approach is too optimistic and hopeful for use in many community contexts where decades of disinvestment and inequality have created significant challenges to community well-being and participation (Emejulu, 2015). While the authors acknowledge these critiques of ABCD, it is important to point out that very few approaches and models of community practice are suitable for every situation and context, which is why many scholars discuss and emphasise the need to combine different practice methodologies and tools in order to address different aims and goals within a community practice scenario (Rothman, 2008; Gamble and Weil, 2010; Brady and O'Connor, 2014).

Our interest in the complementarity of our art-based community development perspective with Kretzmann and McKnight's ABCD nicely synchronises within the larger and historical synergies of ABCD;, and ABCD, in turn, synchronises with more formal organisations and institutions in the US. Around the same time that Kretzmann and McKnight's work was systematised and published another national movement, the Community Arts Network, was established (in 1989) as one of two principal programmes of Arts in the Public Interest (API).[1] The founders of API included long-time artists Linda Burnham, Steven Durland and Maryo Ewell. Active in community-based arts since the 1960s, Burnham and her colleagues described 'community art' as a type of community cultural development in which 'art (was) made as a voice and a force within a specific community of place, spirit or tradition' (Burnham et al, 2004). In 1991, William Cleveland and colleagues created the Center for the Study of Art and Community (Bainbridge Island, Seattle, Washington State). Cleveland and colleagues later formalised the notion of art-based community development (abbreviated as ABCD) as 'arts-centered activity that contributes to the sustained advancement of human dignity, health and/or productivity within a community' (Cleveland, 2002, p 7). Interestingly, much as we have done now, Cleveland explicitly aligned purposes and interests between art-based community development and the other ABCD (asset-based community development) in 2002. Cleveland concurred 'with many in the community development field who feel that a thriving community must be supported primarily from within – by its members, resources and capacities, for the present and future' (Cleveland, 2002, p 7; also see Cleveland, 2005).

Further work yielded influential practice handbooks and case studies of creative uses of community art and community art institutions (Schwarzman and Knight, 2005; Silverman, 2010). Building upon collaborative experiences and work with API, Goldbard provided some of the first theoretical and analytic formulations of what came to be called 'community cultural development' as

> the work of artist-organizers and other community members collaborating to express identity, concerns and aspirations through the arts and communications media. It is a process that simultaneously builds individual mastery and collective cultural capacity while contributing to positive social change. (Goldbard, 2006, p 20)

This is mirrored in our current contemporary conceptualisations and narrative. More recently, arts-based community development and community development have become more or less used interchangeably, with neither much political incident nor academic invective (Curtis Center Program Evaluation Group, 2014; Gant, 2014).

Learning from history: the case of the Mexican voice

The use of arts-based methods for community development has many historical roots. The arts have been integral to all social movements, to the urban social settlements and to trades union organising (Brieland, 1990; Fabricant and Fischer, 2003). These movements have recognised the power of the arts and cultural institutions to bring together and create communities and as a means for carrying powerful messages. In more recent history the arts have been used to foster community development and action by groups, such as the NAMES Project, founded in 1987 and best known for developing the AIDS memorial quilt project. Its work not only generated social activism around HIV/AIDS and gay and lesbian concerns, but also served as a form of community development as it gathered community members together around art (McDonald et al, 2006). These historical examples exemplify how art has the capacity to play a key role in advancing one or more types of community change.

The case of *The Mexican Voice* and its role in the Mexican American Movement (MAM) in mid-20th-century California provides insights in which community journalism can contribute to community development within a marginalised cultural group. The typical scholarship on Mexican-American or Chicano activism in the US often overlooks the work of community organisations that began before the Second World War to bring Mexican-Americans together to question their social conditions (Gutiérrez, 1984; Muñoz, 1989). However, Mexican-American historians now identify the MAM as one of the first community-based organisations developed to advocate for the status of Mexican-Americans in California and the South-west (Muñoz, 1989; Sanchez, 1993).

Early development

The MAM developed from the Mexican Youth Conferences organised by the Los Angeles YMCA (Young Men's Christian Association) in Los Angeles in the mid-1930s (Gutiérrez, 1984; Muñoz, 1989; Tudico,

2010). This YMCA work began when a Mexican–American group worker was hired to create a youth leadership programme in order to reduce 'juvenile delinquency' among Mexican–American youth. As with all YMCA programmes of that era, group–work methods were used to engage young men in 'developing character, good citizenship, and desirable values' (Muñoz, 1989). The programme included an annual weekend conference where young men who had been selected for their leadership potential engaged in educational workshops and sports activities (Sanchez, 1993). One goal of these annual conferences was to develop local and regional groups for Mexican–American youth (Gutiérrez, 1984).

The Mexican Voice was founded by the MAM in 1938 as a way for the participants in the Mexican Youth Conferences to reach out to a greater number of youth and youth organisations in the region. Although the work was initiated under the auspices of the YMCA, this publication developed into a regional publication with increasing autonomy from its original sponsor. The Mexican Voice was edited by Félix J. Gutiérrez, a member of the MAM and the Mexican Youth Conference, who was a student at Pasadena Junior College. His journalism training began in high school and he had served as a writer and art editor of his high school newspaper and yearbook (Gutiérrez, 1984). The first issue was a single duplicated sheet, but by 1941 it was typeset and had original Mexican-themed art on the covers (Gutiérrez, 1984).

The founders of The Mexican Voice wanted to publish an 'inspirational/ educational youth magazine' for the community that would provide 'news of outstanding Mexican youth, his achievements, his thoughts, his ideals, and his aspirations' (The Mexican Voice, March 1940, p 14). Their intent was to counteract the negative image and stereotypes of Mexican-American youth and to encourage young people to continue their education and work toward personal and community improvement. Each issue covered topics focused on the social conditions of Mexican-Americans, news of local and regional clubs, profiles of successful Mexican-Americans, sports news and editorials on current events. When the US entered the Second World War there was coverage of the participation of Mexican-Americans in the armed forces, defence industries and other activities to support the war effort .

Culturally themed art was integral to each issue, with original art created for each cover. Most of this cover art was created by Juan Acevedo, the art editor and a student at Los Angeles City College.[2] These covers, such as the one illustrated in Figure 16.1 from the August 1939 issue, used cultural symbols to inspire young people, using familiar symbols such as the serape, charro tie and sombrero.

Figure 16.1: Cover art, *The Mexican Voice*, vol 2, no 3 (August 1939). Artist: Juan Acevedo.

In 1942 the leadership of the Mexican Youth Conference voted to leave the auspices of the YMCA and to incorporate as an independent non-profit organisation called the Mexican American Movement (MAM).The goals of the MAM incorporated many of the values of the YMCA group workers, such as community, self-education and democracy, in addition to broader goals emphasising improving the conditions of the Mexican-American community.

Although the MAM was relatively short lived, it contributed to the development of the community and its members in many ways. Connecting and bringing together Mexican-American young men and women from Arizona and California through its youth conferences and publications, it contributed to the solidarity of this population. The dialogue that took place also contributed to consciousness and awareness of the conditions of Mexican-American youth and young adults in the region. Equally important was the way in which the organisation enhanced the leadership skills and social development of its participants (Muñoz, 1989; Sanchez, 1993). Many of the participants went on to become educators, group workers and attorneys in the greater Los Angeles area and used the skills they had developed to create new organisations such as the Association of Mexican American Teachers, Parents without Partners and the Mexican American Political Association (Gutiérrez, 1984; Muñoz, 1989).

The historical example of *The Mexican Voice* and its role within the MAM provides insights for arts-based organising. The involvement of members in writing articles and creating art for each issue provided a collective activity through which they could hone their message and voice as a movement. The magazine issues then provided a voice for the movement and encouraged participation and membership. All the issues of *The Mexican Voice* are available in the University of California

Library archives and provide a lasting record of an early community development movement.[3]

The case of youth and the Good Neighborhoods photovoice project

Background

Good Neighborhoods was a major community-change initiative funded by the Skillman Foundation ('the Foundation') between 2005 and 2015, involving an organised effort that sought to create and foster healthy, safe and supportive neighbourhoods that allow for the full development of children and youth. The Foundation expected that initial technical assistance would be provided to six specifically identified and selected Detroit neighbourhoods to help convene and develop collective plans to address problems that impacted on the quality of life and development of children and youth. The Foundation contracted with a school of social work (SSW) at a major state university to co-create a technical assistance centre (TAC) providing technical assistance services. Assistance could include but was not limited to community organising, programme planning, development and implementation, fundraising and communications. Embedded in the work was the reality that all six neighborhoods were largely populated by lower-income African-American families with (at the time) nearly 60% of all children aged 0–12 years. The majority of neighbourhood residents experienced poor high school graduation rates, high unemployment and under-employment, sobering crime rates and extremely poor public schools. At the same time, residents expressed a strong affection for their neighbourhoods, willingness to work hard to improve the communities and great reluctance (but not much ability) to leave their communities (Gant et al, 2009).

The community change process that comprised Good Neighborhoods occurred in three phases: Planning, Readiness, and Transformation. During the Planning phase, residents and community stakeholders were engaged in community-wide planning processes. The product generated was a community action plan owned and driven by the community. It was important that the community owned the process and saw themselves as the community change agents, using the resources and expertise available to them through the Foundation and one of the Foundation's key partners, the TAC. The Foundation and partners met with key community stakeholders, indigenous leadership, faith-based leaders and major service providers in each neighbourhood.

The purpose of the initial meetings was to present the Foundation's theory of change, along with the resources it would make available if these key stakeholders saw value in this process and invited the Foundation and its partners into the neighbourhood to assist residents and stakeholders in implementing the change model. The invitation was made and accepted in all six neighbourhoods. This acceptance initiated the neighbourhood planning process. As a result, relationships were established, roles were clarified within the partnership and the residents and stakeholders in the neighbourhoods began to understand what to expect of each partner and to view TAC as a valuable resource in the process. We discuss one key strategy used to move the planning process forward: the Photovoice Youth Initiative.

Case scenario: youth presence and involvement in community planning

The extensive process of community dialogue and discussion is discussed elsewhere (Hollingsworth et al, 2009). During the initial series of discussions, small but highly vocal groups of youth across the community presentations and smaller community meetings persistently raised questions and expressed concerns about the extent to which children and youth – presumably the primary reason for the initiative – had any means of raising their concerns or issues throughout the community planning process.

Using ABCD in the Good Neighborhoods as youth mobilisation process

At around the same time, a presentation on the use of Photovoice in community development initiatives at the Fall 2007 American Evaluation Association conference prompted the Foundation to propose Photovoice as a youth mobilisation strategy for Good Neighborhoods (Love and Muggah, 2005; Love, 2007). The TAC accepted the Foundation's request to develop the Photovoice project as part of its participant training and education role, for two reasons. First, the co-primary investigator of TAC had previous and extensive experience with the Photovoice technique. Second, the TAC had strong relationships with all the neighbourhoods and could easily oversee and coordinate the project. The Good Neighborhoods Photovoice project was conducted over the summer of 2008 and enrolled 33 youth from five of the six Detroit neighbourhoods.

A team of five second-year Master's students from the TAC's SSW field unit were actively engaged in oversight of this project in which youth between the ages of 15 and 21 collected Photovoice data. The project had the dual advantage of broadening perceptions (strengths and deficits) of the neighbourhood from the perspective of its resident youth while engaging youth in research. Contrary to what was hypothesised, there was not a significant increase in positive attitudes toward civic engagement across the sample of 15- to 21-year-olds. However, there was a main effect for age. Youth in the 18- to 21-year age group showed a significantly greater increase in positive attitudes at post-test compared to the 15- to 17-year age group. Authors considered greater cognitive development and the influence of social circumstances occurring in Detroit during that time to be among potential explanations for the significant finding. (Older youth may have been better able to consider photographic data and their connection with it on a broader level than may have been the case for younger participants.) As a final consideration, some historical context of events in Detroit at the time of the study are worth mentioning. During the summer of 2008 the popular young mayor of Detroit was Kwame Kilpatrick. He was indicted on several federal corruption charges and the trial played out on a daily basis in print, radio and TV media. This was a topic of local and national news, and news accounts were suffused with thinly veiled assumptions about incompetent leadership and corruptionamong African-Americans leading urban (inner) cities. Seeing, hearing and witnessing Detroit – and, by extension, minority residents of Detroit – as laughing-stock communities came up frequently during discussions between youth and Photovoice facilitators in the North End and Chadsey Condon communities. Youth felt even more motivated and inspired to make critics of Detroit – and, by extension, Detroit residents – aware that Black Detroit youth were interested in working hard to improve neighbourhood communities and enhance educational opportunities.

Lessons learned

The project culminated in a public visual display created by the high school-aged youth who had participated in the data collection and the publication of an article in a community practice journal (Gant et al, 2009). The display received considerable local coverage in print and video media (Allen, 2008). However, one of the most critical action points in Photovoice was the actual transition of ownership of the exhibit and trained skill-based participation from the Photovoice facilitators (for example, social work graduate student interns) to the young people themselves (Gant et al, 2009). The Photovoice process was time limited (eight weeks in the summer) and far more resource intensive than either the graduate social work interns or young community residents realised. After the community presentations, both groups of young people were exhausted; for both groups of students, heavy school loads awaited them in September 2008. There was simply neither the energy nor the time to continue the Photovoice process to its logical and desired conclusion. To this day, the Photovoice experience is still discussed and highly regarded as an effective community strategy by the Skillman Foundation, the TAC and community youth and residents from the participating neighbourhoods.

The case of the Oaks

Background

The community known as the Oaks consists of four diverse neighbourhoods within a mid-sized urban city in the South Central region of the US. The Oaks is approximately 4.38 square miles, with a total population of 17,600. It is a richly diverse community with approximately 46% of residents identifying as Latin@, 9.5% as African-American and 6% as Native American (US Census Bureau, 2014). The Oaks is also rich in diverse individual and institutional assets that together hold the key to long-term locally driven asset-based community development.

Within the Oaks are a community centre that has operated for more than 50 years, a brand new state-of-the-art public library with daily programming for all ages, an elementary school of nearly 1,000 youth with nearly 80% bilingual staff, several neighbourhood associations, culturally diverse restaurants, food stalls and markets and large areas of green space. Additionally, within the community is the only Latin@ community development organisation in the state, a Comanche Nation centre and more than 20 places of worship representing many religions and spiritualties. Despite the many assets found within the Oaks, changes in the economy and shifts in urban planning strategies have led to more gentrified and segregated neighbourhoods along the lines of race, age, culture and ethnicity. As a result of these trends, residents of the Oaks seldom interact with one another, except when people come together in free spaces provided by anchor institutions. Within the spaces of anchor institutions all community members are welcome, and as a result, this provided an excellent opportunity for employing ABCD in order to bring together diverse groups within the Oaks for the purpose of community building.

Case scenario

During 2016 social work faculty from a nearby university were approached by a librarian from the Oaks about the possibility of partnership and collaboration related to positive youth and community development. Over several months, members of other local anchor institutions such as the community centre, local neighbourhood associations, churches, an elementary school and the local Community Foundation were drawn into conversations about the Oaks. During these early meetings it was brought to the attention of stakeholders and faculty that the city and county health department wanted to build a new wellness centre that would serve residents of the Oaks. Despite the health department's having conducted needs assessments and analysis of health disparities in the community prior to deciding on the Oaks as the best-fit location for the wellness centre, few credible attempts were made by developers to involve community members, especially non–white residents, in the process. Due to the lack of community involvement in the planning for the wellness centre, stakeholders from anchor institutions wanted to find ways to build community among the diverse groups within the Oaks in order to help bring community members together to have a greater voice in community development efforts.

Using ABCD in the Oaks

Based on initial conversations with anchor institutions and residents, the decision was made to use ABCD, as a result of wanting to promote community member involvement and voice in planning the wellness centre as well as in future local issues. One of the main ABCD principles guiding efforts in the Oaks was that everyone possesses strengths that can benefit the community. Faculty provided training to students, interns and others in appreciative enquiry, a strengths-based interviewing technique, in order to identify positive attributes and strengths among residents. Another principle of ABCD employed in the Oaks was based on the perspective that anchor institutions are vital providers of resources and connections to residents, and serve as important spaces where residents interact. Additionally, respect for inclusivity and diversity in the ABCD process was strongly considered, which meant that decisions related to community programming, events and forums must take into account the diversity represented in the community.

The ABCD principle of gaining an in-depth understanding of local assets was incorporated by having students and community partners not simply map local assets by way of observations or 'windshield surveys',[4] but interact with residents, proprietors and stakeholders about why each place, location, structure or person was an asset in the community. Finally, the ABCD principle of involving community members as active participants in community development was utilised by creating a plan for student interns and faculty members to work with anchor institutions to put on the first-ever community party in order to bring diverse community groups together, while at the same time promoting the collection of asset data in an engaging and inclusive way. While the ABCD work in the Oaks is still in its infancy, early results have been promising for building bridges between anchor institutions, neighbourhoods and people.

Lessons learned

Despite being in its early stages of development, the Oaks' effort has provided preliminary lessons learned. One of the biggest reasons for early success in the Oaks is the investment in and role of anchor institutions. Anchor institutions have provided free spaces to meet, staffing resources for projects, connections to potential funders, supervision for students and interns, and historical and cultural knowledge of the community. An additional lesson learned from this effort is that residents' involvement must be thoughtfully considered in order to be effective and sustained over the long term. In the case of the Oaks, residents were often segregated in their respective neighbourhoods by differences in race, language, culture, income, age and history. In order to build community among residents of each neighbourhood, while also finding opportunities for neighbourhoods to come together, anchor institutions worked with social work faculty and students to organise events with community building in mind. As a result of this experience, community partners also learned that in order to build interconnectedness across difference, it is imperative to organise events that are fun, inclusive and inviting to the entire community. One of the biggest successes early on in the Oaks was the development of the first-ever community party. Social work students reached out to neighbourhoods, anchor institutions and specific identity-based communities that were often left out of community events, such as the Chica@ community, the Honduran community, the Comanche Nation and the Korean community. The party included local food stalls from each major ethnic group in the community as well as music, dance and arts and crafts activities sponsored by cultural anchor institutions. The event brought together all the diverse groups within the Oaks in a way that promoted relationship building and asset development. Free expression boards and community maps were placed throughout the event, and community members indicated where they were from in the Oaks, as well as what they loved or appreciated the most about their community. More than 500 residents attended the party, and the synergy created by the event has led to the creation of several working groups and greater inclusivity in existing groups, such as the wellness centre initiative. Finally, the biggest lesson learned from early efforts in the Oaks is that while funding makes community work easier, the process of struggling along without it can help to develop confidence among community members and partners as a result of figuring out creative ways to undertake efforts without monetary resources. By struggling to secure funding, anchor institutions, partners, faculty and students were forced to pay closer attention to their own unique individual and institutional assets in order to sustain progress during the first year. Overall, ABCD has provided a flexible process for engaging a diverse community in participatory practices that will ultimately help to organise community members and build the capacity of the Oaks well into the future, thus reclaiming community decision making from elected officials and influential stakeholders outside the community.

The benefits of arts-based community development

While much of community development is focused on addressing urgent social problems and needs such as homelessness, health disparities, poverty and economic development, strategies often favour the involvement of social welfare agencies, government and business leaders at the expense of local residents' knowledge and decision making. Often, community development professionals may lack the knowledge and skills for working with diverse communities that include many unique ethnic, racial and cultural groups that are separated by difference. This feat is daunting for any community worker, but especially for those who are outsiders to the community. By considering the ABCD approach to community development, along with a strong emphasis on respecting, appreciating and highlighting diversity in the arts and culture, it is possible for community development professionals to promote the empowerment of community members, identify local assets that could play major roles in efforts and build bridges with and from diverse sectors of the community. These case studies show how this can be achieved through minimal but sensitive interventions.

Notes

1   The CAN project promoted information exchange, research and critical dialogue within the field of community-based arts. It project was active from July 1999 to April 2010. API no longer engages in any active projects or programming other than promoting the High Performance and the CAN archives of stories, essays, interviews and more, available on the internet. The CAN website is now archived on Archive-It, courtesy of Indiana University: http://wayback.archive-it. org/2077/20100906194747/www.communityarts.net/. As of August 2016, API maintains a Community Action Network Facebook site at https://www.facebook. com/communityarts.

2   www.echoesofthemexicanvoice.com/2014/04/29/the-man-behind-the-mexican-voice-cover-art/.

3   Special thanks to Felix F. Gutiérrez, who provided input into this section on *The Mexican Voice*.

4   Brief observations taken while driving round an area.

References

Addams, J. (1910) *Twenty years at Hull-House*, New York: Macmillan.

Allen, E.A. (2008) 'Photovoice: captured photos reflect many voices', *Detroit Metro Times*, August 20–26, pp 12–13.

Brady, S.R. and O'Connor, M.K. (2014) 'Understanding how community organizing leads to social change: the beginning development of formal practice theory', *Journal of Community Practice*, vol 22, no 1–2, pp 210–28.

Brady, S.R., Schoeneman, A.C. and Sawyer, J.M. (2014) 'New directions in critical community practice: assessing and analyzing the damaging impact of neo-liberalism on community practice', *Journal for Social Action in Counseling and Psychology*, vol 6, no 1, pp 36–60.

Brieland, D. (1990) 'The Hull-House tradition and the contemporary social worker: was Jane Addams really a social worker?', *Social Work*, vol 35, pp 134-8.

Burnham, L.F., Durland, S. and Ewell, M.G. (2004) *The CAN [Community Action Network] report: The state of the field of community cultural development – something new emerges*, Saxapahaw, NC: Art in the Public Interest/Community Arts Network.

Checkoway, B. (1995) 'Six strategies of community change', *Community Development*, vol 30, no 1, pp 2–20.

Cleveland, W. (2002) *Mapping the field: Arts-based community development*, Minneapolis, MN: Community Arts Network.

Cleveland, W. (2005) *Making exact change: How US arts-based programs have made a significant and sustained impact on their communities,*Minneapolis, MN: Community Arts Network.

Curtis Center Program Evaluation Group (2014) *Case study evaluation of CPAD [Community + Public Arts: Detroit] in Six Detroit neighborhoods,* Ann Arbor: University of Michigan School of Social Work.

Deepak, A.C., Rountree, M.A. and Scott, J. (2015) 'Delivering diversity and social justice in social work education: the power of context', *Journal of Progressive Human Service,* vol 26, no 2, pp 107–25.

Defilippis, J. and Saegert, S. (eds) (2012) *The community development reader* (2nd edn), New York: Routledge.

Delgado, M. and Staples, L. (2008) *Youth-led community organizing: Theory and action,* New York: Oxford University Press.

Emejulu, A. (2015) *Community development as micropolitics: Comparing theories, policies and politics in America and Britain,* Bristol: Policy Press, esp. pp 85–120.

Fabricant, M.J. and Fischer, R. (2003) *Settlement houses under siege: The struggle to sustain community organisations in New York City,* New York: Columbia University Press.

Fisher, R. (1994) *Let the people decide: Neighbourhood organizing in America,* Boston, MA: Twayne, esp. pp 160–75.

Gamble, D. and Weil, M. (2010) *Community practice skills: Local to global perspective,* New York: Columbia University Press.

Gant, L.M. (2014) 'Personal and societal transformation through social work and the arts: notes and summary', https://sites.google.com/a/umich.edu/social-work-and-the-arts---2014-conference/.

Gant, L.M., Shimshock, K., Allen-Meares, P., Smith, L., Miller, P., Hollingsworth, L. and Shanks, T. (2009) 'Effects of photovoice: civic engagement among older youth in urban communities', *Journal of Community Practice,* vol 17, no 4, pp 358–76.

Goldbard, A. (2006) *New creative community: The art of cultural development,* Oakland, CA: New Village Press.

Gutiérrez, F. (1984) 'Mexican-American youth and their media: The Mexican Voice, 1938–1945', paper presented at the Annual Meeting, Organization of American Historians. Los Angeles, CA, US.

Gutierrez, L. and Lewis, E.A. (1994) 'Community organizing with women of color: a feminist perspective', *Journal of Community Practice,* vol 1, no 2, pp 23–36.

Hollingsworth, L., Allen-Meares, P., Shanks, T. and Gant, L.M. (2009) 'A solution-focused approach to community planning: miracles, dreams, and strategies', *Families in Society,* vol 90, no 3, pp 332–5.

Krajewski-Jaime, E.R., Wiencek, P., Brady, S.R., Trapp, E. and Rice Jr., P. (2010) 'Teaching employable skills to special education youth: an empowerment perspective', *The International Journal of Interdisciplinary Social Sciences*, vol 5, no 1, pp 167–76.

Kretzmann, J.P. and McKnight, J.L. (1993) *Building communities from the inside out: A path toward finding and mobilizing a community's assets*, Evanston, IL: ABCD Institute.

Love, A. (2007) 'Using democratic evaluation principles to foster citizen engagement and strengthen neighborhoods in a place based poverty program', paper presented at the American Evaluation Association Annual Conference, Baltimore, MD, November.

Love, A. and Muggah, B. (2005) 'Using democratic evaluation principles to foster citizen engagement and strengthen neighborhoods', *The Evaluation Exchange* [Harvard Family Research Project], vol 11, no 3, pp 14–15.

McDonald, M., Sarche, J. and Wang, C. (2006) 'Using the arts in community organizing and community building', in M. Minkler (ed) *Community organizing and community building for health*, New Brunswick, NJ: Rutgers University Press, pp 346-64.

Minkler, M. and Wallerstein, N. (eds) (2011) *Community-based participatory research for health: From process to outcomes*, Chichester: John Wiley & Sons.

Muñoz, C. (1989) *Youth, identity, power: The Chicano movement*, London: Verso Press.

Parrott, L. (2009) 'Constructive marginality: conflicts and dilemmas in cultural competence and anti-oppressive practice', *Social Work Education*, vol 28, no 6, pp 617–30.

Piven, F.F. and Cloward, R. (1977) *Poor people's movements: Why they succeed and how they fail*, New York: Random House.

Reisch, M. (2008) 'From melting pot to multiculturalism: the impact of racial and ethnic diversity on social work and social justice in the USA', *British Journal of Social Work*, vol 38, pp 788–804.

Rothman, J. (2008) 'Multi-modes of intervention at the macro level', *Journal of Community Practice*, vol 15, pp 11–40.

Sanchez, G. (1993) *Becoming Mexican American: Ethnicity, culture and identity in Chicano Los Angeles, 1900–1945*, New York: Oxford University Press.

Schwarzman, M. and Knight, K. (2005) *Beginner's guide to community-based arts*, New York: New Village Press.

Silverman, L.H. (2010) *The social work of museums*, New York: Routledge.

Thomas, M.L., O'Connor, M. and Netting, F.E. (2011) 'A framework for teaching community practice', *Journal of Social Work Education*, vol 47, no 2, pp 337–55.

Thompson, C., Hardee, S. and Lane, J.C. (2011) 'Engaging student diversity through a social justice learning community', *Journal of Diversity in Higher Education*, vol 4, no 2, pp 106–19.

Tudico, C. (2010) 'Before we were Chicanas/os: The Mexican American experience in California higher education, 1848–1945', PhD dissertation, University of Pennsylvania, State College, PA.

US Census Bureau (2010) *Overview of race and Hispanic origin: 2010 Census*, Washington, DC: USCB.

US Census Bureau (2014) *Census facts*, American Community Survey, www.census.gov/quickfacts/table/PST045214/00,4055000.

SEVENTEEN

Working with female migrant workers in Hong Kong

Suet-lin Hung and Kwok-kin Fung

This chapter discusses how socio-political forces in Hong Kong shape the situation of new immigrants from mainland China, who are also Chinese but who differ in ethnicity and many aspects of culture, language and life experiences. An overview of responses from the community development field regarding ethnic and cultural diversity is provided to set the context of social services offered to new immigrants to Hong Kong from mainland China (People's Republic of China: PRC). To understand the perspectives and experiences related to this ethnic and cultural diversity, a small-scale qualitative study of community workers who work with these migrants was conducted in Tin Shui Wai North, a Hong Kong community with the second-highest proportion of migrants from the mainland. It is argued that ethnic diversities within the same race (Chinese) are characterised by a complex range of factors, including gender and class, and are emphasised by migration from a 'developing' (the PRC) to a 'developed' (Hong Kong) location. The 'othering' process is also at work through the social construction of new immigrants as different from Hongkongese. We further emphasise the need for community development workers to be self-reflexive when developing ethnic and culturally sensitive community practices that deal with the dimension of 'difference' of new immigrants.

The socio-political context of new immigrants from mainland China

Migrants from mainland China vary in their ethnic, urban or rural, educational and occupational backgrounds. Although the majority are of Han ethnicity, cultural differences can be observed between new arrivals and Hong Kong citizens who have experienced a greatly different economic, social and political environment during the past 60+ years (from 1949 onwards). Migrants from different parts of China speak a variety of dialects and many local studies have highlighted that language is a major barrier to social adjustment for new arrivals from outside the Guangdong province who do not speak Cantonese (HKFWS, 2000), as it is for migrants elsewhere in the world.

The daily quota of migrants from mainland China to Hong Kong was increased from 75 to 105 in 1993, and further to 150 in 1995, and this inflow has aroused increasing public attention. As a result, the number of registered immigrants within Hong Kong increased from 27,976 in 1990 to 61,179 in 1996. The figure dropped somewhat to 48,587 in 2009 as the backlog was gradually absorbed. The proportion of female migrants from 1998 to 2014 was 63–75%, and those aged 25–44 years comprised up to half of all female migrants during that time (HAD, various years). The great majority of these women were married to Hong Kong men and migrated to Hong Kong in order to reunite their family (CSD, 1996, 1999; HAD, 2000). The implications of this immigration for housing, education and social welfare services were considered to be alarming.

The number of local studies related to this target group increased considerably during the late 1990s, but then declined in the 2000s. Nevertheless, local studies over the years have persistently revealed a less than promising picture of the social adjustment of new arrivals from mainland China. For adults in general and women in particular, research studies have revealed difficulties that are experienced in different aspects of life, including family relationships (ISS-HK, 1997; Hung et al, 1999), employment (CCCTW, 2001), community integration (CCCTW, 1998; CCCMCSK, 2003) and seeking help (Commission on Youth, 1999). These studies also revealed that these people suffered from poverty, a lack of social support, poor self-esteem, immense stress and social stigmatisation (HKCSS, 2001, 2003). Children mainly encountered difficulties in education (HKFYG, 1997; HKFWS, 2000), peer relationships (HKFYG, 1995) and family relationships (SSPDC, 1999; CCCTW, 2001).

Hong Kong society generally has strong negative views on new immigrants from mainland China and considers that they are depleting the resources of Hong Kong by relying on welfare and public medical services. This was particularly true before the abolition in 2003 of entitlements to the Comprehensive Social Security Scheme (CSSA) for those residing in Hong Kong for less than seven years, except for children. Despite this change, the public perception persists that women have migrated to Hong Kong to obtain social security benefits. As many of these married migrants are from less economically developed parts of China, there is also a dominant perception that their motivation for marrying Hong Kong men is essentially financial. Discrimination against the new immigrants from mainland China has been well documented in local literature (ISS–HK, 1997; CCCTW, 1998). The impacts of ethnic and cultural difference are compounded when they are linked with migrant status and poverty.

Ethnicities of new immigrants from mainland China

The definition of ethnicity and 'race' is essentially political. The construction of a new identity was initiated in 1996 when the Hong Kong Special Administrative Region (HKSAR) government announced the official term 'new arrival' to refer exclusively to those who migrated from China. This replaced the term 'new immigrant', which had popularly been used in the community, in order to differentiate them from migrants from outside China. (Here, these terms are used interchangeably.)

Although new arrivals are not homogeneous in terms of their place of origin, ethnic group, language, rural or urban hukou (registration), education or occupational background, they are always referred to as a group. As they are of Chinese origin, it is often argued that no racial issue is involved. In this case, the concept of ethnicity is relevant, and allows for a much sharper analysis to be made, especially when racial differences are not appropriate but the divisions between the groups are noticeable and definite. Therefore, the use of ethnicity to understand the circumstances of new immigrants from mainland China allows the exploration of wide differences and helps us to identify the less pleasant ways in which people and groups in Hong Kong respond to ethnic difference (Hutchinson and Smith, 1996).

Mainlanders, as the new arrivals are frequently called, and South Asians (for example, people from Pakistan and Bangladesh), who have received increasing public attention over the last decade, have posed challenges to Hong Kong society overall in terms of social services and public order, but these two groups (categorised as two groups according to local dominant discourses of ethnicity) have been treated differently with regard to social welfare. Different strategies for the provision of welfare apply to new immigrants from the PRC and racial minorities from South Asia. For new arrivals who are also Chinese, cultural differences are minimised for the purpose of promoting integration, and they are encouraged to use mainstream social welfare services. Racial minorities, as South Asians are often labelled, are treated as a separate group and the social services with which they are provided are marginalised and segregated. Due to the poor provision of information in languages other than Chinese, racial minorities can use only those services targeted at them exclusively.

New arrivals being treated as a separate group from the Hongkongese is a familiar phenomenon of 'othering'. The identity of the Hongkongese, however, is equally, if not more, fluid. The temporal dimension is an important factor, in that a requisite for obtaining formal citizenship in Hong Kong is seven years' residence. However, the identities of Hongkongese are not defined merely with reference to time but are culturally and politically constructed. The discussion on the identity of Hong Kong citizens began before Hong Kong sovereignty was returned to the PRC, at which time it was distinguished from that of Chinese (Kuan and Lau, 1997; Lau, 2000). Although it is beyond the scope of this chapter to discuss the identity of Hongkongese, its core characteristics are being born locally, growing up and being educated in Hong Kong, mastering fluent Cantonese, having basic literacy in both English and Chinese (traditional Chinese rather than simplified Chinese characters) and having 'ways of thinking' that are a cultural hybrid of East and West (Chau, 1995). Politically, the term 'new' immigrants from mainland China differentiates them from the 'old' migrants who came to Hong Kong after 1949 but before the cancellation of the 'touch base' policy introduced in 1974. These 'old' migrants are also classified as 'local'. In this way, the identity of Hongkongese is difficult if not impossible to delineate, since it is defined in terms of place of origin and native language – a 'Hong Kong standard' Cantonese accent.

The ethnic and cultural diversity of community work in Hong Kong

While 'local' usually refers to a single characteristic, cultural diversity highlights the existence of not one but many 'locals'. Culturally sensitive/ diversity practice is therefore essential to community development in every society, irrespective of the extent of 'uniformity' or 'universality' that is perceived by the global and/or local communities. Cross-cultural practice that requires cultural competence has become a fundamental aspect of community development to foster multiculturalism and cross-cultural integration.

Community work has been developing in Hong Kong since the 1950s and mainstream community development services have been provided by social workers. Ethnic and cultural sensitivity, however, has not been central to the concerns of the social work profession for socio-political and historical reasons. Although Hong Kong was a British colony for more than 100 years, ending in 1997, high sensitivity to ethnic and cultural issues did not evolve till relatively recently, even though it has long been considered a migrant city with 40% of its population born outside Hong Kong, mostly in the PRC. The reason probably lies in the fact that 95% of the Hong Kong population is defined as Chinese in terms of 'race' and 91% of the population speak Cantonese (CSD, 2006). Chinese people have been the major target groups for social welfare services, whereas Westerners enjoyed a higher social status during the colonial years and have been treated as a separate group. Social work, developed from this unique background, has involved Chinese social workers serving Chinese people. The adaptation of a Chinese 'localised' system of social welfare for racially/ethnically diverse groups in society is relatively recent and less developed, and has only become an issue of concern during the last two decades because of the increasing number of new immigrants from mainland China, as well as immigrants from South Asia.

Working with new arrivals: ethnically and culturally sensitive practices

New immigrants from mainland China predominantly use mainstream services in the Hong Kong context, due to a lack of specialised services. The sensitivity of community workers, who are mainly Hongkongese, towards their situations, which are shaped by ethnicity and culture as well as by gender and class, is therefore important. The Tin Shui Wai community was selected because, for the past few years, it has had the highest number of single-parent families, unemployed families and families with incomes lower than the CSS-. It also has the second highest number of new arrivals from mainland China (Social Welfare Department, 2008). Because of the level of deprivation within the community, its social welfare services have become more substantial over the past two decades.

In 2011 two focus group meetings were conducted, and 12 social workers from 11 community development projects at Tin Shui Wai participated in a larger study on social capital of Tin Shui Wai conducted by the authors. It emerged that cultural sensitivity has been a prominent concern with regard to developing social capital. In order to explore the perspectives and experiences of community workers (who are usually trained social workers) in dealing with new arrivals, the authors followed up by conducting long interviews with three of the community workers who had attended focus group meetings and who had shared a great concern about ethnicities.

Although the number was small, the interviewees were selected to represent diversity in terms of gender, years of working experience and service settings. In-depth interviews of two hours each were conducted that generated rich data that revealed varying perspectives on working with new immigrants from mainland China, and the implications of such diversity for community development practice. The three community workers were:

A – a female social worker who has worked in the community for more than three years and who is now serving in a secondary school;

B – a female social worker who has more than seven years' work experience and has worked in the community for four years, and who is now working in a family service centre;

C – a male social worker who has about 13 years' of work experience, has been working in the community for more than 10 yearsand is now working in a community project.

Understanding ethnicity and culture: differences and commonalities

The three community workers have adopted a cultural perspective when dealing with new arrivals from mainland China, as exemplified by their appreciation of the tension between commonalities and diversities, which is critical to this perspective. All three community workers have identified cultural differences between new immigrants and Hongkongese, which include social behaviour in general, behaviour in seeking help, participation in community activities, worker–service user relationships and parenting styles.

All three community workers admitted that they could easily recognise the new immigrants by their appearance, including their style of dress – either very casual or very well dressed. Some of their social behaviours that were mentioned included a (perceived) rude and casual style of communication, such as speaking loudly and a preference for talking rather than listening; a less caring attitude towards others, such as taking all the food when it is supposed to be shared; not queuing or jumping the queue; dashing into a lift; rushing to get what they want; taking things that do not belong to them; asserting their demands without embarrassment; and poor social manners, such as sitting anywhere and spitting. New immigrants also shared instrumental values as demonstrated by their keen interest in material gain.

The community workers have also often observed diversity between the two groups in terms of behaviour in seeking help and worker–service user relationships. They consider that new arrivals are eager to seek help, mainly in terms of material and tangible assistance. However, they are, less conscientious of their rights than are the Hongkongese, who consider that receiving assistance is a citizen's right and that they should always be given a choice regarding the activities in which they participate. New arrivals are on the whole more grateful to community workers and tend to treat them with trust and respect. They are more passionate and open with a community worker whom they trust who has demonstrated a genuine commitment to help them, and they are ready to repay any favours. The commitment of Hongkongese to worker–service user relationships is much weaker.

Opinions about attitudes towards social participation were also requested and all three community workers felt that a strong orientation towards exchange could be observed among new arrivals.

> "When new immigrants participate as volunteers, they would be calculating in terms of material rewards. Relationship with community workers does not help much to sustain their participation but only tangible rewards." (A)

Community workers A and B emphasised that such a mentality is shaped by the provision of social services within the community:

> "I thought the mentality of seeking help as a right has been developed by the flood of services in the community. Yet, new arrivals' commitment to receiving services is high because they treasure opportunities more than the Hongkongese. They are eager to learn and gain experience." (B)

Only community worker C saw the reason for their 'material mindedness' as being related to their level of poverty, which would explain why Hongkongese, who are generally better off, are always, in his view, less 'calculating'.

The three community workers also observed cultural differences in parenting styles. New arrivals tend to be more authoritarian in parent–child relationships. They use scolding and beating more frequently to discipline their children. Community worker C opined that new-arrival parents tend to trust their environment and leave their children unattended in public areas.

It is evident from these descriptions that the community workers are speaking from a Hongkongese perspective and regard new arrivals from an 'outsider' position when identifying differences. Recognition of differences is significant but may entail a risk of exaggeration, leading to stereotypes. However, the community workers are also aware of the strengths among new immigrants, which include a greater commitment to worker–service user relationships, a greater enthusiasm for developing relationships and treasuring the opportunities offered by social services to learn and widen their experience.

In addition to differences between groups, one community worker was able to identify diversities among new immigrants according to their number of years of residence in Hong Kong and their age.

> "With increasing years in Hong Kong, the differences in living habits are diminishing. Age is also critical. The younger ones are eager to find jobs but the elder migrant women are not keen. They have no clear goals to pursue, and only spend their time participating in various activities." (B)

Community workers also noted that the divide between new arrivals and the Hongkongese is minimised when family affairs and common interests are the topics of conversation (B), and particularly when both have the same place of origin in mainland China, which is considered as sharing the same 'roots' (A). Similarities in backgrounds of class in general and welfare in particular, which is unique to the community due to its high proportion of low-income families, also reduce the diversity of social status and living styles between new arrivals and locals.

Although language always functions as a significant ethnic boundary marker, and early studies on new arrivals have identified language as a major difficulty in social adjustment, the three community workers shared the common view that it no longer constitutes a communication barrier now that Mandarin (Putonghua, the official language of the PRC) is more popular in society. However, it is still a source of tension. One community worker opined that when the Hongkongese complain about language difference it is an expression of disapproval and non-acceptance.

> "Two Putonghua women were in the volunteer group I organized. The other members in the group who are Hongkongese communicated with each other in Cantonese and complained that they did not understand what they [the Putonghua] were saying. The problem is that they do not accept them. The minority Putonghua members and the majority Cantonese members do not communicate during volunteer work but all of them perform the tasks." (A)

Language may not be a barrier in daily life, but B considered that because their accent is 'weird' it affects their chances of employment. C had a different view, that although a great majority of the new arrivals can understand and speak Cantonese, Putonghua has become the dominant language in Tin Shui Wai North because of the ever-increasing number of new arrivals residing in the community. Language is no longer a marker of diversity, but the Hongkongese complain that they have become the minority in the community. All three community workers considered that competition for resources explains the antipathy and feeling of upset of the Hongkongese.

C was also able to identify the many 'locals' and the variations among Hongkongese. He saw that there are also similarities in culture between new immigrants and groups of Hongkongese who are village people: the traditional Chinese culture continues to impact on rural Hongkongese in the community as well as on those from mainland China, while other Hongkongese are more inclined towards the Western notion of individualism.

> "The rural people of Hong Kong and new arrivals share the same values of self-reliance and the street culture of forming close groups to protect each other and exercise justice. Both are committed to relationships and caring for 'insiders'." (C)

However, such similarities have not drawn the two groups together. Some rural people share the dominant view that new arrivals are taking advantage of the Hong Kong welfare system in order to obtain resources (A).

Despite the fact that commonalities increase with years of residence in Hong Kong and new arrivals are keen to take on the identity of Hongkongese, the construction of identities is complex. One community worker realised that the critical divide lies in birthplace: whether or not they were born in Hong Kong.

> "Despite the fact that many new arrivals have been residing in Hong Kong for more than seven years ... they [new arrivals] are conscious of the difference in identity. They clearly know that they are the new arrivals and always mention it. They consider that because they were not born in Hong Kong, they can never be Hongkongese. According to them, the Hongkongese are 'civilised' and have a higher

educational background and therefore their voices can be heard." (B)

Implications for community practices

The community workers considered themselves to be culturally sensitive and were able to appreciate cultural diversity across groups and within groups, and the strengths and weaknesses of new arrivals. They also recognised commonalities across ethnic groups of the same race, although their inferences on appropriate community interventions varied and were closely related to their perspectives on social integration. Two community workers chose to ignore these differences when organising activities that concurred with the dominant notion of 'social integration': differences, they felt, should be minimised and there is a need for migrants to be assimilated into the dominant culture. The best strategy to foster this, they felt, was not to treat them differently, although they considered that special programmes that target social adjustment exclusively are required. All three community workers agreed that there is a need for new immigrants to understand the dominant culture:

> "I have not treated them differently. I have not put any special thoughts into programme design. There are many other parents who are not new arrivals and I would like them to learn about and experience 'what is generally considered as good parenting in Hong Kong'. I will not separate them from the others but group together them with the Hongkongese. Cultural integration is in my mind. By mutual understanding through contacts, they are no longer new arrivals or Hongkongese but residents of a housing estate or mothers of a child. It is a school setting and they are interacting in the role of parents." (A)

> "I would like them to adjust as soon as possible and the best way to do this is not to treat them as new arrivals." (B)

Cultural sensitivity was generally perceived as not applicable to the goal of social integration. However, C emphasised the need to be culturally sensitive. He considered that the retention of one's culture is desirable and has fostered this by designing activities that fit into the culture of immigrants by using more collective forms of activity, such as community kitchens, communal computer stations and sport activities in the streets. He also has a different view of the direction of social integration; that is, instead of new arrivals being assimilated into the Hongkongese culture, Hong Kong people have to adjust to this new era of political domination of Hong Kong by the PRC and the trend of converging life styles between the two areas. The Tin Shui Wai North community is at the forefront of such changes because of the large number of new arrivals.

> "There is a need for them [new arrivals] to understand the dominance but it should be done unobtrusively. There is no need to advocate it by emphasising it." (C)

In his opinion, the integration process should be mutual, or even the dominance [of the majority] should be reversed. According to all three community workers, culturally sensitive community development is important, but less important when working with Chinese people than with South Asians.

Discussion

Identities are constructed socially. New arrivals have been considered as 'others' in the socio–political context of Hong Kong. Many of the prominent differences between new arrivals and Hongkongese that were identified are somewhat negative and superficial, and mainly concern codes of appearance and daily behaviour. It is obvious that community workers practise their profession in a social world and their own ideas about new arrivals are also socially constructed, although these may be modified following personal interaction with them. As part of the social structure, they share the dominant ideas on new immigrants in terms of categorisation, and they may not be aware that the construction of identity is a mutual process that is also influenced by new arrivals who exhibit characteristics that conform to and confirm their classification as 'others' in order to cope and obtain resources. The extent to which gender, class and other divisions did not contribute to their understanding of new arrivals suggests that these are considered irrelevant to the social construction of ethnicity.

The three community workers who participated in this study are committed to serving new arrivals and the community and consider themselves to be culturally sensitive. However, two of them see integration as the assimilation of ethnic minority groups through the acquisition of dominant knowledge, values and expected behaviour patterns and consider this to be the essential and only path to 'integration' into society. This highlights the significance of awareness of ethnic and cultural diversity on the part of community workers in Hong Kong, which hitherto has not been well addressed in the history of community development in Hong Kong. The reflexiveness of community workers is central to this awareness. Without taking the extreme view of cultural relativism or being naïve with regard to multicultural Chinese 'communities', community workers must nevertheless subject their own cultural assumptions to scrutiny (Pakes and Sim, 2007). They must be aware of the social construction of the situation and identities of new immigrants in the socio-political context of Hong Kong, the impact of gender, class and other social divisions on ethnicity, and the complexity of commonalities and differences within and across cultures. Reconsideration of the perspectives and goals of social integration also needs to be included in the reflexive process.

Community development practice is a cultural and political activity that involves social interaction. Cultural sensitivity implies an understanding of both the immigrant and the host cultures (Lee, 2005). Chinese culture is neither singular nor static, and the cultures of Hong Kong Chinese and mainland Chinese are swiftly converging following the return of Hong Kong to Chinese rule, and also because of the rapid economic development of the PRC. The number of cross-border marriages and the extent of cross-border employment have increased. When working with new arrivals, community workers in Hong Kong still need to develop a reflexive understanding of the immigrant culture by examining the political, social and economic changes in the PRC over the past few decades and the impact of economic reform on the Chinese 'new' culture.

Finally, there has been a call to decentre the position of community workers who deal with culturally diverse groups and, in this case, to centre the Hongkongese perspective, arguing that a 'grounded' understanding is required:

> We do not believe that 'cultural competence' has to do only with being sensitive to the different realities of people from different cultures. We believe that competence as a professional from a cultural point of view, means much more than this. For a start, competent professionals need to be able to appreciate the skills and resources of a community, and the ways in which the particular community understands these. What is more, competent professionals then need to be able to play a part in assisting that person, or that community to engage with their own skills and knowledge

in ways that contribute positively to their community. (Bracho, 2000, p 3)

References

Bracho, A. (2000) 'An institute of community participation: the work of Latino Health', *Dulwich Centre Journal*, no 3, pp 1–3.

CCCMCSK (Caritas Community Centre – Mok Cheung Shui Kan) (2003) *Study report on social inclusion of new arrivals*, Hong Kong: CCCMCSK (in Chinese).

CCCTW (Caritas Community Centre – Tsuen Wan) (1998) *Survey report on Hong Kong citizens' impressions towards immigrants*, Hong Kong: CCCTW (in Chinese).

CCCTW (2001) *Study report on opportunities of vocational development for new arrival youth*, Hong Kong: CCCTW (in Chinese).

CSD Census and Statistics Department (1996) *Thematic report no 15: Hong Kong citizens who got married in mainland China*, Hong Kong: CSD, Government of the Hong Kong SAR.

CSD (1999) *Thematic report no 22: Hong Kong citizens who have their spouses and children in mainland China*, Hong Kong: CSD, Government of the Hong Kong SAR.

CSD (2006) *Population by-census: Main tables*, Hong Kong: CSD, Government of Hong Kong SAR.

Chau, K.K.L. (1995) 'Social work practice in Chinese society: reflections challenges', *Hong Kong Journal of Social Work*, vol 29, no 2, pp 1–9.

Commission on Youth (1999) *Support network of new arrivals*, Hong Kong: Commission on Youth (in Chinese).

HAD (Home Affairs Department) (2000) *Survey on new arrivals from mainland China, 3rd Quarter, 2000*, Hong Kong: HAD, Government of the Hong Kong SAR.

HAD (various years) *Quarterly report of database on demographic characteristics of new arrivals from the mainland*. Hong Kong: HAD, Government of the Hong Kong SAR.

HKCSS (Hong Kong Council of Social Service) (2001, 2003) *Study on the cross-cultural impression and acceptance between local people and new arrivals*, Hong Kong: HKCSS (in Chinese).

HKFWS (Hong Kong Family Welfare Society) (2000) *A study of parental stress and coping strategies of mainland Chinese immigrants*, Hong Kong: HKFWS (in Chinese).

HKFYG (Hong Kong Federation of Youth Groups) (1995) *Social adjustment of new arrival youth from mainland China*, Hong Kong: HKFYG.

HKFYG (1997) *Study report on social adjustment of new arrival children from mainland China*, Hong Kong: HKFYG (in Chinese).

Hung, S.L. et al (eds) (1999) *Qualitative study report on situations of married new arrival women from mainland China*, Hong Kong: Caritas Community Centre – Tsuen Wan (in Chinese).

Hutchinson, J. and Smith, A. (1996) *Ethnicity*, Oxford: Oxford University Press.

ISS–HK (International Social Services – Hong Kong) (1997) *A study on the Chinese new immigrants in Hong Kong*, Hong Kong: ISS–HK.

Kuan, H. and Lau, S.K. (1997) *Political attitudes in a changing context: The case of Hong Kong*, Hong Kong: Hong Kong Institute of Asia-Pacific Studies, The Chinese University of Hong Kong.

Lau, S.K. (2000) 'Hongkongese or Chinese: the problem of identity on the eve of resumption of Chinese sovereignty over Hong Kong', in S.K. Lau (ed), *Social development and political change in Hong Kong*, Hong Kong: The Chinese University Press, pp 255–84.

Lee, M.Y. (2005) 'The complexity of indigenization of clinical social work knowledge and practice', *Hong Kong Journal of Social Work*, vol 39, no ½, pp 3–31.

Pakes, K. and Sim, R. (2007) 'Culturally sensitive therapy? Examining the practice of cross-cultural family therapy', *Journal of Family Therapy*, vol 29, no 3, pp 267–83.

SSPDC (Shamshuipo District Council Working Group on New Arrival People and Youth) (1999) *Study report on social adjustment and needs of new arrival families in Shamshuipo*, Hong Kong: Shamshuipo District Council (in Chinese).

Social Welfare Department (2008) Seminar on Yuen Long district community service planning: information on Yuen Long district (unpublished).

Section Five
Working across cultural boundaries: ideological and personal reflections

Introduction

Gary Craig

The two concluding chapters have been given a separate section because they present some very personal reflections from community workers who have confronted the difficulties in practice of working across cultural boundaries in a way that has challenged their view of the object of community development and the ideology that underpins it, and assumptions about their own identity as a community development worker operating within a challenging cross–cultural context.

Belton's view of the value of community development with/to minority ethnic groups, based on widespread experience in countries both with 'developed' and 'developing' economies and with the most marginalised groups, such as the Roma in East and Central Europe, is, perhaps appropriately for such a contested subject, at best ambivalent and at times even highly sceptical. Drawing on the work of liberation writer–activists such as Franz Fanon and Ivan Illich, and on the disciplinary analysis of Foucault, he argues that, without exerting great care and reflexivity, community workers are open to the charge of reproducing the attitudes and practice of their colonial predecessors with communities labelled as suffering from economic, political and social deficits and 'underdevelopment', a stance that is legitimised by racism and prejudice and that dismisses the culture and history of minorities as without value. Those with power thus blame the marginalised for their marginalisation, rather than accepting that they are the victims of the operations of a racist state.

Summersgill writes, in a very moving personal account, about the tensions of moving from a country formally acknowledged as multicultural, in which she was seen as mixed-race and thus, in essence, 'BLACK', to be a community worker in the unique context of a country – New Zealand/Aotearoa, the land of the long white cloud – that, while historically and culturally defined as bicultural (with the Treaty of Waitangi balancing the rights of the indigenous Māori against the power of the imperial invaders from Britain), is now increasingly, in a strictly demographic sense, multicultural, as migrants – both economic and those seeking refuge – have arrived from many new destinations, including Europe, Africa and Asia. Her account describes the difficulty of, first, accepting a new identity as 'white', and then finding a way to work, and an acceptable language, that both acknowledge the cultural and legally established framework, endorsing the rights of the Māori population, and the fact of a demography that is perhaps more multicultural than any other country's in the world. Resolving these tensions at a personal and political level remains work in progress, work that other countries, notorious for their mistreatment of indigenous peoples, have yet properly to begin to address.

EIGHTEEN

Developing communities: do minority groups need development?

Brian Belton

Preamble

This chapter is premised on my involvement with developing practice in South East Asian countries (Belton, 2012a, 2012b) and with Roma communities in London; however, I will also be drawing on understanding and shared practice with regard to on-going research work underway in Germany, Spain, Romania, Malta, Holland and Turkey. I critique the notion of community development in South East Asia (and elsewhere) by looking at responses to Roma groups in the European context, the challenges of professional ascription of community and ambitions to fabricate community. I explore assumptions about shared identity/interest and replication of colonial ethos, drawing on Fanonian perspectives. I consider work premised on suppositions about the need for development, how logically (and effectively if not consciously) these promote 'deficit' models of practice, implying that groups are relatively 'underdeveloped'. This suggests an Illichian analysis of community development as a form of professional iatrogenesis1 that promotes incarnations of 'weak power' (Belton, 2013).

Introduction

What follows reflects attempts to move away from ideas of educational and community development with a number of government agencies in South East Asia, including Malaysia, Bangladesh and Sri Lanka, over the last few years, previously in Hong Kong and Shanghai. This more recent work aimed to develop innovative and progressive responses to particular social and political contexts, rather than to continue what is essentially a colonial conceptual framework premised on the supposed deficit inherent in those national contexts. This chapter also draws on a decade of working within an academic framework of community learning and development in the British and European context, effectively encompassing much the same deficit assumptions; in that sense, 'colonialism has come home'.

Looking to exemplify this situation (to develop a heuristic model), I present a critical analysis of the current perspectives of Roma, the political position of this group and the threats concomitant with the same, given the 'rise of the right' in Europe, demonstrating how political and professional responses to Roma directly impact on them. The 'colonial position' of this population is exacerbated by anti-'Roma' racism. This constitutes a multifaceted set of phenomena, altering over time, place and, arguably, sometimes from person to person. Its elaboration is also dependent on the social position that any particular individual or group of Roma find themselves in relative to the wider community. The nature of prejudice is manifested in and through a range of social, cultural and economic factors. However, this complex web of phenomena is largely ignored or undetected and (simplistically) racism has become the functional means (politically and professionally) to explain disadvantage and the 'development' of officially and professionally defined groups (named and labelled as 'communities'). The plight of Roma is explained via a discourse of racism and, as such, their 'development' is addressed by way of the same.

At an institutional and state level, this stance enables the denial of political responsibility by blaming popular prejudices for failures to act politically and socially. At the same time it corrals groups as 'Roma' and therefore, by definition, 'lacking' in a range of social competences by way of that designation.

Thus Roma are placed within a Foucaultian carceral[2] (Foucault, 1977), dualistically categorised to be focused on (via the professional gaze) with the ambition to reform (discipline), contorted and experienced as an obligation on Roma to become 'integrated' (assimilated/rehabilitated/corrected). The latter is an almost impossible task as it translates to becoming that which one is not (that is, something other than Roma). These circumstances equate to the dehumanising process/experience that Fanon (1963, 1967) suggests might be thought of as the inauguration of a colonial mentality; one cannot be accepted as who/what one is, therefore to be accepted one must be like who one is not – which is of course setting an unachievable agenda, condemning all involved to an existence of angst and frustration. This is clearly a form of punishment, thus completing the Foucaultian circle.

As such, 'development' means 'change' or 'alteration'; a proposed movement from where one is to another – usually designated –

psychological, social place (that might encompass actual physical 'relocation'). But the 'change' that is sought is possible only with the abandonment of ('unacceptable') aspects of identity and the embracing of a counter-identity that evokes 'tolerance' (one becomes 'tolerated' rather than accepted as one is).

Roma access to resources and a voice are increasingly, via a politicised narrative, framed within this colonial ethos, evoking what I have elsewhere called (following Hall, 1991) 'Weak Power'. The latter might be thought of as a resort used by the relatively (otherwise) powerless to gain influence and access to social resources by way of defining oneself as the oppressed pariah. This process confirms notions of the 'born victim', the necessarily oppressed (Belton, 2013) that in turn facilitates or invites professional intervention, confirming the oppressed status of the colonised. This process defines Roma as a discrete racial, ethnic or cultural group; at the level of local community it fosters personal and group alienation. Professional interventions that by and large reinforce these circumstances result in 'iatrogenesis' (Illich, 1976), the treatment taken to alleviate a malady that in actuality promotes pathology.

This situation has its corollaries across the post-colonial world, although, as a sort of phantom hang-over of colonialism, it lurks almost unseen in the fabric of professional and political practice. It has been embedded by contemporary states, maybe to some extent unconsciously, into educational and welfare structures under the banner of 'development' (educational/community) that assumes deficit (under-development). The case of the Roma in Europe exposes how this manifestation of social and cultural malaise has led to social and political agendas being framed *for* (rather than *by*) this group. These ambitions for Roma confirm their status as a political and social 'other'; an entity to be assimilated and reformed within the carceral of ethnic/cultural colonialism.

A good deal of the literature relating to community development, certainly in the (sparsely represented) field of 'race' and ethnicity, promotes and rationalises models of practice that are, in the main, based on hearsay and stories, romantic and/or unconventional political views, guesses and assumptions. Such material often results in workers preaching homespun morality. This echoes the colonial/missionary era, underpinned by forms of instruction and domination. We need to move away from this by avoiding simplistically assigning people to what we designate to be a community, operating on it to somehow 'develop' it. If we are to be of real service to people we are going to need to understand ourselves more as servers (servants) than as authority figures making such decisions; we should exist professionally to work with or serve people to develop their own influence and authority. This is an 'asset assumption'; that people have influence and can potentially use it to gain more control over their lives and social contexts. However, if this is not going to be yet another colonial process, we probably need to grasp that it is we who are defined by them, and not the other way round.

Young people in particular are portrayed as a group (as the colonial 'native' was) to be personally or socially lacking, deficient in terms of education, morality or even the civilising effects that can be accessed only with the aid of the 'informal educator', 'social pedagogue' or 'community development worker'. Various social and ethnic groups are commonly depicted by way of assumptions, developed out of social fears (not unusually inflamed by the media) about declining personal standards and/or moral degeneracy. These groups are frequently portrayed as in need of 'support', 'help', being beset by vaguely described psychological and social problems. As such, they are contradictorily represented, sometimes at the same time, both as a threatening 'enemy within', the seed of moral and social degeneracy, and as a relatively incapable or infirmed group, in need of extensive professional patronage; they are taken, contradictorily, to be both 'weak and vulnerable' as well as 'intimidating and powerful'.

It is this strange duality of response that translates to a social view of particular groups as being 'pathological' relative to the more 'respectable' and/or 'responsible' (less feckless) population. As such, this invites a model of intervention that smacks of a treatment (deficit) model; the overriding aim of much of the work with those categorised as the 'other' is correctional in ethos, being applied to individuals or groups understood and responded to as 'non-conformist' or 'disaffected' (abnormal).

Logical analysis of this suggests that this deficit model of practice relies on convincing workers and their clients that they (the clients) have innate insufficiencies, that there is something inherently impaired in the condition/identity. Apart from being inherently unattractive, this perspective is implicitly oppressive, unavoidably demoralising and ultimately alienating, its stark reality being that some population groups are seen to have 'inborn' inadequacies that need to be treated or compensated for by way of forms of social discipline or reformation. South African anti-apartheid activist Steve Biko saw that convincing people that this lack was real was a means of the continuance of coercive domination. As he remarked, 'The most potent weapon of the oppressor is the mind of the oppressed' (Biko, 1971, p 7), echoed by Bob Marley's plea (in his 'Redemption Song'[3]) paraphrasing Marcus

Garvey's counsel (1938) to 'Emancipate yourselves from mental slavery recognising that none but ourselves can free our minds'.[4]

This being the case, we need to formulate a different approach than one premised on the assumption of developmental need. Such an approach might reject such deficit models and promote instead one that is diametrically opposite – a model that lays emphasis on people as personifying the vibrant hope and potential of any society; a model based on the recognition that the individual is confirmed in their humanity by their contribution in and to their social context

The enigma of community

The community is often seen as the target of professional and academic activity – but where is it? Traditionally communities have been understood as having a geographical basis, such as a rural village or inner-city neighbourhood, but in the contemporary era community is not limited by geography. Communities can arise around common interests or identity, even be virtually based. Refugees, for example, often work within a framework of transnational communities linked across national borders, mainly by common ethnicity or countries of origin. Community does not even seem to be restricted by size, as we now talk in terms of the 'national community', even the 'global community'. Community is everywhere and ever present.

The condition of modern human beings is quite curious when viewed from the perspective of other times. We are now all individuals. We have a notion of 'self' and can describe ourselves in terms of being 'unique'. I can list propensities and characteristics that I perceive to be more or less particular to me. Modern sociology, neurology, psychology and even anatomy seem to confirm this prognosis. I am I, you are you, she is she, he is he. In an age of gender confusion and botoxic agelessness much more is up for grabs. To a certain and growing extent we can become who or what we want to be. We exist in what is a very self-centred universe wherein we are thought to construct ourselves (Nemeth, 2002, p 6). This is comparatively new. The widespread use of the notion of community is a post-Second World War phenomenon. But here we are, each one of us individualised human beings, seeking to express ourselves while at the same time showing a desire to be part of greater wholes. We wish to 'commune' with others.

This anxiety not to be alone is a primal feeling close to other deep-seated drives such as sex and eating. It is the force behind family and tribal affiliations epitomising the basis of our social psychological make-up. It harks back to a time when the individual had no responsibility or identity outside the clan or settlement. One was of one's 'tribe', and later trade, and that is what defined who one was. This 'people trap' might be thought of as the archaeology and the genus of what we think of as community. The wish for community is an echo of a time much less complicated. Ours is an epoch where the individual fills up the space of thought. It was Freud who did much to open up this path laid by industrialisation, individualism and the coming of consumer society. We now account for everything as individuals. Our beliefs, taxes, system of justice, government and financial position are all premised on individual responsibility.

The very basis of the capitalist system is of individual consumers buying things for themselves. But in the same way as our social evolution has outrun our biological evolution, our individualised state appears to be something we have yet completely to manage. The post-modern, individualistic existence has hit us so swiftly that we seem not to have had the time or the space to acclimatise. It seems that many of us do not feel emotionally secure with this state of being, to the extent that we dig up all sorts of archaic attachments. Nevertheless, the idea or the hope of community is exceedingly important to contemporary society. The need or want to belong to a community has been portrayed as a central desire of what might be called post-modern humanity. A yearning for unity, safety and the sense of belonging certainly seems to be associated with community.

The downside

Stating that community exists implies a boundary or a division between people. It establishes those who are a part of it and those who are not a part of it. The defining of a community places some people within and other people outside of that community. The tighter the affiliation of any given community, the more impermeable its boundaries appear to be in terms of entry or exit (Figure 18.1); observe, for example, the American Amish or North London Hassidic Jews.

People in a community have supposedly something in common with each other that distinguishes them in some way as different from members of other groups. The resulting labelling creates an 'inner' and an 'outer' – a them and us. The more binding the connections within a community tend to be, the more distinct is the division between those of the community and those alien to it. This makes the community a difficult place to leave for the threatening and relatively unknown outside world, where the former community member will themselves be foreign. At the same time the interlocked community is

Figure 18.1: Impermeable (closed) community

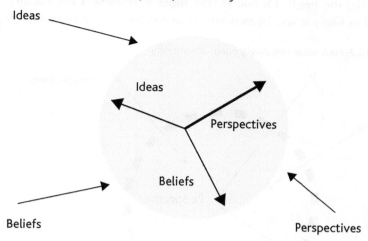

almost impossible to get into, especially if one comes from a similarly comparatively impervious social situation. For example, it would be hard for someone born into a Hutterite community to leave that situation, and even more difficult for them to join and be totally accepted by a group of devout Zoroastrians. Profoundly, while a community can be defined as a place of inclusion it is also a means of exclusion – 'You are not like us, therefore you do not belong'.

In order to be accepted by a community one must, to a greater or lesser extent, subsume oneself into the whole. Certain codes and ways of being that promote acceptability must be adopted and adhered to. Not to do so would mean becoming an outsider or being identified as a member of another community. In order to ensure continued connection, the community member needs to comply with the perceived needs of the community, which tend to override the need of any single member or minority of members or their possible desire to dissent. A very 'solid' community will regard any departure from accepted norms as unacceptable. For instance, not wearing (or wearing) a particular hat at certain times or places, playing disapproved-of music, eating 'unclean' food, looking at someone else in the 'wrong' way.

Is it not strange that we crave the sense of belonging that we believe a community will bring at the same time as we are so 'individualised', demanding a notion of 'self'? We ask the question of who 'we are', and that this be both noted and celebrated. We insist that our 'personality' or 'persona' needs to be understood and catered for. We want to be distinct but also subsumed, and the very last thing most of us want is to be totally and permanently alone; but we also feel reticent about 'following the herd'. Of course, the more permeable a community is, the less likely it will be understood or recognised as a community.

Figure 18.2: Permeable (relatively open) community

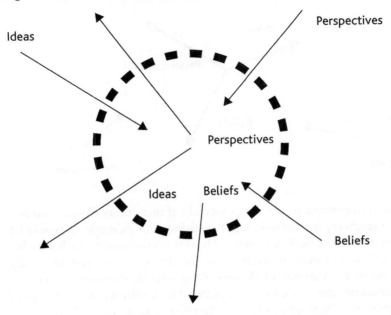

As we study community or 'engage with communities' it might be worth bearing the above in mind. Those obliged to grow up in situations where relatively little knowledge permeates the walls of community have had to live with the often-resulting pooling of ignorance that breeds prejudice towards outsiders. As this is going on, the community, keeping both distant and distinct, invites prejudice against it via stereotyping in the absence of any information coming out of the community (or distortion by others, such as the media) to disprove the same.

It may be telling that it is often those who have never known the crushing nature that closely collective ways of living can promote who seem most avidly to seek to propagate community life, even though from Jonestown to Waco and the Heaven's Gate cult, the whole idea has been shown to be tragically flawed.[5]

Community has the ability to suffocate individual expression and openly persecute those who might seek to move away from the community's beliefs and norms. It is often the site of stereotyping, prejudice, discrimination and exclusion. The whole notion of community is based on the idea of members complying with a particular, sometimes quite rigid, set of norms. To be outside those norms is likely to mean that one will be chastised or expelled from the community, usually to the distress of relatives and friends who might remain in the community. As such, the community rewards those who personify its norms and punishes those who do not reach its collective expectations. The community is authoritarian in this respect. It is reactionary, punitive, tyrannical and not interested in consensus. It is about the rule of the few by the many, the dictatorship of the majority, the creator and oppressor of minorities. It suppresses the wants and needs expressed by the minority to the whims and fancies of the majority.

Community norms come into being – as unwritten laws that impact on people's ways of being, thinking and action. Very often these norms go unchallenged because to challenge them means punishment or shunning. It is much easier to fade into the mass, to be a part of the relatively warm, seemingly friendly, conforming but harmonious throng. I just have to undermine my 'self' for the 'good' of the whole (as defined by elders, priests and so on) and all will be well.

But what of those people who do challenge or kick against the community's standards and expectations, those who rebel against either the codified or unwritten rules that dictate how they should behave? What, at the end of the day, changes for the young person from being shackled to one community (say an urban religious and/ or ethnic minority) and then binding themselves to another (a radical or extremist group for instance)? Why might young people resist their community's rule, only to adopt the regulation of another community? Does rebelling against your community ultimately change anything? If it did, it would not be rebellion but revolution. To what extent does hegemonic thinking affect the way in which professionals engage with communities?

Control and community

Foucault's (1977) ideas relating to the individual demonstrate how people can be categorised and detached from the general social landscape as individuals being labelled as mad, criminal or young and so on. He argues that this arises out of a need that contemporary society has to predict and control behaviour.

Professionals, as agents of the state, look at someone, observe their behaviour and others (for example Roma) who are thought to be like them. Records are then generated that enable us to make predictions about the future behaviour of those we have observed, which means effective control mechanisms can be put in place that will channel and/or deflect their activity into behaviour that we, our organisations, institutions and the state prescribe for them or approve of – community writ large.

Community can be seen as an idea that has evolved out of our society, a social system based on exploitation (which is what capitalism is) as another form of control. The more community controls, observes and corrects behaviour, the less there is for the state to do in this respect. The ambition for community in our society is for it to be used as a corrective instrument (as community police officers, community wardens and 'community watch' exemplify). That is why it is seen by many right-wing community enthusiasts, alongside the family, as having a responsibility in terms of social control.

Foucault would regard community developed and used in this way as an aspect of the 'carceral' society and part of a general control process like prisons, schools or youth projects, which are all locations where 'specialists' and academics are busy observing, recording, naming and predicting behaviour. The end of this process is the desire (albeit sometimes driven by anxiety) to control. This might be for the best or the worst of reasons.

The Roma: some immediate social history

Given the above, it seems fitting to look at how the idea of a Roma community arose and developed; what its potential and actual 'differentiation' is based on. Gypsy slavery was not abolished in law in Europe until well into the second part of the 19th century, but persisted as a social practice well after that date. However, subsequent to the formal ending of slavery, Roma were turned off the lands they had formerly toiled over and evicted from their huts and other dwelling places. This meant that they were without the means of life and labour, literally bereft; a proportion were obliged to become itinerant, looking for work and temporary shelter.

However, many stayed on as a kind of serf labour with their former masters, or simply had no other recourse but to beg for food and shelter, having only their labour to offer in exchange. Thus the former slaves remained trapped in a semi-slave state, labouring on the land or gaining positions as the most lowly of household servants. The majority had no access to any type of formal education or alternative means of survival. The social situation and pariah status of Roma made fertile ground for the unabashed racism that continued for the best part of the next century, even up to today.

Racism discourse

Across Europe the discourse that has become central to research connected with Roma, defining them (historically, presently and in the future), is anti-racism; 'Roma' people and their interests as individuals and as a collective are explained via inequality in terms of culture, race and/or ethnicity. Issues related to Roma have become increasingly addressed by relatively low-cost, moralistic 'solutions' (translated through the language of rights). Roma are essentially seen as 'racially challenged', and this is put at the core of their experience of disadvantage.

Prejudice and discrimination present authentically serious difficulties for the majority of 'Roma' people, but anti-'Roma' racism is a multifaceted set of phenomena, altering over time, place and, arguably, sometimes from person to person, and also dependent on the position any particular individual or group of Roma find themselves in relative to the wider community or society. The nature of prejudice is manifested in and through a range of social, cultural and economic factors; racism has become a functional means to explain disadvantage – unemployment, low life expectancy, slum housing. While it is true that straightforward and implicit or explicit racism towards Roma continues, this has become the simple explanation for a much more multifaceted form of oppression. Racism has been made a 'route one' rationalisation of disadvantage and it is, in the main, what is targeted to alleviate the same. At an institutional and state level, this enables the denial of political responsibility by blaming popular prejudices for failures to act politically and socially.

This essentially reflects the promotion of false consciousness within and towards this group. The story is that what we are confronted with when thinking of Roma is an ethnic discourse, addressable via the promotion of an ethical/moral response, when the marginalisation of this group is the result of a range of issues and phenomena. This simplistic understanding undermines and detracts from the possibility of comprehending this group as essentially the victims and prey of the capitalist social formation; it conflates and camouflages the social imperative of inequality inherent in state-sponsored capitalism.

In this context, issues pertaining, or said to be pertaining, to Roma in particular are made to appear to be almost purely an uncomplicated struggle for rights by and for an oppressed ethnic minority against the ignorance and prejudice of host communities. However, this interpretation prevents the recognition of a process of the reassignment of most Roma to their traditional social position as a reserve of cheap labour, maintained at minimal cost to the state. At the same time, while identity as race, ethnicity and culture in terms of Roma are relatively ethereal categorisations, their disadvantage (in a direct experiential sense) is mechanistic. These categorisations are a consequence of the interplay between the economic and social positions of Roma (along with many other groups). The latter is instrumentally related to the nature of the social formation over and above relative identity. Yes, racism and bigotry are present, but they are at least as much a product of the Roma disadvantage as they are the cause of it.

However, as many Roma often seem to 'ethically disappear' into host communities after achieving a (basic) level of social economic parity, one is left to conclude that, for Roma, their 'race' is at best a secondary causation in terms of their collective experience of disadvantage. The ethnic discourses that have previously been the basis for apartheid and genocide have been effectively reinterpreted by 'enlightened' non-Roma benefactors, helpers, professionals, activists and academics as the supposed means of addressing what are essentially economic, social and/or political sources of their causation. Standing back, it is hard not to understand such efforts as attempts to ameliorate structures fundamental to the economic formation via an ethnic or racial discourse; it is difficult not to feel that this is like trying to stop a leak in the roof by a change of attitude – the application of subtle psychological tactics to solve a hard practical defect. Essentially, this saves on tools and replacement materials, but it will not stop the leak; that will just get worse. This is not quite like buying second-hand water cannon to address a potential rebellion of disaffected youth, but about as pointless.

So, while an increasing number of Roma people are attempting to resist this categorisation (it is doubtful if a majority of this group are seeking or pursuing a unique if collective identity), the social agenda with regard to Roma is dominated by a racial/ethnic narrative. One consequence of this is forms of segregation – Roma are regarded as a 'type'. I wonder how long it will be before we have 'Roma Skills' to match the training programmes in 'Gypsy Skills' being offered in Surrey (England) at the moment? Perhaps in the South East Asian context one could imagine community development initiatives introducing 'Bajau Skills'?

The ethnic discourse has an influence beyond bland identity. Roma access to resources and a voice are increasingly channelled via this narrative, giving rise, as noted, to 'Weak Power' (Belton, 2013) that inclines one to accept one's oppression. This echoes Fanon (1963, 1967) in that it translates as power being maintained by the colonial elite through the sustaining of a sense of relative powerlessness on the part of the 'native' as the 'wretched of the earth'. As academic and professional cadres get behind and reinforce this process they create what Martin Kovats in Budapest has called 'The road to Hell', 'paved with good intentions' (Kovats, 2003, p 4).

A cycle of reaction

This being the case, we may deduce that obvious social and economic mechanisms and circumstances, reinterpreted and understood as almost exclusively arising solely as cultural, racial or ethnic difference (almost alone), give rise to both internal and external pressures on Roma individuals and groups. The consequences are continued discrimination, social exclusion, limited opportunities and social tension. This poses difficult questions to those who follow a community development agenda in that we are obliged to approach this (or any) defined community within similar deficit paradigms and address them in ways that can only energise those same paradigms.

The propagation of Roma ethnic, racial or cultural difference also fits the agenda of the far right-wing in terms of segregating Roma as a group effectively without a political or economic reality; they are merely the result of their own category. All they are is what they are and they are restricted by what they are (not their social economic context – which is understood as just another consequence of what they are). This has led to a working through of 'Weak Power' within an identifiable expression of a Weberian social exclusion dynamic (see Parkin, 1979); the excluded exclude the included, so making the excluded a sort of faint representation of the included. The extent of Roma politics is to identify themselves as Roma and others as not being Roma, which matches the fantasies of the far Right. What is produced is a 'cycle of reaction'. This has been expressed by the International Romani Union's (IRU) 'Declaration of a Nation', the claim that all 'Roma' constitute a single and distinct community that requires its own separate representation. This is antithetical to the objective of equality for Roma people within their home societies, and as such it is probably not surprising that in more 30 years the IRU has failed to generate grassroots support among Roma. However, the IRU has functioned as the forum of a few dozen international activists (Roma and 'non-Roma'), unsurprisingly sustained by the patronage of established political interests. But it is, in reality, a voice for segregation and forms of 'separate development' (apartheid).

However, 'Roma' is simply one political replacement for the generic identity 'Gypsy', which covers a huge number of highly diverse communities with different political needs, aspirations, capabilities and interests, living in a wide variety of economic, political, social and cultural environments. There are of course other minorities that are understood in this way; effectively a form of categorical stereotyping.

This fictional community has no shared language – a tiny minority might use one of the numerous Romani dialects, many of which are so unlike any other that they are incomprehensible to speakers of another parlance, often being used as a second or domestic language. There is also a panoply of cultural, religious, historical and ethnic differences between groups who might be called 'Roma'. Many of these groups do not call themselves or others 'Roma': for example, we can identify Spanish Calé and Gitanos; French Manush (a sub-group of Sinti); and Hungarian Lovari (Lovara) and Romungro (Modyar or Modgar).

Even within countries, Roma minorities are diffuse and diverse and do not function as any kind of clearly definable or actual community. As Liégeois puts it (1994, p 130), 'from the Gypsy point of view there is no such group as the Gypsies'. Similarly, Kovats (2003, p 4) argues, Roma as a category represents:

> the politicisation of the Romantic racial myth of the 'Gypsy people'; this, though intellectually discredited, has been thrown a lifeline due to its political utility. The application of 'Gypsy' identity has traditionally been used to marginalise the status of these communities ...

For him, Roma, being pushed to the degree of separation as a distinct nation,

> accords with this tradition by legitimating the ideology of segregation and suppressing democratic political development in order to sustain the marginalisation and isolation of 'Roma' people ... (Kovats, 2003, p 4)

This situation, promoting the understanding of Roma as a discrete racial, ethnic or cultural group, at the micro-level of local community, fosters personal and group alienation. They are discarded at the margins of society, and society acts like and so becomes the enemy or probably more realistically the constant threat. At the same time society understands Roma as a sort of human peril. This two-way response can manifest itself in the form of crime (for instance, Roma are driven to crime, while they are designated because of their identity as criminal), hostility, family dysfunction and educational disaffection.

Within the corral of mutual intimidation, the institutions of the host society at best 'tolerate' the Roma 'other', at the same time promulgating the perception of difference, the very source of discrimination and prejudice. Professional energy, understanding and focus are dominated by the same in terms of how Roma are approached, and their situation assessed, as a 'community'.

With the huge political shift to the Right in Europe, most notably in its easterly regions, the continued allegiance with racial identification poses a huge danger. The ethnic categorisation of Roma not only asserts the legitimacy of polity premised on ethnicity, it also provides the basis for the ideological, political and institutional dislocation of 'Roma' minorities from 'majority', thus freeing governments from their social and moral responsibility for a whole swath of their citizenry. Thus, Roma ethnic categorisation can be understood as a reactionary phenomenon, resonant of a far right political order in which people are increasingly divided by ethnic boundaries, rather than united by their common interests (à la socialism). When professional intervention is premised on much of the above, it can do little more than exacerbate the situation.

As things stand, Europe-wide, 'Roma' are grossly over-represented among the long-term unemployed. They experience massive inequality in regard to housing and healthcare. Their consequent dependency on shrinking welfare resources and declining public services is an obvious manifestation of growing social inequality. The 'prohibitive' costs of improving these people's living conditions and of returning their labour to 'profitability' provides a strong incentive for the state to define 'Roma' as a distinct racial community, thereby allowing policy to focus on the far cheaper and simplistic promotion of ethnic 'difference'. However, once the majority identify a minority group as incorrigibly distinctive, it is a small step to depicting them as irredeemably defective.

The political delineation of 'Roma' as an ethnic or racial group and the promotion of some essential 'difference' between 'Roma' and everyone else in society exploits traditional prejudices and low expectations. 'Difference' is used to explain Roma impoverishment, social tension and conflicts, migration and the failure of 'integration' initiatives. It conserves the political, social and economic isolation of 'Roma' people and supports the ideology of segregation.

Potential for cohesion; human solidarity (as humans)

Working with Roma, I see possibilities for social cohesion between Roma and the host communities. This is promoted via community and cultural action/solidarity as (first and foremost) human beings (as opposed to types of human being). Such processes can stimulate new interpretations of social relations and promote cultural cross-fertilisation, and so growth, understanding, harmony and community integrity, dignity and civility.

Being part of cross-national and international collaboration, focused on work with and among Roma, but as part of an understanding of these groups having commonalities and overlaps with other marginalised groups/communities, is also progressive both politically and socially. This approach can help to build contemporary models of better political, professional and social understanding and practice, but such work needs to include members of such groups, who should be involved in research as well as the leadership and delivery of practice.

In the light of growing political extremism across Europe, such cooperation, via the promotion of understanding and cultural/ethnic interaction and co-working, also has the potential to alleviate and counter exclusion, prejudice, exploitation and oppression. However, this can be projected only by way of the abandonment and/or rejection of deficit models with a focus on notions about developing this community.

The meaning of 'Roma' is not 'slave'; it means 'man', not in the masculine sense but as a referral to being human; you and me, we are Roma! The world is not made up of those in relative spiritual or inherent but ethereal deficit and those who are not; we all have capacities that are more or less realised. But that realisation is largely blocked in us when we are regarded as by nature an inherent recipient – more of a (undeserving) consumer (of all things good) than a creator (of them).

Notes

[1]   An injury or illness resultant on medical care.

[2]   Imprisonment/incarceration.

[3]   Bob Marley, October 1980, Island/Tuff Gong. Producers: Bob Marley, Chris Blackwell.

[4]   Garvey's October 1937 speech (at Menelik Hall in Whitney Pier, Sydney, Nova Scotia) commented: 'We are going to emancipate ourselves from mental slavery because whilst others might free the body, none but ourselves can free the mind.'

[5]   These were all closed communities which ended with murder and violence.

References

Belton, B. (2012a) *Establishing a professional youth worker association*, London: Commonwealth Secretariat, http://thecommonwealth. org/sites/default/files/events/documents/Establishing%20a%20 Professional%20Youth%20Worker%20Association_1.pdf.

Belton, B. (2012b) *Professional youth work: A concept and strategies*, London: Commonwealth Secretariat, http://thecommonwealth. org/sites/default/files/events/documents/Professional%20Youth%20 Work.pdf.

Belton, B. (2013) 'Weak power: community and identity', in M.W. Hughey (special issue ed), *Race and ethnicity in secret and exclusive social orders: Blood and shadow, Ethnic and Racial Studies*.

Biko, S. (1971) *White racism and black consciousness: The totality of white power in South Africa*, https://studycircle.wikispaces.com/file/view/ White+Racism+and+Black+Consciousness,+Steve+Biko,+Janua ry+1971.pdf.

Fanon, F. (1963) *The wretched of the Earth*, New York: Grove Weidenfeld.

Fanon, F. (1967) *Black skin, white masks*, New York: Grove Press.

Foucault, M. (1977) *Discipline and punish: Birth of the prison*, New York: Viking.

Garvey, M. (1938) 'The work that has been done', in *Black Man*, vol 3, no 10, pp. 7–11

Hall, S. (1991) 'The local and the global', in A.D. King (ed.), *Culture, globalization and the world system*, London: Macmillan, pp 19–40.

Illich, I. (1976) *Limits to medicine: Medical nemesis – the expropriation of health*, New York: Marion Boyars Publishers.

Kovats, M. (2003) 'The politics of Roma identity: between nationalism and destitution', Open Democracy, https://www.opendemocracy. net/author/martin-kovats.

Liégeois, J-P. (1994) *Roma, Tsiganes, Voyagers*, Strasbourg: Conseil de l'Europe.

Nemeth, D.J. (2002) *The Gypsy-American: An ethnogeographic study*, Lewiston: Edwin Mellen Press.

Parkin, F. (1979) *Marxism and class theory*, London: Tavistock.

NINETEEN

Without borders: community development, biculturalism and multiculturalism

Angela Summersgill

E ngā mana, e ngā reo e ngā karangatanga maha, tēnā
koutou, tēnā koutou, tēnā koutou katoa.
(All authorities, all voices, all the many alliances and
affiliations, greetings)

Traditional formal welcome in Te Reo Māori

Today, Aotearoa[1]/New Zealand is considered one of the most
multicultural countries on the planet. The 2013 census revealed
that 'New Zealand has more ethnicities than there are countries in
the world. In total, 213 ethnic groups were identified in the census,
whereas there are 196 countries recognised by Statistics New Zealand'
(Minson, 2013).

Sitting alongside that increasingly diverse reality is the Treaty of
Waitangi's[2] fiercely-guarded commitment to biculturalism, deeply
woven into the fibre of everyday life and thinking. Tiriti o Waitangi
sets out the 'negotiated'[3] agreements, rights and status of the indigenous
peoples of Aotearoa/New Zealand (Māori) and the responsibilities and
gifted status of the Crown and its subjects (British settlers/ Pākehā[4]).

This chapter shares some of the issues, experiences, questions
and practice implications arising for me, the author, a mixed-race,
British-born community development practitioner and social work
educator living in Aotearoa. I have sought better to understand the
issues and questions regarding the coexistence of biculturalism and
multiculturalism; I have sought to question what it might be that we
separately and collectively need to do in order to move forward with
respect and inclusivity.

Through many years' experience of working in and alongside
diverse communities in the UK, exploring models of community

engagement and conflict resolution, I had become convinced that the transformation of hearts and minds occurred through the witnessing of personal narratives and through participation in dynamic and reflective techniques used to reduce prejudice and discrimination. Creating bridges to sustain connection across difference appeared to be a central strategy for increased cohesion and equality in those communities. Given the Aotearoan statistical picture, surely it must follow that strategies for managing diversity and promoting connection need to be an increasing reality for those who work in and alongside communities here?

It is this conviction of the power of narrative, this curiosity, this passion and deep resonance with a transformative praxis[5] that continues to assist my and others' liberation, and it is that brings me to this page, to these words and to this hope-filled curiosity shared here.

This reflects on some of the people, places and events that have presented themselves as moments of awakening on my journey, one that I hoped would lead to a better understanding of a question that was central to my enquiry: could I, with respect for the indigenous culture and practices of Aotearoa, legitimately and authentically continue to use the bridge-building and transformative techniques I had experienced to such powerful effect in multicultural England? In choosing to communicate this journey through a poetic narrative, it is my intention to honour both the oral storytelling tradition fundamentally central to Te Ao Māori (Māori worldview) and the persistent influences of ecofeminist[6] perspectives that continue to provide me with a holistic, inclusive and connected analysis. I am also forever indebted to Gramsci's[7] ideas (including hegemony, coercion and the notion of organic intellectuals) and to a Freirean pedagogy[8] that recognises that 'narratives of the people' – stories that ordinary people tell about their everyday life experiences – hold the key to the theory and practice of social justice.'[9] Storytelling is universally recognised and stories, if considered as 'evidence in themselves, rather than technique for illustrating existing ideas, have a significant contribution to make to the process of personal and social transformation' (Gelman and Basbøll, 2014).

As we sit together in our separate times and spaces, I know nothing of you, the reader, save that in this moment we might connect, however briefly, and in that moment we may begin to seek, understand and heal whatever hurts and mistreatments keep us separated from one another. Perhaps you too yearn for connection and wholeness, seeking to clarify just how we might together take action in our desire to reconnect with and humanise our humanity.

Through these pages I invite you to share in the thoughts, observations, questions and ever-evolving levels of understanding and meaning that have unfolded over time as I transitioned between two lands, worlds apart but intrinsically connected. I enter into this process with an open heart, mind and genuine humility to seek deep and respectful healing that may restore our connections to self, each other and our environment; the shared humanity that has over much time, space and mistreatment been interrupted, violated and discarded.

As both conscious participant and privileged witness, I can tell you that I have experienced connections being forged between individuals and between groups, bridging the divide where there had before existed only an awareness of difference, a tension, at best a passive resistance and mistrust. Through the emotionally intelligent process of creating bridges to sustain respectful connection across difference, stories of mistreatment were shared, discomfort was acknowledged and moved through, myths were dispelled, fears were addressed and commonalities were identified. I knew, in my core, that these were the stepping-stones that could assist me to reach out and begin to bridge the divide, heal the fractured connections that I saw in everyday interactions. These steps assist us to develop the tools to dismantle oppressive structures and ways of being. They gift us the building blocks to help create our shared vision for social justice. They foster a 'unity in difference' so essential to cohesive multicultural communities.

There were many faces, many stories that came from those communities. With each story shared, I was gifted a privileged opportunity to hear of the impacts of injustice. Whether racism, sexism, homophobia, Islamophobia or anti-Semitism, with each story shared, I recall the healing and the change, the discomfort and the realisations, the commitments and the apologies, the appreciations and the reclaimed pride, the resurgence of self and a deep resonance for all concerned. I recall the empowerment, the owning of privilege, the commitment to alliances, the promise of connection.

With each account of the impact of prejudice and discrimination, my heart broke. With each heartbreak came a repair, a rebuild, a piecing together of the composite parts; each witness and storyteller reflecting on their shift and how it was that they, the world and its people looked and felt a little different now. Those people, faces, stories and feelings live as the notes in my heartsong. Within such a framework of conscious compassion, honesty and vulnerability, these moments of connected humanity transcended any differences or conflict, and even as the moments faded and the drift returned, the meaning of the resonance and the awareness of similarities remained and carried forward.

Was there, then, a natural union to be made between the techniques and strategies I had experienced in England and the diverse and multi-ethnic population in Aotearoa? Having no map to navigate the unfamiliar landscape and its people, and feeling a deep sense of disconnected drift, I felt that something in my initial analysis was missing. I knew about diversity. I knew about respectful interactions, I knew about power and identity. Did that knowledge have value and meaning here? What, after a short while, I came to recognise was that the things I didn't know or yet understand held greater importance and significance in terms of my repositioning of self and practice. It was those unknown factors that somehow were likely to hold the key. This sense of drift, the whole and complex process of transplanting oneself from one country to another had left me between two worlds, with no clear place or sense of how to initiate 'docking procedures' and hit the ground running. I realised that in order to map the landscape and find my place I had first to undergo something of the journey.

The transitioning of identity

Travelling light and with as much humility as I could genuinely bring into any given moment, I got underway, hoping that in time I would be able to erect the signposts, know the subtle contours of the mountains and be able to recognise the flow and direction of the life-giving rivers. Only then would I understand how to walk gently on this land and know my direction and place. And so, inevitably, I let go and in doing so came to see myself anew. I surrendered to the rising tide of awareness and to the unknown. I submerged into the experience of 'being'. I dived in, eyes shut, heart wide open.

Six years had passed since I left England bound for this beautiful 'land of the long white cloud'. I departed my other worldlife proud in my reaffirmed and relatively healed and whole mixed-race, well-educated, working-class female body. I had known, first hand, racism, sexism and class oppression for as long and as deeply as my memories and trauma would allow. I had journeyed with others to come to face all of the places and spaces of self that had been systematically targeted over the course of my lifetime and had in rage and joyous tears reclaimed that which had not been there for the taking in the first place.

Passing like spirit through the clouds and time zones, I did not sleep for wondering what this new life in a new land might look and feel like. My body arrived in Aotearoa some two days after departure. It took a good while longer for the rest of me to come to ground. As I stepped off my Emirates waka[10] and the first morning sun warmed my face, everything changed. All that I had held close to me fell away and I stood naked in the stark truth of my privilege, a plateau of white advantage that I had almost and conveniently forgotten existed in England. The harsh and terrifying reality that I had come to realise was that here I could not mask my privilege with mixed-race oppression, I could not distance myself from my white heritage and people any longer. Here, in Aotearoa, I was white and British and that was all that counted. I was told in words, and more, that I was seen only in terms of my white privilege. I was told I was Pākehā because I came from England. I was considered 100% white. There appeared to be no space for my Middle-Eastern other, my often forefronted English identity. Did my mixed-race self and experiences not hold any meaning or commonality here?

In travelling as far away from my birth land as possible, I had in fact and unwittingly come closer to home than ever before. My place in the world, my relationship to myself and others, all that I had known and crafted it to be, fell apart. I let go and surrendered, trusting, hoping, that at some point in time I would resurface, with new knowledge and understanding, with greater awareness and with a toolkit honed to assist me in navigating this unfamiliar landscape in which I felt I was no more than a welcome intruder.

It was then that I realised the full importance of context and environment as a lived experience. By changing my environment, I was experiencing the world through a new lens. As I looked on, for a time, more of a passive spectator than an active participant, I witnessed my identities being restructured, reprioritised and reassigned a value in relation to my geographic location and as a consequence of my colonising ancestors. The bridge I had to build here was multilayered and demanded that I reconnect with the aspects of myself that I had, through guilt, shame, denial and neglect, been privileged enough to be able to archive many, many years ago. These aspects of self were essentially my whiteness in equal measure to my Middle-Eastern heritage, my white privilege and historical denial and convenient masking of that in my mixed-race identity; all that was here and now to be brought centre stage for closer inspection. I could no longer claim sanctuary in my 'I'm not white' proclamation. In coming to face and know more of my privilege as a white middle-class European living in Aotearoa, I have been able to deepen my understanding of context and refine some of my questions regarding how to engage in authentic, culturally sensitive practice here. I have been able to re-envision an anti-oppressive analysis and work towards being an effective ally to others. I had a new vantage point from which to view the landscape.

In this awakening, I began to realise more fully that there was something unique about Aotearoa and its people. Through direct front-line practice, through the development of social work education and the unending willingness and generosity of a diverse range of practitioners, educators, students and community members, some of whom are Tangata Whenua (the indigenous people of the land – Māori), some Pākehā (people who identify primarily as New Zealanders and have British/European heritage) and some Tauiwi (non-indigenous people who don't identify as Pākehā), I have been able to develop something of a deeper understanding of this uniqueness and reflect on my position and practice within it.

I want to own that I started from a very different place. I'd heard much talk, highly charged opinions, reactions, dismissals and demands from a diverse range of people when reference was made to 'The Treaty' and 'Biculturalism'. My initial responses were born out of ignorance, self-preservation, dualistic thinking and a Western training and belief system that exposed 'othering' as oppressive and hegemonic practice. I failed to see the relevance of a document from 1840 that betrayed the Indigenous people and set the stage for the plundering of natural resources and dismantling of a culture. I failed to see why I should accept biculturalism, as it effectively relegated me to a category with all other non-indigenous people living here. There was no mechanism for differentiation across the immense diversity of those of us so easily 'othered'. I wanted to retain my identity as distinct from social work colleagues from India, Argentina or South Africa, for example. I wanted to evidence to my colleagues, who clearly needed to be updated about the demographic of their own country, that we had moved on. We were clearly a multicultural country. Hadn't they read the statistics? It was clear that there was tension and unease, and I could begin to see why. It was clear that colleagues were just struggling to accept the changing face of their country. I could assist with that process because I had skills, tried and tested, brought from England. There was evidence that I could share to support my methods. I could see what I needed to do. The truth is, I couldn't see at all. That was, in essence, the issue.

Challenging my assumptions

I sat in a conference room that, although polished, was saturated in sadness. It echoed the stories and voices of torment that it has witnessed over its many years of providing safe space and potential for reconnection to those families and children who had lost their way, their way of life and sometimes their humanity in a society they no longer recognised. On that day, around the over-large table, sat a group of senior statutory social workers tasked with organising a training and development day for the team. As we shared ideas and honoured, more or less, each other's contributions, it occurred to me very gently that I was the only Tauiwi, and despite my privilege and power elsewhere, in the world and in the communities in which I now worked as a social worker, I had little authority in this room. I was a minority and an immigrant. My Māori Tangata Whenua colleagues held mana whenua[11] because of their innate connection to the particular geographic region we inhabited and because of their indigeneity. With genuine humility I understood and accepted the part I had to play in maintaining the appropriate and correct balance of power.

When it was my turn to speak, I recall trying to articulate two things. First, that my contribution to the pot of ideas was to start to look at the diversity within the team and I had some activities to assist with that process. Second, and as a rationale for my suggestion, I introduced the idea that I had read a statistic somewhere about the increasing multicultural nature of New Zealand. In that exact moment that my words entered the room, a fist from nowhere came crashing down onto the table with such force that I jumped back. From a rage deep within, which for some time I did not understand, an elder practitioner, a fierce and powerful advocate for her people, roared as she rose to her full height and stated her claim that we were 'not a multicultural country'. She thumped the table again and left, saying she would never accept or tolerate 'that word', it made her 'blood boil'. No further words were spoken in the room for what seemed like an eternity. I scanned the faces of my colleagues but I could not interpret their meaning. I had no tools to translate their shared history and differing viewpoints. In any case, I knew enough to know that no one would speak against another's heartfelt korero.[12] No one referred to what had just occurred, even when the discussion resumed. I had learned pretty swiftly that words mattered. They held more than meaning, and no translation could bridge that gap.

In that critical moment, I was gifted a precious insight. Not only a signpost but a flashing beacon to indicate the direction that my journey to greater understanding should take. I needed to move beyond my own limited and Eurocentric perspectives and develop a much more informed understanding of what was clearly contentious and pain filled for my Tangata Whenua colleagues and their people.

As I made a commitment to seek out a better understanding of Te Tiriti o Waitangi and biculturalism as aspects of the uniqueness of Aotearoa that must be understood and integrated into practice,

I acknowledged my whiteness, my privilege and my commitment to figuring out what that positioning actually meant in terms of my relationship to Tangata Whenua and Te Tiriti. With reaffirmed commitment to a practice and enquiry arising from an analysis of power, a commitment to work with humility, respect, hope and integrity, I entered into the unknown, this time with eyes, ears, mind and heart wide open.

Finding place

The Waitangi Tribunal Hearings had come to my new home town to hear claims laid against the Crown for breaches of Te Tiriti. That was all I knew, and as I took my seat in the marae, alongside my Māori colleague who had invited me, I tried to make sense of my surroundings. I felt like I had appeared on a screen set, script and role unknown. As I looked around, I could see that the stage was set, the actors were already in role and playing their parts. The props looked real enough, and whispering through both audience and actors were various inaudible reminders and acknowledgments and the almost hush of anticipation that occurs just before the curtain rises. I had not purchased a ticket and felt sure that at any moment I would be asked to leave. A hand touched mine and, as I turned and traced the hand to its owner, I met the eyes of a Kuia[13] and we smiled. She leaned in to me, hand still resting on mine and spoke straight to my soul, 'whose side are you on?' she required to know. I wanted to say 'yours!' but didn't. I wanted to say 'not theirs!' but didn't. I wanted to say 'there are no sides!' but didn't.

'I am here to witness!' I said as I held her gaze for long enough to communicate to her soul much more than words would ever have accomplished. 'Āe'[14] she replied with a smile and patted my hand. As she let go the proceedings began. But this was not theatre or make-believe, and I could not suspend my disbelief. I was in fact being offered an opportunity to face full-on the real and the everyday lived experience of a people who were trying to heal unfathomable hurt and reclaim what had been stolen from them by white people and sanctioned by the Crown. A man young and proud stood to speak his claim. He explained in exceptionally beautiful poetic detail how he was connected to everything, and that included the family land and the unresolved pain of his ancestors that he carried and that had brought him to this place, to this tribunal, to this claim for recognition and resolution. As his tears fell, so did mine. Not from pity or guilt, but from a place of shared humanity that recognised that his pain and history were intertwined with mine, and yet, we had never met. Our shared tears fell slowly and steadily; his onto the several hundred pages of lived experience that he now presented as evidence for the Tribunal; and mine, scorching a path as they fell drip by drip from my face onto my hands that lay motionless on my lap, in soft remembering of the Kuia's touch. Silently and deeply I let my heart break.

The insight that followed the heartbreak was fundamental to the deepening of my understanding of Biculturalism and Te Tiriti o Waitangi. I came to see that Te Tiriti was viewed by many Māori as an endorsement of the provisions set out in the earlier Declaration of Independence of 1835, a statement (He Whakaputanga o te Rangatiratanga o Nu Tīreni) that has never been rescinded by the representation of Māori leaders who signed it. This was a proclamation to the international world that Aotearoa was an independent state and that full sovereign power and authority resided with the 'Confederation of Chiefs' (the collective name given to the signatories) and the people they represented. The Declaration's clear stand that 'no separate legislative authority' (kawanatanga) would be permitted unless they were appointed and directed by the 'Confederation' was paid little regard after the signing of Te Tiriti in 1840, as both British and New Zealand governments claimed that Te Tiriti overrode its predecessor, the Declaration of Independence. However, at the time of its signing, Te Tiriti was considered by Māori to be an endorsement of the earlier Declaration and an invitation to the British to enter into a relationship with Māori to govern the country peacefully together. Te Tiriti adds a crucial and unique dimension for British peoples here in that it accepts and welcomes Pākehā as citizens in a Pacific nation.

These were not, then, 'someone else's' historic documents; they laid out my responsibilities as Tangata Tiriti – a person of the Treaty – even though my privilege ensures that my survival is not dependent on my participation. Those around me, those whose lands I now sit upon to share my story, their cultural survival, their self-determination, their justice that had been stolen, had recourse through the existence and centrality of these agreements. Over a period of 40 years, and supported by the establishment of the Waitangi Tribunal in 1975,[15] Pākehā and non-Māori have had a greater opportunity, and clearer processes, for acknowledging the implications of Te Tiriti as the basis for nationhood here, and bear witness and answer to the untold breaches and continued abuse of its principles.

What, then, of trust? Such a vital aspect of transformative engagement having been so abused, all I could do was feel my deep sadness and a shame towards my ancestors, which left me in danger of detaching not only from Tangata Whenua but also from my own people. I emerged from this experience with new eyes and fresh heart. I saw now that what often played out as discrimination and resistance before me and towards me, what took time and love and patience and commitment to begin to break through, was the historic and on-going consequence of trauma, disappointment, betrayal and abuse.

Again, what I saw and experienced resonated with my UK-based experiences as yet another powerful example of the way that transformation of hearts and minds occurred through the telling and witnessing of personal narratives. Pain and mistreatment transcend all borders and speak all languages. Here again, through being a privileged witness during the Tribunal hearings, I had experienced the creation and holding of space, so that through storytelling the restorative processes could begin to do their work and assist healing and connection.

What was beginning to blossom within was a sense of familiarity and home in the midst of all this difference and unknown; and a sense that, for Tangata Whenua, engagement in these processes was a healing and justice of sorts in the making.

Absorbing meaning

I took a moment to rest on my journey through the rugged and expansive terrain. In that moment I felt connection. There was no separation, I was intrinsically part of everything that was, is and ever shall be. In that moment everything made sense; safe in my own personal snow globe I gazed with childlike wonder at the sparkles drifting slowly to the ground as the realisations and understanding came. In my journey through time, through the increasingly familiar landscape, I had collected tales and signs of a civilisation almost lost. The rivers and valleys tell of a people who walked softly upon the land, with respect and welcome. A people who knew how to live simply and in harmony with their environment. A people whose social structures and processes were highly developed and sustainable. A people who felt no separation from the land and sky, the ocean and the deepest forest. The same people who tell tales of how the fairylike folk came and took their lands and married their daughters; then banned their language and systematically dismantled their way of life, while simultaneously commodifying their resources and spiritual connection to the land. With my own eyes, I have seen many signposts and desolate ruins, scars both physical and emotional, marking the people and the places already visited by my ancestors.

I slowly began to see that I live in a land as a welcome partner with an Indigenous people who hold in their rememberings that the taken-for-granted aspects of a socially just and functioning society have been destroyed. Traditional rights, obligations, opportunities, security and systems have been invaded and overthrown to ensure the advancement of white privilege and concepts that seek to 'disproportionately support' and legitimise the prevalence of neocolonial structures (Yellow Bird, 2008, pp 282, 288). To consider the 'development' of communities in Aotearoa would be to assume that there is a need for development and that communities are, by implication, 'underdeveloped'. Such a deficit-model approach would be to deny the consequences and responsibilities of history, of my ancestors, of my here and now privilege.

So, while Te Tiriti purports to recognise Māori rights as Tangata Whenua of this land, those rights must be understood in the context of having been and continuing to be a generational right, gifted through generations of Māori living in a respectful and intimate connection with the land.

With that in mind and in a conscious attempt to step outside of any 'compassionate coloniser'[16] behaviours, I want to tautoko (Chile, 2007, pp 35–6)[17] the conceptualising of community development practice in Aotearoa as operating within three 'tikanga' (cultural) strands. The first tikanga consists of state systems and provision. The second tikanga consists of the processes of social change achieved through collective action of individuals and groups to enhance the voice of the marginalised. The third tikanga consists of Tangata Whenua Māori working for tino rangatiratanga, self-determination and liberation. My enquiry and focus to date is concerned with a further, fourth strand, and one that is emerging in response to the current picture of diversity here in Aotearoa. It is here that I have come to ground and my practice has started to take shape. Practitioners located in this strand are actively engaged in seeking appropriate processes and models that are responsive to complexities of the multilayered diversity that they encounter. Feeling as though I had now potentially found my fit, I came to look again at who is appropriate to work with whom and what considerations need to be consciously held in working with groups that are different to me and in a context with deeply entrenched inequalities and mistreatment. What I held close to my heart and knew for sure was that working with Māori requires of Pākehā and Tauiwi a commitment to constant repositioning and reflection in order to consider whether, in any given moment, they are acting as agent of change, compliance or control. This willingness to engage in dynamic and reflective practice was exactly what had been so fundamental to the success of the techniques I had witnessed and experienced in England. The act of committing oneself even more deeply to embrace a reflexivity and a vulnerability that was and is all-exposing and founded on a truthful desire for connection and justice – a unity of praxis[18] (Reason, 1998) – was something I held dear and that I had seen as a determining factor in the transformative processes.

Making connections

I see you Māori, woman, hurting. I see her Pākehā, woman, hurting. I see you triggered by something she said. I watch you as you tell her that she will never know your world but that you have had to fully know hers. I watch her bow down silent beneath the privilege that she would gladly cast off. She does not want to be told that no matter how hard she tries, how good she is, how well she can sing waiata[20] and care for your children as her own, that there are places she will never go to and experiences she will never have, and all because of the colour of her skin and where she comes from. Her privilege holds no currency here, just a mirror. She, like you, is still learning to understand how differences can be similarities and can manifest and serve to connect. She is still learning to listen and be still, as are you. So, listen both, you know what you have to do: you must face the horror of the death of the world, and speak the truth as you know it and see it. And you must listen in wonder to the presence of the world. Listen with both heart and mind and you will know what to do and how to be.

So, what of love and respect, dialogue and connection, storytelling and deep reflection? What of bridge building across difference to support personal and social transformation? For the time being, my journey of enquiry has brought me to a time and place that speaks of an authentic resonance between tikanga Māori values and those of my personal experience of transformative community work practice. I learned of 'whakawhanaungatanga', 'manakitanga', 'aroha', 'kotahitanga' and 'kaitiakitanga' and my heart echoed, 'connection', 'care and respect', 'love and generosity', 'unity' and 'environmental guardianship'. While earlier experiences had shown me that words held more than meaning and translation alone was never enough to bridge the gap, a shared value base and a desire for connection offered a perfect foundation from which bridge building could begin.

Through sharing of personal narratives, we not only come to see ourselves, each other and the world anew, but we make connection where previously we have perceived disconnect; we assert ourselves as part of the process and challenge the supremacy of the scientific paradigm and allow space for the diversity of experience to be heard.

In such a landscape, there exists a language of hope, of love, of mutual enquiry and respect that tells of a journey rather than a destination. A journey of shared intention, honesty and friendship, that seeks reconnection through laughter, tears, stories and rememberings and that guides us through the terrain we must navigate in order to empower each other, affirm our hopes, nurture our relationships and achieve a sustainable and mutual respect for each other.

I want to hear your stories, share your songs and laughter and witness your tears and rage. I want to know what will become of you and me, us, when, after the last word is spoken and we move from this moment in time, high on our new-found connection, exchanging well-intentioned promises that with each turn of the page whisper more and more gently into open spaces until they are but memories, which like the swallows and swifts of springtime circle us from time to time, but seldom come to ground. What is it that you will say passed between us? What is it that you will recall?

It is my humble hope that in sharing here both the questions that currently present themselves to me as important and the subsequent considerations and reflections, that something may resonate for you, assist you, raise a question for you and bring us closer together and help us better to understand why it is that I am sitting here reaching out to you, from a land that I call home, but that, in truth, I only came to know and love a short time ago.

Notes

[1] Most widely known and accepted Māori name for New Zealand, whose literal translation is 'land of the long white cloud'.

[2] Te Tiriti o Waitangi (The Treaty of Waitangi), signed in 1840, formed a covenant between the Crown and Māori hapū (kinship group or tribe). It allowed for peaceful acquisition of land that Māori wished to make available and was created as a means to ensure sustained peace, order and good will between the Indigenous people and the European settlers. See Network Waitangi (2016, p 14).

[3] In signing the Te Reo version of the Treaty, Māori believed they were confirming Māori sovereignty and authority for their people. However, the Crown's English-language version states that Māori gave their sovereignty to the Queen of England. Therefore the notion of its being a negotiated agreement remains something of a controversial issue. Network Waitangi (2016, p 15).

[4] The term is derived from 'Pakepakeha', a mythical human-like being with fair skin and hair. The name was gifted by Māori to the European settlers.

[5] 'A unity of theory and practice capable of social change' emphasised by Paulo Freire. See Ledwith (2016, p 2).

6   An analysis that holds a critical connection between the environment and the feminine.
7   Antonio Gramsci, influential and significant Marxist political theorist and intellectual.
8   A process of empowering education popularised by Paulo Freire that questions everyday life and makes critical connections linking theory and action to promote social change.
9   A central tenet of Freirean practice. See Ledwith (2016, p xiv).
10 Māori term for canoe, often (with a specific name) used to identify one's own or one's ancestors means of arrival in Aotearoa.
11 Customary authority of a tribe over the land in a particular area.
12 Spoken narrative, story or statement.
13 Female elder.
14 To give assent, or say 'yes' in Te Reo Māori.
15 Network Waitangi (2016, p 6). The Tribunal (selected by the Crown) is convened under the Treaty of Waitangi Act 1975, with the power to make recommendations to the Crown regarding compensation or redress to Māori claimants for breaches of the Treaty.
16 'Individuals who are well intentioned but often unwittingly perpetuate colonial injustices through their commitment to Western doctrines and ideologies and their blindness to the interests of Indigenous Peoples'. Yellow Bird (2008, p 283).
17 To support, accept.
18 Gramsci's concept that describes theory and practice becoming an inseparable part of each other in cycles of action and reflection. See Ledwith (2016, p 31).
19 Māori word for song(s).

References

Chile, L.M. (2007) 'The three Tikanga of community development in Aotearoa New Zealand', in L.M. Chile (ed), *Community development practice in New Zealand: EXPLORING good practice*. Auckland: Institute of Public Policy AUT University, pp 35–74.

Gelman, A. and Basbøll, T. (2014) 'When do stories work? Evidence and illustration in the social sciences', *Sociological Methods & Research*, vol 43, no 4, pp 547–70, doi: 10.1177/0049124114526377

Ledwith, M. (2016) *Community development in action: Putting Freire into practice*, Bristol: Policy Press.

Minson, S. (2013) *Census*, Statistics New Zealand, www.stats.govt.nz/census/2013-census/data-tables/totals-by-topic-mr1.aspx.

Network Waitangi (2016) *Treaty of Waitangi – questions and answers* (6th edn), Christchurch: Network Waitangi.

Reason, P. (1998) 'Listen, little man! Reflections one dark morning', in *Original Blessing: A Creation Spirituality Network Newsletter*, vol 2, no 6, pp 6–8, www.aral.com.au/whyar/Reason2.pdf.

Yellow Bird, M. (2008) 'Terms of endearment', postscript in M. Gray, J. Coates and M. Yellow Bird (eds), *Indigenous social work around the world: Towards culturally relevant education and practice*, Aldershot: Ashgate Publishing.

Afterword: messages for community development in working with minority groups

Gary Craig

As will be clear from the chapters in this volume,[1] community development takes many forms: many people practising community development, including a very great number whose job title or role does not even specifically refer to community development, work in a way that would be recognisably community development in terms of its adherence to the core values of the practice, to equality, respect for difference and diversity and so on. (And conversely, many with this title appear not to adhere to the values of community development.) Although the definition of community development in the Budapest Declaration discussed in the Introduction to this book is very wide ranging, reflecting the fact that delegates from more than 30 countries and a variety of policy and practice contexts contributed to it, the values of social justice remain core to it: those values are also core to the struggle against racism. Anti-racist work and true community development are indeed natural bedfellows.

Doing community work is not easy, nor has it ever been. Historically, most community workers have worked on the margins of organisations, poorly financed, poorly supported, often poorly understood and working as much to convince employers of the value of their work as to support their local communities, rarely achieving the satisfaction of significant concrete gains from their work. One of the consequences of the fiscal austerity measures recently put in place across much of the world has been that these pressures on community development have grown and the majority of paid community workers are now increasingly employed by organisations that not only increasingly question the value of community development per se but may, in many cases, be subject to the influences of racism. This makes work in this territory even more difficult, as community workers are often having to face two ways and finding their commitment to the values of social justice, perhaps most of all in this case their professional and personal integrity, under threat.

This is a significant insight because, although I commented in the Introduction on the lack of books about community development and 'race' (the reasons for which – other than, ironically, the impacts of racism in differing ways – remain unclear to me), it is evident from the contents of this book, and indeed from the many other chapters offered to me for which it was not possible to find space in this volume, that there is a very rich seam of anti-racist organising within a community development framework to be mined across the world. A further message to those interested in this area is therefore that one hopes that this will be the first of many similar contributions to the literature: I certainly look forward to more, more diverse and politically salient volumes. It surely has to be the case that much more of the unspoken remains to be spoken about publicly because it is also apparent, simply from a review of the world's media – and despite the attempts of some governments to rule it illegal and the work of many community-based or -connected anti-racist groups and individuals to confront it – that racism is increasing in both scope and depth, whether at individual, structural (that is, policy framed) or institutional/ organisational (practice framed) levels. To take just a few examples of this worldwide that have emerged during the gestation of this book: the successful 'leave' campaign in the UK's EU referendum has released unexpressed racism to the extent that the number of racist attacks on minorities doubled in a few weeks after the referendum; the Hungarian government secured a 95% vote in favour of refusing to allow more migrants to come into the country, which arguably had already taken far fewer than its fair share of refugees; the 45th President of the United States, Trump, who secured substantial public support (if a minority of the popular vote), has done so on a platform that includes building a wall to stop Mexicans entering the country (with Mexico paying for the wall), removing all 'Muslims' from the country and banning others from entering it; Australia has done deals with a number of neighbouring Pacific islands to house asylum seekers rather than allow them onto Australian soil; the German Chancellor's hitherto high levels of political popularity in her country were almost totally undermined by her insistence that Germany should take what is in fact more than their fair share of migrants fleeing the Syrian conflict; and in every continent of the world, inter-ethnic conflicts, whipped up by hostile press and right-wing and increasingly chauvinistic politicians, are a bloody fact of life or, at best, structurally sanitised into policies – as in Malaysia, Botswana and Fiji – that exclude some people from the rights of full citizenship. Publicising the work of community organisers who are addressing the issue of racism is thus a political necessity as an important counterweight to these frightening trends.

Working on issues of 'race' in such a hostile political environment thus presents many challenges and none of the authors of the chapters in this volume would claim to have the complete answers to what is, after all, a wide-ranging political struggle. Interestingly, the practice of social research has faced parallel difficulties over the past decades. For many years, most researchers and most funders claimed that work with minority ethnic groups was too costly and too difficult methodologically: funders would argue that the numbers of minorities were too small, they were difficult to reach (in reality, a criticism to be made of the researchers and not of the researched), that language and cultural difficulties made it expensive to set up projects; and researchers were happy to hide behind these arguments. In recent years, however, and particularly as the size of minorities has grown and the impact of policies on them has become more apparent (not least their continuing presence among the most deprived in most populations), together with the advocacy of minority activists, some academics and those supporting their work, the tide has begun to turn. The battle is not entirely won but some research funders now require grant applicants to demonstrate how they plan to ensure that the views, and involvement, of minorities are reflected in their proposals, and are prepared to fund the extra costs involved, for example in developing booster samples, using interpreters, translating materials into minority languages and so on. There may be a message here for community development, that new projects should be required to demonstrate the extent to which they will engage with minorities, with all the potential difficulties that that might potentially present. A related point is that, as Greenfields chapter (Chapter Eight) showed, researchers can use the values of community development to underpin research work concerned more with process and outcomes than with strict academic research findings.

The other major difficulty facing community workers working cross-culturally is about bridging the inherent gaps – of trust, understanding, acceptance, respect – between the ethnicity of the worker and the ethnicity of the group or groups with which s/he is working. It is obviously the case that any community worker should come to their work armed with a high degree of cross-cultural sensitivity, but that is really only a starting point. And this is not an issue of white workers working with minority communities as has most frequently been the case. Beckford's chapter (Chapter Fifteen) demonstrated that being from a minority background provides no easy way through these challenges, and both he and Gutiérrez and colleagues (Chapter Sixteen) showed the importance of building bridges between minorities as well as between minority and majority populations. Even the work of *sampad*

(Chapter Five), with what might be thought to be a more homogeneous population, suggests that there are as likely to be tensions within as much as between differing ethnic groups. The same issue is reflected by Hung and Fung in Chapter Seventeen, on Hong Kong, where all the parties discussed might be regarded as of Chinese ethnic origin but are actually from quite differing cultural traditions. How community workers approach issues of cultural difference depends to some degree on the significance of that difference. Notcutt (Chapter Ten) and others' quandary (including Beckford's from a male perspective) about coming face to face with the practice of patriarchy is, in their view, probably best dealt with by side-stepping it in the short term, confident that the work itself brings significant gains for the women being worked with and that this in itself will in due course deliver a more effective challenge to patriarchy from the women themselves. Gregory's (Chapter Seven) and others' approach to criticisms of cultural practices among migrants of various kinds might be, for example, by acting as cross-cultural brokers, to argue that this is a two-way street and that there is nothing inherently good or impressive about the practice of host-country nationals. And on an even more positive note, as Sondhi (Chapter Five) and Lathouras and Ross (Chapter Thirteen) demonstrate, there is much about minority culture that, rather than being dismissed by those wishing to assimilate minorities (that is, to turn everyone into black 'Anglos'), has a lot to tell us about the value of other cultures, and ways of living and being. This is despite such cultures being rejected as 'traditional', or different from 'normal', that is 'Anglo', ways. At the same time, when clashes between cultural practices and human rights are apparent, community workers should not be paralysed by fear of being regarded as culturally insensitive.

There will be occasions when community workers armed with the values of social justice, of whatever ethnic origin, should have no option but to intervene to promote those values. Too often, community workers, social workers, the police and others have veered away from facing difficult issues within the community for fear of being labelled as racist (and it has to be said that on occasion minority members have been prepared to play the 'race' card in defending questionable practices): the consequences of this disinterest have been tragic in some cases, for example leading to the deaths of children from beatings and neglect or from witchcraft practices. Culture is not in itself good, and the acid test should be one of fundamental human rights:[2] does a culture impinge on the human rights of its members? Does it challenge the core values of social justice? With this in mind, questions of, for example, female genital mutilation (which is an issue widely ignored or defended as a cultural norm until very recently) or child exploitation are exposed very clearly as attacks on the rights of women and children that are totally unacceptable. And this is really the last and clearest message from this book: that those practising community work have to arm themselves with these core values in theory and in practice. In the turmoil and confusions of cross-cultural work, and in a context of ever-increasing and more violent forms of racism, this remains their clearest and most important line of defence.

Notes

[1] And indeed elsewhere; see for a recent example of a range of forms of community development practised in one region of the world, 'Community development in East and South East Asia', *Community Development Journal*, Special Issue, vol 52, no 1.

[2] I do not take the view that the UN Universal Declaration of Human Rights is a cloak for Western imperial practices. Virtually every country in the world has signed the Declaration.

Index

Note: page numbers in italic type refer to Figures.

R

Taylor, J. 66–7
Taylor, M. 75, 132
Te Tiriti o Waitangi (Treaty of
  Waitangi), 1840 311, 316, 318, 319,
  321, 323n2
Terra Nullius doctrine 5, 219
terrorism 18, 29, 37n1, 50
Thiarai, Kully 103
Third Sector Research Centre (TSRC),
  UK 65
Thomas, M.L. 258
Tin Shui Wai North community, Hong
  Kong 277, 281–9
Tisdall, K. 203
Toronto, Canada:
  leadership roles in community
    development 201, 245–54
  racist stereotypes 248
'transformative participation' 203
translation services 133
'translocational positionality' framework
  112
Transylvania, Romania 206, 207
  see also Romania
Traveller communities:
  official recognition of in UK 172–3
  see also GRT (Gypsy, Roma and
    Traveller) communities
Treaty of Trianon 206
Treaty of Waitangi, 1840 5, 292, 311,
  316, 318, 319, 321, 323n2
Tribhangi Dance Theatre (sampad) 102
Trump, Donald 328
TSRC (Third Sector Research Centre),
  UK 65
Turkish immigrants to Germany 8
Twine, F.W. 43

U

UDMR party, Romania 207, 209
Uganda 4
UK:
  asylum system 138–42
  austerity policies 29–31, 50, 52, 327
  BME community engagement and
    public policies 23, 25–6, 32–6
  history of 26–32
  EU referendum, 2016 1, 3, 7, 8, 31,
    35, 37n2, 45, 125, 133, 328
  far-Right groups 27, 29, 48
  migrant labour 8
  migration from former colonial
    territories 13, 98
  multiculturalism 27, 28, 29, 98–9

racism 1, 6, 42, 43, 47, 48, 50–3, 127
racist violence 26, 27, 29, 42, 45, 46,
  48–9
terrorist attacks 18
welfare state 6
white supremacy 24, 44—45
youth work tradition 204–5
UKBA (UK Border Agency) 138, 139,
  140, 146
UKIP (UK Independence Party) 125,
  130
Ukraine, and ROMED2 189
UN Commission on Population and
  Development, 33rd Session, 2000 3
UN Commission on Sustainable
  Development 67
UN Gateway Programme 232
'underclass' 174
UNHCR (UN High Commission for
  Refugees) 139, 140
United Nations Convention relating to
  the Status of Refugees, 1951 138
Universal Declaration of Human Rights
  331n2
University of Greenwich 81, 85
Urban Programme, UK 27
USA:
  arts-based community development
    (ABCD) 261–72
  First Nations (aboriginal) people 2, 5
  non-profit sector 249
  population profile 257
  terrorist attacks 18

V

VCS (voluntary and community
  sector):
  mainstream organisations and BME
    groups 69, 73–4
  see also BME VCS (voluntary and
    community sector)

W

Wallace, C. 211
Walshe, C. 91
'war on terror' 49, 50
Ware, Phil 61, 65–80
'Weak Power' 293, 295, 304–5
West Asian population, Canada 245
West of Scotland Regional Equality
  Council; Minority Ethnic
  Employment and Training Project
  166